THE WINES OF BRAZIL

THE CLASSIC WINE LIBRARY

Editorial board: Sarah Jane Evans MW,
Richard Mayson and James Tidwell MS

There is something uniquely satisfying about a good wine book, preferably read with a glass of the said wine in hand. The Classic Wine Library is a series of wine books written by authors who are both knowledgeable and passionate about their subject. Each title in The Classic Wine Library covers a wine region, country or type and together the books are designed to form a comprehensive guide to the world of wine as well as to be an enjoyable read, appealing to wine professionals, wine lovers, tourists, armchair travellers and wine trade students alike.

THE WINES OF
BRAZIL

TUFI NEDER MEYER

ACADEMIE DU VIN LIBRARY

Tufi Neder Meyer, a graduate of UFMG Medical School with a PhD in surgery, has studied wines since before college. He was a professor at University of Vale do Rio Verde from 1979 to 2019. Besides his medical and academic career, he has also been a wine educator since the 1990s. Tufi holds the WSET Level 5 Honours Diploma and is a WSET Certified Educator (up to Level 3), as well as a *Formador Homologado del Vino de Jerez* (Certified Educator on Sherry), CPE (Certified Port Educator) and French Wine Scholar instructor. He translated the *French Wine Scholar Study Manual* into Portuguese for the Wine Scholar Guild. He lives and works in Brazil's Southeast region, teaching at The Wine School Brasil (WSET approved) and other institutions.

This work is fondly dedicated to the people I love: Christiane, Lorenza, Emílio, Isabela, João, Beatriz and Rafaela. May it also honour the memory of my son Guido, who lives in our hearts.

Published in 2025 by Académie du Vin Library Ltd
academieduvinlibrary.com

A CIP catalogue record for this book is available from the British Library
ISBN 978–1–913141–86–8

Front cover: © Casa Geraldo vineyards, Minas Gerais.

Photos courtesy of Tufi Neder Meyer unless otherwise stated.

Publisher: Hermione Ireland
Editor: Rebecca Clare
Indexer: Catherine Hall
Illustrator: Darren Lingard

Typeset by Suntec, India
Printed in Great Britain

CONTENTS

ACKNOWLEDGEMENTS

No enterprise, books included, is the work of a single person. This applies particularly to technical works. Many, many people participate in some way and should be thanked. Yet, we all know this, but it must always be remembered: it is impossible to thank everybody deserving of our gratitude. I apologize, therefore, to any and all people not mentioned here. This is exclusively due to faults in my memory and organization.

I am especially grateful to Rebecca Clare for inviting me to write this book and help with editorial matters – many thanks for her trust and support.

The assistance of my homonymous cousin, Tufi Neder Neto, in English revision is gratefully acknowledged.

Many thanks to Adeliano Cargnin (General Director, Embrapa Uva e Vinho) for allowing the use and modification of many illustrations.

I thank particularly the following friends for their unconditional support and invaluable assistance: Fábio Miolo, Jorge Tonietto, Carlos Abarzúa, Edson Andrade, Pedro Candelária, Diego Cartier, Alexandre de Carvalho, Daniel Dalla Valle, Taiana Madeira, Lorenzo Pizzato Michelon, Ricardo Morari, Cláudia Nunes, Eduardo Junqueira Nogueira Jr, Daniel Panizzi, Flávio Pizzato, José Fernando da Silva Protas, Murillo Regina and Átila Zavarize.

I have been warmly received by so many people when visiting wineries. Others have kindly sent me wines to taste or helped me in other manners. For all, my gratitude: Miguel Ângelo Vicente Almeida, Ricardo Ambrosi, Sadi Andrighetto, Eduardo Angheben, Daniel Aranha, Arnaldo Argenta, José and Hortência Ayub, César Azevedo,

Valter Bebber, Cyril Bernard, Guilherme Bernardes Filho, Gustavo Bertolini, Gustavo Borges, Clóvis Boscato, Denise Brandelli, Euclides and Gabriela Brocardo, Roberto Cainelli Jr, Noemir Capoani, Marco Antonio Carbonari, Renato Cárdenas, Juliano and Giovanni Carraro, Roberta Cavalcanti, Vinícius Cercato, Aline Cioto, Gabriel Victor Cogorni, Humberto and Bruno Conti, Analu Couto, Hugo Gonçalves Couto, Lorenzo Cristofoli, Eduardo Cruz, Irineo Dall'Agnol, Fernanda Dall'Astta, Marco Danielle, José Afonso Davo, Gaspar Desurmont, Alexandre Develey, Luís Eduardo Dias, Jorgito Donadelli, Hendrios Draguetti, Lucas Fardo, Giovanni Ferrari, Jorge Fin, Aline e Rubens Fogaça, Lucas Foppa, Vanderlei Gazzaro, Moacir Giaretta, Lucas Giarolla, Eduardo Giovannini, Fábio Góes, Gabriel Gontijo, Julio Gostisa, Henrique Göttens, Guilherme Grando, Joelmir Grassi, Ricardo Henriques, Vaner Herget, Viviane Hilgert, Leo Kades, Patrícia Kaufmann, Edvard Theil Kohn, Walter Kranz, Rubem Kunz, André Larentis, Márcio Lattarini, Marcelo Luchesi, Cláudio Macedo, Daniel Maia Bastos Machado, Sérgio Malgarim, Carolina Martin, Daniel Alonso Martins, Janaína Massarotto, Viviane Mattiello, Guilherme Menezes, Heloise Merolli, Caio Mincarone, Bruno Motter, Michel Motter, René Ormazabal Moura, Francieli de Nardi, Jurandir Nosini, Celso Panceri and his daughters Estefânia and Emanoela, Welles Pascoal, Gilberto and Guilherme Pedrucci, Isabela Peregrino, Fábio and Felipe Marques Pereira, André Peres Jr, Pablo Perini, Thiago Peterle, Gabriel Pianegonda, Rinaldo Dal Pizzol, Silvio Cesar Poncio, Luiz Porto Jr, Gabriela Pötter, Júlia Pozzan, André Previtali, Maurício Rios, Odilete Rotava, Marco Antônio Salton, Jefferson Sancineto, André Luiz Gonçalves dos Santos, Marcos Scatolin, Gabriela Schäfer, Paula Schenato, Bruna Schmidt, Dirceu Scottá, Cristian Sepulveda, Fábio Silva, Gustavo Leme da Silva, Vanessa Bancer Soliman, José Sozo, José Procópio Stella, Jeferson Suzin, Sabrina Suzin, Marcio and Stella Tadashi, Eloiza Teixeira, Luis Toledo, João Valduga, Rogério Carlos Valduga, Marcio Verrone, Artur Viapiana, Rosana Wagner, Amanda Willoweit, Luis Henrique Zanini and Eduardo Zenker.

I could not have written this book without the invaluable help of friends who were important in my wine studies years ago: Eugenio Echeverría, Adolfo Lona and Júlio Anselmo de Sousa Neto. Thanks a lot!

FOREWORD

Most people associate Brazil with its vibrant culture, football, breathtaking landscapes and infectious rhythms. Wine may not be the first thing that comes to mind, especially as Brazil is overshadowed by its South American neighbours Chile and Argentina. However, Brazilian wines are as diverse as the country itself, shaped by distinct microclimates, wide-ranging soil types and numerous grape varieties. In recent years the industry has been going through a steady and exciting transformation; for this reason, this book written by Tufi Neder Meyer is relevant and well timed.

I first encountered Tufi in 2010 whilst lecturing WSET Level 3 in São Paulo, where he came across as studious, thoughtful, curious and a person with great attention to detail. With such competence, focus and professionalism Tufi quickly gained his Level 5 Honours Diploma through WSET. The fact that he resides in Brazil makes him the perfect author for this book at the right time.

Brazil's wine industry has been quietly flourishing for decades; however, a significant transformation has gained pace since producers discovered double pruning, a technique that allows grapevines to yield high-quality fruit during Brazil's dry winter months as opposed to ripening fruit in the middle of a rainy summer.

This revolutionary approach has enabled viticulture to expand into regions previously deemed unsuitable, such as the warmer and arid areas of the central part of the country, especially in the states of Minas Gerais, São Paulo and Goiás. Tufi explains the process in detail and describes how its adoption has enabled producers to expand to new frontiers, not only outlining the physical aspects that govern each grape growing area in depth but also providing individual insights into all relevant producers.

Make no mistake, this is a serious book, written by a serious author for serious professionals and wine lovers. In parts it goes into great depth, which requires a more scientific mind; then the writer switches from detailed technical explanation and offers inviting recommendations about tourism and information about the local cuisine to give a sense of the overall colourful culture that Brazil has to offer.

You will also find insightful explanations of historical events that affected the industry, from the arrival of Portuguese colonists in the sixteenth century, who planted the first grapevines along the coast in São Paulo Estate, to subsequent waves of European immigrants in the nineteenth and early twentieth centuries, particularly from Italy and Germany, that helped shape Brazil's wine industry, focusing on the southernmost state of Rio Grande do Sul.

It pays homage to some of the visionaries who greatly contributed to the progress of viticulture in Brazil, from the nobleman from Porto named Brás Cubas, reputed to be the first person to plant a vine in the Brazilian territory, to Murillo Albuquerque Regina, the professional responsible for adapting the technique of double pruning that has enabled the expansion to new territories that is happening right now, alongside those countless personalities who labour in the cellars with passion and persistence, aiming to propel Brazilian wines onto the world stage.

The book also explores the complexities of Brazil's social and political landscape, including the policies that have both hindered and helped winemakers over the years.

The writer's personal journey through Brazil's wine regions offers readers more than just historical facts and technical details. With a style that blends informative analysis with personal anecdotes, the book brings to life the warmth of Brazilian hospitality, the excitement of discovering a new producer and the pleasure of savouring a glass of wine from a country that has shown resilience and the ability to reinvent itself over the years: a testament to the people who dare to believe that their wines are capable of standing alongside wines from other countries on the world stage.

As you turn the pages of this book, may you discover not only the diversity and quality of Brazilian wines but also the spirit of a nation that celebrates life with immense passion. *Saúde*!

Dirceu Vianna Junior MW

INTRODUCTION

'Give me some more wine, because life is nothing.'

Fernando Pessoa

Many decades have sadly passed, but I can still remember when, as a child, my father allowed me to drink a 'refreshment' (as he called it), at Sunday lunch only, made by mixing a little pink, sweetish wine with a large glass of water and more sugar. The wine was made in São Roque, São Paulo, from *labrusca* grapes and curiously labelled 'Astronauta'. I cannot recall whether it was 'foxy', but one thing is for sure: my fondness for wine started with such long-gone moments. Dad's taste improved; a few years later, there was always a bottle of German wine for Christmas, now devoutly sipped undiluted. I was responsible for selecting and buying it in Belo Horizonte, where I studied medicine. During my studies, I attended the college's library daily; it contained an old edition of *Encyclopaedia Britannica*. As I already appreciated the English language (it had been fundamental for my admission to medical school), I translated the whole entry on wine into Portuguese in order to practise and learn. I made a booklet from the text using an antediluvian contraption called a typewriter. Since then, wine and English have become everyday subjects, and more so after I earned all Wine & Spirit Education Trust (WSET) certifications up to the now defunct Level 5. This enabled me to become a wine educator as a second, less stressful profession.

Although producing the precious liquid since the sixteenth century, Brazil is not well known internationally for its wines. This is unfair, although various reasons may explain such undeserved obscurity: relatively

1

small production volume, few exports, heavy competition from neighbouring wine giants (Argentina, Chile) and a general misunderstanding
of our country's size, geological and climatic complexity, and tremen-
dous vinous advancements. After centuries of near-dormancy, Brazilian
wine has improved dramatically since the 1990s. Everything is in a state
of flux, with new producers sprouting up almost daily. Although trustworthy statistics are not exactly our forte, I may confidently state that
more than 500 producers of *vinifera* grapes (either boasting a winery or
not) and wines exist in the country. The wineries vary from *garagistes*
to huge industries delivering millions of bottles yearly. We are uniquely privileged to have three distinct types of viticulture. A large array of
grape varieties (some genuinely national) and wine types also exist. All
levels of quality are present. For the wine explorer in search of new experiences, *ne plus ultra*.

Books about Brazilian wine are, unfortunately, scarce. So, adding a
brick to the laborious and endless increase in knowledge of Brazilian
wine is a great privilege. Integrating my book into such a prestigious
collection as the Classic Wine Library reinforces that honour and sense
of responsibility. These are further augmented because this is the first
book on a South American country in the series. I hope you, genteel
reader, may effectively enhance your knowledge of our wines after you
finish reading or consulting the book. The text has taken innumerable
hours of work (no typewriter any more), a lot of trips (some adventurous) through this vast country and the tasting of hundreds of wines. As
you may guess, I cannot say this was a tedious undertaking. Quite the
opposite: I have almost always been warmly received by the Brazilian
wine professionals, whom I would like to thank. You know this already,
of course: sitting among people genuinely interested in this most excellent drink, talking endlessly about the subject and tasting so many
wines (alas, spitting out nearly everything) are memories, to paraphrase
the Brazilian singer and composer Milton Nascimento, 'to keep on the
left side of the chest'. We wine lovers know well how closely this blessed
dram is linked to emotion.

Allow me to be objective, though. This book is not a wine guide or
catalogue. A lot of producers (164) are encompassed here. Many, however, are not. I apologize to those who are absent – it would, indeed, be
an impossible feat to include everybody. I have not attributed marks to
the wines or been restricted to vintages (with a few exceptions). My paramount objective was to briefly describe the style of the wines using a

standardized tasting model and organoleptic and structural descriptors. As to quality, the reader may apprehend it from my descriptions.

After this Introduction, I briefly provide relevant general data and information on Brazil. This is essential to understanding what comes next.

Part 1 is introduced by a chapter on the history of wine in Brazil, which begins by describing how the Indigenous peoples made their alcoholic beverages and then covers 500 years to reach the present day. Chapter 2 delineates topography, geology and soils, and includes maps and information on Brazilian soil classification. Chapter 3, on climate, reveals that Brazil is not simply a tropical country but instead has a wide climatic variety. Also examined is the ingenious Multicriteria Climatic Classification (MCC), possibly the best climate systematization for wine purposes. Coloured maps enrich the text. A chapter on viticulture and winemaking looks at the three types of viticulture unique to Brazil: traditional, winter and tropical. The main pests and diseases, training/ trellising systems and rootstocks, vineyard areas and grape production are also analysed in this chapter. Note that not all grape varieties grown in the country are considered; I have written, instead, about genuinely Brazilian cultivars and those which, for one reason or another, have distinctive characteristics and interest here.

In the next three chapters, I describe Brazil's geographical indications, its wine law (which can be quite peculiar and a bit tricky) and (in a condensed way) the Brazilian wine business. The chapters in Part 1 cover the general theoretical matters applicable to the whole country and are followed by the bulk of the book – that is, the chapters on the different regions, in Part 2. These include information about each area: its history, geography, tourism, producers and most relevant wines. Again, maps and pictures illustrate the text.

Rio Grande do Sul, the most important wine-producing state, occupies two chapters. The first focuses on Serra Gaúcha, where a large percentage of Brazilian wines are produced. The second covers all other areas in this state. Then, to conclude the South region, where traditional viticulture is practised, the next chapter is devoted to Santa Catarina and Paraná. Continuing northwards, there is a chapter dedicated to the Southeast, including São Paulo, Minas Gerais, Espírito Santo and Rio de Janeiro. This is the realm (albeit not exclusively) of double pruning and winter harvesting (DPWH), and a rapidly expanding and vast region. This same approach applies to the following chapter, on the Centre-West. Then, we turn to the Northeast (where tropical viticulture reigns).

Finally, Appendices on vintages and importers of Brazilian Wines in Europe and the US, along with a Glossary and some suggestions for further reading conclude this vinous journey through the vastness of Brazil. I hope the reader can find much to explore in this book and augment their expertise in this fascinating drink – made in Brazil.

Saúde!

A note on the text

Wineries who welcome visitors or offer wine tourism experiences are marked with ♀ .

General facts about Brazil

Brazil is huge: with 8,510,418 square kilometres, it is the fifth-largest country in the world, having the seventh-largest population: 203,062,512 people (as of 2022). The extensive surface area, however, allows for a density of just 23.9 humans per square kilometre, positioning it at 182 amongst all countries. Brazil has boundaries with all South American nations except Chile and Ecuador. Its extreme points are: 5°16' N, -33°45' S, -34°47' E and -73°59' W. The equator traverses Brazil across its northernmost portion; 7 per cent of its territory belongs in the Northern Hemisphere. The Tropic of Capricorn cuts the country through its biggest city, São Paulo. Time zones go from UTC-2 to UTC-5. The coastline measures 7,491 kilometres. Spanning such a large latitude and longitude, it's no wonder that we see a wide range of climates, relief and soils. The general view that Brazil is a tropical country *tout court* is, therefore, too superficial. There is vast complexity and heterogeneity here, with a correspondingly large variety of grape-growing terroirs.

Brazil is politically divided into five regions: North, Northeast, Centre-West, Southeast and South. These are subdivided into 27 states, including the Federal District (where Brasília, the country's capital, is located). There are 5,570 municipalities. From a vinous viewpoint, the most important states are Rio Grande do Sul, Santa Catarina (South region), São Paulo and Minas Gerais (Southeast), and Bahia and Pernambuco (Northeast).

Portuguese is the official and almost exclusively spoken language. Brazilian Portuguese, softer, slower and less guttural than the same idiom spoken in Portugal, is remarkably uniform across the country, although accents vary from region to region. According to the official agency the Instituto Brasileiro de Geografia e Estatística (IBGE) – or Brazilian Institute of Geography and

Statistics – in 2021, 43 per cent of Brazilians were (self-declared) white, 47 per cent mixed race and 9 per cent Black; the remaining 0.9 per cent were Indigenous.

In 2023, official data (World Bank) estimated Brazil's nominal gross domestic product (GDP) at US$ 2.17 trillion, the ninth-largest in the world. However, per capita GDP was placed at number 89, at US$ 9,070 (Atlas methodology). The human development index (HDI) was 0.76 (in 2023), also positioned at 89. Despite this large GDP, significant disproportions exist in the national wealth share distribution. There are huge social problems and a sizeable contingent of people with enormous needs. According to the Statista website, in 2021, the upper 10 per cent of the population (about 22 million people) had almost 80 per cent of the country's wealth, with just 1 per cent (2.2 million) of all inhabitants holding 48.9 per cent. The middle 40 per cent (over 87 million) owned 20.6 per cent of the wealth. There is, then, a very large population where wine consumption can grow.

Brazil's currency is the real (BRL).

PART 1
BACKGROUND

1

HISTORY OF WINE IN BRAZIL

Humans have long inhabited Brazil. Archaeological remains from Serra da Capivara, Piauí, have been dated by the carbon-14 method as being up to 54,000 years old, although this is controversial. One of the oldest (about 11,500 years old) human fossil skulls in the Americas (nicknamed 'Luzia') was found at Lagoa Santa, Minas Gerais.

A large population of Indigenous people, still known here (and not in a derogatory way) as 'índios' (estimated at 5 million people), lived in the country in about 1500, when the first Portuguese expedition arrived, or 'discovered' the land. This marks the start of Brazil's written history.

There were no wild vines growing here, as there were in North America. No wine, as such, could exist. Not that the índios didn't consume an alcoholic beverage – they did. It was (and is) called *cauim*. Made from manioc roots, its preparation, interestingly, demanded one step of chewing the cooked pieces of manioc. This task, performed exclusively by female virgins, allowed the contact of manioc's starch with the salivary amylase enzyme, which broke the unfermentable carbohydrate into smaller, fermentable units. The chewed matter was returned to a pan over a fire for a second cooking. The materials were then placed in semi-buried earthenware vessels, where fermentation started and stopped by itself. The beverage was (and still is among preserved cultures) drunk predominately during feasts and ceremonies.

The process of *cauim*-making was described during the sixteenth century by the French voyager Jean de Léry, as well as by the German mercenary and arquebusier Hans Staden (who was kept prisoner by the

*Cauim-making and consumption in Brazil, from Jodocus Hondius's
map of America*

Tupinambás índios for eight months). Léry observed, quite knowing-
ly, that people who perchance felt nauseated by this chewing process
should remember the way wine was then made in Europe. He pointed out that all grapes were foot-trodden, often while wearing coarse
boots, and that the treaders tarnished the grapes in the vats, where
'things less pleasing than the mastication of the women from America'
could occur. According to Dante Teixeira, in 1606 the Flemish engraver
Jodocus Hondius published an updated edition of the atlas from Gerard
Mercator; one of its beautiful illustrations, reproduced here, shows the
making and consumption of *cauim* in Brazil.

The original Latin text (in the upper part of the picture) can be translated as: 'Way of preparing and taking the drink among Americans in
Brazil, whereby virgins, after chewing the roots, spit them, cook them
in pots and offer them to males to drink. Such special beverages are considered delicious among them.'

ARRIVAL OF THE PORTUGUESE AND SPANISH

Wine was a part of Brazil's history from the very beginning. The first
Portuguese expedition, with no less than 13 ships and about 1,500 people, arrived there in 1500. Its leader was Pedro Álvares Cabral, who
disembarked at Bahia on 22 April. Cabral sent one of his ships back
to Portugal, taking news of the important discovery to his king, Dom
Manuel I. The news was conveyed in a letter written by the expedition's scribe, Pero Vaz de Caminha. He describes how the Portuguese
met the índios, this being a peaceful encounter. Wine, amongst other
things, was offered to them: 'Wine was brought to them in a goblet;

they barely put it in their mouths; they didn't like it at all, nor did they ask for more.' Caminha goes on writing, and, after some pages on other subjects, wine is again mentioned by him in a more optimistic mood: 'Some of them drank wine; others could not. But I think they will drink it in goodwill if they get used to it.'

Caminha was right more than 500 years ago. Brazilian people have, indeed, become used to wine, albeit not so much to fulfil the aspirations of those making and selling it – but this situation is changing.

The first Mass was celebrated in the newly discovered land five days after the Portuguese arrived. Wine is an integral part of the Catholic liturgy, and it was (and still is) considered as indispensable as food in many European countries. It is only natural that endeavours always to have wine available began just after white people arrived. Wine stocks were an important part of ships' supplies. Considering the hygiene standards of the 1500s (which would not change much for another three centuries, to say the least) and the conditions under which wine travelled, one can only wonder whether it was drinkable on arrival. Maybe the índios were right to reject the beverage, although documents indicate that the wines came from the prestigious Pêra Manca estate in Alentejo. It is no surprise that a great deal of effort has since been expended in trying to grow vines and produce wine. This happened in all parts of the Americas where the Portuguese and Spaniards, staunchly Catholic, arrived in that far-distant time. Brazil was undeniably already among the first places to produce wine on the new continent, in the sixteenth century, along with Peru, Mexico, Chile and Argentina.

From 1500 to 1530, the Portuguese limited themselves to extracting *pau brasil* (brazilwood or Pernambuco) from Brazil. However, the threat of having the land taken by the French induced King João III to start the actual occupation of the region. He sent an expedition, led by Martim Afonso de Souza, to colonize Brazil. This involved sending craftsmen, including farmers, to plant sugar cane and other commodities. One of the most important people in de Souza's expedition was the nobleman Brás Cubas. Coming from the Douro region, he was a winemaker and brought vine cuttings with him. It is reported that these came from the Douro (Malvasia variety), Alentejo (Galego) and Madeira (Verdelho, Bastardo and Tinta). He tried cultivating vines at São Vicente, on the seaboard of the present state of São Paulo, but the hot, humid climate thwarted his endeavours. Together with his fellow Portuguese João Ramalho (son-in-law to an Indigenous chief), he climbed the coastal range (now Serra do Mar), arriving at the Piratininga region, the present site of São Paulo's metropolis. There, at a higher altitude (around 900 metres), with a more temperate climate, he successfully planted and kept the first Brazilian vineyard of note. From this, he made the first Brazilian wine in 1551 – a fact recorded in the archives of the Carmo Convent in Santos (now a big port and city, it was founded by Cubas). This can be legitimately considered the start of viticulture and winemaking in Brazil, with Brás Cubas as its founding father.

Not that the Portuguese settlers did not try elsewhere. On the island of Itamaracá, in Bahia, the varieties Moscatel, Ferral and Dedo de Dama (called Cornichon in France) were planted, possibly even before the successful attempt of Brás Cubas, in 1542. It is likely, although unrecorded, that regional wines were produced there. On the other hand, it is known that other plantings of the same cultivars were established on another Bahia island, Itaparica, in the seventeenth century. This endeavour was supported by Prince Johan Maurits van Nassau-Siegen, head of the Dutch domination of a part of north-eastern Brazil, sponsored by the newly founded *West-Indische Compagnie* (Dutch West India Company), from 1636 to 1644. Itamaracá's coat of arms included a cluster of grapes, as seen in a painting by Franz Post. The Itamaracá vineyards existed until the first half of the nineteenth century when they were left to their own devices and perished.

The Jesuit priest Manuel da Nóbrega wrote in 1549 that he saw vines and grapes in Brazil's Northeast, observing that they could yield two harvests in a single year. This was Brazil's first register of tropical viticulture, including the characteristic of more frequent crops – something that, importantly, continues to this day. This was endorsed by Gabriel Soares de Sousa, a Portuguese who lived for 17 years in Bahia, where he owned land. He wrote a book, *Tratado Descriptivo do Brasil* (Descriptive Treatise on Brazil), which was published in 1587. The book was revised by Francisco Varnhagen, Viscount of Porto Seguro, and republished in 1879. When writing about the *capitanias* of São Vicente and Santo Amaro (in today's São Paulo), he stated that vines did well there and that some people were making two pipes (barrels) of wine a year. He noted, however, that such wine was green and needed to be boiled to avoid becoming vinegary. Of Bahia, he wrote that there were plenty of vines, always green, with the leaves never falling, and that they produced a crop whenever they were pruned, which was ordinarily twice a year. There, however, ants were rife and could decimate a vine overnight, which was a reason for not establishing more vineyards.

Another important thread in the early history of Brazil's wine was not of Portuguese origin, but rather Spanish. Again, the Jesuits: to convert índios to the Catholic faith, but also to protect them from being enslaved, Jesuit priests led by Padre Roque González de Santa Cruz established, from the early seventeenth century (1626), organized communes in southern Brazil, named *reduções* (reductions, or Missions). There, the índios were taught the practice of agriculture and other professions. Vines were needed among the established cultures in order to generate wines for the Mass. There was a cellar under the main refectory (I have seen it at the impressive ruins in São Miguel das Missões, Rio Grande do Sul). The grapevines probably came from or via Argentina or Uruguay, as did the missionaries. Texts from then and more recently mention at least two varieties: Molar and Tintilla. The *reduções* existed in today's states of Paraná (Guairá) and Rio Grande do Sul (Sete Povos das Missões). All were terminated violently by the action of slavers or due to the rivalry between Portugal and Spain, at the beginning of the eighteenth century. Roland Joffé's movie, *The Mission*, from 1986, shows a part of this sad history.

Also, at Rio Grande do Sul and Santa Catarina, a wave of immigrants from the Azores and Madeira arrived during the eighteenth century. According to the excellent book (in three beautiful volumes) by Rinaldo dal Pizzol and Sérgio Inglez de Sousa, they brought their viticultural traditions with them, establishing vineyards in the region between the Jacuí and Taquari rivers, close to the future state capital, Porto Alegre. Historic registers reveal that commercial wine production existed in the first half of the nineteenth century, thus establishing the area as the cradle of viticulture in Rio Grande do Sul, the most important wine-producing state in Brazil.

Back to the Piratininga vineyards: despite being productive to the point of heavy clusters touching the earth and experiencing proper dormancy due to sufficient cold in winter, no better fate than Itaparica's awaited them, according to some views. Before their decline, however, they became fairly significant. Although most of the wine consumed in Brazil for religious and everyday purposes was imported or smuggled from Portugal and Spain, some from Piratininga arrived in the Northeast and North of the country. Wine production became important enough to be taxed under invigilation. Carlos Cabral, in his delightful book *Presença do vinho no Brasil – um pouco de história*, describes how, in 1640, the City Council of São Paulo de Piratininga demanded that all wine merchants present their products to be tasted and approved. This was the first recording of an official wine tasting in Brazil.

Then, in 1695, gold was discovered in today's state of Minas Gerais, leading to a rush. This reduced manpower significantly in São Paulo. Another result was high inflation, which increased the price of everything. Wine became very expensive, to such a degree that seems hard to understand today. One small barrel (*barrilote*) of wine (possibly 25–50 litres, or what a slave could carry) was sold in the mining region at no less than 200 octaves, or 600 grams, of gold! Notwithstanding this, all agricultural activities in São Paulo were neglected and almost abandoned – vines included. Only a small residual area of the former vineyards survived, and the commercial production of wine almost disappeared. Some scholars, however, do not agree, believing that viticulture and winemaking continued despite the various difficulties (see The Southeast, page 285).

To make matters worse, in 1785 the Portuguese Queen Maria I (known as 'Maria the Mad') prohibited all manufacturing activities in Brazil, including winemaking. The intention was to avoid competition between locally made goods and those coming from Portugal. No wonder the still-incipient wine industry ground to a halt in the country – it was still a Portuguese colony.

NINETEENTH-CENTURY DEVELOPMENTS

Not much later, Europe was thrown into great turmoil by the Napoleonic Wars (1803–1815). Napoleon's troops invaded Portugal when the country was governed by the regent João (son of Maria the Mad). Before they reached Lisbon, the royal family and a great part of the court, supported by the English, fled to Brazil. A new court was established in Rio de Janeiro from 1808 onwards, and João became king as João VI. Although this marked the adoption of European manners and behaviour by the upper tiers of society – including wine consumption – the state of the local winemaking infrastructure did not change significantly in the first decades of the nineteenth century. Most wine, then, was imported, mainly from Portugal.

At such times, the English Lieutenant Henry Chamberlain visited Rio. A good watercolourist and dedicated observer of local costumes, he painted many pictures and wrote a book with interesting accompanying text, *Views and Costumes of the City and Neighbourhood of Rio de Janeiro*, which was published in 1821. Shown below is a picture from the book depicting how slaves then transported wine barrels, on carts or on their backs, in Rio de Janeiro. This state of affairs, of the vile exploitation of men by men, was only to end (at least legally) in Brazil in 1888 when Princess Isabel abolished slavery.

In 1822, after João returned to Portugal, his son Pedro, who remained as regent, proclaimed Brazil's independence from Portugal and became its first emperor as Pedro I.

Another type of invasion then took place, with effects – at least on Brazilian viticulture – comparable to those of Napoleon's on European history. These were long-lasting and have lingered until the present day. This invasion was the introduction of American hybrids in Brazil, especially Isabella (here known as Isabel). Isabel is a Bailey spontaneous

Slaves transporting wine at Rua Direita, Rio de Janeiro, in the early nineteenth century (from Henry Chamberlain's Views and Costumes of the City and Neighbourhood of Rio de Janeiro)

labrusca/vinifera cross. Two versions of this introduction exist. Firstly, Englishman Thomas Messiter bought land in Rio Grande do Sul on the Island of Marinheiros and Serra dos Tapes. He became a dealer and importer. Cuttings of Isabel were possibly sent to him by José Marques Lisboa, a diplomatic counsellor (and later an important admiral in the Brazilian Navy), who served in Washington between 1837 and 1838. Messiter planted the cuttings in the aforementioned locations, from which they would disseminate to other parts of the state and country. Secondly, another Englishman, John Rudge, bought land where São Paulo is located today, planting extensive vineyards of Isabel in around 1830. Whoever the pioneer was, he was certainly English, the deed was done, and Isabel succeeded so well that this variety is the most planted cultivar in Brazil to this day. This is due to its great productivity, disease resistance and ability to thrive in climates where *vinifera* varieties struggle. Isabel (and other American hybrids) are used to produce the majority of wines popularly drunk in Brazil, where they are classified as *vinhos de mesa* (table wine), as opposed to *vinho fino* (fine wine), made from European varieties.

Emperor Pedro I left Brazil in 1831 after abdicating and came back to Portugal to become its king (not without fierce opposition). His son became the second (and last) Brazilian emperor, Pedro II. In contrast to his impetuous father, who reigned here briefly, Pedro II ruled the country for 58 years. After slavery was abolished, increased immigration was called for to provide the manpower needed for agriculture, a trend that began before the abolition of slavery. Portuguese immigration had already existed for a long time, with German immigrants beginning to arrive in Rio Grande do Sul as early as 1824. The coming of people from other European and Asian countries was also promoted in the second half of the nineteenth century: Spain, Italy, Poland, Syria, Lebanon and Japan, among many others. The most important contingent, as it pertains to wine, was not Portuguese but rather Italian.

Although most Italian immigrants went to São Paulo, many settled in Rio Grande do Sul, Brazil's southernmost state. About 84,000 Italians arrived, mainly from northern Italy (Veneto, Lombardia and Trentino). All families received pieces of land, called *lotes*, each measuring 25–30 hectares. Such government-owned land was mostly available in Serra Gaúcha, a mountainous region in north-eastern Rio Grande do Sul. As they did at home, the Italian settlers planted grapevines and made wine. For this, they mainly used Isabel and other resistant hybrids. After a few

Italian immigrants harvesting grapes in Serra Gaúcha (IBGE, public domain)

years, official registers pointed to over 11 million litres of wine being made annually. Although most of it was consumed locally and regionally, some of the wine found its way to other states, like São Paulo. At first, the commerce in such wines was dominated by German immigrants. Later, however, the Italians themselves took charge of transportation and sales. Wine quality in those days was by no means uniform, but those with more knowledge began to fight to produce better wines. This included moving away from Isabel and using either better hybrids (Norton/Cynthiana, Oberlin) or, importantly, classical European varieties such as Barbera and Merlot. The picture above shows Italian immigrants in a grape harvest scene at Serra Gaúcha.

Phylloxera was first diagnosed in Brazil in 1893 in Andradas, Minas Gerais. Its effects have not been as disastrous as in Europe because a significant percentage of wine grapes grown at that time were American hybrids. The same applies to fungal diseases of the same origin.

The first registered winery in the country dates from 1892: J. Marimon & Filhos, in Candiota, Rio Grande do Sul. This place, Quinta do Seival, is now owned by the big Miolo Wine Group and continues to be important in the world of Brazilian wine.

Coincidentally, the first winemaking schools and laboratories appeared at the turn of the twentieth century, such as the first oenological laboratory of Rio Grande do Sul, which was established in 1899. The cooperative movement also started a few years later, motivated by the federal government. The first cooperative was founded in 1911 at Caxias do Sul, in Serra Gaúcha. Others soon followed suit.

THE TWENTIETH CENTURY DAWNS

The first decades of the twentieth century brought two important developments: the quest for better quality and the appearance of more significant négociant enterprises to allow for more widely distributed wine sales and to fight falsification. A group of Italian oenologists, led by Celeste Gobbato (later the author of an important book, the *Manual do Vitivinicultor Brasileiro),* was contracted by the state government and began to teach. This had very important, long-term multiplier effects on Brazilian winemaking, including the constant stimulus to change from Isabel to European varieties – not a very easy task, as the latter are much less resistant and lower yielding.

Wine producers and dealers were empowered through the foundation of the first union, the Sindicato Vinícola do Rio Grande do Sul, in 1927. One of the main objectives of this union was to fight fraud. Here, as everywhere, this was rife. Many wines sold in other states as *vinho gaúcho* (wine from Rio Grande do Sul) were rough mixtures of

First assembly of Cooperativa Vinícola Aurora associates (photo: public domain)

many components, including wines made elsewhere. Their poor quality damaged the reputation of *vinho gaúcho* and needed to be challenged. At more or less the same time, new cooperatives, more stable and lasting than the first, were founded: no less than 52 from 1930 to 1936. These included the Cooperativa Vinícola Aurora, established in 1931 (see photograph, p. 18); it is today, with 1,100 associated families, one of the biggest wine producers in Brazil.

The efforts to replace Isabel with European varieties continued, led by oenologists and oenology schools such as the Estação Experimental de Viticultura e Enologia (EEVE) – Experimental Station of Viticulture and Oenology – at Caxias do Sul. As usual, however, it was the commercial success of a wine that showed growers how converting to *vinifera* could be good for business. The first bottled Brazilian varietal wines sold as such and crafted from European varieties (Bonarda, Cabernet Sauvignon) were branded *Granja União* and made from the 1937 vintage. They were produced by Companhia Vinícola Rio-Grandense from a 150-hectare vineyard in Flores da Cunha. It was a national success, despite the small volume of production, and remained so for decades, signalling the start of varietal culture among wine lovers in the country – pertaining to Brazilian wines, of course. It is interesting to see the names on the labels of a series of wines made during the 1930s in Rio Grande do Sul, as mentioned by Rinaldo Dal Pizzol and Inglez de Sousa: Clarete, Rheno, Porto, Liebfraumilch and Champagne. Almost all of these were made from American hybrids, at a time when (somewhat naively) generalized names of famous European wine types were used to label local products – much as in the US, Australia or South Africa.

According to the same authors, in 1940 Rio Grande do Sul sold 37,357 hectolitres of wine to other Brazilian states, mainly to São Paulo and Rio de Janeiro. Interestingly, 34,184 hectolitres were sold in bulk (barrels), while just 3,173 hectolitres were bottled wines.

Wine exports started in 1958, taking advantage of a great wine shortage in France. Then, Brazil sold 30 million litres of bulk wine to France after various negotiations, which included Count Robert-Jean de Vogüé of Moët & Chandon. Argentina also bought 4 million litres, whereas Switzerland imported another 2 million. This favourably impressed Brazilian consumers, drawing their attention to the domestic wines. Another innovation (for the local market) emerged: a branded wine made by a winery for a third party. Bernard Taillan, a Frenchman who owned vineyards in Algeria, had an import business in Brazil (being instrumental in the aforementioned exports). He died just a little after this transaction was completed, being replaced by his partner Count Guy de Foucauld. The latter planned and, indeed, launched, from 1962, a *vinho fino*, made by Cooperativa Aurora and labelled Bernard Taillan. This brand was important in promoting the new category of superior Brazilian wines amongst a consumer group with influencing power. Some years later, in 1976, Aurora started to produce another brand (for itself) called Conde de Foucauld – which persists to this day. Also during the 1970s, the vermouth-making company Martini & Rossi entered the market of *vinhos finos*, again through wines produced by another firm, the same Companhia Vinícola Rio-Grandense that owned Granja União. For Martini, Companhia started to make the Château Duvalier brand, with enormous commercial success. The names of such brands draw attention to a kind of Brazilian trait, fortunately (but very gradually) waning: foreign words can be more worthy of esteem than local denominations. Many a fine wine made here was so christened, and not only with French influence: Katz Wein, Kiedrich, Nachtliebewein, De Gréville, Baron de Lantier, Clos de Nobles, Majou Tanret, Cave d'Aubigny and many others – a long list.

BIG BUSINESS AND NEW FRONTIERS

The last decades of the twentieth century saw the appearance of family enterprises which later became very successful. To name but a few: Salton, Miolo, Valduga, Dal Pizzol, Valmarino, Lídio Carraro, Don Giovanni and Perini, all of Italian heritage. These coexisted with the arrival of foreign investors: LVMH (through Provifin, later Chandon do Brasil, in 1973 – one of the first wineries of the group outside France), Heublein (1972), Seagram (owner of Maison Forestier), National Distillers (through Almadén) and Martini & Rossi. It was through Martini that the Argentine oenologist Adolfo Alberto Lona arrived at Serra Gaúcha. He achieved enormous success with the Baron de Lantier *vin de garde* and De Gréville sparkling wines. He was also very effective in stimulating and supporting wine associations and wine lovers' movements, disseminating the culture of wine widely. As for Maison Forestier, in the early 1980s it introduced important technological improvements, such as temperature-controlled vessels made of stainless steel with electronic controls. Forestier also launched various varietal wines, including a pioneering Chenin Blanc from São Francisco Valley.

In the 1980s and 1990s, the consolidation of big winemaking businesses and the influence of imported wines (mainly from Chile, Argentina and Portugal) made it mandatory to improve the general quality of Brazilian wines, both through viticulture and winemaking. A much-needed conversion from pergola (here called *latada)* to upright, vertical vine planting and trellising systems (known generally as *espaldeira)* took place, and much higher standards of care provided better grapes. In winemaking, the adoption of stainless steel and temperature control, modern laboratories and, above all, the better training of oenologists improved quality and brought Brazilian winemaking in line with that of any other wine-producing country.

The role of the former Colégio de Viticultura e Enologia (CVE), in Bento Gonçalves, founded in 1959, cannot be overemphasized: it trained the vast majority of Brazilian oenologists, first as technicians and later (from 1995) at college level. Today, it is a part of the network of *institutos federais*, providing professional and technological education nationwide. On a par with this, another institution was developing in the city of Bento Gonçalves: the former Oenological Station (working since 1942) became, in 1985, the Centro Nacional de Pesquisa de Uva e Vinho (CNPUV) – the National Centre for Grape and Wine Research – which is part of Embrapa Uva e Vinho. Empresa Brasileira de Pesquisa Agropecuária (Embrapa) is the prestigious Brazilian Agricultural Research Corporation responsible for many advances in the country's mighty agriculture. Today, both Instituto Federal do Rio Grande do Sul (IFRS) and Embrapa Uva e Vinho are fundamental to the technical and scientific foundations of Brazilian viticulture and oenology.

Until the end of the twentieth century, the only significant wine-producing region in Brazil was Serra Gaúcha. From the 1980s onwards, however, extraordinary developments took place in other regions. The first, still in Rio Grande do Sul, was Campanha Gaúcha, on the Uruguayan border. Brazil was then under a military regime. The state oil company, Petrobrás, was led by a general, Ernesto Geisel, from Rio Grande do Sul, who later became president of the country. National Distillers, an American company dealing in many industries, including petrol and wine, was a frequent partner of Petrobrás. It is said that Geisel challenged (and encouraged) National to establish a winery in the state. Together with the governor and other political figures, the Uruguayan

Juan Carrau (a winemaker himself) acted as a middleman, promoting a meeting between them and National's CEO, a Mr Bell. The decision was taken to start a new wine business through Almadén, owned by National, at Rio Grande do Sul. The first experimental vineyard was planted at Bagé. A few years later, with the prestigious assistance of Harold Olmo from the University of California (Davis), a larger area was chosen at Sant'ana do Livramento. There, Almadén bought land (1,200 hectares) and planted extensive new vineyards, launching ten varietal wines and making one million cases each year. Although changing hands (first to Seagram, then to Miolo), production continues, and, more importantly, has shown the potential of the new region to other makers, thus consolidating this new vinous hub. Also in Rio Grande do Sul, other regions (Serra do Sudeste and Campos de Cima da Serra), which are drier than Serra Gaúcha, have been developed and continue to thrive.

However, another unexpected wine centre was developed very far away: the São Francisco River Valley in Brazil's tropical Northeast. Relying on irrigation from this big river, fruit-producing enterprises appeared in the 1980s. These included grape growing, mainly table grapes, but also wine cultivars. With incentives from the government, the production of wine had already started there in 1984, and always from *vinifera* grapes. Subsequently, other groups and firms established themselves in the region, taking advantage of the particular conditions of tropical viticulture, in which (on average) more than two crops a year are possible.

More or less simultaneously, another significant region arose in Santa Catarina state, at altitude (900–1,400 metres), where the cool climate allowed apple growing. A little later, in 2007, 200 hectares were in production, all planted with *vinifera*. This area has grown considerably and has recently been awarded an *Indicação de Procedência* (IP) or Provenance Indication classification.

INTO THE TWENTY-FIRST CENTURY

The start of the twenty-first century saw the rise of a novel vine-growing technique that has allowed a true revolution in the production of wine in Brazilian regions where this was previously insignificant. Double pruning and winter harvesting (DPWH) management, pioneered by Murillo Albuquerque Regina, was introduced experimentally in Três Corações, Minas Gerais state, in the 2000s. This is a technique (see page 42) whereby a second pruning, usually performed in January, induces a second growing cycle in the vine. This allows the ripening of the grapes during the winter (dry and sunny in Central Brazil). Planting at altitude, DPWH has led to the production of several prize-winning wines in Minas, São Paulo and other states. This has added a new dimension and a third approach to grape growing in the country, besides the traditional viticulture (in the south of the country) and multi-harvest tropical viticulture (Vale do São Francisco) – something unique in the world of wine.

In parallel, the introduction of origin certification is an ongoing process. The first IP, for Vale dos Vinhedos in Serra Gaúcha, was granted in 2002. Since then, ten other IPs and two DOs (*Denominação de Origem*) have followed suit, contributing to improved wine quality.

According to the International Organization of Vine and Wine (OIV), Brazil is presently one of the 15 biggest producers of wine in the world (with a total annual volume of 3.6 million hectolitres) and has the twenty-second-largest vineyard (considering all grapes, including those used for eating and raisins). Per capita consumption is still small (an annual figure of about 2.64 litres per person based on 2021's figures), but is growing. Most importantly, the production, consumption, quality, sales and exports of *vinifera* wines have increased remarkably in recent decades.

Today, Brazilian wine is poised to continue growing in variety, originality, quality and quantity. This growth is supported by an increasingly robust internal market, growing interest abroad, new regions and original techniques. Therefore, the history of more than 500 years of wine production in Brazil points to a promising future.

2

LAYOUT OF THE COUNTRY

TOPOGRAPHY

Many people wrongly believe that Brazil's terrain is mostly lowlands. This is perhaps due to the Amazon and Pantanal, two very large areas of low, wet terrain with incredible biological diversity, plus the long area of flat terrain along the coast, which is embroidered by hundreds of beautiful beaches and dunes, lagoons and mangroves (the *mangues*).

This impression is reinforced because Brazil is remarkably rich in rivers, along which many lowlands exist. There are eight major drainage basins. One is the largest (in length and discharge) river on the planet, the Amazon, and its many tributaries (for example, Juruá, Purus, Madeira, Negro, Tapajós, Xingu and Tocantins). All river basins cover an immense territory, about 46 per cent of the whole country, including a significant number of other mighty watercourses (Paraná, São Francisco, Jequitinhonha, Grande, Paraíba and so on). Brazil has one of the largest freshwater reservoirs in the world. The São Francisco River, 1,609 kilometres long and whose basin covers nearly 8 per cent of the country's surface, is the most significant in vinous terms. It is here that tropical viticulture flourishes.

The truth, however, is that a large portion of the country is formed by highlands, here called *planaltos*. When it comes to vine growing, the lowlands are unsuitable – they are too hot, too humid and a hostile environment for vines. For viticulture, it is the highlands that matter. These are roughly divided into two groups. The first, Guiana Highlands, is home to the two highest peaks in Brazil: Pico da Neblina, at 2,995 metres, and Pico 31 de Março at 2,974 metres. Situated in the part of the country in the Northern Hemisphere, which is warmer due to its proximity to the equator and is sparsely populated and remote, such highlands have not been cultivated significantly. There are no vineyards here. The other group is far larger, and, as regards wine, is the one deserving interest. The ensemble of such highlands is known as the Brazilian Highlands, or *Planalto Central Brasileiro*, and has an average altitude of about 1,000 metres. Map 1 indicates its approximate contour in red. It is usual to divide this vast area of about 5 million square kilometres into smaller units, as the geographer Aroldo de Azevedo devised in 1949. These are as follows:

Map 1: Relief map of Brazil. Also shown are the altitudes of some vineyards in several Brazilian states. RS: Rio Grande do Sul; SC: Santa Catarina; PR: Paraná; SP: São Paulo; MS: Mato Grosso do Sul; MG: Minas Gerais; GO: Goiás; MT: Mato Grosso; BA: Bahia; PE: Pernambuco.

- *Planalto Central* is the area around the country's centre, the capital Brasília and neighbouring regions, such as Goiás state.
- *Planalto Meridional* (Southern Highlands) in the states of Paraná, Santa Catarina and Rio Grande do Sul.
- *Planalto do Meio-Norte* in the states of Maranhão, Piauí and Ceará, in the Northeast region.
- The comparatively small *Planalto Nordestino*, or *da Borborema* (in the north-eastern states Alagoas, Pernambuco, Paraíba and Rio Grande do Norte).
- *Serras e Planaltos do Leste e do Sudeste*, or Eastern and Southeastern Ranges and Highlands, the largest area of Brazilian Highlands, encompassing many states (south to north: Paraná, Santa Catarina, São Paulo, Rio de Janeiro, Espírito Santo, Minas Gerais, Goiás and Bahia).

The topography, in all Brazilian highlands, is by no means homogeneous. Although the terrain is very old, and the extremes of altitude are only moderate (no part of the country reaches 3,000 metres), most of the highlands show hills of varying gradients, mountain ranges (here known as *serras*), elevations with a more or less flat top, or *chapadas*, gorges, ravines, cliffs and large, rocky outcrops. There are, however, extensive areas that are relatively regular, called *cerrados*. This type of savanna totals 2 million square kilometres in central Brazil, mainly inside the Brazilian Highlands. Although some of its areas are pretty dry, there is great biological variety. As in much of the highlands, winters are sunny and dry, an essential component of double pruning and winter harvesting (DPWH), one of Brazil's three climatic types of viticulture.

A long range of mountains runs along the east coast, more or less from Minas Gerais to Paraná – this is the Serra do Mar, which has a series of subdivisions and ramifications, as well as some of the highest peaks in the country, such as the Pico da Bandeira (2,890 metres). One part of this system, the Serra da Mantiqueira (in the states of Minas Gerais, São Paulo and Rio de Janeiro), is becoming important in Brazilian wine-growing, again due to DPWH.

In the Northeast, where the climate is much drier than in other parts of Brazil, the *cerrados* give way to the *caatinga* – large areas of relatively flat terrain with a semi-arid tropical climate. Here, agriculture depends on irrigation. Despite the high temperatures, viticulture has developed, and the conditions permit more than one harvest yearly.

With very few exceptions (the most important being Campanha Gaúcha, in the extreme South), viticulture has been successful in Brazil only at significant altitudes. Be it in the South, the realm of traditional viticulture, the Southeast and Centre-West, where DPWH is growing fast, or the Northeast, home of tropical viticulture, vineyards are planted at elevations of around 370 metres to more than 1,200 metres above sea level (see Map 1, page 25). This counterbalances temperatures that can be higher at low altitudes than is desirable for grape growing.

GEOLOGY

When we see a physical map of South America, with the high elevations of the Andes, and learn about earthquakes in countries around it, we may assume that Brazil also has geological and volcanic activity of note. This would mean a more recent geological history. Yet, this is incorrect: the terrain is much older. More than 36 per cent of Brazil is on Precambrian rocks, formed more than 541 million years ago. Some are even older, from about 3 billion years ago, formed during the Archaean aeon.

In some areas, however, volcanic activity occurred during the Palaeozoic (251–539 million years ago), when the Gondwana super-continent still existed. Such was the case for terrains that today lie in the north-eastern states of Maranhão and Piauí and the southern Paraná state. During the late Palaeozoic, all supercontinents on Earth united to form the single land unit of Pangea. During the Cretaceous period of the Mesozoic era, Gondwana began to break down, thus separating South America from Africa. Remains of such cleavage can be found in Pernambuco, São Paulo and Paraná. Geological activity gradually diminished, ending at the present general picture of very old terrain at low altitudes and nearly no seismic occurrences.

Brazil has no earthquakes of note, except for some activity in its westernmost areas (like the state of Acre), nearer to the Andes. Looking at the tectonic plates on Earth, Brazil is entirely contained within a single plate, the South American Plate, with borders distant from the country. These are, in fact, along the Pacific coast of South America (meeting the Nazca Plate), in the middle of the southern portion of the Atlantic, midway between Brazil and Africa (where the African Plate begins), to the south of Cape Horn (marking the appearance of the Antarctic Plate) and far away north of the country (where the North American and Caribbean plates begin). No wonder maps of tectonic and volcanic activity show Brazil as a very calm part of the world. NASA research pointed to 358,214 epicentres of seismic events in the whole world in the period 1963–1998. Of these, only about 20 (0.006 per cent) were in Brazil. There are no active volcanoes in the country; those extinct a very long time ago now look more like steep hills.

There is a relationship between soils and geomorphic surfaces, which implies that the older the latter, the more homogenous the present soils. This could explain why, in Brazil, despite the great number of soil types, some more comprehensive orders are predominant, such as the *latossolos*. These soils, notwithstanding their significant clay content, high acidity and low fertility, have good drainage and may be suitable for viticulture.

SOILS

There used to be two views on what primarily determines wine quality and attributes when the viticultural site is the focus. The first was the Old World (predominately French) approach, which stressed, first and foremost, the so-called terroir. Even when geology and landscape were the main factors, the soil was also an integral component, sometimes with unfounded exaggerations (as, for instance, believing that the taste of wine could come from minerals directly absorbed by the vine from the soil). The second was the New World version, with a stress on climate, water and nutrient supply rather than soil types. Although these two views are more diffuse currently, when terroir is being increasingly sought after in New World countries (note the appearance of 'terroir experts' like Pedro Parra in Chile), this duality of thought remains valid.

One way or the other, however, as Robert E. White described in his excellent book *Soils for Fine Wines* (2003), it is impossible to escape from expert management of the soil if grapes and wines of good quality are the aim. Viticulturists should never forget that vines have a long productive life (sometimes reaching five decades), so their relationship with the soil in which they are planted must be the best. It is the soil that, in very different ways according to its type and composition, will provide water and nutrients, hence determining such fundamental properties as vigour, balance, yield and, ultimately, grape quality. On the other hand, the soil is also home to pests and diseases, which can deeply influence the biology of the vines and, again, the quality of grapes. Successful viticulturists must, therefore, know their soils well and keep them in good condition. This is achievable, inevitably, through a sound knowledge of pedology.

Soil classification systems

It is impossible to adequately study a subject as complex as soils without a solid classification system. Classifying soils allows growers to understand their characteristics and limitations, predict their behaviour, exchange technical information, and pinpoint their most correct or suitable use. Therefore, this is not merely an academic exercise.

Wine books commonly describe soils in a somewhat simplistic way, often considering single factors (for example, granitic, basaltic) or mixing classification criteria in an isolated manner (such as describing a region as having sandy, silty and chalky soils – the first two are textures and the last one mineral composition). Sometimes, superficial generalizations are made – for instance, stating that all sandy soils are loose and well drained, when some of them may have a solid, cemented subsoil that is difficult to drain. I have, therefore, opted for a more scientific, complete and complex system of soil classification, as described below. Needless to say, this is more demanding to understand but allows for greater precision.

Given the size of the country, its geological features and the variety of climates, it is no wonder that Brazil has a multitude of soil types. The country has its own classification of soils. This has been developed by Embrapa, a 40-year-old federal organization responsible for developing, in their own words, a genuinely tropical model of agriculture and animal farming. This institution will appear in the book several times, and for good reason: it is one of the main factors in Brazil's ascent to agricultural powerhouse. It has a vine and wine division called Embrapa Uva e Vinho. Significant developments in the Brazilian wine sector are always arising from their work, such as the Multicriteria Climatic Classification (MCC) of grape-growing regions, breeding new varieties, or the establishment of geographical indications.

The Sistema Brasileiro de Classificação de Solos (SiBCS) – or Brazilian System of Soil Classification – now in its fifth edition, has some similarities with the international World Reference Base for Soil Resources (WRBSR) and the American Soil Taxonomy. It covers the entire national territory and is a hierarchical system with categorical levels of soil properties: orders (first level, with 13 classes), suborders (second), great groups (third), subgroups (fourth), families (fifth) and series (sixth). The combination of all levels results in a very large series of complete classification types; the detailed soil map of the whole country has no less than 713 types. This high-resolution map is very interesting to study (search the internet for 'IBGE solos 1:5.000.000').

Morphological and analytical data are used to classify soils in SiBCS. Morphological criteria include colour (such as red, red-yellow, yellow) and texture. Analytical data are more numerous and may be, for example, the percentage of mineral materials, the activity of the clay fraction, pH, rate of silt to clay, and the content of ferrous oxides, aluminium and organic matter, among other criteria. The first level (order) and second level (suborder) appear in abbreviations as upper-case letters. Features of the third level or below appear as lower-case letters. Here are some examples:

- Order: L – *latossolo*, P – *argissolo*, R – *neossolo*, F – *plintossolo*
- Suborder: A – *amarelo* (yellow), H – *húmico* (humic), N – *nátrico* (rich in sodium), V – *vermelho* (red)
- Great group: a – *alumínico* (rich in aluminium), d – *distrófico* (dystrophic, or infertile), e – *eutrófico* (fertile), n – *sódico* (rich in sodium), x – *coeso* (cohesive), and so on

In this way, a soil classified as PVAd is *argissolo* (P) *vermelho-amarelo* (VA, or red-yellow) *distrófico* (d, or infertile). Incidentally, this is the most common type in the country, occupying more than 1.5 million square kilometres.

The 13 orders of soils (*solos*, in Portuguese) in Brazil, according to SiBCS, are (in descending order of percentage of occurrence): *latossolos* (31.6 per cent), *argissolos* (26.9), *neossolos* (13.2), *plintossolos* (7.0), *cambissolos* (5.3), *gleissolos* (4.7), *luvissolos* (2.9), *planossolos* (2.7), *espodossolos* (2.0), *nitossolos* (1.1), *chernossolos* (0.4), *vertissolos* (0.2) and *organossolos* (0.03). Seventy-two per cent of Brazilian territory comprises just three orders of soils: *latossolos*, *argissolos* and *neossolos*. The first two add up to 58 per cent of the whole. Map 2, opposite, shows the distribution of the 13 orders of soils in the country.

This section will now look briefly at the first level (orders) of the Brazilian System of Soil Classification and the three most frequent orders in Brazil.

Latossolos (ferralsols in the WRBSR classification, or oxisols in the American taxonomy), the most frequent order in Brazil, are very old and intensely weathered (greatly changed when compared to the parental rock). They are deep (1–2 metres or more), are more common

Map 2: Distribution of the 13 orders of soils in Brazil (redrawn courtesy of IBGE)

on flat terrain or rolling hills, and usually have low fertility and high aluminium content, demanding correction (with lime, fertilizers). They have a red, yellow or yellow-red colour derived from iron oxides. They are usually strongly acidic, with low base saturation. They have suitable porosity and permeability, hence waterlogging is not a common problem. Rocks are usually absent in the topsoil and subsoil, making *latossolos* suitable for cultivation; they are not prone to erosion. Despite occurring more frequently in tropical areas, and hence being less favourable to wine growing, they also appear in subtropical parts of the country, where most of the viticulture occurs. Their total area in Brazil is 2,681,566 square kilometres.

Argissolos (WRBSR's acrisols, or American ultisols) are those showing an accumulation of clay (*argila*, in Portuguese) in the 'B' horizon (the second most superficial layer of the soil). The clay has moved from the 'A' to the 'B' horizon. Hence, there is more sand in the former than the latter. They may have different colours (red, red-yellow, yellow, grey), and they tend to occur on terrains with a relief rougher than those where *latossolos* predominate. A high aluminium content is frequent, and such soils are mostly acidic. As many are also dystrophic, correction is needed when cultivated. They also demand protective measures against erosion, as the topsoil contains less clay. Total area: 2,285,371 square kilometres.

Neossolos (WRBSR's fluvisols, or American entisols) are, as the name suggests (*néos* means new in Greek), young, shallow soils, which may show many characteristics from the base rocky material. The origin may be alluvial or from Precambrian rocks. They are more common in areas with strong inclination, although they may also occur along rivers. They are very prone to erosion on slopes. Total area: 1,122,594 square kilometres.

Soils and wine growing in Brazil

Some general points to note about soils and the bearing they have on wine in Brazil are:

- The country's most frequent soil types have a significant clay content. In many books, clay soils are described as poorly draining, hard or sticky. This is not the case in Brazil, where most clay soils have a good structure and, even when completely dry, do not harden too much.

- Many of these soils require fertilizers.

- Most Brazilian soils are acidic (pH less than 7.0). This makes it challenging to accumulate calcium carbonate. Limestone or chalky soils, therefore, are not common except in some semi-arid regions, where the soil pH is alkaline.

- Acidity correction, therefore, is very frequently needed in the country.

- The sheer dimensions of the country do not allow oversimplifications, such as, for example, expressions like 'the Northeastern soils' or 'the soils of Minas Gerais' (a vast state, larger than France).

3

CLIMATE

Like the topography, Brazil's climate can be misunderstood. The common understanding is that this is wholly a tropical country: hot, wet and covered in rainforest. Again, as explained earlier, this can be due to the Amazon and the Pantanal, very large, well-known areas of low, wet terrain of incredible biological diversity, and to the remarkably beautiful coastline.

Few people outside the country realize that it snows regularly in some parts of Brazil (including a wine region, Serra Catarinense). Outside the lowlands and the coast, a large range of climates exists. This benefits wine and allows Brazil to be unique in having three types of viticulture, as distinguished by the climatic classes.

Climatic variability is linked to the vastness of the land. Brazil's latitudes span a vast expanse: from 5°16' N to 33°45' S. It's the same for longitude: from -34°47' E to -73°59' W. Both the equator and the Tropic of Capricorn traverse the country. Knowing that a large segment of the country is at altitude is fundamental because each 100 metres of elevation leads, in general, to a decrease of about 0.65°C, so placing a vineyard at 800–1,000 metres above sea level has a significant effect on viticulture.

Studies on Brazilian climate started in the late 1800s, when Henrique Morize (1889) and Frederico Draenert (1896) published the first in-depth works on the subject. In 1922, Morize published a tentative classification of the country's climates, incorporating concepts by the Russian-born (but mostly working in Germany) scientist Wladimir Köppen and using data from 106 weather stations.

In this book, I use two classification systems. The first (Köppen classification) has general applications and was not devised for vinous purposes. It helps determine the general characteristics of Brazil's climate. The second, the remarkable Multicriteria Climatic Classification (MCC) system, co-authored by the Brazilian scientist Jorge Tonietto, is meant precisely for viticultural applications.

Köppen developed and published the first complete version of his climatic classification system in 1918, revising it later (1936). Rudolf Geiger made some subsequent changes; this is why the system is also known as Köppen-Geiger. It continues to be widely used and is easy to understand. The system relies significantly on the types of vegetation in each analysed region. It serves well, therefore, to know how strongly climate determines a biome. There are five main groups of climates identified by a first letter: A (tropical), B (arid), C (temperate), D (continental) and E (polar). Each group's second letter designates rainfall and a third letter indicates temperature. In Brazil, the nomenclature of the climate classes in this classification is a little different but maintains clarity and meaning. The table opposite shows the climate classes in the Köppen classification according to Brazilian nomenclature.

In 2014, Brazilian researchers (Alvares and collaborators) published the paper 'Köppen's climate classification map for Brazil'. They used data from 2,950 weather stations to obtain high-resolution maps (temperature, elevation and Köppen classes). This remains a very detailed and useful study; its main results are now summarized. They found the following percentages of the first three groups: A (tropical) 81 per cent; B (arid) 5 per cent; and C (temperate, or humid subtropical) 14 per cent. Twelve Köppen classes of climates were identified, of which three (Cwc, Csa and Csb) are rare. The frequency of the significant classes was, in decreasing order: Am 27.5 per cent, Aw 25.8, Af 22.6, Cfa 6.5, As 5.5, Bsh 4.9, Cfb 2.6, Cwa 2.5, and Cwb 2.1. Map 3, on page 36, redrawn and modified from this paper with permission, illustrates Brazilian climatic conditions.

From a viticultural standpoint, the C group (temperate or subtropical) is the country's most important, occurring in the main wine-producing states in Brazil: Rio Grande do Sul, Santa Catarina, Minas Gerais and São Paulo. Both traditional viticulture and DPWH are practised in regions belonging to one of the C subclasses. Tropical viticulture in Brazil, however, occurs in Bahia and Pernambuco in places with a B (arid) climate, demanding irrigation.

Climate classes

Class shorthand	Brazilian nomenclature
Af	Tropical, without dry season
Am	Tropical, monsoon
Aw	Tropical, dry winter
As*	Tropical, dry summer
BWh	Dry, arid, low altitude and latitude
BWk	Dry, arid, mid altitude and high altitude
BSh	Dry, semi-arid, low latitude and altitude
BSk	Dry, semi-arid, mid latitude and high altitude
Csa	Humid subtropical, dry summer, hot summer
Csb	Humid subtropical, dry summer, temperate summer
Csc	Humid subtropical, dry summer, short and cool summer
Cwa	Humid subtropical, dry winter, hot summer
Cwb	Humid subtropical, dry winter, temperate summer
Cwc	Humid subtropical, dry winter, short and cool summer
Cfa	Humid tropical, oceanic, without dry season, hot summer
Cfb	Humid tropical, oceanic, without dry season, temperate summer
Cfc	Humid tropical, oceanic, without dry season, short and cool summer
Dsa	Temperate continental, dry summer, hot summer
Dsb	Temperate continental, dry summer, temperate summer
Dsc	Temperate continental, dry summer, short and cool summer
Dsd	Temperate continental, dry summer, very cold winter
Dwa	Temperate continental, dry winter, hot summer
Dwb	Temperate continental, dry winter, temperate summer
Dwc	Temperate continental, dry winter , short and cool summer
Dwd	Temperate continental, dry winter, very cold winter
Dfa	Temperate continental, without dry season, hot summer
Dfb	Temperate continental, without dry season, temperate summer
Dfc	Temperate continental, without dry season, short and cool summer
Dfd	Temperate continental, without dry season, very cold winter
ET	Polar, tundra
EF	Polar, frost

* Not always found in classifications

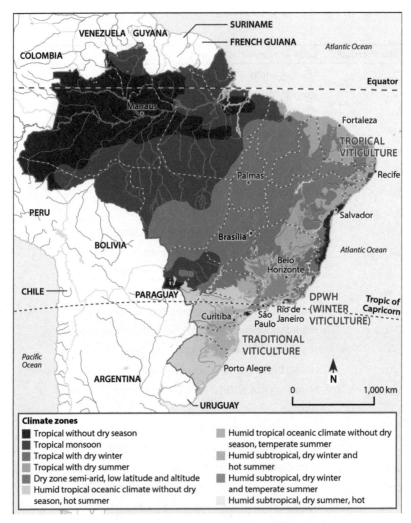

Map 3: Köppen-Geiger climate zones and main viticultural macro-regions in Brazil (modified with permission from Alvares et al., 2014)

Apart from in semi-arid areas in the Northeast (where there can be as little as 390 millimetres of rain a year), there is plenty of rainfall in Brazil, especially in summer. In some regions, this may reach more than 4,000 millimetres. This has been one of the main viticultural difficulties in the country, so careful site selection is of paramount importance. Brazil has no shortage of fresh water (except in the Northeast). For vines, much to the contrary. Too much rain in the growing season was one of the main reasons for fundamental developments in the Brazilian

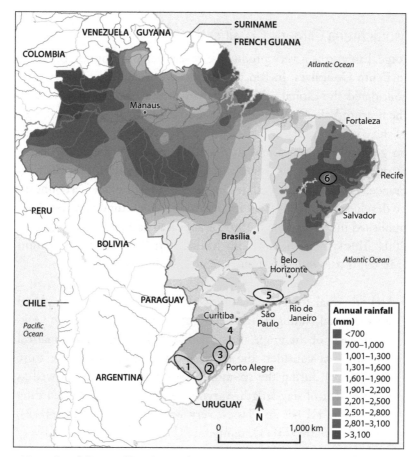

Map 4: Rainfall map of Brazil (modified with permission from Alvares et al., 2014). The circles/ellipses denote wine regions (1: Campanha Gaúcha; 2: Serra do Sudeste; 3: Serra Gaúcha; 4: Serra Catarinense; 5: main DPWH area; 6: Vale do São Francisco)

wine scenario: tropical viticulture, DPWH and agronomical improvement in the traditional areas. Map 4, again redrawn from Alvares and co-workers, summarizes rainfall in the country. I have made a change: inserting circles or ellipses to locate the main wine regions in Brazil. The reader may correlate their position with the climatic conditions.

Climate change in Brazil, up to now, has been at times a *bon problème* (good problem). In Rio Grande do Sul, for example, the number of good vintages has increased. However, the other side of the coin is the greater frequency of weather extremes, such as the devastating floods that provoked enormous damage to the same state in 2024. Other regions have been relatively spared.

Multicriteria Climatic Classification

Jorge Tonietto is a very productive researcher working for Embrapa in Bento Gonçalves, in Rio Grande do Sul state. The town may be considered the capital of Brazilian viticulture, ensconced as it is in the heart of Vale dos Vinhedos, the most traditional winemaking area of the country. Tonietto is presently engaged in very important work on geographical indications in Brazil. He earned a doctorate degree at the École Nationale Supérieure Agronomique de Montpellier, in France. There, together with his mentor, Professor Alain Carbonneau, he developed a novel system for classifying viticultural climates. First published in Portuguese in 1999, it appeared as a paper in English in 2004. This system was called the Multicriteria Climatic Classification (MCC). It uses three synthetic viticultural climatic indices:

- Heliothermal (or Huglin) Index (HI): this relates to the global heliothermal (sunlight, temperature) conditions during the vegetative cycle of the grape. It is calculated through a mathematical formula that considers the mean and maximum air temperature (in Celsius) during the six-month period of the cycle, as well as a coefficient of day length, varying from 1.00 to 1.06 according to latitude. HI has six classes: very warm (HI+3), warm (HI+2), temperate warm (HI+1), temperate (HI-1), cool (HI-2) and very cool (HI-3).
- Dryness Index, or DI: also calculated for a six-month period, this mirrors the potential water balance of the soil, derived from Riou's drought index. It allows the characterization of the fundamental water component of a given region's climate. It considers the rainfall (precipitation), the potential transpiration and the direct evaporation, which lead, also through a mathematical formula, to the estimate of soil water reserves. DI has four classes: very dry (DI+2), moderately dry (DI+1), sub-humid (DI-1) and humid (DI-2).
- Cool night Index (CI): this is the minimum air temperature (in Celsius) during September (Northern Hemisphere) or March (Southern Hemisphere), the months of grape maturation. It can be an indicator of grape quality pertaining to wine colour and aromas. There are four classes: very cool (CI+2), cool (CI+1), temperate (CI-1) and warm (CI-2) nights.

Jorge Tonietto

The MCC system divides the grape-growing regions into groups, using the three indexes. In theory, the combination of these classes would allow 96 different climates. In practice, however, some combinations do not happen. In the paper mentioned, Tonietto and Carbonneau identified 36 groups. It is important to note that the characterization may change from year to year, according to the harvest conditions.

Besides being a research tool when evaluating the potential of novel regions for viticulture, as well as for winemaking zoning, MCC permits the study of the relationship between the climate and the quality and typicality of wines produced in a given region. It goes deeper, therefore, than other systems used for viticultural purposes, such as the Winkler Scale. The MCC system also allowed, once published, the development of new concepts:

- Viticultural climate: the set of three indexes characterizing a given geographical area.
- Climatic group: the ensemble of vineyards, zones or regions sharing the same class of viticultural climate.

- Viticultural climate (with intra-annual variability): applied only to regions where more than one grape harvest is possible, the climatic class can change according to the time of the year. Such is the case in the São Francisco Valley in Brazil.

Here are three examples of the application of the MCC in Brazilian locations:

- Vale dos Vinhedos (Rio Grande do Sul, 640 metres above sea level): HI+1, DI-1, CI-1, or temperate-warm, sub-humid, with temperate nights.
- São Francisco Valley (Bahia/Pernambuco, 366 metres above sea level, average – this has intra-annual variability): HI+3, DI+1, CI-2, or very warm, moderately dry, with warm nights.
- Três Corações (Minas Gerais, 839 metres above sea level, where winter harvest is practised): HI+1, DI-1, CI+2, or temperate-warm, sub-humid, with very cool nights.

Climate, like soil, is not a simple subject. Studying it seriously demands different approaches, as we have seen, which are more in-depth than simply describing a climate as, for example, tropical, desert, temperate, dry, and so on. This is more so with viticulture: the MCC system states itself how important it is to delve into details when someone wants to know more about how to classify the climate of a given location, be it a vineyard, denomination, town, region, state or whatever geographical unit is chosen.

4

VITICULTURE AND WINEMAKING

THREE TYPES OF VITICULTURE IN BRAZIL

Brazil's large size and variety of climates allow, perhaps uniquely in the world, three types of viticultural practice. Jorge Tonietto and co-workers have summarized this subject well in several publications. They divide Brazilian viticulture into three macro-regions, each with its own particular characteristics. I will describe them briefly here.

Traditional viticulture

Here, the practices are the same as those used in most wine regions worldwide. The vines are pruned once a year and there is only one harvest. The usual physiology of the vine is followed. As a plant originally from, and most adapted to, cooler climates than the tropics, the vine has the well-known vegetative cycle of dormancy, budding, flowering, veraison, harvest and leaf fall. Due to climatic conditions, achieving more than one production cycle per year is impossible. Still the largest (in terms of planted area and production volume), this type of viticulture is practised in a macro-region with a mostly temperate, or humid subtropical, climate. Altitudes range from 50 to 1,400 metres. No irrigation is needed. Most Brazilian vines are managed in this way in Rio Grande do Sul, Santa Catarina, Paraná and some parts of São Paulo, Minas Gerais and Espírito Santo.

Tropical viticulture

When average temperatures are above 22°C, there is no true dormancy, and the vegetative growth continues throughout the year. It is possible to have more than one vegetative cycle in a single year. Since the 1970s, for table grapes, and the 1980s, for wine grapes, a system with two prunings and two (or even more) harvests a year has been practised. Irrigation is fundamental not only for water needs but also for controlling the cycle. The producer can, for example, reduce water supply and use a phytoregulator, such as ethephon, to end a growth cycle and force the vines to lose their leaves. Otherwise, the combination of pruning, irrigation and hydrogen cyanamide (to force bud break) will lead to a new cycle. Staggered parcels, control of irrigation and pruning allow the production of grapes throughout the year. This can be very advantageous in commercial terms and permits a better use of winemaking facilities. A steady flow of grapes for processing is better than working with a huge load of grapes in traditional harvests. The figure opposite shows how a producer can manage six parcels during the year. This very technological type of viticultural management is still in development. Fundamental to this are, for example, selecting the best-adapted varieties (such as Chenin Blanc, Itália, Syrah) and rootstocks (such as Paulsen 1103 and IAC 766, 313, 572), precise irrigation, control of bud load and selecting the best pruning techniques. Tropical viticulture is concentrated in Pernambuco and Bahia, in the São Francisco Valley. This macro-region has a tropical semi-arid climate; altitudes range from 350 to 420 metres.

Winter viticulture (DPWH)

This recent development started in the early 2000s in Três Corações, south of Minas Gerais. Here, besides the usual pruning in August, known as 'formation pruning', there is another pruning (in January or February) called 'production pruning' – hence, 'double pruning' (also known as 'inverted pruning'). The first pruning is severe, leaving single-bud spurs. A green harvest eliminates clusters in October or November. The production pruning is followed by hydrogen cyanamide application to break bud dormancy and avoid apical dominance. The grapes mature fully in the winter – hence, 'winter harvesting' (June to August) and my proposed acronym DPWH (double pruning and winter harvesting).

There are two growth cycles and one harvest per year (there is no significant production in the 'normal' cycle). The oldest commercial

DPWH vineyard, in Três Corações, is now 21 years old and still going strong. Although it is presently impossible to know whether such management reduces the vine's lifespan, the great health of the pioneering vineyard points to a significant useful commercial life. Winter in this macro-region is dry and sunny, with warm days and cool to cold nights (high diurnal variation). This maintains acidity and promotes a good level of polyphenols and aroma precursors. The macro-region is very large, coinciding with the Brazilian Highlands, and the vineyards lie mostly at altitude (600–1,200 metres). The predominant climate is temperate (subtropical), with Köppen types Cwa and Cwb. Many Brazilian states have such areas: Minas Gerais, São Paulo, Bahia, Goiás, Rio de Janeiro, Espírito Santo, Mato Grosso and the Federal District. The expansion of vineyards and wineries has been very fast and continues.

This unique trio of viticultural regimens has allowed Brazilian winemakers to extend their terroirs remarkably. The knowledge base and possible technologies have increased, placing the country and its viticultural researchers at the forefront of these developments. This benefits consumers, brings new options to wine lovers who appreciate new possibilities, and allows for a potential increase in Brazil's exports. Although there are some producers using the principles of organic and biodynamic viticulture, the generally humid climate poses great difficulties, so that these practices are seldom encountered in Brazil. Map 3 (see p. 36) gives an idea of the location of the macro-regions.

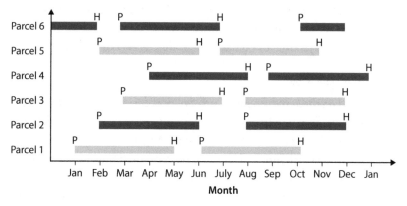

Example of management of six parcels. P: pruning; H: harvest; black bars: red grapes; grey bars: white grapes. Translated and redrawn with permission from Pereira, Tonietto et al., 2020.

VINE PESTS AND DISEASES

The vine is an imported plant in Brazil, where wild examples like those in North America have never existed. So are its diseases, which are much the same as elsewhere. A detailed study of this subject is beyond the scope of this book, so here we will be limited to the most frequently encountered problems and where they are more critical.

A scientific paper published in 2017 in OenoOne, featuring vintners from all over the world (including Brazil), pointed out that the most important vine troubles were downy mildew, powdery mildew, bunch rots like grey mould (botrytis), trunk diseases and virus diseases. This very interesting work also linked geography (including climate) and diseases.

Downy mildew

Brazil, where many places are not arid or dry, has significant troubles with downy mildew (caused by the fungus *Plasmopara viticola)*. The infection is highly favoured by warmer temperatures (20–26°C) and high humidity (from 70 per cent), which are extremely common here. Even when the air humidity is lower, the disease progresses if the soil is humid or when free water (rain, dew or fog) occurs for over three hours in a row. In Brazil, where it is known simply as *míldio*, it has been reported in all viticulturally important states. The severity is, of course, lower in the semi-arid regions. Even here, however, rain arrives during the first semester, propitiating surges of downy mildew during one of the growth cycles. Where DPWH is practised, the disease is very significant during the first months of the cycle, when it rains significantly. Control is achieved through frequent sprays of systemic or contact fungicides, as everywhere else.

Powdery mildew

Caused by *Uncinula* (or *Erysiphe) necator*, powdery mildew is also widely prevalent in Brazil, where it is known as *oídio*. As it does not depend on high humidity, it is also very notable in the São Francisco Valley, the realm of tropical viticulture. Here, the damage may lead to losses of up to 80 per cent of a single harvest. Conditions that favour the growth of the fungus are temperatures around 25°C and 40–60 per cent humidity. Dry, warm and cloudy periods are the worst. They may happen frequently where DPWH is practised. To control the disease, both sulphur and systemic fungicides are sprayed alternately.

Bunch rots

Bunch rots encompass several diseases affecting the grape bunches and leading to significant quality and yield losses. Grey mould – the 'bad' botrytis, another fungal disease – is caused by *Botrytis cinerea*. This agent also leads to a benign, desired form of infection, 'noble rot', which is fundamental for producing legendary sweet wines like Tokaji and Sauternes. Such an advantageous form, unfortunately, has not been reported in Brazil, whereas grey mould, the disease, is common: *podridão cinzenta*. Temperatures between 18°C and 28°C, plus high humidity, increase the severity of this problem. As everywhere, the countermeasures include fungicides, but vine management is also fundamental and is practised here. Bunch thinning, de-leafing and changing from overshadowed training/trellising systems like *latada* (pergola) to others allow for better canopy management. Other forms of bunch rot have been reported in the Campanha Gaúcha: ripe rot (*Glomerella cingulata*) and bitter rot (*Greeneria uvicola)*, which are worse in American varieties, as well as acid rot, more prevalent in *Vitis vinifera*.

Trunk diseases

Trunk diseases cause the decline and eventual death of the plant and are a growing problem everywhere. It has been estimated that the yearly cost of replacing vines affected by trunk diseases may surpass US$ 1.5 billion. They may be collectively called *declínio e morte da videira* in Brazil. Those already reported are Esca/Petri's disease (*Phaeoacremonium*), black foot (*Cylindrocarpon* or *Campylocarpon*), dieback (*Botryosphaeriaceae*), Eutypa dieback (*Eutypa lata)* and excoriosis (*Phomopsis*). *Eutypa* has been reported in Rio Grande do Sul (from 2004) and São Paulo. In the Northeast (tropical viticulture), at least four such diseases have been reported, starting in 2009. There, losses of up to 60 per cent in vine nurseries have occurred.

Other pests and diseases

Brazil is also by no means free of phylloxera. Hence, the use of resistant American rootstocks is mandatory. Due to the climate, an extensive series of pests may attack vines and, especially, the grapes: weevils, fruit flies, caterpillars, wasps, bees, trips, bugs, mealy bugs and mites. There has been a trend for using biological approaches to reduce their damage. Another important agent causing potentially heavy losses during grape ripening is birds. Netting is often indispensable to avoid their attacks; this is routine, for example, in southern Minas Gerais.

There have been reports of a possible association between the decline and death of grapevines in Brazil and infestation by the insect *Eurhizococcus brasiliensis* (*Margarodidae*), better known as 'ground pearls' or 'earth pearls'. It is frequently found at the vine's roots in decaying plants and is native to the country's southern states. However, it has also been found in São Paulo and the São Francisco Valley. Still, it's unlikely that the insect is a cause of decline per se, as many plants heavily infested with earth pearls do not show signs of decline. It is more likely that it may act as a co-factor (as nematodes do), damaging the roots and allowing the penetration of fungi.

As for grapevine virus diseases, Brazil also mirrors the rest of the world: they are a growing concern. It may be that correct diagnosis, rather than increases in incidence or prevalence, explains the impression of a worsening of this problem. Viruses may have been one of the leading causes of a significant reduction in Serra Gaúcha of the area planted with Cabernet Franc. The following viruses have already been detected in Brazil: GVA, GVB, GLRaV (leafroll-associated), GRSPaV (stem pitting-associated), GFLV (fanleaf-associated), GFkV (fleck-associated), GRVFV (vein feathering-associated), TFDaV (temperate fruit decay-associated), CEVd (citrus exocortis viroid) and HSVd (hop stunt viroid). As elsewhere, the use of uncertified propagation materials may have been a cause of the increase in virus diseases. This has improved in the last decade, with new nurseries with the necessary certifications appearing in both Minas Gerais and Rio Grande do Sul.

Another notable fungal disease in the country is anthracnose (*Elsinoe ampelina*), known in Brazil as *varíola* or *olho de passarinho* (bird's eye). It is widespread in the country but particularly affects the southern regions. Ideal conditions for the microorganism are temperatures between 24°C and 26°C, plus rainy springs, mist, air humidity of 90 per cent or more and cool winds. The disease affects American and European cultivars, and rootstocks. Losses may be total if not treated correctly. There are 12 fungicides registered at the Ministry of Agriculture for treating anthracnose.

Other diseases affecting the grapevine in Brazil are bacterial canker (*Xanthomonas campestris*), especially in the São Francisco Valley, and grapevine rust (*Phakopsora euvitis*), first reported in 2001 and since widespread.

TRAINING AND TRELLISING

Until the 1980s, nearly all Brazilian wine was made in Rio Grande do Sul. Its viticulture was founded and developed by Italian immigrants and their descendants, who brought with them the traditional training/trellising systems adopted in Italy in the nineteenth century, above all the *tendone* or *pergola* method, known in Brazil as *latada*.

When I visited wineries in Rio Grande do Sul in the 1990s, their proprietors were proud to show that a large-scale conversion was under way: from *latada* to *espaldeira*. The latter is a general name in Portuguese for vertically oriented training/trellising systems, or vertical shoot positioning (VSP) systems. This has been an important part of the technological revolution that started in those days in Brazilian viticulture and winemaking. It has taken a long time and is still happening in some places. This is not to say, however, that *latadas* have disappeared.

Latadas are horizontally oriented systems, with spur pruning alone or associated with some type of cane pruning. The vines are planted in rows, the inter-row distance usually being 2.5 metres. The inter-vine distance is 1.5–2.0 metres, depending on soil fertility and cultivar vigour. The production zone is high, at 1.8 metres above ground. Embrapa recommends a bud load of between 100,000 and 140,000 buds per hectare. This allows for a dense occupation of the terrain by the canopy, a large number of clusters and high yields. There are disadvantages, however, with *latadas* demanding higher implantation costs (posts, wires and so on); they may also lead to excessive vigour and shadowing of clusters, requiring more canopy work. Humidity in the fruit and consequent fungal diseases may also be issues: the quality of the grapes can suffer. This system is mainly used for non-*vinifera* varieties, like the omnipresent Isabel.

For *vinifera* varieties, in Rio Grande do Sul, in 2015, *latadas* still had 2,920 hectares versus 3,102 in *espaldeiras,* 279 in 'Y' and 54 'lyre'. In the Northeast, however, where too much sunlight and heat may be problematic, *latadas* can mitigate these issues. New *vinifera* vineyards are systematically planted using *espaldeira* systems in most regions, including those managed according to DPWH, except in the São Francisco Valley.

VSP systems – the *espaldeiras* – are the norm for European varieties. The usual spacings vary. Inter-row distance may be as low as 1.00 metre in short, low, manually managed vines, which is uncommon. More commonly, the production zone is 1.0–1.2 metres above ground and the vine's total height is 2.0–2.2 metres. The inter-row distance is usually 2.5

metres, allowing for mechanization. However, the rows may have a larger spacing (3.0 metres) in drier climates such as the São Francisco Valley. Bud load goes from 65,000 to 80,000 buds per hectare. Both cordon and Guyot, the latter more so, are used. Variations on the VSP theme, such as lyre or 'Y' systems, are adopted less often. Important advantages of *espaldeiras*, as mentioned by the growers and Embrapa, include: a lower cost of implantation than *latadas*; building the trellising systems does not demand specialized knowledge; allows for good ventilation; enables mechanization; and most varieties adapt well to it. *Espaldeiras* are widespread in the country and adopted whenever a greater quality of *vinifera* grapes is desired. In the DPWH areas, only VSP systems are used.

Rootstocks

In Rio Grande do Sul, the rootstock Paulsen 1103 is by far the most used for *vinifera* varieties: 58 per cent in 2015. SO4 followed it, with 21 per cent. Other rootstocks, like Solferino and 101-14, were used in small percentages in the same year.

In the Northeast, research indicated that Paulsen 1103 led to a very good balance in Syrah and Chenin Blanc. The rootstock IAC 766, however, also offered a satisfactory performance with both cultivars. IAC stands for Instituto Agronômico de Campinas, a research institute founded in 1887 and owned by the state of São Paulo.

The rootstock Paulsen 1103 (*Vitis berlandieri* × *Vitis rupestris*) suits most Brazilian regions well because it increases vigour, delays maturation, and shows good resistance to downy mildew, fusariosis and phylloxera. It also tolerates dry soils, preferring those with large quantities of clay. It has adapted very well to states as diverse as Rio Grande do Sul, Santa Catarina, São Paulo, Minas Gerais, Bahia and Pernambuco.

VINEYARD AREAS

According to the International Organization of Vine and Wine (OIV), in its *State of the World Vine and Wine Sector 2023*, Brazil had 83,000 hectares of vineyards in 2023 (1.5 per cent more than in 2022). This information differs from that supplied by the IBGE, the national statistics institute, as reproduced by Embrapa. The newly created Cadastro Vitícola Nacional (www.embrapa.br), which is linked to the Ministry of Agriculture, states that the total harvested area in the 2022/23 vintage was 75,553 hectares. The statistics may diverge because OIV also counts vineyards that are not yet producing, whereas IBGE's data are restricted to the harvested area. OIV's data place Brazil as the twenty-second country in planted area.

Importantly, OIV and IBGE both provide data on the total vineyard area, whether the purpose is to produce table grapes, raisins, grape juice or wine. In this sense, some countries (like Turkey, India, China and Iran) have very large vineyard areas, although these are mostly dedicated to purposes other than wine. This also applies to Brazil.

Until a few years ago, the only organized statistics system for planted areas belonged to Rio Grande do Sul. For a long time, this represented the actual situation, as this state was home to nearly all vineyards in the country. With the expansion of viticulture to other states, there was a need to create a more comprehensive system. The above-mentioned Cadastro Vitícola answered such a need. It works through the Sistema de Informações da Área de Vinhos e Bebidas (SIVIBE) – or Information System on the Wine and Drinks Area. As with all data banks, it is only as good as the input it receives. Despite the heavy educational and promotional work being done by Embrapa, led by researcher José Fernando Protas and his team, SIVIBE is still a work in progress. As it is, in any case, the only available system to consult, I will use it here, along with the last available data (2015) on Rio Grande do Sul.

Statistics must always be taken with a pinch of salt. Sometimes, the same source throws up conflicting data. Such is the case with OIV: the 2022 report mentions that Brazil's planted area increased from 2021 to 2022 after declining for eight consecutive years. However, another OIV publication (*Focus OIV – Distribution of world's grapevine varieties*) states that Brazil had a total vineyard area of 87,000 hectares in 2017. Notwithstanding possible conflicts, all such data are enough for the wine consumer or student to understand Brazil's size and importance in the grapevine arena.

Within the country, the bulk of vineyard area is concentrated in the South region (73 per cent of Brazil's total in 2021), especially in Rio Grande do Sul (62.4 per cent). The other two states in this region had roughly 4,000 hectares each in the same year. Nearby São Paulo state (Southeast region) had 8,022 hectares in 2021 and 8,436 in 2022/23. In the same region, Minas Gerais registered a 4.8 per cent increase in planted area in 2021 compared to the previous year, reaching 1,270 hectares. This process went on to reach 1,350 hectares in 2022/23. This was most likely due to new areas of DPWH viticulture. In the Northeast region, a land of table grapes and tropical viticulture, Pernambuco is the largest producer, with 8,256 hectares. In the same region, Bahia state had 2,119 hectares in 2021, a 7.6 per cent increase on 2020. The remaining states have much smaller vineyards. The Centre-West region is investing in producing *vinifera* wines made by DPWH and also in oenotourism. Besides the state of Goiás (78 hectares) and Mato Grosso (52), the Federal District, around Brasília, has 57 hectares of vines.

Grape production

In 2021, according to Embrapa, Brazil produced 1,697,380 metric tons of grapes, a significant increase over 2020 and also relatively higher than 2018 and 2019. It is important, however, to point out that the quality of grapes for winemaking was exceptional in 2020, a great vintage. Climatic conditions helped a great deal in increasing yields in 2021. As expected, the biggest states were Rio Grande do Sul (951,767 tons, 56.1 per cent of total Brazilian production), followed by Pernambuco (390,640), São Paulo (147,359), Bahia (61,274), Santa Catarina (59,638), Paraná (57,000) and Minas Gerais (19,571). The year 2022 saw less favourable conditions, with a total national production of 1,502,371 tons. Estimates from IBGE point to a recovery in 2023 to 1,664,757 tons. Many other states also produce grapes, albeit in much smaller amounts. Approximately half the total amount consists of table grapes, the other half being processed into wines, juice and other products. Brazil does not produce raisins.

In Rio Grande do Sul, there were 14,417 properties in 2015. The average surface area was 17.5 hectares. In the most traditional region, Serra Gaúcha, with its rugged terrain, this was 13.8 hectares. In newer, flatter areas, like Campanha Gaúcha and Serra do Sudeste, the average size of the properties was significantly larger. Depending on the microregions, this ranged from 95 to 564 hectares. Such were the sizes of the properties, not the vineyard areas. When the latter are considered, the average size in the state was just 2.8 hectares. Again, the average vineyard surface varied from 4.3 to 26.1 hectares in the newer areas. There is much room for expansion.

When the indicator 'share of national agricultural crop area under wine grapes' is examined in Brazil, it shows only a small share. This is due to the vast tracts of land occupied by other agricultural products. Brazil is the world's largest producer of coffee, soya beans, orange juice and sugar, besides being one of the leading producers of corn, beans and cotton. The relative status of the grapevine is similar to that of other large countries, such as the US, China, Russia and India.

GRAPE VARIETIES

Considering the number of planted varieties, Brazil cannot be accused of monotony: there are about 120 *Vitis vinifera* varieties (70 red, 50 white) and over 40 *Vitis labrusca* cultivars in its vineyards. In 2016, 85 per cent of the country's vineyards consisted of red grapes, versus 60 per cent in 2000, according to Kym Anderson and Signe Nelgen. In their useful data compendium, it can be seen that the share of French varieties in Brazilian vineyards grew from 15 to 35 per cent in the same period. Although very detailed, this work mentions that Cabernet Franc is Brazil's second most planted grape. This, unfortunately, is not true, as can be seen from the table shown overleaf which gives the most planted varieties in 2017, in decreasing order (OIV, 2017).

The most important *vinifera* grapes, in terms of processed volumes, are:

- Southern states: Cabernet Sauvignon, Merlot, Pinot Noir, Tannat, Cabernet Franc, Ancellotta and Egiodola (reds); Chardonnay, Moscato Branco, Riesling Itálico, Trebbiano, Glera (Prosecco), Moscato Giallo and Malvasia de Cândia (whites).
- Northeast: Syrah, Alicante Bouschet (reds) and Chenin Blanc, Moscato Canelli and Itália (whites) lead the list. DPWH areas: Syrah dominates by far, followed by Sauvignon Blanc and other varieties.

In Rio Grande do Sul, the most planted grapes in 2015 were Isabel (26.1 per cent of the vineyards), Bordô (23.1), Niágara Branca (6.7), Concord (5.4), Niágara Rosada (5.0), Seibel 1077 (3.7), Jacquez (2.7), Cabernet Sauvignon (2.6), Chardonnay (2.5), Isabel Precoce (2.0), Merlot (1.9), BRS Violeta (1.6), Moscato Branco (1.3), Moscato Embrapa (1.2), Pinot Noir (1.1), and BRS Lorena (1.0). In the same year, *Vitis vinifera* varieties occupied 6,354 hectares. The most planted, in descending order, were Cabernet Sauvignon and Chardonnay (more than 1,000 hectares each), Merlot (760), Moscato Branco (540), Pinot Noir (443), Tannat (323), Riesling Itálico (293), Trebbiano (180), Glera/Prosecco (170), Cabernet Franc (164), Moscato Giallo (146) and Malvasia de Cândia (130). In 2015, the *vinifera* cultivars with the largest newly planted areas were, in descending order: Chardonnay, Pinot Noir, Riesling Itálico, Glera and Tannat. This reflects the importance of sparkling wine production in the state, as the first four are mainly used to craft base wines.

Planted varieties (OIV, 2017)

Variety	Colour	Area (hectares)	Percentage of total vine-yard area	Trend
Isabel	Red	13,000	14.9	Decreasing
Niágara Rosada	Pink	11,000	12.6	N/A
Bordô	Red	10,000	11.5	Increasing
Itália	White	9,000	10.3	N/A
Niágara Branca	White	3,000	3.4	Decreasing
Concord	Red	2,000	2.3	Decreasing
Alphonse Lavallée	Red	2,000	2.3	N/A
Couderc Noir	Red	2,000	2.3	Decreasing
Jacquez	Red	1,000	1.1	Decreasing
Cabernet Sauvignon	Red	1,000	1.1	Decreasing
Other varieties		33,000	37.9	
Total		87,000		Increasing

Main vinifera varieties (SIVIBE, 2022)

Variety	Planted area (hectares)
Chardonnay	918.6
Cabernet Sauvignon	770.6
Merlot	664.3
Moscato Branco	648.5
Pinot Noir	520.7
Lorena	477.6
Tannat	419.4
Moscato Embrapa	395.5
Muscat Blanc à Petits Grains	390.4
Prosecco (Glera	317.3
Trebbianos	302.9
Riesling Itálico	296.7
Malvasias	284.3

SIVIBE data from 2022 confirms this importance and shows, on the other side, a decline in Cabernet Sauvignon's planted area. Many producers I talked to complained about the variety's difficulties in ripening properly in several areas, hence they opted for changing to other, more reliable cultivars. The second table opposite, built from SIVIBE data, shows the *vinifera* varieties with larger planted areas in Brazil (2022). To note: Moscato Branco, as explained later in this chapter, is not Muscat Blanc; Muscat Blanc à Petits Grains, in Brazil, includes several Moscatos (Giallo, Nazareno and so on); Trebbianos and Malvasias are plural because there is more than one name beginning with these words in the SIVIBE information.

Other vinifera varieties (SIVIBE, 2022)

Variety	Planted areas (hectares)
Alicante Bouschet	195.6
Cabernet Franc	176.6
Sauvignon Blanc	117.4
Malbec	113.7
Syrah	95.5
Marselan	86.3
Viognier	77.9
Itália	76.7
Tempranillo	59.7

Another group of less frequently seen varieties is outlined in the table above, with the data also from SIVIBE (2022), including declared planted areas above 50 hectares. It is important to note that it is highly likely some grapes have a much larger area. Such is the case, for example, for Syrah, which is by far the most planted variety in DPWH projects. The scarcity of SIVIBE data on Minas Gerais contrasts with information from the Associação Nacional de Produtores de Vinhos de Inverno (ANPROVIN), the association of winter wine producers. Also of note: Itália is predominately a table grape in Brazil, but it is vinifera and used to craft sparkling wines, especially in the Northeast.

Using SIVIBE data, I retrieved a total planted area of *vinifera* varieties in 2022 of 7,967.5 hectares, which covers the 53 most planted cultivars. Taking into account the already mentioned and very likely incompleteness of data inputs to the system, as well as additional varieties and sources, it is possible to speculate, quite conservatively, that Brazil may have about 9,000 hectares of planted *vinifera* varieties to make *vinhos finos*. This is growing steadily, especially in new regions, such as, for example, all DPWH (Minas Gerais, São Paulo, Goiás, Rio de Janeiro, Federal District and Bahia), and north-west of Rio Grande do Sul, among many other scattered areas.

BRAZILIAN GRAPE CULTIVARS

Since 1977, Embrapa has developed a genetic improvement programme (*Uvas do Brasil*, or 'Grapes of Brazil'). This aims to develop grape varieties better adapted to Brazilian conditions to produce table grapes, juice and wine. Until now, 20 new cultivars have been attained. Some desirable characteristics are high-yields, diverse production cycles and high resistance to vine diseases. Embrapa maintains the largest vine germplasm bank in Latin America, boasting 1,400 accessions. Besides the more commonplace *Vitis vinifera* and *Vitis labrusca*, Embrapa also has a large series of wild tropical species and interspecific hybrids. Much research has been and is being done using classical and state-of-the-art technological tools. This programme is akin to the European trials to obtain fungus-resistant hybrids, or PIWI (an acronym for *Pilzwiderstandsfähig*). In a world beset with environmental concerns, good-quality varieties demanding fewer agrochemical inputs and offering higher yields are a noble pursuit. At Minas Gerais, Empresa de Pesquisa Agropecuária de Minas Gerais (Epamig) – the Embrapa equivalent for Minas Gerais state – has started to make (experimentally) wines from PIWI varieties (of Italian origin) planted in the south of the state. Eight different cultivars (four red, four white) were used to make wines, which were assessed by a multidisciplinary tasting panel. The results have been favourable. In Brazil and abroad, PIWI varieties with at least 85 per cent of *vinifera* genes are considered *vinifera* cultivars.

The Embrapa varieties have grown significantly in the country. According to Anderson and Nelgen, the planted areas of the most important genuinely Brazilian varieties, in 2016, were Moscato Embrapa (683 hectares), Violeta (636), Cora (570), Lorena (500), Niágara Red (469) and Carmem (328). The total vineyard area of all 15 such varieties planted was, in the same year, 3,596 hectares. Compared to 2010 (1,714 hectares), the growth is very significant.

France, Italy, Brazil, Portugal

Portugal controlled Brazil from 1500 to 1822; a large portion of the population of the country is of Portuguese descent. Italians flocked to the country, especially during the nineteenth century, while French immigration was minute. Portugal and Italy, therefore, have been much more important than France in shaping Brazil. However, when analysing which grape varieties are the most planted, France is the champion by far. Italy comes second, followed by Brazilian grapes, but Portugal has just a few examples.

Why? In my opinion, there are several reasons. Historic registers mention some grape growing and Portuguese varieties in the early centuries after Portugal claimed Brazil in 1500. In 1785, the Portuguese queen Maria the Mad prohibited winemaking in Brazil. This may have increased the already existing hostility of Brazilians to things Portuguese. In the nineteenth century, American hybrids became dominant due to their greater yield and disease resistance, and the old Portuguese grapes almost completely disappeared. The Italian immigrants brought their varieties, such as Barbera, Moscato and Trebbiano, but they were not extensively cultivated, as hybrids were more economically viable. When a movement to promote *vinifera* started in the early twentieth century, the preferred cultivars to be imported were French, or 'international'. Quality French wines, such as those from Bordeaux, Burgundy and Champagne, were far better known than Italian and Portuguese wines. This same preponderance happened in all New World wine-producing countries.

However, aromatic Italian grapes have always been important in producing Asti-like sparkling wines. They have been followed by similar Brazilian varieties. There has been a recent renaissance of Italian grapes to craft still wines. Among others, Barbera, Fiano, Garganega, Montepulciano, Nebbiolo, Sangiovese and Teroldego have entered (or re-entered) the stage. Glera became relevant in the making of Prosecco-like sparklers. As for Portuguese varieties, a welcome trend to plant Alvarinho and Touriga Nacional can also be observed.

Moscato Embrapa

Moscato Embrapa, or BRS UV10693, is a July Muscat × Couderc 13 hybrid (*Vitis* interspecific crossing) with 75 per cent *Vitis vinifera*, obtained in 1983. After years of evaluation by growers, wineries, oenologists and consumers, it was considered fit for making wine and launched in 1997. It has high vigour (requiring de-leafing) and yield, reaching up to 35 tons per hectare (using the *latada* system), and is resistant to downy mildew and grey rot. It has an average sugar content, at harvest, of 19 Brix, with a total acidity of around 90–100 mEq per litre. It produces white wine which is aromatic (Muscat-like) and mostly medium dry with low acidity. According to Brazilian wine laws, Moscato Embrapa cannot be used to make monovarietal wines labelled as *vinhos finos*. This occurs despite the wines not showing any *labrusca* character. Depending on the percentage, however, it can be part of a blend of a *vinho fino* – for example, Asti-like aromatic, sweet sparklers.

Lorena

Lorena, or BRS UV12731, is a white crossing Malvasia Bianca × Seyval, obtained in 1986 and officially launched in 2001. It is very productive: the yields can reach 25–30 tons per hectare. It is tolerant to powdery mildew, anthracnose and grey rot and moderately tolerant to downy mildew. As basal gems are not productive, long pruning is advised. It is well adapted to vertical and horizontal training systems, although the first is preferred for quality. Compared to Moscato Branco, Lorena brings 35 per cent more sugar and demands 40 per cent fewer agrochemicals. It may reach 22 Brix at harvest when acidity is 100–110 mEq per litre. It is aromatic and suitable for both still and sparkling wines. The agreeable, fruity wines can be reminiscent of other aromatic varieties, such as Gewurztraminer or Muscat, albeit less weighty. Properly vinified, their antioxidant content can be three times higher than in most other white wines. Embrapa has developed a process to achieve this, including a specially isolated and developed yeast (*Saccharomyces cerevisae* 1vvt97) and a maceration protocol. The wine has been dubbed 'Lorena Ativa'. Cultivating Lorena has been shown to improve growers' income, due to the good sugar content (which influences the prices paid for the grapes) and to high yields. For such reasons, Lorena is gaining ground among both growers and winemakers. The variety is not limited to the Southern states. It is already planted in the Southeast (São Paulo, Minas Gerais, Espírito Santo) and Northeast. This is indeed a true Brazilian original. According to SIVIBE, Brazil had a total area of 503 hectares planted to Lorena in 2023.

BRS Bibiana

BRS Bibiana is a white variety with 68.2 per cent *vinifera* genetic material, the balance comprising several other *Vitis* species. It is a crossing of Lorena with Embrapa's CNPUV 149-156 (Moscato Branco × IAC 1897-16), obtained in 1999. It is moderately vigorous and does not need extensive canopy work. Yields can reach up to 25 tons per hectare.

It is moderately resistant to the mildews, and no cases of grey rot or anthracnose have been observed. Even in difficult, rainy vintages, it can attain 21–22 Brix. The average acidity is 117 mEq per litre, with a pH of 3.3. Analyses of the wine have detected both thiols and terpenes, with ethyl octanoate predominating. The wine's aromas and flavours show Muscat-like components and some echoes of Sauvignon Blanc, albeit with a subtler personality with good acidity. A few wineries in Rio Grande do Sul (for instance, Buffon and Cainelli) produce Bibiana wines.

BRS Margot

BRS Margot is a red variety, a crossing of Merlot × Villard Noir. Its genetic material is about 74 per cent *vinifera*. The wine has no 'foxy' aromas and flavours, reminiscent of Merlot, with a medium level of acidity and tannins and a young, fruity style. Its commercial production is still incipient. Vinícola Gilioli, at Flores da Cunha, has produced a Margot wine.

IAC Ribas and IAC Máximo

In parallel with Embrapa, the Instituto Agronômico de Campinas (IAC) has developed its programme of breeding new varieties with the same purposes. Two of their best results are IAC Ribas and IAC Máximo. IAC Ribas is a Syrah × Seibel 7053 crossing (hence, it has a complex pedigree) developed in the 1950s by Walter Ribas. It has taken a long time for IAC to study it, including experimental vineyards and vinifications, so it was launched only recently, in 2021. It is a white grape with a medium mildew tolerance, requiring less spraying than most *vinifera* varieties. The yield is 7–15 tons per hectare, depending on the rootstock and training system (higher with the 'Y' configuration), as well as on the climate and type of viticulture. It has adapted well to DPWH: despite a lower yield, the quality of grapes is superior. It matures to 19–20 Brix with traditional viticulture and to 23.5 in DPWH, when its juice may have a pH as low as 3.12. The wines are very fresh and light, with aromas and flavours of tropical fruit. Among other producers, Mantovanello (Indaiatuba) and Bella Quinta (São Roque) wineries (both in São Paulo) have already made commercial wines from this cultivar.

IAC Máximo is a crossing of Seibel 11342 × Syrah bred by Santos Neto in 1946. It is considered by some to be the best red variety bred by IAC to craft wines. Being a hybrid, however, its wines must be labelled as *vinho de mesa* (wines not made from *vinifera* varieties). Vinícola Terrassos (Amparo, São Paulo) produces a wine from Máximo.

OTHER 'SPECIAL' VARIETIES IN BRAZIL

Although possibly or certainly not originating in Brazil, some cultivars have developed special characteristics here, are used in a distinctive way or are hard to find elsewhere. Despite the sometimes minute planted area, they can be a good experience for intrepid wine lovers wishing to tread less common paths.

BRS Moscato Branco

Moscato Branco – do not be misled by the name – is not the grape known in Italy as Moscato Bianco or internationally as Muscat Blanc à Petits Grains. Research by Embrapa scientists, led by Patricia Ritschel, has shown that Moscato Branco has a unique genetic profile when compared to more than 5,000 accessions from the Brazilian grape germplasm bank and the French grape germplasm collection. These included the aromatic grapes Moscato R2 (a clone of Muscat Blanc à Petits Grains), Moscato Giallo, Muscat of Hamburg, Muscat of Alexandria and Itália (table grape). Its DNA fingerprinting is also different from the Malvasia group. The studies indicated that Muscat of Alexandria and Almafra (a rare Portuguese grape) have probably participated in Moscato Branco's pedigree. The French ampelographer Jean-Michel Boursiquot, who became famous after identifying Carmenère in Chile, has also been to Brazil. He endorsed Moscato Branco's singularity. It is a likely candidate for becoming a uniquely Brazilian *vinifera* variety. It is, by far, the most planted Muscat-like cultivar in Rio Grande do Sul. The growers prize its early budding (which reduces the risk of spring frost damage), high yields and good commercial acceptance. Research amongst specialized tasters showed that the most frequent descriptors of its sparkling wine are, in decreasing order: 'sweet aromas'; fresh non-tropical fruit; floral; fresh tropical fruit; and nuts/almonds. Interestingly, it retains a welcome acidity in Serra Gaúcha. The total planted area in 2023, according to SIVIBE, was 646 hectares.

Goethe

Edward Staniford Rogers created this hybrid cultivar in Salem, Massachusetts, in 1851. It is a crossing of Muscat of Hamburg and another hybrid, Carter. The grape was probably brought to Brazil in the nineteenth century. It is cultivated and vinified only in Santa Catarina state, where an IP is exclusively dedicated to it, albeit tiny. Here, there are two clones, Goethe Clássica (pink skin) and Goethe Primo (white), with the same genetics. This has been studied by Schuck and collaborators, who found, interestingly, that the Goethe grape from Santa Catarina has a DNA profile that does not match any other available in large grape genetic databases. This indicates that it is a unique variety instead of the original American crossing. However, this requires more research. The vines are mainly trained to a 'Y' system in the IP, where the total planted area is 55 hectares. Goethe generates a white wine without *labrusca* character, which is fresh, fruity (citrus, peach, tropical fruit), floral and mineral. Skin contact (one to three days) is usual, imparting a higher content of flavours and polyphenols to the wine. Goethe is used to produce still and sparkling white and pink (Clássica) wines.

Riesling Itálico

Riesling Itálico is the Brazilian name for Welschriesling, a variety that probably originated in Croatia and is widely planted in Eastern Europe. One of its parents is unknown; the other is the obscure Coccalona Nera, a rare Italian grape. Interestingly, Coccalona is also a parent of Barbera. This famous variety is then at least a half-sibling of Riesling Itálico. The synonym Graševina is adopted in the book *Wine Grapes* by Robinson, Harding and Vouillamoz, as the authors suggest a Croatian origin. This seems unlikely, as Coccalona Nera has not been present there at any time, as stated by Raimondi and co-workers in a very interesting paper published in 2020. According to Embrapa, the grape was brought to Rio Grande do Sul by the Agronomical Station of Porto Alegre, the state capital, in 1900. It is easily adaptable and very productive, having found a good niche in Rio Grande do Sul (being the seventh most planted *vinifera* cultivar in 2015). The grape does not mature to high sugar content and keeps acidity well, besides being subtle and delicate in aromas and flavours (apple, pear, stone fruit and white flowers), with a soft texture. Such traits make it suitable for making sparkling wine blends or (less commonly) to play the solo part. It is even used by Chandon, a producer with a long tradition in such wines. Still varietal wines are also made, such as Aurora's version from IP Pinto Bandeira or Almadén's entry-level rendition from Campanha Gaúcha. SIVIBE statistics point to a total planted area of 290 hectares in 2023.

A beautiful cluster of Itália grapes

Itália

Itália is a crossing of Bicane (an obscure French white grape) with Muscat of Hamburg, obtained in 1911 by Alberto Pirovano, in Rome. Its correct Vitis International Variety Catalogue (VIVC) accession name is Muscat Italia, and it has 27 synonyms. Luciano Poletti brought the variety to Brazil in the 1930s, but only after 15 years did Sussumo Ussui succeed in cultivating it. And what a success: today, Itália is one of the most important table grapes in the country. No wonder: its big, beautiful, firm, fleshy grapes are delicious. It is *Vitis vinifera*, with an expected Muscat character, which makes it very important for crafting sweet sparkling wines in the São Francisco Valley. Here, a mutation was observed in the 1990s, with improved aromas and flavours, nicknamed 'Itália Melhorada' (Improved Itália). Embrapa has collected planting materials and submitted them for antiviral treatments, and started to propagate them commercially in 2015.

Peverella

There has been some confusion about this grape, but Brazil can likely boast of being one of only two countries with it in the whole world. According to Robinson, Harding and Vouillamoz's *Wine Grapes*, the variety known in Italy as Peverella would be, in truth, Verdicchio (based on unpublished research by Grando and Vouillamoz). It refers specifically to a grape called Peverella cultivated in Trentino/Alto Adige. These authors state, moreover, that Brazilian Peverella would be identical to Verdicchio, according to a work developed by Brazilian and American researchers led by Patricia Leão, published in 2009. This work, however, studied only genetic material obtained from a germplasm collection belonging to Embrapa Semi-Árido, Bahia. The authors themselves recognize that much of this is from an unknown origin. Generalizing, then, that the genetic material from Peverella kept in this collection would represent this grape at a national level seems inadequate. The geneticist and writer Ian D'Agata, in his much-quoted book *Native Wine Grapes of Italy*, had already expressed doubts about this. A very recent work by Cisilotto and co-workers, published in the demanding scientific journal *Vitis* in 2023, points to another – and much more interesting – direction. The researchers collected plant material from vines grown by two producers (Salvati & Sirena and Foresti) at Serra Gaúcha. Genetic studies from such materials performed at the University of Caxias revealed that this Peverella was, in fact, the obscure Italian grape Boschera. They proved that it was not Verdicchio. Boschera grows in Veneto, not Trentino, and the planted area is minute. Ampelographic comparisons, moreover, as published in this paper, show that Verdicchio and Boschera have distinct differences in the skins and leaves. Cisilotto informed me (via personal communication) that the ampelographic characteristics of Peverella grown by other producers are the same as those of their collected materials. Brazil has, then, a very rare cultivar.

According to recent SIVIBE statistics, the planted area is less than 6 hectares. The present scarcity of Peverella plantings contrasts with its abundance during part of the last century. According to Camargo, the grape was introduced to Rio Grande do Sul by João Dreher at the start of the twentieth century, becoming the main white *vinifera* grape at Serra Gaúcha until the early 1970s. The market preference for international varieties and irregular yields explains its decline. A few producers, fortunately, have not eliminated it, their vineyards becoming a source of planting material for other growers. In any case, the fact is that an opportunity exists to take advantage of this scarcity and promote a very unusual wine. This is indeed a Brazilian speciality. 'Indeed' because, although a few Italian producers from DOCG Colli di Conegliano use the variety, it is only part of a blend with Glera, Verdiso and other grapes. An orange Peverella wine by Era dos Ventos has achieved high praise from the Brazilian specialized press. Vinified without skin contact at low temperatures and in protected conditions, the product is a delicate, fresh, piquant wine with hints of white flowers, and aromas and flavours of melon, pear and a touch of spice and honey. It takes well to a short time in oak.

Rebo

Rebo is a Merlot × Teroldego crossing, obtained in 1948 at San Michelle all'Adige, Trentino, by Rebo Rigotti. About 39 hectares were planted in 2000 in Italy, predominately in Trentino. It is much less usual outside its mother country. In Brazil, a growing number of producers (about 20) cultivate it. SIVIBE statistics point to a planted area of 25 hectares (2023). Rebo wines are deeply coloured, rich but fresh, and display evident fruitiness, both red and black berries, with a good structure of fine, soft tannins and hints of herbs to add complexity.

Ancellotta

The variety Ancellotta has a large acreage in Italy, mainly in Emilia-Romagna, where it is used as a blend component of red Lambrusco or to produce concentrated must to improve the colour of anaemic wines. In Rio Grande do Sul, it is increasingly used to craft varietal wines. These have a deep colour, rich, ripe fruit, fresh acidity and usually soft tannins. The wines pair well with Italian pasta dishes.

Marselan

This Cabernet Sauvignon × Grenache crossing was developed in France in 1961. It has a good resistance against fungal diseases. A growing number of wineries produce varietal wines from this grape, especially in Rio Grande do Sul. In Brazil, the wines have lots of colour and aromas. These bring ripe red (cherry) and black (cassis) fruit. They are well structured in acidity and fine-grained tannins and take oak well. Many products are of high quality and are ageworthy.

YIELDS

According to Statista, the average five-year (2018–2022) yield in Brazil was 20.7 tons per hectare. Assuming an average of 700 litres of wine per ton of grapes, the theoretical yield would be 144.9 hectolitres per hectare. The yield data, however, includes table grapes and American hybrids. It is better to rely on information provided directly by producers. In Rio Grande do Sul, Bruno Motter (Don Guerino) mentions 6–10 tons per hectare (42–70 hectolitres per hectare), whereas Ricardo Morari (Cooperativa

Garibaldi) claims a yield of 12–25 tons per hectare (84–175 hectolitres per hectare). The reason for the much higher figure from Cooperativa is likely to be because they produce many inexpensive wines, a great percentage being sparklers from high-yielding varieties (Moscato, Glera). Monte Agudo yields 5–7 tons per hectare (35–49 hectolitres per hectare) in Santa Catarina. Heloise Merolli from Legado, Paraná, told me that her Fiano vineyard has average yields of 7.4 tons per hectare, or 51.8 hectolitres per hectare. According to Murillo Regina, most DPWH vineyards yield 6–8 tons per hectare (42–56 hectolitres per hectare). In the Northeast, Ricardo Henriques (Rio Sol) reports 14 tons per hectare (98 hectolitres per hectare) for white grapes and 7–8 tons per hectare (42–56 hectolitres per hectare) for red varieties. These are general, average data – as Adolfo Lona stresses, the most important information is the yield per vine; the standard is 2–3 kilograms per vine. He says one bottle of a good, delicate white wine demands about 1.5 kilograms of grapes, as only the free-run juice is used. Inexpensive reds can use up to 80 per cent of the weight of grapes with hard pressing. Brazilian yields can be compared to those of other countries: Germany, New Zealand and South Africa produce over 80 hectolitres per hectare; the USA and Australia over 70; Italy 68; France 58; Argentina, Austria, and Chile 50; Spain 42 and Portugal 33 (source: *BKWine*).

BRAZILIAN WOODS FOR WINE AGEING

There is a long tradition of ageing *cachaça* (a sugarcane juice spirit) in Brazilian wooden vessels. Using these for wines is an exciting and promising new development. Some producers and several academic works attest to the feasibility of replacing oak. The alternative Brazilian species studied and tried include *amburana (Amburana cearensis), bálsamo* or *cabreúva (Myrocarpus frondosus), castanheira do Pará (Bertholletia excelsa), cumaru (Dypterix odorata), grápia (Apuleia leiocarpa), ipê amarelo (Tabebuia vellosoi), jaqueira (Artocarpus heterophyllus), jequitibá rosa (Cariniana legalis),* and *putumuju (Centrolobium tomentosum).*

Amanda Andrade, in her MSc dissertation, studied Merlot wines matured in oak, *amburana* and *jequitibá*. The experimental wines were submitted to both laboratory analyses and controlled tastings by consumers. The latter preferred the wines aged in *amburana* and then in *jequitibá*; oak came in third. António Jordão and co-workers also found a consumer preference (as well as a higher phenolic content) for wines having contact with *ipê*, *jaqueira* and *amburana* cubes, compared to oak. Suzana De Carli and her team studied the anatomical, physical and chemical properties of *amburana* and *jequitibá rosa*. They found that the latter had more similarities with oak, both having properties supporting their use in cooperage and wine ageing.

Must weight scales

Nearly all producers in Rio Grande do Sul evaluate the must weight in the field through refractometers (here called *mostímetros*), using the Babo scale instead of Brix. The Babo scale is named after its inventor, August Wilhelm von Babo, an oenologist of German descent who worked in Austria at the Klosterneuburg viticulture school. This scale, better known as *Klosterneuburger Mostwaage* (KMW), is used predominately in Austria and other countries in Central Europe. It is possible that Brazil adopted it because many Italian immigrants to Rio Grande do Sul came from Veneto, which was ruled by the Austro-Hungarian Empire until 1866. However, this is just conjecture. The Babo scale reflects the sugar concentration in musts better than Brix, as it considers only sugars, whereas Brix considers all solids. To convert Babo into Brix, use Brix = Babo/0.85.

Two producers have advanced significantly in their trials of these woods. Gaspar Desurmont, from Vinhetica (Campanha Gaúcha) started his experiments ten years ago. He told me that, in his view, some woods – *amburana*, *bálsamo* and *grápia* – are not usable as they are too overpowering and mask the wine's aromas and flavours. He loves the marriage of *jequitibá rosa* and Sauvignon Blanc, as this wood brings a fresher finish than oak, with a charming, slightly bitter, tang. Desurmont also praises *putumuju*, which raises the black fruit notes in reds such as Syrah or Saperavi, and *castanheira do Pará* used to improve the structure of Cabernet Franc wines without adding vanilla flavours. *Ipê amarelo*, as he says, imparts honey, beeswax and yellow flower flavours to white wines. Desurmont is trying a series of other woods from Pará state besides *araucaria* and some eucalyptus. Giovanni Ferrari from Arte Viva (Serra Gaúcha), another indefatigable oenologist, produces several wines using Brazilian woods. He employs cubes and staves, in addition to barrels (made by Tanoaria Mezacasa, Monte Belo). He likes *grápia* and Sauvignon Blanc despite this species' strong spicy and woody notes. Arte Viva's Juju Rosé is made predominately from Marselan, ageing with *jequitibá rosa*; slight notes of aniseed, caramel and molasses are

Brazil sparkles

It is undeniable that sparkling wines are a very important part of the Brazilian wine mix, and their importance is growing significantly. Although statistics must always be handled with some scepticism, the country likely crafts almost 50 million bottles of these wines annually. Between 2019 to 2024, according to WineXT, sales of non-Moscatel sparkling wines grew 23 per cent and Moscatel grew by a whopping 49 per cent. Since 2015, about 80 per cent of all sparklers sold in the country have been made in Brazil. They are the most important component of Brazil's wine exports and have earned many prizes in international contests. This success is due to several factors:

- Although there is no such thing as a single style of Brazilian sparkling wines (this is a huge country), all share some desirable characteristics: they are mostly fresh and fruity, very easy to enjoy and affordable.

- Moscatel-based sparklers are immensely successful, exhibiting some desirable traits: high aromaticity, low alcohol, and sweetness balanced by fresh acidity. They are usually less sweet than Asti.

- Sparkling wines made using the tank (Charmat) method are also fruity, easy drinking, inexpensive and of increasing quality.

- Traditional method examples also show an increasing level of craftsmanship and a great variety, from simple and fruity to very complex, top-quality wines with years of autolysis.

- As in Champagne, the climate in Serra Gaúcha, the most important production area, favours the making of base wines with low alcohol and high acidity, suitable for sparklers.

- Human expertise in producing these wines is a fundamental cause of their success. Skilled, experienced master oenologists like Adolfo Lona, Gilberto Pedrucci and Mario Geisse, among many others, have guaranteed the high quality of these wines.

imparted by this wood, improving the wine's complexity. *Castanha* contributes pepper and nutmeg to his Geodésis red blend. Flávio Pizzato, on the other hand, is still sceptical in this regard; he says that, so far, no Brazilian wood has impressed him so much as to justify its use.

This is a work in progress. A much larger 'critical mass' of examples is needed to produce clearer, more significant findings. These preliminary results, however, are promising, pointing to an original Brazilian contribution to winemaking.

5

GEOGRAPHICAL INDICATIONS

The history of geographical indications (in Portuguese: IGs, or *Indicações Geográficas*) for wine in Brazil is recent. Studies to make them feasible began in the 1980s, when Embrapa researchers consistently verified, in Rio Grande do Sul, that wines from different origins had distinct characteristics – the terroir effect. Embrapa catalysed other contributions (from producer associations and universities), developing the theoretical and practical background to build the structure of IGs in the Brazilian wine sector.

It was only in 2002 that the first *Indicação de Procedência* (IP), or Provenance Indication, was granted to Vale dos Vinhedos. Ten years later, the area obtained a *Denominação de Origem* (DO), or Denomination of Origin. Others soon followed suit. This is an ongoing process, with the most recent IP arising in February 2025.

LEGAL FOUNDATIONS

IGs in Brazil are granted by a federal government autarchy, the Instituto Nacional da Propriedade Industrial (INPI) – or National Institute of Industrial Property – a part of the Ministry of Development, Industry and Services. Created in 1970, the INPI grants and registers brands, designs, software, patents, geographical indications and other modalities of intellectual property. IGs are conceded to products, like wine and other foodstuffs, with characteristics that allow a link to their origin, imparting reputation, value and identity and hence distinguishing them from similar products with different origins. The idea, as everywhere, is that these wines show unique qualities connected to terroir: soil, vegetation, climate and know-how (within which tradition is interspersed). Whenever an association or union of producers wishes to obtain IP or DO status, it must petition the INPI in a detailed process, whose final answer may take years.

The legal documents which are the foundations of IG concessions are the *Lei da Propriedade Industrial* (Industrial Property Law), from 1996, and its regulation, the *Portaria INPI/PR no.4*, from 2022. IGs in Brazil, according to such norms, are of two kinds:

- *Indicação de Procedência* (IP): a geographical name with a very elastic area (can be a locality, region, state or even country) known, in the case of wine, by a given product.
- *Denominação de Origem* (DO): a geographical name designating a product whose qualities and characteristics are closely connected to the geographical environment, including natural and human factors.

After a geographical indication is granted in Europe, it is inspected and overseen by organizations such as the Institut National de l'Origine et de la Qualité (INAO) in France or the Instituto da Vinha e do Vinho (IVV), Instituto dos Vinhos do Douro E Porto (IVDP) and Instituto do Vinho, do Bordado e Do Artesanato da Madeira (IVBAM) in Portugal. In Brazil, the IGs take care of themselves in terms of the observance of rules. This happens through a regulating council which ranges from five to ten members; in all but one (Monte Belo), the majority of these councils are made up of growers or winemakers. There are always members from technical or scientific bodies; only two (Vales da Uva Goethe and Vinhos de Inverno do Sul de Minas) include a consumer representative. As a rule, wines to be labelled with the IP or DO seal must first be approved by a tasting committee which tries to ensure that the originality and typicity of wines are always kept, thus benefitting themselves and consumers.

Brazil had 11 IPs and two DOs in the wine sector as of February 2025. The following is some key information on these.

Map 5: Geographical indications. Modified with permission from Embrapa.
Prepared by Tonietto, Prado, Ribeiro and Falcade (2022)

DO VALE DOS VINHEDOS

Location: Vale dos Vinhedos, Serra Gaúcha, Rio Grande do Sul, townships of Bento Gonçalves, Garibaldi and Monte Belo do Sul

Total area: 72.45 square kilometres

Producers' association: Aprovale – www.valedosvinhedos.com.br/

This pioneering area was granted IP status in 2002. Ten years later, in 2012, the INPI granted DO status. *Latadas* (pergola systems) are forbidden. Maximum yields are 10 tons per hectare for still and 12 for sparkling wines. Harvesting must be manual. Sparklers can only be crafted by the traditional method, from Nature to Brut, using at least

60 per cent Chardonnay and/or Pinot Noir (Riesling Itálico is optional), with a minimum of nine months' autolysis. The date of *dégorgement* must be stated on the label. White still wines must use at least 60 per cent Chardonnay, blended or not with Riesling Itálico; they must age for at least six months. Varietal wines must have at least 85 per cent of the named grape. Reds must use at least 60 per cent Merlot, which can be blended with Cabernet Sauvignon, Cabernet Franc and Tannat; the minimum ageing is 12 months. Neither ageing has to be in oak; if used, however, it must be in barrels, oak alternatives (such as oak chips) being forbidden. The same applies to chaptalization (though the regulation council can authorize this in exceptional instances).

IP PINTO BANDEIRA

Location: Serra Gaúcha, Rio Grande do Sul, townships of Pinto Bandeira, Farroupilha and Bento Gonçalves
Total area: 81.38 square kilometres, with altitudes above 500 metres
Producers' association: Asprovinho – www.asprovinho.com.br/

IP status was granted in 2010. Altitude leads to a milder climate, with a longer growth cycle and later harvest. Above all, the area is renowned for its sparkling wines, but good Chardonnay and Pinot Noir varietals exist. Eight red and twelve white varieties are authorized for still wines; for sparklers, the list is shorter: Chardonnay, Pinot Noir, Riesling Itálico and Viognier for the traditional method, and four Moscatos, plus two Malvasias, for *moscatel espumante*. Open *latadas* are authorized. Maximum yields are 12 tons per hectare for *latadas* (but 14 for *moscatel espumante*) and 9 tons for VSP systems (*espaldeiras*) to craft the other wines. Up to 15 per cent of the grapes can come from outside the IP.

DO ALTOS DE PINTO BANDEIRA

Producers' association: Asprovinho – www.asprovinho.com.br/

DO status granted in 2022. The location is the same as the IP Pinto Bandeira, but the area is smaller: 65 square kilometres, of which about 77 per cent is in the homonymous municipality. The name *Altos* (heights) is due to the high altitude. This is a geographical indication exclusive to traditional method sparklers made from Chardonnay, Pinot

Noir and Riesling Itálico (25 per cent maximum). Only vertical train-
ing/trellising systems are allowed. The maximum yield is 12 tons per
hectare, but the regulating council may authorize up to 20 per cent
more in some vintages, as in Champagne's *plafond limité de classement*
(PLC). Only grapes produced within the DO can be used; manual harvesting and whole-cluster pressing are mandatory. Oak can be used to
ferment/mature the base wine. The maximum juice yield to produce the
base wines is 65 litres per 100 kilograms of grapes. Reserve wines can
have a maximum of five years. The *liqueur de tirage* may increase the
final alcohol to a maximum of 1.7 per cent; the *liqueur d'expédition* up
to 0.5 per cent. The minimal time on lees is 12 months. Final residual
sugar ranges from Nature to Demi-sec. Vintage wines must have at least
85 per cent of the grapes from the declared year.

IP ALTOS MONTES

Location: Serra Gaúcha, Rio Grande do Sul, townships of Flores da Cunha and Nova
Pádua
Total area: 174 square kilometres, with altitudes reaching 885 metres
Producers' association: Apromontes – (+55) 54 99657 9496

IP status was granted in 2012. Altitude ensures a cooler climate, with a
longer growth cycle and later harvest. Only *espaldeiras* (vertical systems)
are allowed. At least 85 per cent of the grapes must come from the IP.
Hand harvesting is mandatory. Maximum yields: 8 tons per hectare for
dry white still wines, 9 for reds, 10 for white grapes used to craft base
wines for sparklers (but 9 for Pinot Noir) and 13 for aromatic, sweet
sparkling products. The regulating council may authorize up to 25 per
cent more in some vintages. Fizzy wines can be sweet (from Moscato
Branco, Moscato Bianco R2, Moscato Giallo, Muscat of Alexandria and
the Malvasias) or drier – the *espumantes finos* (Chardonnay, Pinot Noir,
Riesling Itálico, Trebbiano). Dry white wines come from Riesling Itálico,
Malvasia de Cândia, Chardonnay, Sauvignon Blanc, Gewurztraminer
and Moscato Giallo. Rosés are made with Pinot Noir and Merlot. Reds
use Cabernet Franc, Merlot, Ancellotta, Cabernet Sauvignon, Pinot
Noir, Refosco, Marselan and Tannat. However, up to 15 per cent of
other *vinifera* grapes can be used if their production follows IP regulations and they come from its territory. Chaptalization is forbidden for
still wines, but, again, the council may, in certain years, authorize it up

to 1% abv in the final wine. Sparkling wines can be made both by tank and traditional methods. Dry pink or red varietals must have at least 85 per cent of the stated variety, while still white varietals must be 100 per cent. Must concentration to craft red wines is forbidden. Oak chips are not allowed.

IP MONTE BELO

Location: Serra Gaúcha, Rio Grande do Sul, townships of Monte Belo, Bento Gonçalves and Santa Tereza
Total area: 56.09 square kilometres, with an average altitude of 485 metres
Producers' association: Aprobelo – (+55) 54 3457 1173

IP status was granted in 2013. Both vertical systems and open pergolas are allowed. All grapes must come from the IP. Hand harvesting is mandatory. Maximum yields (between brackets are *latada* yields): 8 (12) tons per hectare for dry white and red still wines, 12 (18) for white grapes used to craft base wines for sparklers (but 10/14 for Pinot Noir) and 18 for aromatic, sweet sparklers. According to the vintage conditions, the regulating council may increase or decrease the minimum sugar concentrations of harvested grapes (here measured in degrees Babo, not Brix).

Fizzy wines can be sweet, made from a minimum of 70 per cent of Moscato varieties; the authorized cultivars are Moscato Branco, Moscato Giallo, Muscat of Alexandria, Muscat of Hamburg, and the Malvasias Bianca and de Cândia. The drier *espumantes finos* have a characteristic profile, as they must contain a minimum of 40 per cent Riesling Itálico and 30 per cent Pinot Noir, with up to 30 per cent Chardonnay and 10 per cent Glera (Prosecco). Dry white wines come from Riesling Itálico and Chardonnay, obeying the 85 per cent rule for varietals; blended whites must contain at least 60 per cent Riesling Itálico and 20 per cent Chardonnay. Reds are made from Merlot, Cabernet Franc, Cabernet Sauvignon and Tannat if varietals; these must have at least 85 per cent of the declared cultivar. The red blends must be 40 per cent Merlot, plus a maximum of 40 per cent Cabernet Sauvignon, 30 per cent Cabernet Franc and 15 per cent Tannat, Egiodola or Alicante Bouschet. Although sparkling wines can be white or pink, no still rosé wine production is allowed in this IP. Traditional method sparklers must remain at least nine months on lees. The region has its own selected yeast strain, *Saccharomyces cerevisiae* 24MB-CM06, which contributes to the identity of the wines.

Chaptalization is allowed up to 2% abv. For sparkling winemaking, regulations allow both tank and traditional methods; at least nine months of autolysis must happen in the latter. The sweet, Muscat-based fizzy wines may not surpass 80 grams per litre residual sugar.

IP FARROUPILHA

Location: Serra Gaúcha, Rio Grande do Sul, townships of Farroupilha (99 per cent), Caxias do Sul, Pinto Bandeira and Bento Gonçalves

Total area: 379 square kilometres – within this large surface area is a more limited region, the ADPM (delimited area of production of Moscatel grapes)

Producers' association: Afavin – (+55) 54 98404 1147

IP status was granted in 2015. This is a very particular IP restricted to *vinhos moscatéis* made only from aromatic grapes, predominately Muscat. This IP produces about half of all Muscat grapes in the whole country. Of note, however, is that most of it is Moscato Branco, whose exact pedigree is unknown, although genetic research suggests that Muscat of Hamburg is likely one of its ancestors. As we saw in the chapter on Viticulture (see p. 58), this cultivar has a good chance of being planted only in Brazil. The authorized varieties are Moscato Branco, Moscato Bianco, Moscato Giallo, Moscato Rosado, Muscat of Hamburg, Muscat of Alexandria, Malvasia Bianca and Malvasia de Cândia. Only grapes grown in the IP can be used, of which 85 per cent must come from the ADPM. Both open *latadas* and VSP systems (*espaldeiras* and 'Y') are permitted. Maximum yields are 25 tons per hectare for Moscato Branco (a very productive variety) and 20 for all other grapes. As in other IPs, the regulating council may, in certain vintages, authorize a 20 per cent increase in production. Hand harvesting is mandatory and irrigation can be performed only in newly planted vineyards or in exceptional years, after permission. The Moscatel products that can be crafted are still wine, *frisante* (lightly sparkling), sparkling, *licoroso* (14–18% abv, dry or sweet), mistelle and brandy. Sparklers are made in tanks through an Asti-like process of a single fermentation, resulting in a wine with 7–9% abv, pressure equal or superior to 4 atmospheres and total residual sugar between 60 and 90 grams per litre. The still wines follow the Brazilian classification of sweetness levels. *Frisantes* cannot be gasified; their pressure is 1.1–2.0 atmospheres. Permitted sweetening agents are fresh must, concentrated must and sucrose, but this may vary according to the category of wine. Varietals must have a minimum of 85 per cent of the variety stated on the label.

IP CAMPANHA GAÚCHA

Location: In the *pampas* (flat fields interspersed with some low, rolling hills), in the southern half of Rio Grande do Sul, this region is very different from Serra Gaúcha. It borders Argentina and Uruguay, with the altitude averaging 150–160 metres
Total area: An extensive IP, Campanha Gaúcha comprises 44,365 square kilometres and encompasses 14 townships
Producers' association: Associação Vinhos da Campanha – www.vinhosdacampanha.com.br/

This is a more recent wine-growing area, with plantings starting in the 1980s. In 2015, the area had 1,560 hectares of *vinifera*, dominated by Cabernet Sauvignon, Chardonnay, Merlot, Tannat and Pinot Noir. The IP originated, then, 31 per cent of the entire Brazilian production of *vinhos finos*.

IP status was granted in 2020. All grapes used for the wines must come from the area. VSP systems only are allowed to grow no less than 36 *vinifera* varieties. These include cultivars uncommon in other Brazilian regions, such as Alfrocheiro, Alvarinho, Longanesi, Ruby Cabernet and Touriga Nacional. Maximum yields are (in tons per hectare) – 15 for base wines to produce sparklers, 12 for whites, and 10 for reds (except Tannat and Alicante Bouschet: both 12). As elsewhere, the regulating council may extend such limits in some vintages. Allowed products are still white, pink and red wines, as well as sparkling wines. The 85 per cent rule must be observed for variety and vintage when stated. Sparklers can be made using the tank and traditional methods. Chaptalization can be made up to 2% abv.

IP VALES DA UVA GOETHE

Location: Santa Catarina, South region, and encompassing eight townships, the most important being Urussanga. The altitude varies between 140 and 290 metres
Total area: 458.9 square kilometres
Producers' association: ProGoethe – (+55) 48 3465 1491

IP status was granted in 2021. This distinctive IP is dedicated to a single grape, Goethe, which has been traditional in the region since the beginning of the twentieth century (see page 59). This rare hybrid is cultivated mainly in pergolas; other systems, however, are authorized. Two clones exist in the IP (Goethe Clássica and Goethe Primo). All wines must be 100 per cent Goethe and made within the IP. Allowed products: white still wines (*seco, suave, leve seco, leve suave),* sparklers (made either by the tank or the traditional method) and *licorosos.* Cork closures are mandatory.

IP VINHOS DE ALTITUDE DE SANTA CATARINA

Location: Santa Catarina, where the IP corresponds to a large region encompassing 29 townships
Total area: 19,676 square kilometres, at high elevation (900–1,400 m), with a cool climate
Producers' association: Vinhos de Altitude Produtores & Associados – www.vinhosdealtitude.com.br/

IP was granted in 2021. More than in Rio Grande do Sul, altitude propitiates a cool climate, with a longer growth cycle and later harvest. About 300 hectares of *vinifera* vines are grown using *espaldeira*, or 'Y' systems. All wines must be made with grapes from the region. In total, 26 varieties are authorized. The most used rootstock is Paulsen 1103. Harvesting is manual. The regulations allow a maximum yield of 7,000 litres per hectare of wine. The regulating council, however, may authorize up to 25 per cent more, depending on the vintage, training/trellising system and other criteria. Charmat (tank) and traditional methods are used to make sparkling wines. The minimum time on lees for the latter is 12 months, and the maximum juice yield for making base wines is 60 per cent. Both varietal and vintage statements must obey the 85 per cent rule. Allowed wine types are dry whites, rosés and reds (*finos, nobres), licorosos,* and sparklers (Moscato-based or the drier styles). Rosés must be made from at least 85 per cent of red grapes. Chaptalization is permitted for base wines to make sparklers and *vinhos finos*, up to 1.5% abv. Oak alternatives are allowed, provided they are at least domino size (chips are forbidden).

IP VINHOS DE BITURUNA

Location: Paraná, exclusively in the municipality of Bituruna
Total area: 1,228.29 square kilometres, with an average altitude of 900 metres
Producers' association: Apruvibi – michele.enologia@gmail.com

IP was granted in 2022. It is dedicated to table wines made from two non-*vinifera* varieties: Martha, also known there as *Casca Grossa* (thick skin), and Bordô. They may be grown in *latadas* or 'Y' systems. The maximum yield is 20 tons per hectare. Both red and white *vinhos de mesa* can be produced, from *seco* (dry) to demi-sec. Varietals must be 100 per cent from the stated cultivar.

IP VALE DO SÃO FRANCISCO

Location: States of Pernambuco and Bahia, Northeast region, covering five townships
Total area: 25,138 square kilometres – the climate is tropical and semi-arid, and the altitude ranges from 350 to 420 metres
Producers' association: Vinhovasf – gualberto@botticelli.com.br

IP was granted in 2022. This is the first Brazilian IP for tropical viticulture. It is located in a low-latitude region (between 8°S and 9°S). Irrigation (from the mighty São Francisco River) is mandatory. According to Embrapa, about 500 hectares of *vinifera* varieties were planted in 2017 for wine production. The particular conditions allow two or more harvests per year (considering an average of several years). There are 23 authorized varieties, all *vinifera*. All grapes used must come from the IP. Both pergola (which may be of benefit in a region with high levels of sunlight and heat) and vertical systems are approved. Maximum permitted yields vary widely, from 10 tons per hectare in *espaldeira* systems for still wines to 40 for sparkling Moscatel. As usual, the regulating council may sometimes authorize 20 per cent more. Due to the region's specificities, harvest and vinification may happen throughout the year. Varietal wines must be made with at least 85 per cent of the stated variety. Sparklers may be made either by tank or traditional method. Chaptalization is permitted for red *vinhos finos* (not for white or pink), up to 1.5% abv. Considering the peculiarities of tropical viticulture, there is a maximum age to allow the sale of wines using the IP seal: one year for sparkling Moscatel, two for still whites and rosés and other sparklers, and four for red still wines. Total annual production averages 8 million litres, made by seven wineries.

IP VINHOS DE INVERNO DO SUL DE MINAS

Location: state of Minas Gerais, Southeast region, comprising ten townships, with a total area of 4,239.6 square kilometres. The climate (Köppen-Geiger) is predominately Cwb (dry winter, temperate summer) and the altitude is (by regulations) at least 800 metres.

Producers' association: ANPROVIN-SM – Núcleo Regional dos Produtores de Vinho de Inverno – José Afonso Davo (WhatsApp: (+55) 11 97497 8454)

The IP was granted in 2025, making it the first Brazilian IP for DPWH wines. It is located in the south of Minas Gerais, the pioneering region for this style of vineyard management. There are 13 authorized varieties, all *vinifera*. All grapes used must come from the IP. Only vertical systems are approved and protective plastic coverage is forbidden. Irrigation and fertigation (mixing fertilizers with irrigation water) are allowed. The maximum permitted yield is 10 tons per hectare. The minimum Brix at harvest is 20° for white and pink wines and 22° for reds. No chaptalization is allowed. IP protection covers only still wines; their minimum alcohol content must be 12% abv. The regulating council may sometimes authorize other varieties, different training or trellising systems, higher yields and other *vinifera* products distinct from still wines. Varietal wines must contain at least 75 per cent of the stated variety. The regulating council has eight members. All wines must pass through a tasting board.

6

BRAZILIAN WINE LAW

A delicious Brazilian fruit called *jabuticaba* is typical of the country and cannot be found elsewhere. Here, whenever something exists that you cannot encounter anywhere else, it is heralded as such. In many ways, Brazilian wine law is a kind of *jabuticaba*. The rules are similar to those in other countries in many respects, but are very specific in others.

All Brazilian regulations pertaining to alcoholic drinks, vinegar and grape products have been consolidated in the *Norma Operacional* (Operational Norm) no. 1, 24 January 2019, issued by the Ministério da Agricultura e Pecuária (MAPA) – the Ministry of Agriculture and Livestock. This *norma* in itself is very short, just one page. Its substance lies in the Annex (2,035 pages). I will examine what is most relevant to wine from this very detailed text.

In Brazil, the term 'wine' has been defined (since 1988) as 'the drink obtained by the alcoholic fermentation of simple juice of healthy, fresh and ripe grapes'. According to this definition, it is forbidden to label anything made from any other fruit, even *jabuticaba*, as 'wine'. There is also some mandatory information that must appear on the label of all Brazilian wines:

- Producer's name, address and CNPJ (National Registry of Legal Entities) number. When a third party makes the wine, their name may or may not be shown, but at least the expression 'produced and bottled under the responsibility of' who contracts the party must appear. The consumer will then know that the wine has been made by a third party, even if they do not know who this is. The name of the oenologist responsible for the wine, or equivalent, also appears.

- The product's registration number at MAPA.
- The brand or name of the wine.
- The classification (class) of the wine according to Brazilian regulations. For example, *vinho fino tinto seco* (fine dry red wine).
- Ingredients: usually just grapes and preservatives.
- The statement '*Indústria Brasileira*' (Made in Brazil).
- Volume of contents on the main label, expressed in international units (usually millilitres or litres).
- Alcohol content, in percentage by volume (for example, 12.5% abv).
- Lot number (can be a barcode).
- Expiration date: in wine, albeit invariably written '*indeterminada*' (indeterminate), this is mandatory. Usually accompanied by the expression 'if kept in a cool, dark, dry place with the bottle on its side'.
- Warnings: whether the wine contains gluten; that 'excessive alcohol consumption is to be avoided' (mandatory only for wines with an alcoholic content of 13% abv or more); and that the wine may contain residues of specific allergenic inputs (such as eggs or fish), if used.

The illustration below indicates how to read the label of a Brazilian wine. Given the preponderance of Isabel, Bordô and other rustic American or hybrid cultivars, it is no wonder that, in Brazil, the law divides wines into two main categories. These are the *vinhos de mesa* (table wines), which can be made with such grapes, and the *vinhos finos* (fine wines), made from *vinifera* varieties. The law, however, is confusing, as

Front and back labels of a Brazilian wine bottle.

it also allows *vinhos de mesa* to be made from *vinifera*. It is hard to imagine why any producer would make a *vinifera* wine and label it as *vinho de mesa*. This category is recognizable, after all, from the organoleptic attributes of American and most hybrid cultivars, including the peculiar 'foxy' aromas and flavours, and by the low price points.

The regulations also state that *vinhos finos* are those made from *Vitis vinifera* grapes of the 'noble' group – but a regulation from 2018 considers all *vinifera* varieties as 'noble'. The producer may also add the expression *de mesa* to a *vinho fino*. Things become more confusing as the law also designates a category of wine named *nobre*, or noble, but this has nothing to do with any *vinifera* variety or with noble rot, but rather with alcohol content. To paraphrase a dictum, *confundit lex, sed lex* (confusing though the law is, it is the law).

Let's now consider some important regulations as determined by said law.

- Sugar content: to be considered dry, or *seco*, a still wine, or a *frisante* (sparkling wine with up to 2 atmospheres of pressure), must have up to 4 grams per litre of sugar. From above 4 up to 25 grams per litre, the wine is *demi-sec*, or *meio-seco*. If the content exceeds 25 grams, the wine is *suave* or *doce*. If still wine is made from American grapes, there is no upper limit for sugar. If, however, a *vinho de mesa* is crafted from *vinifera* varieties, or if any wine is presented as *vinho leve*, it cannot have more than 80 grams per litre. If a winemaker wishes to make a wine sweeter, the law allows the use of the following sweetening agents: sucrose (solid) and simple, concentrated or rectified/concentrated grape must.
- Colour: *branco* (white); *rosado, rosé* or *clarete* (pink); *tinto* (red).
- Alcohol content: regulations divide still, unfortified wines into *leves* (light), 7–8.5% abv; *de mesa* and *finos*, 8.6–14% abv; and *nobres*, 14.1–16% abv. There is a tolerance of ± 0.5.
- Varietal character: if a single cultivar is to appear on the label, the wine must be crafted from at least 75 per cent of this grape. If more than one variety has been used, they should be mentioned in decreasing order of percentage.
- Vintage: at least 85 per cent of the grapes must be from the declared vintage.
- Maturation: both *vinhos finos* and *vinhos nobres* may be labelled as: *Reservado* (despite the name, this is young, unaged, minimum 10% abv); *Reserva* (minimum 11% abv – reds: aged at least 12 months,

whites and rosés – aged at least 6 months, wood ageing being optional); *Gran Reserva* (minimum 11% abv; wood – not necessarily oak – mandatory in recipients with a maximum capacity of 600 litres; reds: aged at least 18 months, of which at least 6 in wood; whites and rosés: 12 and 3 months, respectively).

- Oak alternatives: when oak chips are used instead of barrels, the wine cannot be labelled according to the above-mentioned ageing categories.

The law classifies Brazilian wines into several categories, officially called *classes*, some of which have already been mentioned. This is a summary of the classes and their attributes:

- *Vinho de mesa*: still; made from American, hybrid or *vinifera* grapes; 8.6–14.0% abv; any colour; *seco* (dry), *meio-seco* (demi-sec) or *suave/ doce* (sweet, up to 80 grams per litre for those made from *vinifera*, no upper limit otherwise).
- *Vinho leve*: still; 7.0–8.5% abv; any colour; *seco* (dry), *meio-seco* (demi-sec) or *suave/doce* (sweet, up to 80 grams per litre). The law states that this wine cannot be made from *vinho de mesa*. This apparently means it can be made from the juice of grapes other than *vinifera*, as juice is not wine.
- *Vinho fino*: still; exclusively from *vinifera* grapes; 8.6–14.0% abv; any colour; *seco* (dry), *meio-seco* (demi-sec) or *suave/doce* (sweet, up to 80 grams per litre). Can be Reservado, Reserva or Gran Reserva.
- *Vinho nobre*: still; exclusively from *vinifera* grapes; 14.1–16.0% abv; any colour; *seco* (dry), *meio-seco* (demi-sec) or *suave/doce* (sweet, up to 80 grams per litre). Can be Reservado, Reserva or Gran Reserva.
- *Vinho frisante*: sparkling (natural or gasified), pressure 1.1–2.0 atmospheres; 7.0–14.0% abv; any colour; *seco* (dry), *meio-seco* (demi-sec) or *suave/doce* (sweet, up to 80 grams per litre). The label must state whether the sparkling character has been achieved naturally or through gasification (carbon dioxide injection).
- *Vinho moscato (Moscatel) espumante*: sparkling (natural), from Moscato (Moscatel, Muscat) grapes, pressure 4 atmospheres; 7.0–10.0% abv; white or pink; 20 grams per litre minimum residual sugar. When made from Moscato Embrapa, a hybrid, the expression *fino* cannot be used, as it may be in the case of, for example, Moscato Branco and Moscato Giallo.
- *Vinho espumante* (or just *Espumante,* or *Espumante natural*): sparkling (natural, traditional or tank method), minimum pressure 4

atmospheres; 10.0–13.0% abv; any colour. Sugar content must be on the label: *Nature* (up to 3 grams per litre); *Extra-brut* (>3.0–8.0); *Brut* (>8.0–15.0); *Sec/Seco* (>15.0–20.0); *Demi-sec, Meio-seco* or *Meio-doce* (>20.0–60.0); *Doce* (>60.0). The law does not expressly mandate that such wines must be made from *vinifera* varieties, but most examples are. Interestingly, one winery, Peterlongo from Garibaldi, Serra Gaúcha, can legally use the term 'Champagne' on the label. Since the early 1900s, its use predates the actions taken by the Comité Interprofessionnel du Vin de Champagne (CIVC), the powerful inter-professional committee from that French region.

- *Vinho gaseificado*: sparkling (gasified with carbon dioxide), 2.1–3.9 atmospheres; 7.0–14.0% abv; any colour; *seco* (dry, up to 20 grams per litre residual sugar), *meio-seco* (demi-sec, >20.0–≤60.0) or *suave/doce* (sweet, >60.0). The wine can be crafted from any grape, unfermented juice, *vinho leve, de mesa* or *fino,* or from a mixture of any.

- *Vinho licoroso*: still; 14.0–18.0% abv; natural or fortified; any colour; either *seco* (dry, up to 20 grams per litre residual sugar) or *doce* (sweet, >20). If fortified, any alcohol of agricultural origin can be used. It can be sweetened with concentrated must, mistelle (unfermented juice to which alcohol is added) or sucrose. The colour can be corrected with caramel. Interestingly, in a country with immense Portuguese influences, *vinho licoroso* cannot be fortified to more than 18.0% abv, whereas Port or Madeira usually have 19–20% abv. Before the *vinho nobre* class was instituted, any Brazilian dry wine having more than 14% abv had to be labelled as *vinho licoroso*.

- *Vinho composto*: still; 14.0–20.0% abv; any colour; *seco* (dry, up to 40 grams per litre residual sugar), *meio-seco* (demi-sec, >40.0–≤80.0) or *suave/doce* (sweet, >80.0), with the addition of macerates or concentrates of vegetal or animal origin (such as vermouth or wines with quinine, egg yolk, *jurubeba* – a bitter medicinal plant). The wine can be sweetened with concentrated must, mistelle or sucrose. The colour can be corrected with caramel.

- *Filtrado doce*: made from grape must (partially fermented or not), with the permitted addition of *vinho de mesa*; can be (and almost always is) gasified (up to 3.0 atmospheres); up to 5.0% abv; any colour; 60.0–100.0 grams per litre residual sugar. Adding sugar is forbidden.

7

WINE BUSINESS

Brazil's population in 2022 was 203.1 million, the seventh largest on the planet. According to the central statistical bureau, IBGE, the biggest city was São Paulo (11.40 million inhabitants), followed by Rio de Janeiro (6.21), Brasília, the capital (2.82), Fortaleza, Salvador, Belo Horizonte, Manaus, Curitiba, Recife and Goiânia. There are 15 cities with more than one million residents and 41 with over 500,000 inhabitants.

Despite the significant disproportions in wealth share distribution, a large percentage of Brazil's population belongs to the middle class and above. About 109 million people belong to class C (earning BRL 4,180–10,450 monthly). Classes A and B make up 14.4% of the population (approximately 30.4 million people). As noted on page 5, the sum of these social strata (more than 139 million people) represents an important contingent in which wine consumption can grow.

Please refer to the Chapter 4 for information on vineyard areas and grape production.

WINE PRODUCTION

According to OIV estimates, world wine production in 2023 was around 237.3 million hectolitres (almost 10 per cent less than in 2022). OIV also estimated production in Brazil to be 3.6 million hectolitres, considerably more (12 per cent) than in 2022 and a very significant 31.4 per cent more than the last five-year average. The vintage in 2022 had already been bountiful, with some commentators comparing its quality with the outstanding 2020, a superb year. This placed Brazil among the 14 biggest wine producers in the world.

Although official statistics on Brazilian wine production in the whole country are lacking, those from Rio Grande do Sul are available for the 2021 vintage. As this state crafts about 90 per cent of all wine in Brazil, such numbers are very significant. In that year, the state produced 174 million litres (number rounded) of *vinho de mesa* (from non-*vinifera* varieties and the mainstay – in volume – of Brazilian wine production). The total production of *vinhos finos* (from *Vitis vinifera*) was 43.5 million litres, an increase of 34 per cent compared to 2020. However, this total does not include base wines for sparklers, either Muscat-based or not. Rio Grande do Sul sold 31 million litres of sparkling wines in 2021. Add this to the *vinhos finos* and the state's grand total will be about 75 million litres.

Estimating the production of other significant regions is a stimulating exercise, although subject to significant errors. The IP Vale do São Francisco, according to SEBRAE (a private entity that supports small businesses), makes 8 million litres a year from about 500 hectares. The IG Vinhos de Altitude de Santa Catarina, having 300 hectares and an allowed yield of 7,000 litres per hectare, may produce around 2 million litres annually. All DPWH (double pruning and winter harvesting) vineyards in several states, totalling about 500 hectares and having lower yields (5,000 litres per hectare), may possibly craft about 2.5 million. These three origins add up, then, to 12.5 million litres. Add Rio Grande do Sul, and the total would be about 87 million litres of *vinifera* wine made in Brazil annually. This would still keep Brazil as South America's third biggest *vinifera* wine producer.

WINE CONSUMPTION AND MARKET

In 2020, with the COVID-19 pandemic, Brazil experienced a big jump in wine consumption. With most people constrained to home activities and able to buy online, many Brazilians started to drink wine or increase the amounts they drank. In that year, about 430 million litres of wine were purchased by Brazilians, over 18 per cent more than in 2019. Despite a post-pandemic fall, wine consumption in 2022, according to OIV, increased almost 12 per cent to reach 400 million litres.

According to Wine Intelligence, about 36 per cent of Brazilian adults – around 40 million people – now drink wine regularly, expanding the wine-drinker base. WineXT estimates a larger number:

44 million. Although this is approximately the same proportion seen in the US, it is far less than in European countries with more mature markets. Portugal, for example (remember that Brazil belonged to that country for centuries), drank 600 million litres of wine in 2022 (OIV). Note that Portugal has 10.4 million inhabitants versus Brazil's 203.1.

It was estimated that the Brazilian per capita consumption of wine (considering the population of legal drinking age, that is, 18 years or more) in 2021 was 2.6 litres per year. Although this is still low, when compared (OIV, 2022), for example, to Portugal (67.5), Argentina (23.8) or the US (12.6), it must be noted that Brazil increased the per capita consumption very significantly from 2020 onwards. In 2019, for example, it was 2.1 litres. This was a remarkable 24 per cent jump. Per capita consumption, however, decreased after the pandemic to 2.4 litres (according to WineXT).

In 2021, more than 489 million litres of wine were sold in Brazil, a mere 2 per cent less than in the first year of the pandemic. This amount considers all wines sold, imported or locally produced, and was 27 per cent higher than in 2019. In 2022, on the other hand, there was a 10 per cent decrease in sales compared to the previous year. Even then, in volume, Brazilian-made wines encompassed almost 70 per cent of all sales. When the sparkling wine sector is examined, Brazilian leadership grew, with 83 per cent of all sparklers sold in 2022. From 2019 to 2022, the Brazilian wine market showed an increase of about 55 million litres, even considering the reduction from 2021 to 2022.

In 2021, the number of wine drinkers in Brazil was more than twice that of 2010. The trend towards better wines was also important, with a reduction, albeit modest, in the amount of more rustic and inexpensive *vinho de mesa* in favour of *vinho fino*. The sales of Brazilian *vinhos finos* increased by 23 per cent in 2021, even compared to the atypical 2020.

Wine imports also increased by 5 per cent in 2021. Brazil is placed number 15 among the biggest wine importers in the world. It leads in South America, with no less than 64 per cent of all its wine imports. The country imported, in 2022, almost 200 million bottles of wine, almost 25 per cent more than in 2019, before the pandemic. The total value of wine imports in 2022 was US$ 448 million. Chile is the largest exporter of still wines to Brazil, followed by Argentina and Portugal – no wonder, considering the physical proximity of the first two countries and the many historic ties with Portugal, besides commercial agreements between these countries and Brazil.

The country was, up to 2022, concerning wine consumption, one of the very few among the largest twenty wine markets where this is not stationary or going down, but rather on the ascent. According to International Wines and Spirits Research (IWSR), only Brazil drank more wine that year than five years earlier.

Although Brazil is still a minor player in wine exports, these are growing too. In 2021, the country exported almost 900,000 cases (of 9 litres, or 12 bottles, each) of wine (still and sparkling), versus 564,000 in 2020. The growth of exports from 2016 to 2021 was no less than 500 per cent. It must be observed, however, that exports, in volume, decreased in 2022 and were less than half the volume exported in 2013. In value, however, 2022 was the best year ever, at US$ 13.6 million. In 2023 and 2024 an annual reduction to a little less than US$ 11 million was seen. The leading destination (in volume) is Paraguay (which acquires mainly *vinhos de mesa* from a single maker, Fante*)*. For sparkling wines, however, the US is the principal buyer and Salton is the leading exporter by far. Other significant purchasers are Uruguay, China and the UK. Compared to external wine sales from Argentina and Chile, Brazil's exports are a tiny fraction. There may be several reasons for this difference. Those two countries produce roughly four times more wine than Brazil. Both, especially Chile, craft more wine than the internal market can absorb. They have a long tradition of exportation, so their wines are far better known abroad than Brazilian products. Brazilian wines deserve more exposure, as bodies such as Wines of Brazil and Apex are working to achieve. This book may help their task.

Wine Intelligence placed Brazil as the fourteenth most attractive wine market globally in September 2021. This service provider forecasted a continuing growth of the Brazilian wine market in the subsequent years, if at a slower rate. According to WineXT, the Brazilian wine market, as a whole, had sales of US$ 3.9 billion in 2022. It is fundamental to remember that Brazil is not yet a mature wine market (like the UK). There is vast growth potential here, which includes, of course, the local industry. Besides the growth of the wine-drinker base, several factors compound the ascension of the wine market in Brazil.

Wine is readily available to buy, be it online or physically. Many consumers are connected to the internet – over 78 per cent of all inhabitants in 2021. E-commerce is very well developed in the country. Mobile phones are widely available. In 2022, more than half of online sales were made using apps rather than websites. According to Wine Intelligence, more than 25 per cent of drinkers bought wine online before the pandemic; following this, online sales have grown even more. The number of digitally active wine sales channels has also increased exponentially. This includes wineries themselves; many have had such services for a while, such as Miolo. Others are following suit: Pizzato, for example, opened its direct-to-consumer online sales channel in 2023.

Two illustrative examples of the boom of online wine sales are wine.com.br (not related to the American homonymous firm) and evino.com.br. Both started modestly, but in a few years, they became big concerns with several owners and investors, growing by buying more traditional physical wine sellers. In doing so, and opening physical shops, these and other wine sellers entered the 'phygital' (physical + online) world. This seems to be another current trend, as is the use of quick delivery channels, such as iFood, by wine sellers who still lack service. Brazilian wine buyers who make their purchases using apps are willing to pay more for the convenience of fast delivery. At the same time, omni-channel players became important, including wine among their products, examples being Magalu (Magazine Luiza) and Lojas Americanas, not to mention the South American equivalent of eBay, Mercado Livre (today a commercial giant). This has contributed significantly not only to availability and variety but also to the price reduction of imported and Brazilian wines and to making this drink more popular.

Brazil is well placed amongst other countries in terms of the willingness of consumers to try new beverage options, an important consumer trend. To many Brazilian consumers, wine is a new option, as most alcohol buyers still drink beer or spirits (like *cachaça*). According to IWSR, the number of such consumers in Brazil is the second largest amongst several countries (second only to China). Not only this, among those who are already wine drinkers in Brazil, no less than 70 per cent (Wine Intelligence) state that they are ready to experience 'new types and styles of wines'. This marketing category of 'adventurous' drinkers favours the expansion of the wine market. So does the sector of highly involved drinkers, which has also grown in Brazil.

Unlike more mature markets, wine is not widely available on-trade in Brazil. Good restaurants have large and well-furnished cellars and wine charts, albeit the prices are not exactly palatable. Many restaurants, especially low-priced ones or those selling food by weight instead of à la carte – the '*comida a quilo*', immensely popular in the country – have very small wine offerings, if any. Therefore, the consumer's on-trade exposure to wine is low, which is a favourable factor for maintaining online wine-purchasing habits. This may be changing, however, as there is a growing tendency for bars to sell wine, either by the glass or in full bottles. The sales of wine through this channel grew significantly in 2022.

Wine is expensive in Brazil, whether it is made in the country or imported. The drink is heavily taxed in both cases. Brazilian producers must pay a long and tiresome series of different taxes, which may add up to more than half the price of a bottle, depending on several factors. The national tax system is overwhelmingly complicated and has a cascading effect, with some taxes applied both at point of origin (sales) and destination (purchase), plus each state has different local taxes – which provokes a kind of perpetual tax war. Many refer to this as a *manicômio tributário* (tax asylum), which is a good description of its complexity. A tax reform has recently been approved, but its effects will take many years to appear.

Exporting to Brazil is not exactly a simple operation due to excessive bureaucracy, high port service prices, hefty taxes, the need for laboratory analyses of all wines, and a series of other factors. Even then, Brazilian wine is often placed at a disadvantage regarding taxation. For example, wines imported from Argentina or Chile are far from being as heavily taxed as those made locally, due to customs agreements. Brazilian winemakers complain bitterly and with good reason. As always, the consumer pays for all of this, inhibiting a more accelerated growth of the wine market.

This subject was studied academically by Kelly Bruch and Jaime Fensterseifer from the UFRGS (Federal University of Rio Grande do Sul) in 2005. These researchers undertook a very detailed study (freely available online) on all taxes imposed on Brazil's productive wine chain. Their conclusions endorsed the claims of producers. Some of them are very illustrative and are summarized here. The total taxes on a bottle of wine in Brazil depend first on its type. *Vinhos de mesa* are the least taxed, followed by *vinhos finos* and sparkling wines. Taxation also depends on the specific state, as state taxes, as noted above, are not uniform. The study compared the states of Rio Grande do Sul (the biggest producer) and São Paulo (the largest consumer), finding that taxes are heavier in the latter. Taxation levels also depend on the type of profits a firm falls into. When taxes on profits (as income tax) are calculated on real profit, they are lower than when calculations are based on presumed profits (these two tax types exist in the country; the majority of small firms work with the second, as the first demands more expensive specialized personnel or advisers). No less than 19 different sorts of taxes were found. Total taxes ranged from 36 per cent (table wine, Rio Grande do Sul, real profit) to 56 per cent (sparkling wine, São Paulo, presumed profit). The average total was 45 per cent. Another work from Instituto Brasileiro de Planejamento e Tributação (IBPT) corroborated these findings, although their calculations arrived at a higher average tax total: 55 per cent.

PART 2
BRAZILIAN WINE REGIONS

INTRODUCTION TO THE REGIONS

As we've already seen, Brazil has three different types of viticulture: traditional, tropical and DPWH (double pruning and winter harvesting). Where each is practised depends fundamentally on the climate. This section is divided into several parts: the South (traditional viticulture in the first three chapters), DPWH regions (the Southeast and Centre-West) and the Northeast (tropical viticulture with some DPWH).

In each chapter, after providing some general facts about the region, I present a selection of wine producers, giving information on the location, website address or Instagram account, planted areas, varieties, viticultural and winemaking details, oenotourism and also, of course, their wines. I have tried to select the most representative producers, based on factors such as (among others) tradition, renown, reliability, typicity, originality and variety as well as their disposition to have their wines tasted and presented in this book.

The comments are not the same as those found in guidebooks, in which, wine by wine, vintage by vintage, marks, detailed tasting notes, and so on, are given. Instead, a more general approach is adopted, whereby I describe some of the wines made by the producer and their characteristics and special attributes, as well as commenting on what they taste like, their ageing potential and other points of interest.

While still more concentrated in Rio Grande do Sul, wine production in Brazil has extended considerably to other states, especially following the rise of tropical viticulture and DPWH. Map 6 summarizes where wine is made in the country (as of 2024). The regions and the most significant geographical indications already demarcated, or well known as such, are shown as small coloured areas. The burgundy circles indicate townships where viticulture and winemaking are active. The states that craft wines are named.

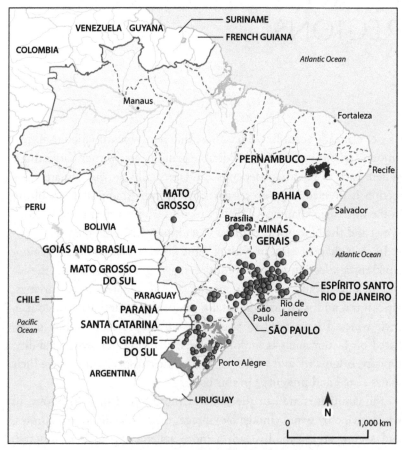

Map 6: Wine regions and municipalities in Brazil

8

RIO GRANDE DO SUL: SERRA GAÚCHA

'The Great River of the South', the southernmost state in Brazil, measures 281,707 square kilometres and has a population of 10.88 million (as of 2022). The human development index (HDI) was 0.787 in 2017 (versus 0.759 for Brazil as a whole). The demonym here is *gaúcho*, derived from long-lasting traditions of riding, cattle raising and open-air work. This is the land, par excellence, of barbecue: *churrasco*. If you travel through Brazil – and even abroad – almost all steak houses, or *churrascarias,* are managed by *gaúchos.* People are traditionalists, not only in their folkloric dances and music but also in their eating and drinking preferences. Everywhere you will find, in all weathers, people sipping

---

The South region

The South region encompasses the states of Paraná, Santa Catarina and Rio Grande do Sul. Due to latitude and altitude, temperatures are generally cooler than in other states, favouring viticulture. DPWH is seldom practised, or even not feasible in most parts, nor is the South a region of tropical viticulture – this is traditional, with the usual growth cycle. There is a strong European influence (especially Italian and German, but also Polish, Ukrainian, Dutch and, of course, Portuguese). This reflects on customs, cuisine, culture, and wine production and consumption. No wonder Brazil's most significant share of wine production comes from here. All three states are agricultural powerhouses with an essential livestock business. They also have important industries. The South region is the wealthiest and most highly developed area of Brazil.

chimarrão, an infusion of mate leaves, from pretty bowls, the *cuias*, using an elaborate metallic pipe called the *bomba*. Rio Grande do Sul remains, by far, the most important state in wine production in Brazil. This has deep cultural roots; per capita wine consumption is twice the national average (4.46 litres per person in 2019).

Rio Grande do Sul offers a lot for the wine aficionado, as oenotourism is well developed and growing. There is no lack, however, of non-vinous tourist attractions in the state (as in the whole country). Rio Grande do Sul receives more than 2 million foreign tourists every year. If you love beaches, go to Torres, Tramandaí or Capão da Canoa. Mighty canyons? They are within the Aparados da Serra and Serra Geral National Parks. Astounding Jesuitic ruins can be visited at *Região das Missões,* a UNESCO World Heritage site, the missions having been important in early winemaking (see *History of wine in Brazil,* page 13). The twin mountain cities of Gramado and Canela offer many attractions – especially, but not exclusively – at Christmas. Porto Alegre, the state capital and main airport hub, is a cosmopolitan city with 1.33 million inhabitants. As for eating, there is much beyond barbecue, including the traditional Italian (predominately from Veneto) dishes in the Serra Gaúcha wine region.

The main historical factor explaining the predominance of Rio Grande do Sul in Brazilian wine was the arrival and settling, in the nineteenth century, of 84,000 Italian immigrants, mainly from Veneto, Lombardia and Trentino. Their families received pieces of land (25–30 hectares) called *lotes* from the government, mainly in the mountainous Serra Gaúcha. They followed their traditions, planted grapevines and made wine. Due to the humid subtropical climate, this was crafted primarily from Isabel and other resistant hybrids. Before long, those with more knowledge began the fight to improve their wines, moving away from Isabel and planting *vinifera* varieties like Barbera and Merlot. It was also in Rio Grande do Sul that the first winemaking schools and laboratories appeared at the turn of the nineteenth century. The cooperative movement also began here a few years later, in 1911. The Cooperativa Vinícola Aurora – today, with 1,100 associates, one of the biggest wine producers in Brazil – was founded in 1931. Varietal wines appeared in 1938. Big wine businesses started in the 1980s and 1990s and were owned by traditional Italian families or multinational companies. Serra Gaúcha remained Brazil's only significant wine-producing region until this time. The state's role as the leader of the Brazilian wine industry was reinforced in the late 1990s when new areas were developed: Campanha Gaúcha, Serra do Sudeste and Campos de Cima da Serra (see Other areas of Rio Grande do Sul, pages 164–218).

This leadership continues. Teaching, training and research facilities are very important. Embrapa has a specialized division at Bento Gonçalves, in Serra Gaúcha: Embrapa Uva e Vinho. It has made significant advances, such as the Multicriteria Climatic Classification (MCC) system and the theoretical and legal foundations of geographic indications, both led by Jorge Tonietto. It is also there that the federal government maintains Brazil's most important graduate course on viticulture and oenology.

The state can be roughly divided, in terms of geological origin, into four regions or geomorphological provinces. Put simply, the extensive Basalt Highlands, as the name implies, mostly have soils of volcanic origin. The Central Depression shows a significant amount of alluvial soils. In contrast, the Crystalline Shield has ancient rocks of igneous or magmatic origin and a complex mix of other soils formed more recently. The Coastal Plains, a low terrain, have the most recent soils, including unconsolidated sand, silt and clay. The state has a few areas above 500 metres. It is not the altitude but the latitude that makes Rio Grande do Sul so important in Brazilian viticulture.

According to the Brazilian System of Soil Classification (SiBCS), the most common orders of soils in Rio Grande do Sul are *latossolos, planossolos, argissolos* and *vertissolos*. All other orders, however, also exist – no wonder, considering the large size of this state.

Most of the state's climate is classified (Köppen-Geiger) as Cfa (humid tropical, oceanic, without a dry season, hot summer). In the Northeast, however (Serra Gaúcha and Campos de Cima da Serra), it is Cfb (which is the same as Cfa, but with a temperate summer). The state experiences abundant rainfall – even the driest regions have at least 1,500 millimetres of rain a year. This can reach up to 1,900 at Serra Gaúcha. Extreme weather events are becoming more common. In May 2024, the state fell victim to devastating floods. Apart from more than 200 deaths, material losses were heavy. It is estimated (Emater-RS) that about 500 hectares of vineyards were destroyed.

Map 7 (overleaf) shows the wine regions of Rio Grande do Sul (state capital: Porto Alegre).

SERRA GAÚCHA

Brazil's biggest (in volume) and most traditional wine region, Serra Gaúcha, has its hub in Bento Gonçalves, 120 kilometres north of Porto Alegre. Bento, as it is affectionately known, had 123,151 inhabitants in 2022. Besides wine, it is important in furniture-making. The tradition of celebrating a national wine festival, *Fenavinho*, began in 1967, for which special installations were built, nicknamed 'Fenavinho Park'. Despite some interruptions, the festival continues to take place (the last one in 2022). The same park is also home to other important wine events, such as the yearly *Avaliação Nacional de Vinhos* or 'National Wine Evaluation', whose thirtieth event occurred in 2024. The large fair Wines of South America/Vinitaly also happens here. There is a charming train trip between Bento and nearby Carlos

Map 7: Wine regions of Rio Grande do Sul (redrawn with permission from Embrapa)

Barbosa. A steam locomotive pulls the old train; during the short trip, passengers can enjoy a band playing and singing traditional music and sparklers being served. At Carlos Barbosa, they can visit the large and attractive retail facilities of Tramontina, where every sort of household cutlery, appliance and tool can be purchased. Other important cities in the Serra Gaúcha include:

- Garibaldi (population 34,355): at a mere 13 kilometres from Bento, but with so many buildings and signs of human activity between them that both cities almost intermingle, this pretty town has many wineries, some of which are the region's oldest.
- Caxias do Sul (population 463,338): this regional metropolis has direct flights from São Paulo (beware of frequent cancellations due to weather conditions). The city is home to lots of industries. At just 44 kilometres from Bento, it is a convenient centre from which to explore the region.
- Farroupilha (population 69,885): the cradle of Italian immigration to Rio Grande do Sul (from 1875 onwards) is known as *Capital Brasileira do Moscatel* or 'Brazilian Muscat Capital'. It is the centre of the homonymous IP (Provenance Indication) specializing in Moscatel sparklers.

Serra Gaúcha was officially delimited by the Ministry of Agriculture in 2006 as a *Zona de Produção Vitivinícola* (Wine Production Zone), having 31 townships. When Pinto Bandeira became a municipality, the number increased to 32.

Except for the IP Campanha Gaúcha, Serra Gaúcha includes all the geographical indications of Rio Grande do Sul. Their limits can be seen in Map 8, overleaf.

Climate and soils

The climate of Serra Gaúcha as a whole, according to the MCC, is HI+1 (2,362), DI-2 (317), CI-1, or temperate-warm, humid and with temperate nights. Using the Köppen classification, the climate is Cfb – humid subtropical with a moderate summer. Annual rainfall is 1,900–2,200 millimetres. The average altitude is about 640 metres, but vineyards can be found from 300 to 850 metres. Spring frosts are a risk, especially for early-budding varieties (such as Chardonnay and Pinot Noir). Hail is not uncommon and may be very damaging. As humidity

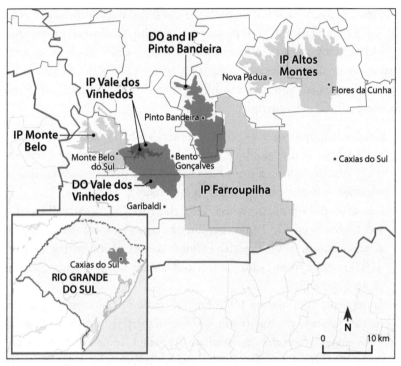

Map 8: Location, IPs and DOs of Serra Gaúcha (modified and translated from Embrapa)

is high, fungal diseases are always a threat, requiring constant attention; the most common are downy mildew and cluster rots.

Serra Gaúcha, as the name implies, is a hilly region. It is beautiful to see: the vineyards are surrounded by extensive native woods with many Brazilian pine trees (*Araucaria angustifolia*). Everything is green wherever you look.

The prevailing soils are naturally fertile, with medium to high organic content. Aluminium and organic matter contents range from moderate to high. The soil is acidic, demanding correction. Clay is a very important textural characteristic: over 90 per cent of cultivated soils have a 21 to 60 per cent clay content. The two most frequent SiBCS soil orders are *argissolos* and *neossolos*. As the region's relief is mountainous (and both orders are more frequent in this type of relief), and due to plentiful rain, erosion is an important concern. The relief also prohibits overt mechanization. Manual harvesting predominates and manpower from outside the area is frequently needed. These facts impact the cost of the wines.

Planted areas and grape varieties

Just as I began writing this section, the SIVIBE – Sistema de Informações de Vinhos e Bebidas (Information System on the Wine and Drinks Area) – became accessible online. As it includes information on planted areas detailed by variety, I could retrieve updated data (2022) for Serra Gaúcha (and elsewhere). Isabel and other American hybrids continue to dominate the region, delivering large volumes of inexpensive wine to all Brazilian states and also exported, mainly to Paraguay. This book, however, focuses on *vinhos finos* (made from *vinifera)*, although I include some Embrapa creations, especially Lorena, Moscato Embrapa and (despite the tiny planted area) Bibiana, as their quality compares well with European grapes. However, Brazilian laws mandate that their wines be labelled as *vinho de mesa*.

According to SIVIBE and excluding *labrusca* and similar, the most planted varieties (more than 100 hectares each) at Serra Gaúcha, in 2022, were: Chardonnay (496 hectares), BRS Lorena (448), Moscato Branco (444), Merlot (382), Moscato Embrapa (358), Cabernet Sauvignon (311), Glera/Prosecco (305), Malvasias de Cândia and Bianca (229), Trebbianos (225), Riesling Itálico (217), Pinot Noir

Vale Aurora's vineyards, as seen from the Estrelas do Brasil winery

(200), Tannat (190), Alicante Bouschet (164), Moscato Giallo (143) and Moscato Bianco/Canelli or Muscat Blanc à Petits Grains (104). A group of varieties with planted areas of 40–100 hectares were as follows: Cabernet Franc (88), Ancellotta (47), Egiodola (45), Marselan (41), Viognier (40) and Malbec (40).

The list of cultivars with a smaller planted area is long. Here we find (in descending order of hectares): Sauvignon Blanc, Teroldego, Pinotage, Muscat of Alexandria, Colombard, Moscatel Nazareno, Ruby Cabernet, Alvarinho, Petit Verdot, Nebbiolo, Riesling, Barbera, Syrah, Sangiovese, Gewurztraminer, Peverella, Tempranillo, Pinot Gris, Carmenère, Saperavi, Chenin Blanc, Montepulciano, Semillon, and BRS Bibiana. There are many others, however, each with a very small hectarage.

The total planted area of white grapes (3,100 hectares) is about twice that of reds (1,604). If all Muscat or Muscat-like varieties are taken together as a group (Moscatos Branco, Embrapa, Bianco, Giallo, Alexandria, Nazareno), an impressive total of 1,074 hectares is obtained. If we add other aromatic grapes (Malvasias, Viognier, Gewurztraminer, Sauvignon Blanc), the grand total increases to 1,366. This shows the importance of aromatic white cultivars at Serra Gaúcha and endorses its vocation for fresh, flavoursome, sweet, delicious white sparkling wines – as well as aromatic, light, dry still whites. The preponderance of Chardonnay and the significant planted areas of Pinot Noir and Riesling Itálico, on the other hand, stress the relevance of classical dry sparklers – for many, the best wines of this region.

The reds, however diverse, are dominated by Bordeaux varieties. These (Merlot, Cabernet Sauvignon, Cabernet Franc, Malbec, Petit Verdot, Carmenère) make up 831 hectares. Merlot has overtaken Cabernet Sauvignon as the most planted red grape (reversing the situation in 2015), which is only natural due to climate and soil. Pay attention, however, to Tannat, crafting ageworthy reds that are lighter and fresher than those from Campanha Gaúcha and Uruguay. Pinot Noir is also noteworthy for still red wines, especially from Pinto Bandeira. These are fresh, fruity, moderate in alcohol and of ever-improving quality. Except for premium wines, and as a general rule with increasing exceptions, do not expect a deep colour in reds from the Serra; aromas and flavours have a medium intensity, with fruit predominating over subtle vegetal notes. Alcohol and body are medium, and the wines have moderate to high acidity. Most are best consumed within four to five years. In top vintages, however, they keep and improve in the bottle for much longer.

In 2022, all those varieties taken together comprised a total of 4,704 hectares. Despite this impressive number, it is dwarfed by Isabel (8,165) or Bordô (7,399). This gives a good idea of how successful the wines made from such American grapes, however 'foxy', are in Brazil.

Prominent wine types

Serra Gaúcha produces the most significant part of Brazil's Muscat-based sparkling wines. Due to the Italian influence, they are crafted by the Asti process, with a single tank fermentation, having low abv (7.5–8.0%) and being sweet but fresh and aromatic, revealing floral (jasmine), fruity (peach, papaya, citrus) and some spice (cloves) components. They are moderately priced and hugely successful in the Brazilian market; many have won prizes and high ratings in local and South American wine guides (such as *Descorchados*). Most have a lower sugar level (65–75 grams per litre) than Asti.

Serra Gaúcha also produces the majority of traditional and tank-method (Charmat) sparkling wines which are made more in the image of Champagne, that is, based on Chardonnay and Pinot Noir. Riesling Itálico is also important in this respect. Serra Gaúcha crafts large quantities of tank-method non-Moscato sparkling wines using the three grapes (and also Trebbiano or Viognier). As with Moscato, these are moderately priced wines of good quality whose consumption is rising in the country. The *crème de la crème* of Brazilian sparklers is made using the traditional method within the Serra, especially (although not only) at the DO Altos de Pinto Bandeira, where altitude, climate and know-how lead to world-class products. Such fine Brazilian sparkling wines have a unique style, combining freshness with fruit (tropical, ripe, but never overripe) and, in the best cases, complex notes due to long autolytic periods.

Chardonnay dominates white still wines. The general style, although evidently fruity, veers more towards elegance than weight, whether oaked or not. Other still, dry whites from the region are made with Moscato Giallo (very aromatic, light and fresh), Riesling Itálico (less aromatic, but keeping lightness and freshness), or from less likely varieties such as Peverella (Boschera), Viognier or those unique to Brazil like the aromatic and soft BRS Lorena or the fresh, crisp BRS Bibiana. Generally, the low or moderately priced still, dry whites are lightly coloured, youthful and crisp, with medium alcohol and body, and not meant for ageing.

The climate and soil of Serra Gaúcha make Merlot a better option than Cabernet Sauvignon. Merlot does better on cold, clayey soils than its Bordeaux companion; it also ripens earlier. It is the main red grape of the DO Vale dos Vinhedos. Some of the best red wines of several important producers embody this fact – for example, Pizzato's DNA 99, Miolo's Merlot Terroir and Valduga's Storia, among others. The warm temperatures might make some people compare Serra Gaúcha's Merlot wines with those from, for example, Napa. In fact, more rain and different soils make the wine less ripe, less fruity, less plush and less alcoholic, with less body, more savouriness, more elegance and tannins that are less soft – a more classical, Bordeaux-like demeanour. Serra Gaúcha Merlot has a style of its own and can be considered, as a whole, the best red wine made in this region.

There are a lot of other red wines at Serra Gaúcha, however. As we've seen, the number of varieties is large. Keep an eye on Tannat and Pinot Noir, but also on Alicante Bouschet, Ancellotta, Cabernet Franc, Barbera, Egiodola, Marselan, Nebbiolo and Teroldego.

There is every scale of production at Serra Gaúcha. The biggest makers of *vinhos finos* (Aurora, Miolo, Salton) may deliver more than 10–15 million bottles of wine annually. The smallest can, indeed, be small, artisanal and even garage-level – but there is gold to be mined here. The following Serra Gaúcha producers are grouped according to geographical indication or city (🍷 : open to visitors).

DO Vale dos Vinhedos wineries

Vinícola Almaúnica 🍷

Bento Gonçalves

www.almaunica.com.br/

Almaúnica was founded in 2008 by twins Magda and Márcio Brandelli, from the fourth generation of a traditional winemaking family (see Don Laurindo, page 108). Sadly, Márcio died prematurely in 2020. Although there is a vineyard, most wines are made from bought grapes. Annual production is 100,000 bottles, focusing on premium wines, under the oenologist Denise Brandelli. The beautiful, state-of-the-art winery has a good oenotouristic set-up. Visitors are welcome to taste the wines (paid for, with no booking needed) or take a guided tour with tasting (reservations required) seven days a week.

Gabriel Gontijo, an oenologist and sommelier, graciously hosted me when tasting their wines. Reserva Chardonnay is a textbook rendition of the variety: with ripe, sweet fruit, it is textural, dense, unctuous, buttery and lengthy. Reserva Merlot brings ripe black fruit and an overt oak character; it is fresh, moderately tannic and elegant. Reserva Malbec is very dark, displaying ripe plums, blackberries, chocolate, some pepper and good savouriness. It has vital acidity and a strong tannic structure and will age well. It is more Cahors than Mendoza. Reserva Cabernet Sauvignon is made from a specific clone which ripens earlier than usual; they also prune it earlier. Despite being very ripe (cassis, just a hint of capsicum), it has a rewarding acidity and fine-grained tannins. Reserva Syrah is one of their specialities, as this variety is uncommon in Serra Gaúcha. It is spicy, savoury and ripe (blackberries), bringing notes of smoke and being slightly barnyard-like. Complex, fresh, elegant and with deftly managed oak, it has a northern Rhône accent – more Côte Rôtie than Hermitage.

Tannat (Campanha Gaúcha) is well balanced and ripe, with a grippy tannic structure, demanding additional time in the bottle. Quatro Castas is an excellent blend, at the same time elegant, well structured, balanced and complete – a true delight. Cabernet Franc (Campanha Gaúcha), made from raisined grapes, is so ripe, with warming but well-integrated 15.7% abv. It is a strong product, dense and layered.

Then came a sequence of memorable reds. Parte 2 is their premium Merlot. The 2018 was the last wine crafted by Márcio before he passed away. Incipient tertiary notes add complexity to ripe fruit (still quite clear), chocolate, fine oakiness and such soft tannins. Leaving it in the glass for a while promotes a peacock's tail of aromas and flavours. The current edition is riper, bigger and more layered, and its sinewy tannins require bottle ageing; it is very suitable for cellaring. A wine for meditation is Eterno Syrah; spending five years in oak, it is concentrated, full, dense, rich and complex. Parte 2 Cabernet Sauvignon is very ripe (so much cassis) and warm at 15% abv. It is minty and has very fine tannins and fresh acidity. Cellar it and you will be rewarded. Corte Bordalês (magnum only) is like a Saint-Émilion Grand Cru Classé A: ripe but firmly structured, rich but savoury, layered and complex; it lacks nothing. S8 Syrah, another wine to drink by itself and consider how good life can be, is matured in French and Slavonian oak barrels. It brings all Syrah's usual flavours in great concentration, and the oak is fine.

Brut Chardonnay is very creamy, with clear autolytic notes, bringing freshness and balance. Nature White is darker, as 20 per cent of the base wine stays for one year in French oak barrels; it is complex, savoury, crisp and bone dry. Nature Rosé is very well structured, with some tannic grip; layered and bone dry; it should be savoured with good food.

Cooperativa Vinícola Aurora ♀

Bento Gonçalves

www.vinicolaaurora.com.br/

Founded in 1931, this large cooperative has 1,100 associates, producing 70 million kilograms of grapes annually, of which 20 million are *vinifera*. The total area of vineyards from all members is 2,400 hectares. No wonder, then, that Aurora is one of the largest producers of Brazilian wine. Currently, Aurora produces 8 million litres of still *vinhos finos*, plus 6 million of sparkling wines. It has pioneered exports (from the 1950s) and oenotourism (from the 1960s).

Aurora has successfully made varietal wines since 1986. A new winery was built at Vale dos Vinhedos in 2019. A team of 14 oenologists led by Nauro Morbini crafts an extensive list of wines, including 13 brands and 220 products. Some are national sales champions, such as the entry-level varietal line of *vinhos finos* Marcus James Reservado or the *vinhos de mesa* Sangue de Boi and Mosteiro. But do not think that Aurora has no upper-level products – it does.

Oenotourism is very important. You can visit the Vale dos Vinhedos premises, where three types of tastings are offered, or Aurora Città, their original winery in the centre of Bento Gonçalves, where three different activities can be booked.

Oenologist Jurandir Nosini, who is in charge of sparkler winemaking, was my host when tasting some of Aurora's products at Città. Some of the best Aurora wines are made with grapes from Pinto Bandeira, where the cooperative owns 14 hectares of vineyards. They are bargains due to moderate prices and a high level of quality. Riesling Itálico is crisp (no malolactic fermentation), with moderate aromas and flavours of citrus and white flowers; after lees contact and *bâtonnage* for six months, it has a good texture and body. Chardonnay brings ripe pear and cashew, showing clear vanilla and spice (part of the wine stays for three months in used American oak barrels). Not undergoing malolactic conversion, it is taut and fine. Aurora Extra-Brut (Chardonnay, Pinot Noir, Riesling Itálico), 12-month autolysis, displays ripe pear and pineapple amidst bread and dough; with 5 grams per litre sugar, it is dry and crisp. Gioia Sur Lie Nature, crafted from the same three grapes, is undisgorged, hazy, bready, tense (but keeping good fruit) and a gastronomic delight. Aurora Extra-Brut Rosé is predominately Pinot Noir (60 per cent), with 12 months' autolysis, offering ripe red berries and considerable structure; it has a long, fruity length.

Outside Pinto Bandeira, Aurora also has many other noteworthy products. From Campanha Gaúcha, I tasted three Gran Reserva reds. Touriga Nacional is very ripe and true to the variety, with blackberry, violet and hints of mandarin; the wine is elegant and its tannins are polished, with oak complementing but not dominating the fruit. Tannat is inky and ripe, with moderate black fruit, earth, mushroom and oak aromas. Its solid tannins ask for a good *churrasco*. Cabernet Sauvignon is ripe (so much cassis) and minty, with just a touch of capsicum, fine-grained tannins and evident vanilla and spice from 12 months in French and American oak barriques.

Serra Gaúcha, the origin of Aurora, also brings great experiences. Malvasia Aromática is an exciting wine: very intense in aroma (white flowers, papaya), dry and very fresh – and, again, a genuine bargain. Conde de Foucauld (a brand launched in 1976) Cabernet Sauvignon is ripe, albeit less than the Campanha rendition; it is agile and lively, with sleek tannins and well-integrated oak. Millésime Cabernet Sauvignon (with 10 per cent Alicante Bouschet), after 16 months in American and French oak (which is quite evident), is ripe, layered, complex and long. Gioia (premium line with just two wines) Merlot DO is so ripe (15% abv) and plummy, and it also brings blackberry, cigar box, chocolate and coffee. It has such a strong structure and will age wonderfully for a long time. It is a great Vale dos Vinhedos Merlot. Conde de Foucauld Brut is made from Trebbiano, Riesling Itálico and Viognier by a short Charmat method; it is easy going, floral, zesty and well made. Moscatel is a sweet, Asti-like sparkler made from Moscato Branco; it is, as expected, very aromatic (floral, fruity), with a low 7.5% abv, sweet (75 grams per litre) and fresh (titratable acidity 7 grams per litre).

To my pleasure and surprise, Jurandir opened a genuine rarity: Clos de Nobles Cabernet Franc from 1986! Garnet in colour but limpid, Port-like aromas arose from the glass, together with earth, leather and truffles; fresh acidity made it still quite alive. It demonstrates that Brazilian reds can stand the test of time.

Vinícola Canto dos Liivres

Bento Gonçalves

@cantodosliivres

Sadi Andrighetto, a former partner of the now-defunct Milantino, founded a new winery with his wife, Jacqueline. She will graduate in oenology shortly. They make their wines (currently at Pizzato) from 12 hectares of vineyards. Sadi is keen to talk about his wines and his trajectory in the vinous realm.

Chardonnay is fermented one-third in tanks, one-third in second-use French oak barrels and one-third in American oak barriques. It is fresh, elegant and savoury. Pinot Noir is perfumed, ripe and lively, with good oak integration. Malbec is ripe, plummy, elegant and lighter than the average Argentinean product. Merlot is perfectly ripe, with rounded tannins, mouth-watering and gastronomic. Cabernet Sauvignon is varietally true: ripe cassis, capsicum, sleek and fine-grained tannins; it is ready to drink but may gain tertiary complexity within a few years. Cantoria Gran Reserva is a blend of five red grapes and several vintages from 2012 to 2017. It is inky, complex, layered and overtly oaky.

Vinhedos Capoani ♀

Bento Gonçalves

www.vinhedoscapoani.com.br/

This winery was started in 2009 by Noemir Capoani, who owns a furniture factory. His father Volmir already had a vineyard. Today, Noemir and his sons, Wilian and Renan, manage the business. They produce 140,000 bottles of wine annually – sparkling (50,000) and still (90,000) – using grapes from their 13 hectares of vineyards, plus bought fruit. Franco Caldart and Cristian Zeni are the oenologists. They are unique in cultivating Malvasia Nera, which is an integral part of the blend of their most expensive red wine. Capoani boasts a modern and beautiful oenotouristic set-up, including a restaurant (Trattoria Sagrantino); booking is requested for tastings or a picnic.

It was a pleasure to talk to the enthusiastic Noemir and taste his wines. Frizzante Chardonnay is unusual: a sparkling wine made using the traditional method but from riper grapes and less yeast. The result is a low-pressure sparkler that is prickly and racy and keeps the varietal character. Oaked Chardonnay (clone 67, six-month stage in new

American oak, medium toast) is quite aromatic; you can identify ripe pear, pineapple, vanilla and coconut. It is rich, textural and long.

Gamay Nouveau, from semi-carbonic maceration, is delicious, claret-like and fruity; drink it cold. Pinot Noir Cachos Inteiros (whole cluster) is a refreshing wine with some agreeable vegetal notes and ripe red berries, but austere in style, having a firm tannic structure. Merlot Vale dos Vinhedos is unusually unoaked; it shows ripe, sweet plums and blackberries. Cabernet Franc is ripe (over 14% abv), yet it retains freshness, showing very few pyrazines and good integration with oak. Cabernet Sauvignon (grapes from Quaraí, Campanha Gaúcha) has ripe cassis, little capsicum, good acidity and a fine tannic structure, being ready to drink and also suitable for cellaring. Petit Verdot (Candiota, Campanha Gaúcha) is, again, very ripe but fresh, overtly spicy and with an excellent structure; a long-term wine of high quality. Corte Bordalês (Merlot, the two Cabernets, Petit Verdot) is complex, well balanced, powerful and ageworthy, again of high quality. Red Blend (Merlot, Petit Verdot, Merlot, Malvasia Nera) is, indeed, spectacular: very complex, full, ripe but fresh, strongly structured, layered and long. Riesling Renano Estilo Eiswein, partially made from frozen grapes, is true to this noble variety; it is mouth-watering, well made and not too sweet (28 grams per litre sugar). This is not a true *Eiswein*; Capoani wanted to have something in the style (hence its name), so the grapes are artificially frozen and then immediately pressed, thus obtaining a more concentrated, sweeter must.

Adega Cavalleri ♀

Bento Gonçalves

www.cavalleri.com.br/

This family winery was founded in 1987. Its diversified product line focuses on sparklers (including an unusual red). More uncommon still: they have 9 hectares of Muscat of Hamburg. Annual production is 533,000 bottles; a significant parcel is sold to third parties. Visitors are welcome seven days a week for guided tastings (booking is advised).

The inexpensive Graciema Trebbiano Toscano is pale, sharp and light, like its Italian counterparts. La Vie Pinot Noir rosé is medium pink, fruity, bone dry and textural. Chardonnay is ripe, fresh, moderately oaky and well balanced.

Alicante Bouschet has the expected deep colour, with ripe dark berries, a full body and considerable structure. Super-premium Nilso Cavalleri Cabernet Franc is a very well structured and typical version of this variety: so fresh, dry and savoury. Gran Reserva Cabernet Sauvignon is a very ripe example of this variety in Serra Gaúcha, with excellent varietal character. Prosecco Brut (100 per cent Glera) is light, floral, taut and fruity. Tereza Nature (Chardonnay, Pinot Noir) spends 36 months in autolysis, being ripe, taut and complex, a real bargain. Sur Lie, made from the same two grapes, undisgorged, is hazy, savoury, complex and satisfying. Sparkling Moscatel Rosé is their speciality: 100 per cent Muscat of Hamburg, it is very aromatic (white flowers, red fruits), fresh, well made and not cloying (75 grams per litre residual sugar). White Moscatel (Moscato Giallo) is a pure, elegant and aromatic dessert sparkler.

Don Laurindo Vini di Gerazioni ♀

Garibaldi

www.donlaurindo.com.br/

The Italian Veronese immigrant Marcelino Brandelli arrived at Serra Gaúcha in 1887 and started growing grapes. Like many, he sold the grapes to wineries. His son Cezar and his grandson Laurindo Brandelli did the same for decades, selling to Brazilian firms such as Dreher, Salton and Dal Pizzol. At the start of the 1990s, however, these wineries drastically reduced their purchases and the prices paid for the grapes. Pushed by this inescapable fact and under the strong influence of his son, the oenologist Ademir Brandelli, Laurindo (who died in 2014) founded the winery in 1991. It has been led by strong-minded, vineyard-focused Ademir since its inception. Today, his sons Lucas (agronomist) and Moisés (oenologist) manage the business. The average annual production from 15 hectares (plus bought grapes) is 120,000 bottles. Visitors are welcome at a pretty wine bar with a view of the vineyard. Four different types of tastings can be booked.

The Brandellis – Lucas, Ademir and Moisés – welcomed me on a tour of their excellent winemaking facility and to taste their wines. Malvasia de Cândia, one of their specialities, is a pretty wine that is so aromatic (white flowers, lychees), fresh, dry, light and elegant. Chardonnay DO has a clear varietal expression, with ripe pear and hints of pineapple, plus some butteriness from malolactic fermentation, with an excellent texture and volume. Doracy Chardonnay, on the other hand, brings intense flavours of vanilla, toast, spice (12 months in new French oak), butter and very ripe fruit. It is long, with a slight tannic grip.

Pinot Noir (grapes from nearby Monte Belo) has ripe red berries and some earth and forest floor, well integrated with oak; it is lively and well structured in tannins and alcohol. Cabernet Franc (grapes from Via Trento) has ripe black fruit balanced by fresh acidity, spice, coffee and vanilla, with no capsicum showing up. Memorável, so called to honour the late Laurindo, is a premium single-vineyard Merlot. It brings ripe blackberry and plums, chocolate, coffee, vanilla, spice and coconut (18 months in French and American oak barrels). A solid structure of acidity and muscular but amicable tannins will allow it to age splendidly. This is Vale dos Vinhedos Merlot at its best, underlining the variety's importance at this DO. Estilo is a blend of Tannat, Malbec and Ancellotta, spending 18 months in French oak; the wine I tasted (2018) had slight tertiary notes, keeping a powerful structure of

Lucas, Ademir and Moisés Brandelli

tannins and acidity. Complex, long and ageworthy, it is a bargain. Don Tannat was a surprise crafted by Lucas and Moisés to honour Ademir; 100 per cent Tannat, it spent 24 months in new oak. This translates into evident vanilla, cedar and spice, well integrated into ripe dark berries, tobacco and earth. This big wine needs time. Três Dons is another great Merlot, with very ripe fruit and all other typical Merlot characteristics. Again, it is strongly structured and requires some years to come together and round up.

Brut Chardonnay, with 24 months in autolysis and 10 grams per litre residual sugar, is crisp, with clearly ripe fruit and moderate autolytic aromas and flavours; it is elegant and light. Nature, with 30-month autolysis, has just 0.2 grams per litre residual sugar. Bone-dry, laser-like and sharp, it rewards the drinker with good notes of bread and brioche.

Tenuta Foppa & Ambrosi ♀

Garibaldi

loja.tenutafa.com.br/

Lucas Foppa and Ricardo Ambrosi, both oenologists, met in 2012 while studying at Instituto Federal, in Bento Gonçalves. After making their first wine in Ambrosi's garage, they worked in Napa Valley for a year. Returning to Brazil, they founded Tenuta in 2019, moving to an old, historic building at Garibaldi in 2021. Innovatively, they also established a winemaking operation in the Napa Valley. Today, from grapes bought at Serra Gaúcha and Serra do Sudeste, 20 different labels are crafted. Total annual production is 60,000 bottles. Five different tastings are offered, by reservation only, seven days a week.

Brazilian Collection Alvarinho (Serra Gaúcha) is a multi-vintage blend spending six months with French and American oak staves. Moderately aromatic (ripe peach, citrus, vanilla, hints of honey), it has a crisp acidity and a savoury, saline finish. Tra Nodo Marselan (Serra Gaúcha) spends eight months with French and American oak staves and cubes. It is inky and purplish, showing ripe plums, blackberries and notes of dust, earth, vanilla and tobacco. The tannins are chalky on the tongue but agreeable. Cultura Touriga Nacional (Serra do Sudeste) is partly matured for ten months in American and French oak barrels. It is very dark and full of floral aromas, ripe black fruit, vanilla and coconut, plus hints of mandarin. Relatively fresh, its tannins are alive but very fine. It is an ageworthy example of this noble variety.

Viticcio Brut (Chardonnay, Pinot Noir, Riesling Itálico), made by the Charmat method with six months of autolysis, has delicate bubbles and shows ripe apple and pineapple amid hints of bread and caramel. It has agreeable aromas, reminiscent of those enjoyed on entering a winery.

Vinícola Giaretta ♀

Guaporé

www.vinicolagiaretta.com.br/

Like many other landowners of Italian ascent, Moacir Giaretta grew vines and sold the grapes. In 2007, however, the family opened a winery. They have grown steadily since then, increasing the volume and variety of the wines they produce. The winery pioneered wine in cans and became important in this industry sector, so much so that other wineries use their canning line for their products. Some wines are also sold in bag-in-box. They started using grapes from Campanha Gaúcha in 2022. Giaretta also have their own beer brand and make *vinhos de mesa* and grape juice. Visitors are welcome for tours and tastings (booking required).

Pinot Noir is ripe, fruity, varietally authentic and easy drinking. It is a bargain. Syrah has a moderate colour, medium body and alcohol – but is loaded with black pepper. Fresh, savoury and soft, it is a great everyday wine. Gran Reserva Homenagem, a blend of Ancellotta, Cabernet Sauvignon and Tannat, spending 12 months in French and American oak barrels, has clear vanilla, tobacco and chocolate amidst ripe black fruit. The tannins are soft and caressing, and the wine is layered and savoury. Extra-Brut (Chardonnay/Trebbiano, traditional method) is pale and lemon-green, showing delicate bubbles. Aromas and flavours bring fresh green apple, pear, citrus, bread and toast. It is bone dry and sharp, with mineral hints.

Bodega Iribarrem ♀

Serra do Sudeste

www.bodegairibarrem.com.br/

Founded in 2020 by Ramiro Iribarrem, of Basque heritage, this winery has 15 hectares of vineyards at Serra do Sudeste. Today, the wines are made by third parties (90,000 bottles a year). The winery at Vale dos Vinhedos is close to completion, ready to start making wine in 2025. Their touristic set-up was close to completion at the time of writing.

They have, however, an open shop where visitors can taste the wines (Thursday to Saturdays, with booking required).

Reserva Chardonnay is a balanced, well-made example of oaked Chardonnay with ripe fruit, moderate acidity, good texture, butteriness, vanilla and toast. Reserva Cabernet Franc has high varietal typicity: moderate ruby colour, ripe cassis, capsicum, pencil shavings, charming acidity and firm tannic structure, all wrapped in vanilla and cedar from 18 months in new French oak barriques. Reserva Touriga Nacional is dark and elegant, with ripe blackberry, violets and a solid structure of acidity and tannins.

Vinhos Larentis ♀

Bento Gonçalves

www.larentis.com.br/

The Larentis were among the first families to grow Chardonnay and Cabernet Sauvignon in Brazil during the late 1970s, selling to other parties. In 2001, they opened their winery, which continues as a family business. André Larentis is the oenologist, crafting 120,000 bottles annually. They welcome visitors for tastings, guided tours and picnics at the vineyard (booking required). Their new oenotouristic set-up is ready to welcome visitors and is set in beautiful surroundings.

Gran Reserva Viognier is precisely what you expect from this variety: aromatic, floral, peachy and dense (almost oily). Some vanilla and spice come from a part (25 per cent) being oaked. Arcangelo Chardonnay (from a selected parcel) has not undergone malolactic fermentation and is matured for 12 months in new and used French oak barrels. It is true to the variety: crisp, savoury and elegant.

Marselan is very ripe, full of blackberries and fruit preserve, with hints of aniseed; its tannins are robust but soft. Teroldego is inky, floral, spicy and savoury, with vanilla and toast from 12 months in French oak and a firm tannic structure. Tannat + Viognier Cofermentado has Tannat's usually fierce tannins effectively softened by Viognier, making it ready to drink. Merlot DO (grapes from Santa Lúcia, Serra Gaúcha) is ripe, meaty and full of blackberries, plums, hints of earth and chocolate; the sinewy tannic structure needs time to come together. Mérito Gran Reserva, a blend of four grapes, is a big wine, so ripe, oaky, concentrated, full and complex that it will age gracefully. Brut Chardonnay, made by the tank method, is fruity, fresh and straightforward.

Lídio Carraro Vinícola Boutique 🍷

Bento Gonçalves

www.lidiocarraro.com/

Founded in 2001, Lídio Carraro owns 7 hectares of vineyards at Vale dos Vinhedos. Most grapes, however, come from their vineyards at Serra do Sudeste (38 hectares), also started in 2001. Here, on granitic soil, with ample diurnal variation, the grapes have fewer vegetal characteristics and less astringency than at Serra Gaúcha. This winery has been competent at promoting its wines at places and events that provide good visibility: duty-free shops, car races, the FIFA World Cup and the Olympic Games, both held in Brazil in 2014 and 2016. As a house philosophy, no wine is oaked, even the most expensive. Almost 80 per cent of their wines ferment spontaneously, not undergoing corrections or deep filtration. Lídio Carraro is open seven days a week for tastings, and reservations are advised for small groups and required for those over ten people.

The brothers Juliano and Giovanni Carraro (the oenologist) warmly welcomed me at their agreeable oenotouristic facilities to taste some of their wines. Dádivas Chardonnay brings sweet, ripe pear and pineapple; it is bone dry and refreshing. Despite no malolactic fermentation, it is textural, with a good volume in the mouth and even some fat from 12 months on its fine lees. Faces Rosé is made by direct pressing from 80 per cent Pinot Noir, 15 per cent Merlot and 5 per cent Touriga Nacional harvested at several passes in the vineyard to improve complexity. It is fruity (red berries), floral and bone dry. This is an excellent rosé with considerable structure.

Dádivas Pinot Noir is very ripe and fruity; it is a lively wine, so crisp (no malo), with a sapid finish. Dádivas Cabernet Sauvignon/Merlot is so gastronomic, again ripe but alive, with a good varietal typicity. Giovanni said he prizes acidity very much, trying to preserve it to the maximum. Agnus Tannat has muscular tannins, so strong, being ripe (15% abv) and complex; it will age very well. Elos Cabernet Sauvignon/Malbec is sold only after five years; notwithstanding this, it is very fruity, plummy, agile and well structured. Singular Teroldego, now 11 years old, is inky and ruby-coloured, and does not show its age. It is full of ripe blackberries, earth, tobacco and coffee, with some animal notes. It has a solid tannic structure and is long and ageworthy. Quorum Grande Vindima Corte is a blend of six different wines from four varieties (all from Vale dos Vinhedos). The structure of acidity and tannins is sturdy, allowing a long ageing time. It is very complex despite being unoaked – a very good wine indeed.

Dádivas Blanc de Blancs (Chardonnay) Brut, made by the Charmat method from base wines of three vintages, stays with the lees in the tank for six to nine months; it is very fruity and dry (about 8 grams per litre), and also fresh.

Maximo Boschi Vini Singolari ♀

Bento Gonçalves
www.maximoboschi.com.br

This winery was founded in 2000 by Renato Savaris (grandson of Maximo Boschi) and Daniel Dalla Valle (chief oenologist at Valduga – see page 121). They craft their products using grapes from Serra Gaúcha, Serra do Sudeste and Campanha Gaúcha. The Biografia line is aimed at the top tiers of the market. Visitors are welcome for tastings (booking required).

Racconto Cabernet Franc (Serra do Sudeste) is a ripe example of this variety, unveiling sweet raspberry, hints of mint, red guava and pencil shavings, plus vanilla and cedar from 24 months in oak. Its tannins are also ripe. Racconto Marselan (Campanha Gaúcha) is a big wine: inky, ripe and sweet fruit, full bodied, with 14.4% abv and a sinewy tannic structure. It offers ripe black and red berries, tobacco, vanilla and spice.

Biografia Chardonnay spends 12 months in oak barrels with *bâton-nage*. Its aromas and flavours are complex, fine and ripe: apple, hints of pineapple and pear, moderate vanilla, spice and butter. It is textural, dense, powerful yet well balanced, and lengthy in the mouth.

Biografia Cabernet Sauvignon benefits from aeration to open up and show ripe cassis, mint, vanilla, cedar and hints of capsicum, leather and earth. Its tannins are sleek, almost caressing, and the acidity is fresh. Biografia Merlot (Campanha Gaúcha) displays ripe blackberries, plums, chocolate, cedar and toast. It has a firm tannic structure and shows some incipient tertiary flavours (leather, tobacco), keeping its varietal character.

Biografia Extra-Brut (Chardonnay, Pinot Noir), with 40-months autolysis, is pale, with very fine bubbles. Ripe pears and apples mix with bread and brioche. It is finely creamy, savoury, long and satisfying. This a fine and elegant sparkler.

Michele Carraro ♀

Bento Gonçalves

www.michelecarraro.com.br

The brothers Carlos Miguel, Ivair and Vilson Carraro, great-grandsons of the Venetian immigrant Michele Carraro, founded their winery in 1987. They own 11.9 hectares of vineyards. The fourth generation of this Carraro family branch continues to lead the business. Tastings and tours are available through prior booking.

Reserva Ancellotta, as it pertains to this variety, is inky, bringing ripe black and red berries. Discreet vanilla and toast combine with some savouriness. The wine is rich, fresh and soft. Reserva Malbec is ripe, showcasing plums, spice, overt vanilla and cedar. The tannins are fine and the wine is easy drinking. 1875 Rebo exhibits ripe blackberry, sweet spice, vanilla, toast and hints of dust, earth and herbs. The wine is fresh, has firm but fine-grained tannins, and is savoury and food friendly. 1875 Marselan has ripe red and black fruit amidst spice (cinnamon and white pepper). It is rich, full bodied and caressing.

Miolo Wine Group ♀

Vale dos Vinhedos (various locations)

www.miolo.com.br/

Like many in Serra Gaúcha, the Miolos have Italian roots. Giuseppe Miolo arrived here in 1897. Like other immigrants, he received a piece of land, or *lote*, where the DO Vale dos Vinhedos is situated today: Lote 43 (a name honoured on the label of one of their top wines). His descendants, as usual, grew vines. Until 1989, they were just growers, selling *vinifera* grapes to local wineries. When these stopped buying, the family, then led by Giuseppe's three grandsons (Darcy, Antonio and Paulo), decided to start making wine – the alternative would be to go on selling grapes, but at ridiculously low prices, or just let them rot on the vines. Despite a series of difficulties, they sold some assets (a truck and a tractor) and managed to build a small winery. Their first wine, the 1990 Reserva Miolo, was launched in 1992. Reserva was a stunning commercial success: from bottling 70,000 litres in 1994, they skyrocketed to 300,000 in 1998 and 500,000 in 2000. Three sons of Darcy (who died in 2020) became the leaders: Adriano, an oenologist who graduated from Mendoza; Fabio, established at São Paulo to look after commercial affairs; and Alexandre (at Serra Gaúcha). From then on, Miolo grew very fast, not only buying

Fábio, Alexandre and Adriano Miolo

more land and planting vineyards at Serra Gaúcha but also expanding to other regions: the Seival estate at Candiota, Campanha Gaúcha; Ouro Verde/Terranova estate at Vale do São Francisco (in association with the Benedetti family); and then, in 2009, the large Almadén complex at Sant'Ana do Livramento, Campanha Gaúcha (in partnership with the Benedetti and Randon families).

The Miolo Wine Group holding now owns 1,000 hectares of vineyards, crafting 13.3 million bottles annually. The Miolo family is the controller, and the Benedettis and Randons continue their involvement. The group is the largest Brazilian maker and a significant exporter of *vinhos finos,* bottling over 100 labels from four origins. This is, indeed, an interesting success story in Brazilian wine.

Today, the main production of Miolo, in volume terms, comes from outside Vale dos Vinhedos. Here, however, a series of prestige labels continue to be made at their principal winery, processing local grapes and also many from other provenances. Miolo owns 100 hectares of vineyards at Serra Gaúcha. There is a busy oenotourism development, receiving thousands of visitors and offering several activities. Their tasting room is exemplary. Miolo is open seven days a week; booking is necessary for special tastings and activities.

Adriano Miolo hosted a tasting of some of their Vale dos Vinhedos wines and gave an illustrative talk. Cuvée Giuseppe (CG), a brand started in 1997, is exported in significant quantities (over 110,000 bottles). In 2025 they will launch a lot which is presently maturing under water.

Adriano says this is a tentative way of obtaining constant conditions for ageing. CG Chardonnay is barrel fermented, after which it stays in the barrels on lees with *bâtonnage*; no malolactic fermentation is allowed, to retain freshness. It is varietally true, ripe (pear, pineapple), having a good texture, plus savouriness, vanilla and toast from oak. CG Red (Merlot/ Cabernet Sauvignon) was the first wine to obtain DO status years ago. It is a very good, ripe, well structured, round Bordeaux blend. Merlot Terroir, one of their '7 Lendários' (The Legendary Seven), is made from several distinct terroirs, including Monte Belo, Garibaldi and Graciema. It is a typical Vale dos Vinhedos Merlot at its best: ripe blackberry, chocolate, hints of truffles, mint and aniseed, all framed by ripe tannins and agreeable freshness. Lote 43, also 'Legendary', is crafted only in top vintages. This means ten times in 25 years. A Bordeaux blend where Merlot predominates, the wine is so fine and typical, at once ripe, fresh, well structured and ageworthy. It will reward you after many years of cellaring.

Cuvée Nature (Pinot Noir/Chardonnay) is made using reserve wines that are two to three years old; it is very fresh and sharp but fruity, with bread and dough aromas from an 18-month autolysis. Millésime is their top vintage sparkling wine, using grapes from the best parcels; also undergoing an 18-month autolysis, it is well structured, complex, savoury, developed and elegant, showing how good Brazilian sparklers can be here.

For more on the Miolo Wine Group, see also pages 179 and 322.

Miolo vineyards, Vale dos Vinhedos

Pizzato Vinhas e Vinhos 🍷

Bento Gonçalves

www.pizzato.net/

Pietro Pizzato, the scion of this family, arrived in Serra Gaúcha in the late nineteenth century. His son, Antonio, was one of the founders of Cooperativa Aurora in 1931. Antonio's grandson Plínio, a well-known viticulturist, and his family dedicated themselves to growing grapes for selling to third parties. From 1999 onwards, however, Plínio and his four children began making wines, and what a remarkable start they've made: their Reserva Merlot was a resounding national success. The gentlemanly patriarch, Plínio Pizzato, has led the business with two sons and two daughters. Ivo, responsible for the 1999 Merlot, sadly and prematurely died in an accident. Brother Flávio, also an oenologist, has since taken on the job of producing wines very competently. Commercial affairs are conducted at São Paulo by Jane and at Vale dos Vinhedos by Flávia – all having inherited their father's amiable manner. They continue to rely mainly on Merlot as their flagship grape – but not solely, as their still and sparkling Chardonnays are very good too, as is the Semillon (a variety which, sadly, has almost disappeared from Serra Gaúcha – and Brazil, for that matter).

Flávio Pizzato on his barrels

Pizzato owns 36 hectares of vineyards at Santa Lúcia (close to their winery), plus 23 hectares at Dr Fausto, Dois Lajeados, 50 kilometres to the west but still included in Serra Gaúcha. In both, the soil is basaltic and clayey, with small pebbles. Pizzato crafts 500,000 litres of wine annually, mostly from their own grapes. They gladly welcome visitors for tastings at their pretty oenotouristic space; reservations are advised but not required for small groups.

Lorenzo Pizzato Michelon, Plínio's grandson, received me enthusiastically for a technical tasting at their wine bar. Fausto Chardonnay is unoaked, crisp (no malolactic fermentation), youthful and fruity (pear, pineapple). Pizzato Chardonnay, also unoaked, stays for five months with lees and *bâtonnage*. It has a high varietal typicity, is again racy (no malo either), ripe, well structured and textural – a textbook Serra Gaúcha Chardonnay. Legno is their oaked Chardonnay; it is fermented in French oak barrels (new and second-year), staying there for 10 to 11 months with lees and *bâtonnage*. It is golden, unctuous and buttery (100 per cent malo), mineral, and overtly oaky, but with a seamless integration and a long length. Pizzato Sauvignon Blanc stays on lees for two months, with *bâtonnage*, bringing a mix of tropical fruit (white guava) and grassy aromas without being overly aromatic – veering more towards elegance than power. One of their jewels is Pizzato Semillon. It is golden, crisp (pH 3.33) and ripe (melon, stone fruit, honey). Part of the wine (40 per cent) matures for 12 months in barrels of French oak and acacia, imparting vanilla, spice and light toast to this excellent wine.

The Allumé line is made both from their grapes and purchased fruit; it was once specially made for a large supermarket chain (Pão de Açúcar). Allumé Pinot Noir is fruity, perfumed and floral, with hints of undergrowth, and so fresh that it is hard to stop drinking. Pizzato Merlot DOVV is their highly praised flagship wine made from small vineyard parcels, exhibiting clear varietal characteristics, such as ripe plums, blackberries and cassis. The structure of acidity and tannins is firm, and the deftly managed oak (11 months in French oak barrels, new and second-year) imparts complexity to this ageworthy wine. Alicante Bouschet is another Pizzato speciality, as they have pioneered this variety here. It is inky, very ripe (plums, *jabuticaba*, blackberries), complex (mint, earth, chocolate, spice), full bodied, well structured and long. Concentus Gran Reserva, a blend of Merlot, Tannat and Cabernet Sauvignon vinified separately (the proportions change according to each vintage) is so ripe, complex and complete, with an array of flavours including black fruit, cigar, chocolate, vanilla, spice and more. It is concentrated, full bodied and very long. This wine's ageing ability was demonstrated by an 11-year-old 2013 that I tasted: earth, *sous-bois,* mint, dried fruit, fresh acidity and lively tannins make up a harmonious, complex whole. Verve Gran Reserva, Fausto's top wine, is made from the best parcels at Dr Fausto's vineyard, with the same blend as Concentus. It is very ripe, boasting a robust structure of acidity, alcohol and tannins; the aromatic palette is complex, including ripe fruit, spice, earth, toast and chocolate, with a savoury finish.

Pizzato's iconic wine is DNA99 (since 2005, named to honour the legendary 1999 Merlot), a single-vineyard Merlot from Vale dos Vinhedos with grapes harvested later than most. It is generally considered one of the best Brazilian red wines, and for good reason: it's brimming with very ripe red and black fruit and also offers spice, vanilla, chocolate, toast, tobacco and cedar. Full-bodied, intense and concentrated, DNA99 has a solid structure of sinewy but fine-grained tannins, allowing it to age gracefully for many years. How does it behave then? I tasted the 2011: intense, complex tertiary flavours of leather, tobacco, dried fruit, undergrowth and mushrooms are framed by a very lively colour and tannins that are still strong, but so very fine grained, allowing cellaring for at least five years more. This is, indeed, an exceptional wine.

Pizzato also crafts excellent vintage sparklers, such as Brut Rosé (80 per cent Pinot Noir, the balance being Chardonnay). The clear ripeness of Brazilian berries interacts well with elegant bread and toast (15-month autolysis); it is mouth-watering and a great food wine.

Vinícola Torcello ♀

Bento Gonçalves

www.torcello.com.br/

This is another winery founded by a member of the Valduga family, Rogério Carlos, in 2000. Their annual production, including still and sparkling wines, is 45,000 bottles. One of their specialities has been producing tank-method sparklers on lees for a long time (*Charmat Lungo).* Torcello is conveniently located at the start of the Vale do Vinhedos, close to Bento Gonçalves. There is a brand-new tasting room. Tastings and guided tours are available through prior booking.

Rogério Carlos is an enthusiastic host, keen to provide details about his products. From low-yielding vines (1 kilogram per plant), Torcello

Chardonnay undergoes full malolactic fermentation and stays for four months in new American oak barrels (medium toast). It is very textural, even unctuous, and full of ripe fruit, vanilla and coconut.

Torcello Pinot Noir uses grapes from Cotiporã, 65 kilometres to the north-west, grown at 830 metres under plastic sheet protection. Such cooler conditions ensure a longer maturation. Its must is 20 per cent concentrated by *saignée* (what is taken off is used to create base wines for rosé sparklers). It is dark for Pinot Noir, well structured, ripe but fresh, and shows evident but well-integrated American oak (six months) characters. Perfetto Merlot (made with grapes from Vale dos Vinhedos) is partially (just over 20 per cent) fermented and matured (12 months) in American oak barrels. It is a very complex wine with flavours of smoke, tobacco, chocolate, ripe blackberry and hints of capsicum. It is long and develops a great deal in the glass. Perfetto Ancellotta (Vale dos Vinhedos) undergoes a similar oak treatment, but for 18 months. Rogério explained that he lowers the fermentation temperature to about 16°C at the end of this process to avoid over-extraction. It is inky, brings ripe black fruit, and integrates very well with oak. Perfetto Alicante Bouschet, recently launched, is inky, evidently ripe and fruity, and has an excellent tannic structure.

Famiglia Valduga ♀

Bento Gonçalves

www.casavalduga.com.br/

This large winery was founded in 1972 by Luiz Valduga (who died in 2004). They produced wine to sell to Dreher, a distillery. In 1985, however, they began making wines under their own brand. Today, Luiz's sons, Juarez, João and Erielso, lead the enterprise, which also includes several other products, such as *grappa*, brandy, juices, fine food, artisanal beer, wine imports (Domno) and grape-based cosmetics. This is one of the biggest Brazilian wineries, crafting 3–3.5 million bottles of wine annually. Daniel Dalla Valle leads a team of 28 oenologists. Valduga has expanded out of Serra Gaúcha to Serra do Sudeste and Campanha Gaúcha. The ensemble of vineyards comprises 300 hectares. They also acquired (in 2007) large installations from Domecq at Garibaldi, where the products of a new brand, Ponto Nero (for Charmat method sparklers and fizzy wines), are made. Wines are divided into a series of lines.

Oenotourism is very important here; in fact, they pioneered this activity from 1992. A series of guided tours and tastings, a beautiful

Erielso, Juarez and João Valduga

restaurant (Maria Valduga) and a comfortable guesthouse are available. Wine courses are also offered. Booking is required.

The Valdugas are superb hosts, sparing nothing to make you comfortable. João and Eduardo, Juarez's sons, welcomed me to taste some of their best wines. Gran Chardonnay stays 12 months in Romanian and French oak barrels; it is delicate, exquisite and full of finesse. João attributes this to the Romanian oak.

Gran Pinot Noir (Serra do Sudeste, clone 777) has a deep colour for such a wine, with an excellent structure of fresh acidity, perfect ripeness and considerable tannins. It is complete, varietally faithful and very good. Pretérito, a blend of three red grapes, has a portion of the fruit deep-frozen and pressed, hence concentrating the solids. It is very ripe indeed, dense, strong and Amarone-like. Raízes, a red blend from several origins where Merlot predominates, is a big wine: high alcohol, very ripe fruit and muscular tannins. Cellar it. Storia Merlot is inky, complex, layered, strongly structured, and full of aromas and flavours: plums, chocolate, cigar box, vanilla and much more. This is one of the best Merlots from Vale dos Vinhedos and Brazil. Luiz Valduga Corte 2, made from more than five varieties, is dense, strong, very ripe and baroque, with an extensive palette of flavours; this is another great wine. Villa-Lobos (in honour of the great Brazilian composer) Cabernet Sauvignon from Campanha Gaúcha is so ripe, devoid of pyrazines, and fresh, with a solid structure that allows it to age well.

The 130 Brut (Chardonnay), one of their most famous sparklers, is quite fruity, with ripe pineapple mixed with an evident autolytic character; it is very fine and balanced. Maria Valduga, their top sparkler, is very autolytic, complex, savoury, long and layered, exuding class and quality.

Vallontano Vinhos Nobres ♀

Bento Gonçalves
www.vallontano.com.br/

Established in 1999 by oenologist Luis Henrique Zanini (see Era dos Ventos, page 148), Vallontano crafts 60,000 bottles of wine (still and sparkling) each year. Visitors can shop, taste the wines or enjoy a snack or *risotto* at their restaurant (booking required; closed Mondays).

Reserva Tannat is deep purple, with moderate aromas of ripe blackberry and plum, violet, vanilla, cedar and tobacco. As expected, its tannic structure is strong, even drying, with a slightly bitter finish. This wine cries out to be served with a barbecue! Reserva Merlot has a medium ruby colour and it openly shows aromas and flavours of ripe blackberries and cassis, fruit cake, tobacco, chocolate, vanilla and spice. It is fleshy and soft, with ripe tannins and high varietal typicity.

Brut Rosé (Chardonnay, Pinot Noir, Riesling Itálico) has a beautiful, medium-pink colour and delicate bubbles. A mix of ripe apple, pear and red berries is compounded with tangy acidity, good structure and some savouriness, making it food friendly. LH Zanini Nature (Chardonnay/Pinot Noir) showcases a high intensity of ripe pineapple, apple, pear and red berries; it is dry, crisp and creamy. Bready notes from a 24-month autolysis underline the evident fruitiness.

Also in Vale dos Vinhedos

- Vinícola Dom Aldino (domaldinovinho@gmail.com)
- Audace Wine (www.audacewine.com/)
- Vinícola Santa Bárbara (cescavinhos@yahoo.com.br)
- Vinícola Barcarola Boutique (www.vinicolabarcarola.com.br/)
- Vinícola Battistello (www.vinicolabattistello.com.br/)
- Adega de Vinhos Dom Bernardo (www.vinicoladombernardo.com.br)
- Bodegone Vinhos e Vinhedos (contato@bodegonevinhos.com.br)
- Vinícola Calza, Monte Belo do Sul (www.vinicolacalza.com.br/)

- Vinícola Dom Cândido (www.domcandido.com.br/)
- Vinícola Videiras Carraro (@videirascarraro)
- Cavalleri Vinhos Finos (www.cavalleri.com.br/)
- Vinícola Cave de Pedra (www.cavedepedra.com.br/)
- Cave do Sol (www.cavedosol.com.br/)
- Chamon Garbin Vinhos Clássicos (contato@chamongarbin.com.br)
- Dom Eliziário Vinhos Finos (www.domeliziario.com.br/)
- Gran Legado/Maison Forestier (www.granlegado.com.br/)
- Marco Luigi Vinhos Raros (www.marcoluigi.com.br)
- Monte Chiaro Vinhos Finos (@montechiarovinhosfinos)
- Vinícola Peculiare (www.peculiare.com.br/)
- Famiglia Tasca (www.famigliatasca.com.br)
- Terragnolo Vinhos Finos (www.terragnolo.com.br/)
- Vinhos Titton (www.vinhostitton.com.br/linha/vinhos-finos/)
- Treamici Vinhos (www.treamicivinhos.com.br)
- Cavas do Vale (www.cavasdovale.com.br)
- Casa Zottis (casazottis@gmail.com)

IP Pinto Bandeira and DO Altos de Pinto Bandeira wineries

Vinícola e Pousada Don Giovanni ♀

Pinto Bandeira

www.dongiovanni.com.br/

This beautiful property was once an experimental viticultural centre of the defunct Dreher group. From 1910, besides wine, they also made a well-known brandy (sold to Heublein in 1973). Don Giovanni is owned by Ayrton Giovannini (ex-commercial director at Dreher) and his wife, Beatriz Dreher (granddaughter of the previous proprietors of the old firm). At 720 metres, their terroir (like most vineyards in Pinto Bandeira) favours varieties with a shorter ripening cycle (like Chardonnay and Pinot Noir), hence their primary focus on sparkling wines. Cabernet Franc also does well here. An impressive 150,000 bottles of wine are made yearly from 19.5 hectares of vineyards and bought grapes. A complete oenotouristic set-up includes a restaurant (Nature) and a guesthouse in a refurbished mansion from the 1930s. They offer five types of tastings, a whole-day experience and a night programme (including transportation to and from Bento Gonçalves). Reservation required.

Daniel Panizzi, the manager, received me at their beautiful and historic special tasting room to learn about some of their products. Pinot

Vineyards, native woods and Araucaria trees in Pinto Bandeira

Noir is fruity, ripe, perfumed and fresh, with velvety tannins and a very good integration with moderate vanilla and spice (the wine was barrel fermented and spent a year in used oak). DG Cuvée Quarto Acto, a luxury blend of four grapes, is inky and very ripe, with a vigorous structure of high alcohol and a high concentration of fruit and solid tannins. Several layers of flavours mix well with an agreeable oakiness from 18 months in French barriques. This is a big, ageworthy wine.

Stravagganza Rosé Brut (12-month autolysis) is fruity, ripe and fresh, offering what is typically expected from a good Brazilian sparkling wine. Nature (Chardonnay, Pinot Noir, 24-month) is bone dry and sharp, with a delicate mousse and discreet fruit. Its autolytic character is elegant. Brut differs from the former in the sugar level (about 8 grams per litre) and because its *liqueur d'expédition* has a small amount of brandy. Don Giovanni, remember, originated from Dreher, so brandy production is in its blood. The Brut is autolytic and bready, with ripe fruit, fine and long, and has great gastronomic attributes. After a 60-month autolysis, Extra-Brut Ouro is golden, with less fruit and more brioche and dough, being bone dry, very savoury, balanced and complex – a great sparkler indeed.

Daniel also offered me a classic: a 1994 Cabernet Franc. After 30 years, it is garnet-coloured (not amber) and limpid, bringing a strong, complex, layered spectrum of sweet spice, caramel, earth, dried fruit and nuts. In the mouth, it is soft, elegant, satisfying and very long.

Quite alive, it attests to the longevity of Brazilian wine – but note that enormous progress has taken place since 1994.

Família Geisse Vinhedos de Terroir ♀

Pinto Bandeira

www.familiageisse.com.br

The Chilean oenologist Mario Geisse came to Brazil in 1976 to manage the newly established Chandon facility. One of the first professionals to recognize the potential of the high region of Pinto Bandeira, he purchased some land there and founded Cave Geisse in 1982. His sparklers met with enormous success. He pioneered long maturation on lees in Brazil; his 1998 vintage had 12 years on lees when launched (and there are still some magnums with more than double the time and doing very well). They own 30 hectares of vineyards, managed with a *lutte raisonnée* philosophy. Native yeast is increasingly used.

The quality of their craftsmanship and wines has been recognized by world-famous writers (including Jancis Robinson, Julia Harding and Oz Clarke) and magazines (*Decanter*) and has earned them many prizes and high scores. Despite visiting Brazil very frequently, Mario Geisse lives in Chile. Daniel Geisse is at the helm locally, together with the oenologist Carlos Abarzúa, who has worked for them for 30 years. Annual production is 400,000 bottles from 45 hectares of vineyards. Geisse's products are certainly included amongst the best Brazil can make (really world class), confirming the potential of Serra Gaúcha as an excellent origin for sparkling wines. Visitors are welcome and several activities are offered (advance booking advised).

Carlos welcomed me to enjoy some Chilean-style *empanadas* and other tasty finger foods while we sampled their products at their wine bar, surrounded by gardens and woods. He had driven me through their vineyards and then up to a gazebo atop a hill. Here, besides affording a comprehensive overview of the vineyards, it is possible to see just how beautiful the Pinto Bandeira region is. I spotted two of their resources: a hail cannon (hail is frequent here) and a wind turbine with an integrated heating system to fight frosts (see photograph, page 128). Although very common in Europe, this is seldom found in Brazil.

As all Geisse sparklers are vintage dated, they never use reserve wines. The base wines wait for the following amount of time before the second fermentation is initiated: Cave Amadeu line, three months; Geisse line, five months; and top products, five to eight months. All wines are submitted to an internal tasting panel before being launched. They try to work at the lowest legal limits of sugar content – for example, 8.5 grams per litre for Bruts. This varies, of course, according to the base wines. Carlos informed me that, to improve the quality of the bubbles, it's important to leave a small amount of proteins.

Geisse Brut, their top seller (70 per cent Chardonnay, plus Pinot Noir), follows the house style: a clean, balanced sparkler with clear, but not overwhelming, ripe fruit, so well integrated into a good autolytic character, very fine and round. Blanc de Blancs Brut comes from the best base wines of Chardonnay; it is racy, with ripe pear and green apple and a great elegance. Blanc de Noirs Brut (best lots of Pinot Noir) has more structure, with the expected fruit profile of ripe but fresh red berries deftly integrated into the autolytic notes; it is a very food-friendly wine. Extra-Brut, made from equal parts

Mario Geisse (left) and Carlos Abarzúa

Wind turbine with an integrated heating system at Geisse

of the same two varieties, with a 36-month autolysis, has 5 grams per litre of sugar and undergoes malolactic fermentation. It offers a very clear autolytic character, while still retaining elegance and freshness. Extra-Brut Rosé (Pinot Noir, direct press, 20 per cent barrel fermented, up to three months in used barrels) is pale pink, savoury and well structured, again a gastronomic treat – an excellent wine. Geisse Terroir Nature (again 20 per cent barrel fermented, 48-month autolysis, 52 per cent Pinot Noir) is made only in selected vintages; it brings strong brioche and patisserie aromas and flavours, being very textural and well structured; so complex, long and satisfactory. Terroir Rosé (Pinot Noir, direct press) is 100 per cent barrel fermented, staying for six months in the barriques. It is very complex, layered, well structured and lengthy. These Terroir products from single parcels are, indeed, exceptional wines and tasting them a great hedonistic experience.

Vinícola Valmarino

Pinto Bandeira 🍷
valmarino.com.br/

Although vineyards were planted in 1978, this familiar winery was founded in 1997 by the oenologist Orval Salton. Sadly, he passed away a year later, and his sons, Marco, Guilherme and Rodrigo, took over. They make 250,000 litres of wine annually (including bag-in-box) from their grapes (21 hectares and 18 varieties) and bought fruit. Cabernet Franc is important for them; it was the first *vinifera* grape they planted. Pay close attention to their products made from this variety. Visitors can have a guided tasting, a guided tour with tasting (reservation required), or just sit in their open-air space (an astounding view!) and ask for wines and small platters (seven days a week).

Marco Salton, MSc, Valmarino's oenologist, took me on a Sunday afternoon to tour the winery and taste some of their many wines. Malvasia (legally a varietal; it has 15 per cent Chardonnay) is very concentrated in the mouth: white flowers, lychee, textural, but keeping freshness. Shiraz (grapes from their Pinto Bandeira vineyards) is deep ruby, ripe and savoury, with notes of blackberry, olives and smoke, besides vanilla and toast from 16 months in American oak barrels. Cabernet Franc Ano XXVI is so ripe but fresh, showing notes of raspberry, slight capsicum, vanilla and caramel. V3 Corte 1 (50 per cent Sangiovese, plus equal parts of Cabernet Sauvignon and Merlot) is a full, concentrated, well-structured wine with complex flavours, including sour cherry, cassis and chocolate; it is fresh and long. Reserva de Família, a blend of seven varieties, is a big wine with everything in full: concentration of ripe fruit, oakiness, alcohol and tannic structure. It is spicy and very long, demanding more time in the bottle.

Marco informed me that they usually harvest grapes to craft base wines a little riper (16 degrees Babo, or 18.8 Brix) than the usual 17.6 Brix. He aims to have riper, more structured base wines without excessive acidity. All their sparkler labels give the *dégorgement* date. Valmarino Rosé Brut (12-month autolysis, 8 grams per litre sugar) is made from equal parts of Sangiovese and Pinot Noir; with an onion-skin colour, it is very perfumed and ripe. Tradicional Brut (Chardonnay, Pinot Noir) is pale, crisp, complex, elegant and a real bargain. Blanc de Blancs Brut is so light, crisp, clean and elegant; after a 22-month autolysis, bread and brioche are present. Blanc de Noirs Brut (22-month, 8 grams per litre residual sugar) has more weight, structure and body, besides some tannic grip; it is a very gastronomic wine. Rosa Maria Rosé Brut has a beautiful pink colour; the base wine is made from the direct pressing of grapes harvested at 20 Brix. This shows up as ripe red fruit, a clear tannic grip and a fuller body. Sur Lie Nature, currently with 50-month autolysis, is hazy and complex, with so much bread dough and brioche, savoury, textural and long, with a slightly saline touch on the finish. Tinto Nature Sur Lie is a very unusual red undisgorged sparkler (Pinot Noir, Sangiovese); it has a complex array of sour cherry, ripe red berries, autolytic and savoury notes, with soft tannins. Hard to imagine a better wine to have with *feijoada*, the hearty, cassoulet-like dish of fatty pork and black beans famous in Brazil.

The Val & Churchill line is made in association with Nathan Churchill, the owner of PASP (São Paulo), an importer of oak barrels. Nature Prestige is made from base wines partially barrel-fermented and matured in new American oak. This translates into evident vanilla, coconut and some tannic grip; it is fresh and long.

Also in Pinto Bandeira

- Vinhedos Altos da Pinta (armaciel@gmail.com)
- Vinhos Foresti ((+55) 54 99627 8021)
- Vinícola La Grande Bellezza (www.villalagrandebellezza.com.br/)
- Résistance (resistancechardonnay@gmail.com)
- Vinícola Terraças (contato@terracas.com.br)
- Vita Eterna (contato@vitaeterna.com.br)

IP Altos Montes wineries

Vinícola Família Bebber ♀

Flores da Cunha

www.familiabebber.com.br/

Oenologist Felipe Bebber, father Valter and brother Rafael produce wines that display youth, lightness and elegance, using grapes purchased from Serra Gaúcha, Serra do Sudeste and Campos de Cima. The annual production is 225,000 bottles. A very original offering is Conecto, a kit with two bottles of different wines from Cabernet Franc/Petit Verdot, one aged in concrete, the other in oak, plus a graduated cylinder, allowing buyers to make their own blends. Visitors are welcome (Monday to Saturday) to their cosy, pretty wine bar, garden, various tastings and lunch. Book in advance.

Valter Bebber and the oenologist, Juliana, kindly hosted me while I tasted their wines. Chimango Cuvée Chardonnay is a blend of terroirs (Serras Gaúcha and Serra do Sudeste) and vintages, spending 18 months in used and new French and American oak. Aromas emerge easily from the glass: pineapple preserve, ripe pear, vanilla, coconut and butter. It underwent malolactic fermentation, being textural and soft. Oak flavours have a great length in the mouth.

Família Bebber Reserva Cabernet Franc (Serra Gaúcha) is fresh, well structured, elegant and varietally true. Bah is 93 per cent Tannat, the balance being Touriga Nacional (Serra do Sudeste); it has a deep colour, with violet and black fruit aromas. Its solid tannic structure will allow it to age well. Maragato is a complex blend of six red varieties, three origins and several vintages. It spends (80 per cent of the wine) 18 months in French oak and the balance in concrete eggs. This excellent wine is very complex, layered (ripe black fruit, spice, toast, chocolate, tobacco and more), well structured and ageworthy. Conecto Concreto (Petit Verdot/Cabernet Franc) stays 18 months in concrete eggs. It is spicy and ripe, with hints of earth and dust; good acidity, firm tannins and high, well-integrated alcohol allow it to age well. Conecto Carvalho is the same wine matured in oak instead of concrete; it is, again, very ripe, well structured and spicy, with excellent oak integration. Buy the kit and make your blend! Luigi Bossa, 100 per cent Teroldego (Serra do Sudeste), presents ripe black fruit, spice, herbal hints, a high acidity and muscular tannins. Oak (24 months, French and American) is very well integrated. This ageworthy wine is complex and structured.

Vero Brut Rosé is made by the traditional method from Pinot Noir and Chardonnay (Serra Gaúcha), spending 12 months with lees. It has a pretty onion-skin colour and is fruity, mouth-watering and easy drinking.

Boscato Vinhos Finos ♀

Nova Pádua

www.boscato.com.br/

Founded in 1983 by brothers Clóvis and Valmor Boscato, this winery initially made *vinhos de mesa* to sell to other wineries. In 1986, however, they started to produce *vinhos finos*. Currently owned by the oenologist, Clóvis, and his wife, Inês, they have 8 hectares of vineyards (having pioneered the installation of an irrigation system) and purchase grapes from other growers. The annual production is 350,000–380,000 bottles. They boast technological advancements, such as two Italian horizontal fermenters/macerators and an automated wine analyser, which can quickly test up to 75 parameters. Clóvis likes to sell some wines that are already matured and ready to be drunk without further cellaring. They have a near-perfect tasting room, built with due attention to every detail. Several types of tastings are available to visitors, who can also enjoy meals at their restaurant (booking required).

Clóvis, assertive and knowledgeable, took me to his exemplary tasting room to taste some of his products. Cave Chardonnay brings ripe pineapple; albeit fresh, it is unctuous, with some cream and butter. Gran Cave Merlot remains for 6 months in barrels and 16 in the bottles; it displays a rich palette of aromas and flavours: plums, blackberries, violets and tobacco. It is pretty fresh (pH 3.57) and well structured. Gran Cave Cabernet Sauvignon also spends six months in oak; it is very dark and perfectly ripe, with firm but fine-grained tannins and clear acidity. Clóvis suggests waiting two years, when, he says, the wine will be at its best (although it is already nine years old).

Vinícola Gazzaro ♀

Flores da Cunha

loja.gazzaro.com.br/

The Gazzi family has made wine since 1925. For a long time, this was not a full-blown activity. The winery proper was founded in 1993 by brothers Vanderlei, Ademir and Ladair, who first made only *vinhos de mesa* at third parties. A disused winery was bought in 1999. *Vinifera* Charmat sparklers were launched in 2004 and still wines in 2005. Vanderlei is the oenologist, guiding the annual production of 80,000 bottles of *vinhos finos*. They have a good set-up for visitors, with open-air tables and a bistro, Casa Gazzaro. Tastings can be paired with platters. You can show up seven days a week. Vanderlei was keen to show me his wines and tell stories about his family.

Unoaked Chardonnay is very ripe, with moderate acidity, concentrated and textural. Marselan 1896 is ripe, fruity, plummy and just a bit warm; spending six months in used and new oak, it has a savoury finish. Brut Charmat (Chardonnay) is fruity (apple, pineapple), fresh, round and well made.

Luiz Argenta Vinhos Finos ♀

Flores da Cunha

www.luizargenta.com.br

In 1999, brothers Deunir and Neco Argenta bought a property at Flores da Cunha, the pioneering vineyard of Sociedade (later Companhia) Vinícola Rio-Grandense, of the Granja União brand – producers of the first successful varietal wines in Brazil (see p. 19). A completely new vineyard was developed; today, it covers 50 hectares in the urban perimeter of Flores da Cunha. Except for Teroldego, all the wines are made using grapes from this vineyard. A high-tech winery was opened in 2009 and is now under the direction of oenologist Edegar Scortegagna. Today, the firm (named after Deunir's father) is managed by Deunir and his daughter Daiane (who introduced beautiful and unusual bottles for some wines). They produce 600,000 bottles a year. Oenotourism facilities are well developed; visitors can book various guided tours and tastings, and there's also a restaurant for lunch (closed on Mondays).

The oenologist Hendrios Draguetti was my host for a technical tasting at the beautiful wine bar, from which a view of the vineyard can be enjoyed. Ripiano is an unusual blend of Riesling Itálico, Trebbiano and Pinot Noir (vinified as a white). It is citric, very dry, sharp and light. LA Friulano is perhaps the only wine in Brazil made from this variety. Hendrios informed me that this cultivar is not easy to grow; it always demands cane pruning. The wine is aromatic and well structured, with some unctuosity but keeping fresh acidity; it is long, rich and honeyed. LA Gewurztraminer shows nicely how this exuberant variety performs in Brazil: very aromatic (flowers, lychee) but fresher, lighter and less dense than in Alsace. LA Cave Chardonnay is barrel fermented, spending at least eight months on lees with *bâtonnage*. They use new special Séguin-Moreau barrels devised for white wines. No malolactic fermentation leads to a lively acidity. Elegant oak, savouriness and finesse make this excellent wine European in style.

LA Cave Cabernet Franc is true to the variety: ripe raspberry and cassis, hints of capsicum and pencil shavings, rewarding acidity and firm tannins,

Part of Luiz Argenta's vineyard in Flores da Cunha, viewed from the tasting room wine bar

plus vanilla and toast. It is harmonious, balanced and elegant – another wine of excellence. LA Cave Cuvée is a Bordeaux blend, including Petit Verdot. A portion of the Merlot grapes were dried in boxes, becoming raisined. The wine has ripe and rich black fruit, well-integrated oak and a charming spiciness. Its sinewy tannins and high concentration mean it will age well. LA Clássico Rosé (Pinot Noir, traditional method, 24-month autolysis) is crisp and well structured, its ripe red berries marrying well with moderate bread and brioche flavours. LA Cave Brut (Chardonnay) has a long, 48-month autolysis; no wonder bread, yeast and dough are abundant; it is at once complex and elegant, fine and layered.

Marzarotto Vinhos & Vinhas ♀

Nova Pádua

www.vinhosmarzarotto.com.br/

Janaína Massarotto, the first female oenologist to lead a winery in Brazil, and also a sommelier, makes small batches of artisanal wines using grapes from selected terroirs: Serra Gaúcha, Serra do Sudeste and Campanha Gaúcha. The oenotouristic activities include tastings with or without charcuterie (reservation necessary).

Pleno Peverella displays ripe peach, melon and some fine herbs; it is crisp and piquant in the mouth, with good concentration and mineral hints.

Vinícola Viapiana ♀

Flores da Cunha

vinhosviapiana.com.br/

The Italian immigrant Antonio Viapiana started producing wine in 1920 at the site where the present winery has existed since 1986. Their first *vinho fino*, a Cabernet Sauvignon, was made in 1999. Marselan appeared in 2009, marking a close association between the variety and this winery. They make wines from their 24 hectares of vineyards and purchased grapes. Elton Viapiana is the oenologist, making 100,000 bottles of *vinhos finos* annually. They like 550-litre Italian (Garbelotto) barrels. Viapiana crafts something rare: an orange wine from Gros Manseng. Visitors can enjoy several different tastings at their modern, pretty wine bar and *trattoria*, Gazoldo (booking required).

Artur Viapiana welcomed me to taste their wines. Chardonnay Tostatura Assente, as the name indicates, matures in untoasted oak barrels. Made from Serra do Sudeste grapes, it is very ripe (pear, apple,

pineapple) and the fruit is mixed with clear oak flavours. Having undergone complete malolactic fermentation, it is textural and a bit buttery
but retains freshness. Exóticos Laranja Gros Manseng (a variety seldom
found in Brazil) stays for 6 months on skins, plus 14 months in used
French and Slavonian oak barrels. It is indeed orange, complex (dried
fruits, honey, dust, chamomile), layered, quite tannic, and long.

VIA1986 Pinot Noir (Altos Montes) stays 12 months in new Slavonian
oak barrels. It displays a light ruby colour, and is savoury, well structured,
elegant and complex. VIA1986 Nebbiolo was fermented at 29°C with
some 32°C peaks for better extraction; it stayed for two years in French
oak barrels. It is varietally true: moderate colour, high acidity, strong tannic structure, full body and flavours of red berries and roses. This is a very
gastronomic wine. Viapiana Barricas Selecionadas Lote VI, a Cabernet
Sauvignon-dominated Bordeaux blend with a dash of Teroldego, clearly shows the predominant variety: cassis and capsicum. It has a strong
structure of acidity and tannins, and the ripe fruit is seamlessly integrated
into the oak. VIA1986 Cabernet Franc (Altos Montes) has a strong but
charming varietal character (pencil shavings and capsicum amidst ripe
fruit, fresh acidity and evident tannins). After staying for 15 months in
two sizes of French oak barriques, the ensemble is well integrated, making
it an excellent example of Cabernet Franc from Serra Gaúcha. VIA1986
Blend is Cabernet Sauvignon and Merlot in similar proportions, undergoing an oak regime of 24 months in new French barrels of medium
toast. Round, fine and elegant, it reminds me of a good red Graves.

Blanc de Blancs Nature 575 (Chardonnay, Riesling Itálico) is made
from base wines staging six months in French oak and a 575-day autolysis. It is crisp, mineral, bone dry and fine, with vanilla and brioche
aromas. Blanc de Noirs Nature 584 is Pinot Noir only, with the same
oak treatment and 584-day autolysis. It is also bone dry, racy, toasty and
well structured.

Also in Altos Montes

- Cave de Angelina Vinhos & Vinhedos, Nova Pádua (www.
  cavedeangelina.com.br/)
- Caetano Vicentino Vinhas & Vinhos, Nova Pádua (caetanovicentino.
  com.br/)
- Vinícola Debon, Nova Pádua (vinhosdebon@vinhosdebon.com.br)
- Casa Eva Vinhos e Vinhedos, Flores da Cunha (casaeva.com.br/)
- Vinhos Fabian, Nova Pádua (www.vinhosfabian.com.br/)

- Fante Bebidas, Flores da Cunha (www.fante.com.br/)
- Vinícola Gaio, Flores da Cunha (@vinicola_gaio)
- Vinícola Galiotto, Flores da Cunha (galiotto@vinicolagaliotto. com.br; (+55) 54 3279 3200)
- Cantina Gelain, Flores da Cunha (www.cantinagelain.com.br/)
- Vinhos Gilioli, Flores da Cunha (vinicolagilioli@vinicolagilioli.com. br)
- Vinhos e Espumantes Hortência, Flores da Cunha (vendas@ vinhoshortencia.com.br)
- Vinícola Madre Terra, Flores da Cunha (@vinicolamadreterra)
- Adega Mascarello, Flores da Cunha (www.adegamascarello.com.br/)
- Vinícola Mioranza, Flores da Cunha (www.mioranza.com/)
- Vinícola Monte Reale, Flores da Cunha (www.montereale.com.br/)
- Vinícola Panizzon, Flores da Cunha (www.panizzon.com.br/)
- Pauletti Vinhos e Vinhedos, Flores da Cunha (contato@ paulettivinhosevinhedos.com.br)
- Salvattore Urban Winery, Flores da Cunha (www.vinicolasalvattore. com.br)
- Terrasul Vinhos Finos, Flores da Cunha (www.vinhosterrasul.com.br/)
- Família Ulian, Flores da Cunha (www.familiaulian.com.br/)
- Famiglia Veadrigo, Flores da Cunha (www.veadrigo.com.br/)
- Casa Venturini Vinhos e Espumantes, Flores da Cunha (www. casaventurini.com.br/)

IP Monte Belo wineries

The pretty little town of Monte Belo do Sul, on a hilltop (there is a belvedere just before you arrive in the centre), is the heart of this IP. A series of small family wineries produces limited quantities of wine. Monte Belo is a good place to visit, eat and stay to enjoy its bucolic charms. Pay attention to wines made from BRS Lorena, which is exclusive to Brazil. It was in Monte Belo, at the excellent Francesco *trattoria*, that I first tasted a Lorena years ago – a startling surprise.

Casa Marques Pereira ♀

Monte Belo do Sul

casamarquespereira.com.br/

Felipe and Fábio Marques Pereira, from Canoas, started growing grapes in 2004. Initially making wines for their family's own consumption, they founded a boutique winery. Their first wines were launched in 2016. The present annual production is 50,000 bottles, under oenologist Marcos Vian. They use only grapes from their 8 hectares of vineyards. Unlike most wine businesses in Rio Grande do Sul, the owners are descendants of Portuguese immigrants. The vineyards are located on basaltic soil at an average altitude of 500 metres. One parcel, Cru Jerivás, lies on a subsoil containing semi-precious stones (agate and amethyst). They have a very agreeable wine shop and bistro beside the main church of Monte Belo do Sul, in a restored building from the 1950s. Here, visitors can buy wines, have guided tastings and enjoy platters of charcuterie and cheese seven days a week. Book in advance.

Segredos da Adega Alvarinho is very textural, full bodied and round but also fresh; it stays ten months in new French oak barrels. Segredos Chardonnay spends 12 months in new French oak, being very ripe (pear, pineapple). It is full, unctuous, buttery and long, with clear vanilla and spice. Tannat Reserva is ripe and spicy and does not display this variety's usually unyielding tannins; it is a more elegant, easy-drinking version. Segredos Merlot is mature, with soft, round tannins and complex aromas mixing oak and tertiary hints; it is ready to drink (after 24 months in new French oak barriques, plus 12 in the bottle). Quinta da Orada Corte VI, a blend of four grapes, has very ripe fruit and sweet oak, being complex, rich and long.

Also in Monte Belo

- Avvocato (www.avvocato.com.br)
- Vinícola Calza (www.vinicolacalza.com.br/)
- Eduardo Mendonça Vinhos Livres (@eduardomendoncavinhoslivres)
- Vinícola Faccin (contato@faccinvinhos.com.br)
- Vinhos Faé (vinhosfae@futurusnet.com.br)
- Casa Angelo Fantin (www.casafantin.com.br)
- Helios Vinhos Finos (www.vinicolahelios.com.br)
- Vinícola Megiolaro (@vinicolamegiolaro/)
- Vinícola Monte Bello (www.vinicolamontebello.com.br/)
- Moro Vinhos Finos (@morovinhosfinos)
- Negroponte Vigna (negropontevigna@gmail.com)
- Adega de Vinhos Finos Reginato (@adegareginato)
- Dom Riccardo Vinhos Finos (@domriccardovinhosfinos2021)
- Vinícola Somacal (www.somacalvinhos.com.br/)
- Adega Giovanni Tasca (adegagiovannitasca.com.br/)

- Vallebello Vinhedos & Vinhos (www.vallebello.com.br/)
- Domínio Vicari (dominiovicari.wixsite.com/home)
- Vinum Terra (www.vinicolavinumterra.com.br/)

IP Farroupilha wineries

Adega Chesini ♀

Farroupilha

www.adegachesini.com.br/

The *adega* was founded in 1960 by Felippe Chesini. Today, the third generation, his grandsons, manage the winery, which was modernized in 2001. They are one of a few wineries producing wines from BRS Carmem, a variety bred by Embrapa. They also work with this agency on the Lorena grape. Oenotouristic activities include vineyard visits, tastings, accompanying platters and a complete meal of typical colonial cuisine (reservations are required).

Lorena Ativa is very aromatic and true to the variety: white flowers, lychee and citrus, being textural and even a bit unctuous. 'Ativa' means a higher antioxidant content, achieved using a special yeast, Embrapa 1VVT/97, and special vinification techniques. Moscato (Giallo) is delicately aromatic, perfumed and elegant; bone dry and delicious, it is a bargain. Gênese Chardonnay, which spends six months in French oak barrels, is ripe, buttery and overtly oaky. Gênese Petit Verdot is dark, spicy and ripe with black fruits. It is full bodied, with firm tannins and moderate vanilla and cedar.

Casa Perini ♀

Farroupilha

www.casaperini.com.br/

This winery was founded by Benildo Perini in 1970 and made a giant leap forward in 2005 by purchasing the former equipment of Bacardi-Martini at Garibaldi, including a series of Vinimatic rotofermenters (perhaps unique in Brazil), which they still use. Farroupilha continues, however, as their administrative and viticultural centre. They have an extensive variety of wines distributed into several lines. *Vinhos de mesa* and craft beers are also made. Perini makes 12 million litres across all products annually. The wines are mainly produced from Vale Trentino (Farroupilha) grapes, but some use fruit from other provenances, such as Campanha Gaúcha. There is a very well-structured variety of oenotouristic activities, from simple tastings and visits (no need to book in advance) to a whole-day programme at harvest time (reservation needed).

Fração Única pink Pinot Noir (Campanha Gaúcha grapes), made by direct press, is fermented at 16°C and has a blush colour and high concentration of ripe red berries. It is crisp, fine and elegant. Fração Única Pinot Noir displays sweet, ripe red fruits framed by evident vanilla and coconut. Its tannins are very soft. The Solidário red blend brings ripe blackberry, cassis and plums, plus hints of vanilla and spice. The tannins are fine grained and soft. Fração Única Cabernet Franc shows ripe and fresh blackberry, cassis, capsicum, pencil shavings, vanilla, coconut and tobacco. Its tannins are firm but amicable. Qu4tro is a blend of Cabernet Sauvignon, Merlot, Tannat and Ancellotta, and spends nine months in new French oak barrels. The fruit is black and ripe, blending well with vanilla, spice and cedar. The wine has sinewy tannins, demanding some additional time to soften. It is complex, concentrated, lengthy and ageworthy.

Brut Barrique Vintage (100 per cent Chardonnay) has 20 per cent of the base wine fermented and matured in oak barrels for two months. It is made by a long Charmat process (18 months on lees with *bâtonnage* in the autoclave), showing ripe apple, pear and pineapple, plus hints of vanilla and brioche. Brut Rosé de Noir Vintage (100 per cent Pinot Noir) is blush-pink and exhibits fresh red berries amidst hints of bread, flowers and pomegranate. Also made using the long Charmat method, it has fresh acidity and good structure, making it food friendly. Prosecco Brut is pale, crisp, floral and fruity (fresh apple and pear), perfect for a summer afternoon. Brut Rosé (Chardonnay/Gamay/Pinot Noir, short Charmat) is youthful, showing fresh red berries as well as good structure and concentration. Moscatel is made using the Asti process, with a short time in the tank (25 days); it has intense aromas of white flowers, grapes and peaches. It is not cloying (75 grams per litre residual sugar), and is crisp (pH 3.15), youthful and delicious. Aquarela is a pink version made from three varieties: Moscato Branco, Moscato Giallo and Moscato de Hamburgo. It has aromas and flavours of ripe but fresh mandarin, grapefruit, some strawberry and jasmine. A vibrant acidity balances its 82 grams per litre of sugar. This would go splendidly with a strawberry tart.

Vintage Moscatel Liqueur is golden; in making this superb wine, a 24-hour skin maceration took place and a 120-day sojourn in the tank with *bâtonnage*. It has a high intensity and concentration, brimming with layers of fruit (grapes, peaches), white flowers, and notes of honey and caramel. It is mouth coating and long, but at the same time refined and elegant. A real beauty!

Also in Farroupilha

- Cave Antiga (www.caveantiga.com.br/)
- Vinícola Basso (www.vinicolabasso.com.br/)
- Vinícola Belmonte (vinicolabelmonte.com.br/)
- Vinhos Cappelletti (www.vinhoscappelletti.com.br/)
- Vinícola de Cezaro (contato@vinicoladecezaro.com.br)
- Casa Onzi (adm@casaonzi.com.br)
- Cooperativa Vinícola São João (www.cooperativasaojoao.com.br/)
- Vinícola Tonini (www.vinhostonini.com.br/)

Wineries in other areas of Serra Gaúcha

Amitié Espumantes e Vinhos ♀

Garibaldi

www.amitieloja.com.br/

This business was launched by partners Andreia Gentilini Milan (sommelier) and Juciane Casagrande Doro (oenologist) in 2018, starting with sparkling wines and then extending to still wines in 2020. They have no vineyard or winery but, as clever négociants, devise, order and sell their products themselves. Their operational base is in Serra Gaúcha, but they also offer wines from almost all Brazilian regions, as well as some from Maule, in Chile. Amitié has recently opened a shop at Vale dos Vinhedos, where visitors are welcome for tastings and lunch (booking advised).

Amitié Sauvignon Blanc is pale, fresh and typical. Oak Barrel Viognier is perfumed and has a soft acidity, a good body and slight vanilla and cedar from four months in French oak. Oak Barrel Chardonnay is ripe, fruity and overtly oaky from one year in new French oak barriques. Amitié pink Merlot rosé is pale, fresh and fruity in the Provençal style. Colheitas de Verão is a Cabernet Franc from Serra Gaúcha; with clear varietal character, it is fresh, well structured and food friendly. Oak Barrel Pinot Noir has a fine varietal character, with a good structure and clear, albeit non-intrusive, oakiness from eight months in French oak. Oak Barrel Montepulciano shows deep colour, ripe blackberry and plum, and a strong tannic structure.

Amitié Brut Charmat (Chardonnay, Malvasia) is fresh, with sweet floral and fruity characters. The Rosé version (same grapes, plus Merlot) is ripe, fruity and easy going. Cuvée Brut Charmat (Chardonnay, Pinot Noir) is overtly fruity, creamy, refreshing and elegant. Amitié Nature is a traditional method sparkler from Chardonnay; bone dry, citric, sharp, and biscuity from an 18-month autolysis. Sur Lie Nature (Chardonnay) also spends at least 18 months with the lees before being sold; undisgorged, it is hazy, complex, bready and long.

Angheben – Adega de Vinhos Finos 🍷

Bento Gonçalves

www.angheben.com.br

Idalêncio Francisco Angheben, a descendant of Giacintho Angheben from Trentino, is a much-respected figure in the Brazilian wine scene, especially in viticultural matters. He has had a double career, both academic (teacher at the Instituto Federal, in Bento Gonçalves) and professional (having worked extensively for Cooperativa Aurora and Chandon Brasil). He was very prominent in the development of the new Serra do Sudeste wine region. Eduardo, his son, an oenologist now at the helm of the winery, told me that he undertook a very detailed climatic study of the region as part of his studies. Professor Idalêncio took advantage of this; he selected one of the first areas in the region to be sold to a winery (Chandon) in 2000.

In 1999, Idalêncio founded his winery together with Eduardo. It is a family operation with 15,000 bottles being made annually, with a focus on quality rather than quantity. Angheben has been instrumental in introducing the Teroldego cultivar to Brazil. They use grapes from Serra do Sudeste and Serra Gaúcha. Wine lovers can visit their pretty shop within a restored old house in Monte Belo, from Wednesday to Sunday, for tastings (booking required).

It was there that, on a rainy day, Eduardo showed me some of his products and we had a very agreeable conversation. Chardonnay (Serra Gaúcha) keeps freshness despite malolactic fermentation, being elegant and savoury, with well-integrated oak (spending just three months in French oak) and hints of salinity and minerality.

Barbera, one of their specialities, uses grapes from Encruzilhada do Sul (Serra do Sudeste). It is very ripe but mouth-watering. With a charming rustic character (there are some animal notes), it has amicable tannins and demands to be drunk with Italian food. Cabernet

Franc, from Pinheiro Machado (Serra do Sudeste), is more 'modern' in style: very ripe in fruit, no pyrazinic aromas and well structured – it may age well. Cabernet Sauvignon (Serra Gaúcha) is proof that this variety can ripen properly in the region. It offers ripe cassis (again no pyrazines) and is fresh and well structured, while its fine-grained tannins allow long ageing. Tannat (Guaporé, in Serra Gaúcha) is inky, displaying very ripe berries, cigar box and chocolate; despite the proverbial strong structure, it is an elegant rendition of Tannat, as usual in the region.

Traditional method Brut sparkler (12-month autolysis), predominately Chardonnay, is fresh, ripe, savoury and quite autolytic, elegant and well balanced.

Arte da Vinha

Carlos Barbosa

www.artedavinha.com.br

Founded and led by Eduardo Zenker, a self-taught winemaker, and his wife, Gabriela Schäfer, a biologist, this winery specializes in natural, minimal-intervention wines. They use grapes from Serra Gaúcha and Serra do Sudeste. The wines are produced in small batches; hence, it's important to check availability.

Magmatic Sauvignon Blanc spends ten months in used oak barrels. Oxygen influences are clearly shown by its golden colour and flavours of honey and toast. The varietal character is dimmed in the nose but evident in the mouth as a tangy acidity; it ends with a savoury, saline finish. Francamente Franc Cabernet Franc (grapes from Campos de Cima da Serra) is purple in colour and has a high aromatic intensity: raspberry, blackberry, graphite, floral and hints of capsicum. It is fresh and savoury, with a good tannic structure, and should be enjoyed with food.

Arte Viva 🍷

Bento Gonçalves

www.vinicolaarteviva.com.br

Founded in 2019 by a young and restless oenologist, Giovanni Ferrari, this winery specializes in products made from Serra Gaúcha and Campanha Gaúcha grapes. Their annual production is 70,000 bottles. Giovanni is trying out Brazilian woods such as *jequitibá, cabreúva, grápia (garapeira), amburana, bálsamo* and *acácia negra*, as well as oak of various origins, to bring complexity and spice to the wines. The woods are used chiefly as staves or smaller sizes, but some are used to make barrels. Giovanni takes advantage of the expertise of Tanoaria Mezacasa (a cooperage in Monte Belo), where electrical resistance heater strips instead of flames are used to toast the barrels. He is also investigating the insertion of basalt chips in tanks; he thinks basalt 'polishes' the wine and imparts some minerality. Another area of research is the use of geodesic fermentation tanks to improve the movement of the must inside. Various tastings are offered to visitors (book first).

Giovanni, who has worked at Ruinart and Quinta do Seixo, has a pretty wine bar and tasting room at Caminhos de Pedra (between Bento and Farroupilha). There, we discussed his new alternatives while tasting some of his wines. Sinônimos Sauvignon Blanc (Campanha Gaúcha) is – like many wines here – a product for the brave and adventurous, having spent at least six months in *grápia* barrels. It is so spicy and complex, the usually exuberant fruit quite attenuated by the wood. Rosé, made by *saignée* from four red varieties, is dark pink and very savoury, with a strong structure and some puzzling flavours.

Tinturè, made from five red grapes, has some *amburana* chips treatment. This is a very strong, idiosyncratic wood, imparting a very long length to the wine; again, one of a kind. Marselan is fermented with *cabreúva* and *castanha* chips, maturing thereafter in American, French and Slovenian oak, where it undergoes malolactic fermentation. It is very ripe, fruity, spicy and oaky. Geodésis, their premium red blend of three Italian varieties from two vintages, ferments in a geodesic stainless-steel vat. Afterwards, it receives some treatment with *castanha do Brasil* wood, which imparts pepper and nutmeg. This is a complex, layered wine.

Brut Pinot Noir Método Ancestral is made from grapes harvested at 22 Brix; the fermentation starts in vats and goes on in the bottle without disgorging. The wine is hazy and pink, exuding yeast and dough aromas; it is complex and long.

Cainelli Vinhos Artesanais ♀

Bento Gonçalves (Tuiuty)
vinicolacainelli.com.br/

This family winery was founded in 2012 by Roberto Cainelli and his homonymous son, the oenologist Roberto Jr. They craft their wines from 6 hectares of vineyards and bought fruit. Annual production reaches 45,000 bottles, of which 9,000 are Bibiana and Lorena. Cainelli has a small museum in an old colonial house (1929). Cainelli is one of the few producers of varietal BRS Bibiana wine. They offer a variety of oenotouristic activities: tastings, meals, picnics, tours, harvesting, and more. Booking is necessary.

Bibiana is citric, peachy, floral, fresh and textural. Lorena is aromatic, with a high intensity and concentration of white flowers, grapes, papaya and lychee. It is soft and concentrated, reminiscent of both Muscat and Gewurztraminer. Tempo Petit Verdot exhibits a deep purple colour, ripe black fruit, spice, vanilla and cedar. It is fresh and bone dry, and has sturdy tannins, requiring bottle ageing. Tempo Merlot/Alicante/ Malbec brings ripe blackberries, plums, fruit cake and chocolate. It is rich and fleshy, with firm tannins. Tempo CS/Marselan/Ancellotta displays ripe cassis, blackberries, capsicum, earth, vanilla and cedar. It has fine-grained tannins and is savoury, fresh and food friendly.

Casacorba Vinhos e Espumantes ♀

Nova Roma do Sul

casacorba.com.br/

Founded in 1999, this winery, now led by Marcos Scatolin, has recently been refurbished. Within a 60-hectare property, they own 30 hectares of vineyards (plus olive groves) on clay/basalt soils at an altitude of 700 metres. Under oenologist Tiago Bergonzi, three lines of still wines are made, besides sparklers. Olive oil, grape juice, brandy, *cachaça* and *grappa* are also produced. There is a good set-up for oenotourism, including three different tastings, and cottages to stay in. Reservation is required.

Terroir Chardonnay is fresh and showcases ripe apple and pineapple amidst vanilla and toast from 12 months in French oak barrels. The oak is well integrated and elegant. Terroir Tannat is inky, exhibiting clear notes of vanilla and coconut (12 months in French and American oak barrels). Ripe blackberries and tobacco are framed by warming alcohol and solid tannins. This is a good wine to accompany a barbecue. Vicenzo red blend (Tannat/Merlot) is also deeply coloured, presenting ripe black fruit, fruit cake, chocolate, coffee, vanilla, spice and coconut. It is rich, fleshy, powerful and full bodied, strong in tannins, layered and complex. This is a big wine in the New World style.

Cândida Brut (Chardonnay, traditional method, 36-month autolysis) has fresh apple, pineapple and pear, with yeasty, bready flavours and a few hints of caramel. It has a good density and is rich and savoury.

Chandon Brasil ♀

Garibaldi

www.chandon.com.br

Part of the LVMH group of luxury brands, Chandon started life in Brazil in 1973 as a joint venture (Provifin) with the Monteiro Aranha group and Cinzano. Since then, the French group has become the sole owner. Oenologist Mario Geisse (see Cave Geisse, page 126) was brought from Chile to lead the winery, where he worked for several years. Here, under strict quality controls and with a reliability that made other brands in the group famous (such as Moët & Chandon, Veuve Clicquot and Dom Pérignon), only Charmat-method sparklers are produced after 50 years of operating in Brazil. This is no small production: 3 million bottles are made annually. The grapes come from their Serra do Sudeste vineyards (30 per cent) and from other growers. Before being launched, all wines are tasted by an internal panel of five oenologists. Chandon has a strong focus on sustainability, from the vineyards to the final product. Oenotouristic activities, including several types of tastings (booking mandatory), take place in beautiful gardens with a view of a small vineyard.

Philippe Mével leads the oenology team. He has worked here almost since Chandon began. After having known him in the early 2000s, it was a pleasure to meet Philippe again and taste his products, accompanied by oenologist Franciele Santos. Brut Réserve is, by far, their main product in terms of volume. The base wines are made from Chardonnay, Pinot Noir and Riesling Itálico. It stays for four months with the lees in the tank and has 10 grams per litre residual sugar, being overtly fruity (citrus, apple, pineapple) and fresh. Blanc de Noirs (Pinot Noir from Serra do Sudeste) Extra-Brut (6 grams per litre sugar) has a longer, six-month autolysis. These two additional months are enough to make bread and brioche more perceptible, albeit the wine is also very fruity. Excellence is their top product, spending no less than 18 months with the lees (but this can go up to 36 months). No Riesling Itálico is used and residual sugar is 8 grams per litre. Golden, creamy and well structured, it is intense, complex and long, being a striking example of how good a Charmat sparkler can be. Passion is completely different: made from Moscato and Malvasia, with a dash of Pinot Noir, it has a beautiful pink colour and is very aromatic and sweet (35 grams per litre sugar).

Courmayeur Espumantes e Vinhos ♀

Garibaldi

www.courmayeur.com.br

Established in 1976, this winery was bought by Cinzano in 1986. The Verzeletti family then took control in 2003. The business is predominately led by women. They make 930,000 bottles of wine annually, 80 per cent Charmat sparklers, from their vineyards or bought grapes. They also sell Chilean wines under their own label. Visitors can tour and taste or have a picnic (booking advised).

Essencial line: Chardonnay has clear varietal typicity; 100 per cent undergoes malolactic fermentation, bringing moderate acidity, good texture and some butteriness. After five months in French oak barrels, it gains structure, vanilla and spice. Rosé (Pinot Noir, Marselan), made by *saignée,* is medium pink, fresh and well structured.

Ancellotta, aromatic with very ripe blackberry and cherry, good acidity and a low level of tannins, is a juicy, straightforward wine. Marselan is dark and bone dry, and has a good grip and some savouriness. Alicante Bouschet is inky, with very ripe black fruit, a full body and a solid tannic structure.

Brut White is 90 per cent Chardonnay and the balance is Pinot Noir; it is fresh, fruity and easy going. Quintessencial line: Cuvée Extra-Brut (Chardonnay, base wines spending two months in oak) stays 12 months in the tank with its lees, plus two years in the bottles; it is quite complex for a Charmat, with clear autolytic notes. Rosé Extra-Brut (Pinot Noir) undergoes the same treatment as its white companion (except it spends two-and-a-half years in the bottles). It has an excellent structure, exhibiting riper fruit and fewer autolytic characters than the white version, but keeping complexity and depth. Moscatel is a blend of Moscato Branco, Moscato Giallo and Malvasia; very aromatic, fresh and fruity, its 75 grams per litre residual sugar does not impart any cloying character.

Cristofoli Vinhos de Família ♀

Bento Gonçalves

www.vinhoscristofoli.com.br/

The Cristofolis have planted vines and made grapes for decades at Faria Lemos, a district of Bento Gonçalves. Italian varieties have always been important for them. Brothers Loreno and Mário founded the winery

38 years ago. Winemaking is led by oenologist Lorenzo Cristofoli. A restaurant was opened in 2002, improving the already good oenotouristic set-up. Groups of up to eight people can go straight there for a tasting. Other activities are also offered and groups are welcome by reservation (closed Sundays).

Moscato de Alexandria is a somewhat unusual variety in Brazil, especially for making a dry wine. Cristofoli's version is pale, delicate in aromas, textural and even a bit fat in the mouth, where flavours of white flowers and papaya open up. Sangiovese Rosé is crafted from grapes especially harvested (earlier than for the red wine), directly pressed, with brief skin contact and fermentation at 16°C. It is very pale, with overt aromas and flavours of ripe raspberry and cherry, bone dry and fresh. Drink it cool in the summer – it is delicious. Sangiovese is full of ripe cherry, with hints of herbs and dust. With a medium body and alcohol, it is crisp, bone dry, savoury and food friendly. Dodici Brut (traditional method, 12-month autolysis) from Chardonnay shows ripe apples and pears amidst bread and brioche; it is crisp, dry and elegant.

Enos Vinhos de Boutique

Criciúma

www.vinicolaenos.com.br

This small winery was founded by Leo Kades, a book editor, in 2016. Although the winery's administrative centre is located at Criciúma, in Santa Catarina, the wines are made at Serra Gaúcha, using grapes from Serra and several other areas under the baton of oenologists Alejandro Cardozo and Fernando Camargo. Their annual production is about 20,000 bottles. However, this varies because some wines are produced only in outstanding vintages. All the wines I tasted were well balanced and devoid of excessive oakiness, and so carefully crafted, with beautiful labels and imaginative names, always linked to literary works.

Alvarinho (Serra Gaúcha) is golden and displays complex aromas and flavours of ripe peach, citrus and toast, plus hints of nuts, vanilla, spice, honey and minerality. It is rich, textural, crisp and layered – a truly good Alvarinho. Alice Merlot (Serra Gaúcha) is a well-made example of this variety and origin: ripe blackberry and plum, hints of fruit cake, fresh acidity and a tannic structure which allows some years of bottle ageing. Alice Cabernet Franc (Serra do Sudeste) unveils ripe black fruit, vanilla, cedar and hints of capsicum and graphite. It is fresh, spicy and well structured, with an excellent balance and gastronomic merits.

Enos Gran Reserva Teroldego (Campanha Gaúcha) honours this high-quality variety: a deep colour and complex flavours of ripe black fruit, vanilla, spice, fine herbs and earth. It is savoury, fresh and concentrated, with a firm tannic structure that allows it to age gracefully. Gran Blend Cabernet Franc is an interesting mix of grapes from two origins (Pinto Bandeira and Pinheiro Machado) and three vintages. It is deep in colour and concentrated in flavour: ripe black fruit, vanilla, cedar, pencil shavings, leather and earth. The tannins are sinewy but fine grained. 1984 is a blend of Tannat, Cabernet Franc and Malbec from Serra Gaúcha, displaying an attractive mix of ripe black fruit and fine oak, and tertiary traits (leather, tobacco, earth) within a solid tannic structure. It is layered, complex, long and ageworthy.

Era dos Ventos

Bento Gonçalves

eradosventos.com.br/

This *sui generis* winery makes all its white wines on skins. They pioneered the orange wine style in Brazil, achieving much fame after their orange Peverella earned several prizes. Most wines come from their vineyards, covering about 13 hectares, at Caminhos de Pedra, in Serra Gaúcha. Luís Henrique Zanini (see Vallontano, page 123) and Talise, the owners, have a taste for ancestral vinification methods.

Peverella is indeed orange, showing complex aromas and flavours of dried fruit, dried herbs, earth and caramel notes. It is dry, fresh, savoury and layered. The wine has a good length, ending with some tannic bite and a slightly bitter tang.

Estrelas do Brasil ♀

Faria Lemos (Bento Gonçalves)

www.estrelasdobrasil.com.br/

This small, high-end winery was founded in 2005 by two oenologists: Irineo Dall'Agnol (Brazilian) and Alejandro Cardozo (Uruguayan). The latter provides technical support to many wineries in Brazil, Uruguay, Chile and Peru. He also owns a custom crush facility at Serra Gaúcha. Although Estrelas produces still wines, their primary focus is on fizzy products – hence the name. And this has been successful, as they have earned a lot of prizes at several competitions and achieved significant acclaim among wine critics in Brazil and South America. Varieties used include Riesling Itálico, Trebbiano and Viognier, so deviating from the usual. Although today the annual production is small (30,000 bottles), it can reach 300,000. Estrelas has oenotouristic facilities on top of a hill, from which an astounding view of Vale Aurora can be enjoyed. There is also a life-size statue of Dom Pérignon. Book first.

Dall'Agnol Chardonnay 365 Dias is spontaneously fermented in fourth-use American oak barrels, where it matures with skins and seeds for a whole year. It is orange, fresh, complex, savoury, grippy and food friendly. Pink Prosecco Brut (12 grams per litre residual sugar), made by the Charmat method from Pinot Noir, is fruity, crisp and straightforward. Brut (traditional method, Chardonnay, Riesling and Trebbiano) has a 40-month autolysis; it is complex, fresh, elegantly autolytic and again, so food friendly. Extra-Brut Rosé (Swiss A10 clone of Pinot Noir) has an onion-skin colour, being well structured, 'leesy', spicy and grippy.

Irineo likes to use Trebbiano Toscano to craft base wines due to its aromatic neutrality, moderate sugar levels and high acidity. Trebbiano sparkler (ancestral method, now 58-month) is aromatically distinct: candied citrus, thyme, basil, bread and biscuit, and well structured with a caressing mousse – try it with sushi or seafood. Nature Rosé (Pinot Noir, 40-month) is very complex and complete, with an excellent structure and clear patisserie amidst ripe red berries and a great freshness.

Cooperativa Vinícola Garibaldi ♀

Garibaldi

vinicolagaribaldi.com.br/

Founded in 1931, this cooperative has 450 family members, caring for 1,200 hectares of vineyards (for *vinhos de mesa, vinhos finos* and grape juice). There are 15 different lines of products, including the historical Granja União, a brand they acquired from Cordelier in 2010. This is one of the biggest Brazilian producers, crafting 8 million bottles of *vinifera* wines annually (6.5 million are sparklers). They use grapes from several regions in Rio Grande do Sul. Oenotourism is a strong component; several types of tastings are offered through booking. The facilities are new and include a small walk-through museum. Wine prices are very attractive, as the general quality level is high.

Ricardo Morari, the chief oenologist, is a past president of Associação Brasileira de Enologia (ABE) – the Brazilian Oenology Association. He welcomed me to taste some wines from Cooperativa's extensive line of products. I started with a rarity: a wine from Pálava. This variety of Moravian origin, a crossing between Gewurztraminer and Müller-Thurgau, is seldom found outside the Czech Republic. Unoaked, it is quite aromatic (green apple, nectarine, floral), fresh, light and charming. Granja União Riesling Itálico (quite inexpensive) is lively, floral and fruity – ideal for everyday use. Reserva Alvarinho (grapes from Pinto Bandeira) is crisp, peachy and mineral. Oak staves are used for five months, translating into very discreet vanilla and spice. Very faithful to the variety, this is a genuine bargain. Acordes Gran Reserva Chardonnay comes from the ENTAV-INRA 95 high-quality clone. After spending eight months in new French oak barrels, the wine is golden, savoury, ripe and well balanced. Vinícola Garibaldi's Marselan (Campanha Gaúcha grapes) is ripe, floral, smoky and fresh, with soft tannins. Acordes Merlot is ageworthy: concentrated, with good acidity and a stout tannic structure. After remaining for 18 months in French and American oak, it is full of vanilla and coconut.

Prosecco Brut is floral, fruity, creamy and so fresh; at 12 grams per litre residual sugar, it is light and delicious. Garibaldi sparkling Chardonnay (Charmat method) Brut has the same sugar level, is overtly fruity and has a good varietal character. Vinícola Garibaldi's Nature Blanc de Blancs is also Charmat, but with 12-month autolysis in tanks, from base wines with less acidity than those destined for products with higher sugar levels; it is bone dry and sharp. Vinícola Garibaldi's Rosé is made in a similar way but now uses Pinot Noir; it displays ripe but fresh red berries amidst very light autolytic aromas. Traditional method sparklers are a minor fraction of their production; up to 2018, they were finished by Geisse, but now the whole process happens at the Cooperative. Acordes Extra-Brut, predominately Chardonnay (24-month autolysis), has good ripe fruit mixed with brioche and patisserie; it is fine and elegant. The recently launched Sur Lie, undisgorged, is so savoury, bready, complex and long.

Vinícola Don Guerino ♀

Alto Feliz (Serra Gaúcha)

www.donguerino.com.br

Members of the Motter family (from Trentino) have been at Serra Gaúcha since the 1880s. In the 2000s, Osvaldo and Salete Motter and their sons, Bruno (who graduated in oenology at Mendoza), Maicon and Lucas, bought land at Alto Feliz and started their winery. It is named after Osvaldo's father, Guerino Motter, who made and sold wine in bulk in the 1970s and founded another winery, Casa Motter (in Caxias do Sul). Don Guerino owns 60 hectares of vineyards, planted at 450 metres on red, iron-rich, clayey soil. Their modern winery was finished in 2007 and refurbished in 2018. Earthwaren amphorae are a part of their wine paraphernalia. Several lines of wines are made, also using bought grapes (for example, from Campanha Gaúcha). Bruno Motter directs the winemaking, Maicon oversees administrative affairs, and Lucas, chef and sommelier, takes care of the restaurant and wine bar. Oenotourism is strong, with several experiences on offer. Booking is not required for simple tastings (closed on Sundays), but tours, tastings and the restaurant (weekends only) should be booked in advance.

Monteolivo Alvarinho is intensely aromatic, bringing ripe peach, citrus and mineral notes. It is crisp and textural, with some vanilla hints and a saline finish, so remains true to this high-quality variety. The three following reds share some common traits: a deep purple colour, perfectly ripe fruit, high alcohol and a strong concentration of flavours. Terroir Selection Malbec Vintage has sweet plums, violets, chocolate and vanilla. It is full bodied and has voluminous but soft tannins. Le Franc Cabernet Franc brings ripe cassis and blackberries amidst discreet hints of capsicum and pencil shavings. Its fresh acidity pairs well with a sturdy but fine tannic structure; this is a big, ripe Cabernet Franc. Cemento is a red blend (Cabernet Franc, Malbec, Tannat) and aged 12 months in concrete eggs. Black fruit, dust, earth and violets form its complex palette of flavours. Its structure is solid: high alcohol, great concentration and sinewy tannins allow it to age well. Traços is an expensive and complex blend of five red varieties, predominately Tannat and Teroldego, aged for 14 months in several sizes of French oak foudres and barrels. Cassis, blackberry and hints of herbs and earth are well integrated into deftly managed oak aromas of vanilla, cedar and toast. The wine has a long length and, again, will reward cellaring.

The unusual Brut Rosé is made, using the Charmat method, from Malbec only. It brings fresh plums and red berries, keeping some of Malbec's varietal traits. It is well structured and has a drying and fresh finish, with a slight tannic bite, being a very gastronomic wine.

Vinícola Mena Kaho ♀

Bento Gonçalves

www.menakaho.com.br/

Despite the exotic name, reminiscent of the Maori language, this is another winery of Italian descent: the Roman family has used the Mena Kaho nickname since the seventeenth century. Members of this clan migrated to Brazil during the late nineteenth century, establishing themselves at the very place where the present winery exists. Here, they restored a very old, historic *casarão* (big house), which includes good oenotouristic facilities (including a guest house). Total annual production is 80,000 bottles, including both *vinhos de mesa* and *vinhos finos* (some organic). Visitors are welcome – the winery is part of the tourist route *Cantinas Históricas*. Booking in advance is required.

Di Dio (80 per cent Rebo, plus Merlot) is deep ruby and offers vanilla, cedar, ripe black fruit and chocolate. It is crunchy, rich, full bodied and concentrated in flavour, having a firm but fine tannic structure, which allows it to age gracefully. Brut Riesling (Itálico), made using the traditional method (12-month autolysis), has fresh citrus and green apple, moderate autolytic flavours, and is crisp, fruity and lemony.

Casa Motter ♀

Caxias do Sul

www.casamotter.com.br/

Guerino Motter founded this winery in 1974. Expanded in 1998 and 2017, it still belongs to the Motters. Two generations work here, with oenologist Michel Motter overseeing the winemaking. Their annual production of *vinhos finos* is 100,000 bottles. Grapes from Campanha Gaúcha and Serra do Sudeste are also used, besides those from Serra Gaúcha. The winery is located within beautiful surroundings at the *Estrada Municipal do Vinho* (City Wine Road) of Caxias. You can taste the wines at their shop and wine bar (open Monday to Friday, and at weekends by reservation).

Valentino Motter Chardonnay Reserva is ripe, well balanced and textured, with clear, but not intrusive, vanilla and spice from six months in second-use French oak barriques. Valentino Motter Syrah Reserva (grapes from Serra do Sudeste) is dark, very ripe and peppery, with hints of bacon; after 12 months in oak, there is good integration of the wood and other flavours; it finishes dry and savoury. Roque Motter Tannat is a big wine: inky, fresh, full bodied and savoury, with a muscular tannic structure and 14% abv; it will age very well. Nobre Brut Charmat, made from 100 per cent Chardonnay, is fresh, fruity and easy going.

Casa Pedrucci Espumantes Clássicos 🍷

Garibaldi

www.casapedrucci.com.br/

Gilberto Pedrucci is considered an important maker of Brazilian sparkling wines. He has worked at both Cave Geisse and Peterlongo. At the latter, he was instrumental in reviving the decaying business and earning prizes for their products. Besides this, he has also presided over the Brazilian Association of Oenology and other important associations. Gilberto started his winery, mainly dedicated to sparklers, in 2001 when he bought a 130-year-old, stone-built pavilion in a bucolic, rural location at Garibaldi. It was refurbished and equipped and now produces his multi-prized Charmat, Asti-like, and traditional method sparkling wines. The base wines, with original blends, are made in association with other wineries from selected bought grapes. Annual production is 60,000 bottles, and the quality is always very high due to his exacting standards and expert craftsmanship. Visitors can enjoy three different types of tastings (booking required).

Guilherme, Gilberto's son, was my host when I visited to taste some of their sparklers. Reserva Nature (0.5 grams per litre residual sugar), made from Chardonnay, Pinot Noir and Riesling Itálico, offers very good ripe fruit (citrus, pear) and an evident autolytic character (24-month autolysis). It is delicate, crisp and elegant. Extra-Brut comes from the same blend, albeit with more Riesling, having the same autolytic period. Still very dry (4.5 grams per litre), it is steely, fine and elegant. Elegance and finesse, by the way, are hallmarks of Pedrucci's wines. Fatto a Mano Sur Lie Rosé is pale pink, strongly autolytic, savoury, dense and full. Guilherme suggests drinking this in two stages. First, leave the bottle upright, and the lees will collect at the bottom; pour the clear wine and enjoy it. Second, mixing the lees will make the wine hazy; you can then savour its structure and complexity. Millésime Brut (8 grams of sugar per litre) is also made from the same trio of grapes, but the Chardonnay base wine spends four months in oak. It is golden, well structured, complex (there are so many layers) and long – a memorable sparkling wine!

Vinícola Peterlongo ♀

Garibaldi

www.peterlongo.com.br

This historic winery was founded in 1915 at Garibaldi by Manoel Peterlongo Filho, who named it Estabelecimento Vinícola Armando Peterlongo. The name honoured his only son (a brother to nine sisters), Armando, who took over in 1924 when the family's patriarch passed away. He built a new winery with an underground cellar, always aimed at making sparkling wines. As Manoel started to use the name 'Champagne' on his labels as early as 1915, the Brazilian Supreme Court, in 1974, authorized the winery to go on doing so for some products. Armando died suddenly in 1966 while visiting Italy – his first (and last) trip to Europe. The winery was sold by the Peterlongo family in 2001 to Luiz Carlos Sella and Adilson Luiz Bohatczuk. Today, they produce predominately (95 per cent) sparkling wines, using grapes both from the Serra Gaúcha area and outside it. Annual production can reach 300,000 bottles under the guidance of oenologist Gabriel Carissimi. The historic, stone, castle-like building and the cave, with its small museum, make for an immensely successful and interesting visit. The guided tour (available seven days a week) includes a tasting (booking required).

Armando Memória Chardonnay (grapes from Serra do Sudeste) stays (half the wine) for six months in French and American used oak barrels, which impart clear notes of vanilla, coconut and spice. It is well balanced, ripe and textural. Armando Memória Signature Touriga Nacional (Campanha Gaúcha) brings this variety's well-known aromas of violets, ripe blackberry and mandarin; it is fresh and elegant, with fine tannins. Armando Winemaker Merlot (Serra do Sudeste) is ripe and plummy, with a solid structure of acidity and tannins.

Prosecco Brut is, as expected, fresh, fruity and floral. Brut Chardonnay stays in the tank with its lees (and is constantly agitated) for a whole year (long Charmat process). It is evidently fruity, but autolytic notes of caramel and toast are also present. Privilege Extra-Brut (Chardonnay, Pinot Noir) is fruity, floral, ripe and fresh, with moderate bready notes from at least one year with lees. Champagne Elegance Nature Chardonnay has a portion of the base wines (15 per cent) ageing in French oak. After a 36-month autolysis, it combines ripe fruit with crisp acidity, being bone dry, savoury and saline.

Vinícola Pinhal Alto ♀

São Valentim do Sul

www.vinicolapinhalalto.com.br/

Pinhal Alto has grown vines for over 30 years, but wine production and sales only started in the mid-2000s. Their products, which include grape juice and spirits, are crafted by oenologist Lucas Fardo from 6 hectares of vineyards planted at an altitude of 550 metres. They welcome visitors seven days a week. Booking is necessary for large groups.

Trebbiano Toscano is pale, crisp, citric and simple, highly reminiscent of a good Frascati. Retratos Malbec is ripe, mouth-watering and clean, with slight vanilla and cedar from 12 months in used French oak barrels. Retratos Marselan also spends the same time in oak; it shows ripe black fruit and has a firm structure of acidity and tannins; it will age well. Super-premium Vestígios Ancellotta has a somewhat surprisingly (for this variety) potent tannic structure; it is ripe and quite oaky from one year in American oak, a style prized by many consumers. Vestígios Corte (luxury price level), a blend of Cabernet Sauvignon, Merlot and Alicante Bouschet, is a very ripe, complex, full-bodied wine boasting a sinewy structure; it undergoes a 15-month maturation in new French and American oak; good for cellaring.

Vinícola Dal Pizzol ♀

Bento Gonçalves

www.dalpizzol.com.br/

Atílio Dal Pizzol, a descendant of Italian immigrants who arrived at Serra Gaúcha in 1878, founded the former Vinícola Monte Lemos, today Dal Pizzol, in 1974, together with sons Antonio (who died in 2021), Valter, Valdair and Rinaldo. Rinaldo Dal Pizzol has been a very important influence on Brazilian wine. He presided over União Brasileira de Vitivinicultura (UVIBRA) – the Brazilian Viniviticulture Union – managed several important wine firms, and, as a scholar, wrote (together with Sérgio Inglez de Sousa) the excellent three-volume book on the history of wines from Rio Grande do Sul, *Memórias do Vinho Gaúcho*.

Dal Pizzol has made only *vinhos finos* from the start. They buy all their grapes from selected and closely supervised growers of several Rio Grande do Sul origins. The oenologists Dirceu Scottá (who entered the firm when he was 17 years old) and Marcos Zonta craft about 250,000 bottles of wine and juice yearly. Vinícola Dal Pizzol has a beautiful thematic park and a strong focus on oenotourism. Besides a wine museum, they also carefully maintain the *Vinhedo do Mundo* (World Vineyard), which started in 2005. This is a live ampelographic collection of 400 planted grape varieties from 35 countries. Several different types of tastings (including blind) are available, as well as picnics, a garden experience, or tasting by the fireside during winter (it can be chilly here). They are open seven days a week (booking advised).

Privatum Trebbiano Toscano is a good example of how the judicious use of oak can benefit a neutral variety. After six months in French oak, the wine gains colour and flavours of vanilla, spice, nuts and some savouriness, keeping a citric, crisp acidity.

Cabernet Franc shows ripe raspberry and plums, capsicum and pencil shavings; it is fresh, youthful and varietally true. Privatum Ancellotta showcases ripe blackberries and plums, hints of earth, good acidity and soft, caressing tannins; it is rich, juicy and food friendly. Privatum Touriga Nacional is a rare example of unoaked wine from this noble variety; ripe black fruit, violets and hints of mandarin and earth reveal themselves easily. Its high-quality tannins are very fine and elegant, as is the wine. 45 Anos, a blend of Marselan, Petit Verdot and Alicante Bouschet from Serra Gaúcha and Campanha Gaúcha, has a deep ruby colour and intense aromas of ripe black fruit, spice, toast and some leather. The tannins are ripe, and the wine, like the former, is rich and juicy; however, it has more structure and complexity. Vinum Mundi, their top blend of two vintages, is a field blend of 286 varieties from their World Vineyard, spending 12 months in new French oak barrels. It is inky and displays intense vanilla, cedar, ripe black fruit, tobacco, chocolate, leather and spice. The flavours are concentrated, and this great wine is full, rich, well structured, layered, complex and ageworthy.

Vinícola Salton ♀

Bento Gonçalves (Tuiuty district)
www.salton.com.br

This is one of the oldest Brazilian wineries, founded in 1910 by seven sons of the Italian immigrant Antonio Domenico Salton, who, up until then, vinified his grapes informally. Although now a publicly traded company, the Saltons, now in the fourth generation, continue as its controllers. They expanded commercially to São Paulo in 1948. One of the company's most successful products, the Presidente brandy, continues to be produced there. They started making *vinhos finos* in 1999 and production increased quickly. This demanded an entirely new industrial facility, which was completed in 2004 at Tuiuty (Bento Gonçalves), with huge installations, shown below. From 2005 onwards, they have been a national leader in sparkling wine sales. They expanded to Campanha Gaúcha in 2012–2014, owning 110 hectares of vineyards in this region. Salton exports 800,000 bottles of sparklers annually to 25 countries; still wines included, exports reach one million bottles.

Salton have a large and diverse portfolio. They sold 24.5 million bottles in 2022 (still and sparkling wines, plus non-alcoholic beverages), with a total value of just a little less than US$ 100 million. *Vinhos finos* (still and sparkling) have an annual production of 15 million bottles. The most significant part, by far, is comprised of Charmat-method sparklers, which are sold in all the country's supermarkets. Their Tuiuty winery has ample oenotouristic facilities, offering several categories of tastings and guided tours, with or without a traditional meal. Besides this, they have recently added a restaurant, *Casa di Pasto,* at Caminhos de Pedra, where tastings, with or without platters, are offered. Enoteca Família Salton, where their wines can be bought or tasted, is conveniently located in São Paulo, Brazil's largest city (they also offer courses and other activities there). Reservations are required for most oenotouristic activities.

At one of Salton's tasting rooms, oenologist André Peres Jr accompanied me to taste some of their products. Salton Brut, their sales

Salton's impressive ensemble of Charmat autoclaves

champion (three million bottles a year), is made by a short Charmat method from Trebbiano, Glera and Chardonnay. It is fruity, fresh and simple, with perceptible residual sugar (14 grams per litre). Salton Ouro Extra-Brut (6–7 grams per litre), crafted by a longer Charmat process (at least six months of autolysis) from Chardonnay, Pinot Noir and sometimes Riesling Itálico, is also clearly fruity, but some slight autolytic aromas appear.

Évidence is their traditional method line. Rosé (Chardonnay, Pinot), 24-month autolysis, is made from 30–50 per cent reserve wines, exhibiting a mix of ripe red berries and bread/brioche. Domenico (Campanha Gaúcha) is crafted from Marselan (unoaked, for fruit) and a smaller proportion of Tannat (oaked, for structure). Still youthful, it is a good marriage of ripe fruit and a robust tannic framework; it will age well. Talento (also Campanha Gaúcha), a Bordeaux blend plus Tannat (not co-fermented) spends 12 months in new French Nadalié oak; it is a solid wine in structure and flavours; again one for cellaring.

Vinícola Sotterrani ♀

Bento Gonçalves
www.sotterrani.com/

Guilherme Menezes, an oenologist, founded this garage winery in the subsoil of a house in Bento Gonçalves. He made his first wine in 2005, but only as a hobby. The commercial winery was opened in 2020 and now occupies more space. He buys grapes from several origins, crafting micro-lots of several wines. The total annual production is 3,000 bottles. Visitors can have a guided tasting with the owner (book first).

Chardonnay (Serra do Sudeste) ferments and matures in new French oak barrels. Not undergoing malolactic fermentation, it is crisp and has a good structure (slightly astringent); the ripe fruit is not overwhelmed by the evident oak. Orange Riesling Itálico (Serra Gaúcha), after 30-day skin contact and 30 months in used American oak, is amber in colour, with an agreeable tannic grip and overt oak character.

Ciclos Cabernet Sauvignon (Serra do Sudeste) has ripe cassis and some capsicum; it is fresh and easy drinking. Ciclos Marselan (Pinto Bandeira) is ripe, full of plums and blackberries, having a good tannic structure. Sotterrani Tempranillo (Serra do Sudeste) has a clear varietal character, with ripe red berries, some earth and tobacco, and soft tannins; all are well integrated with vanilla and spice from used French oak. Sotterrani Tannat (Serra Gaúcha) is unoaked, with a deep colour, and shows ripe cassis and plums, plus leather and earth, amidst a solid tannic structure. It is hard to find an unoaked Tannat of this quality. Sotterrani Merlot (Serra Gaúcha) spends two years in French oak barrels, which is consistent with its strong tannic structure; it is quite Bordeaux-like.

Extra-Brut Riesling Itálico, after 36-month autolysis, is citric, crisp and elegant, with clear yeast and dough.

Atelier Tormentas

Canela

www.tormentas.com.br

Gramado and its twin town, Canela, are two of the most sought-after tourist destinations in Rio Grande do Sul – but not exactly for vinous reasons, despite being only a short distance (about 130 kilometres) from Bento Gonçalves. It was there, however, that Maurício Heller Dani, who nicknamed himself Marco Danielle, established this artisanal, small-batch winery inspired by the *Vin de Garage* model and the natural wine movement. With his wife, Érica Mazziero, he buys grapes (from conventional viticulture) and craft wines with minimal intervention (spontaneous fermentation, unfiltered, not stabilized, no additions except low amounts of sulphur dioxide).

Many of the red wines are made by semi-carbonic (whole-cluster) maceration and foot treading. Although the variety of the small batches is very large, Marco admits that he prefers to work with those varieties that seem more akin to his approach to winemaking, such as Pinot Noir, Gamay, Cabernet Franc and Nebbiolo. This appears to be the reason behind some lack of consistency in their blended wines, which vary greatly in composition and style according to different vintages, as Marco himself pointed out. The only sales channel is their website. Their bottles can be found on the wine lists of several prestige Brazilian restaurants.

Fulvia Pinot Noir 2018 (Serra do Sudeste) is garnet-coloured, mixing ripe red fruit with tertiary notes (leather, undergrowth) and vanilla and toast from 18 months in oak barrels. It is complex, layered and savoury. Cabernet Franc (from Campos de Cima da Serra, harvested late, and Campanha Gaúcha, harvested early) has a highly typical ensemble of flavours: raspberry, cassis, pencil shavings, capsicum, minerality and some chalky notes. It is ripe and fresh, with a firm tannic structure, allowing it to gain tertiary complexity with bottle ageing. It is a very savoury and gastronomic wine. Nebbiolo (Serra do Sudeste) also has a great varietal typicity: light colour, highly aromatic and with an intriguing intensity of ripe red berries, roses, earth and vanilla. Its acidity is high and the tannins solid and dry. This complex, balanced, high-quality wine can age for many years.

Valparaiso Vinhos e Vinhedos ♀

Barão

www.valparaisors.com.br

This property was purchased by the oenologist Arnaldo Argenta in 2006. Once (in the 1970s) considered the largest continuous vineyard in Brazil (with 42 hectares of table grapes), it has been revitalized and replanted, boasting a totally refurbished winery. They grow nine *vinifera* varieties, focusing on Italian cultivars. The vines are protected by plastic sheets, which help promote better maturation and allow for fewer chemical inputs. No grapes are bought. Annual production is 30,000 bottles. Arnaldo leads the work together with his daughter Naiana. Their philosophy is to craft natural wines, so they may well be the largest Brazilian producer of this type of wine. Some unusual offerings exist, such as Garganega, Rondinella and Torrontés. Visitors are welcome to tour and taste (book in advance first).

Vitale Garganega, spontaneously fermented, is golden. It displays ripe peach and pear, plus hints of citrus, honey and nuts. The wine is bone dry, crisp and textural, with a slightly bitter bite on the finish. Naturo Torrontés (spontaneously fermented) is strongly aromatic (jasmine, papaya, lavender), fresh, textural and mouth coating. It is lengthy and very faithful to the variety. Naturo Nebbiolo has a pale ruby colour, is overt in the nose, with ripe strawberries, roses and some Port-like aromas. Its acidity is high and the tannins are sturdy, albeit fine; the wine is true to this noble variety.

Vivente Vinhos Vivos

Colinas

www.vivente.bio

Although the small town of Colinas is not officially within Serra Gaúcha, it is so close that this winery is listed here. The owners, Diego Cartier (musician) and Micael Eckert (architect), were formerly lovers of Lembic (spontaneous fermentation) beers. Diego was, indeed, a 'beer hunter'. However, during his trips to Europe, he grew to admire wine, especially natural wines from Jura and Loire. The partners, sharing a desire to make truly natural wines, founded the winery in 2018, opting to have a biodynamic vineyard. They have earned Demeter certification for their vineyard, which is small (1 hectare of Pinot Noir and Riesling). They also buy grapes from Campos de Cima da Serra and Serra do Sudeste vineyards, which are either organic or in the process of gaining biodynamic certification. Vivente winery produces 22,000 bottles a year, which are all natural or low-intervention wines made through spontaneous fermentation. They want their wines to be fruit-focused, fluid and food friendly. Some have already earned national prizes. About 70 per cent of their wines are still, the balance being sparklers. They have succeeded in placing their products at top Michelin-starred Brazilian restaurants, such as Oteque, DOM, Mani, Lasai, Tuju and Casa do Porco. There is no oenotourism at the present time.

Sauvignon Blanc, a bit hazy (unfiltered), is a complex, savoury rendition of this characterful variety; with a tangy acidity, it is bone dry and mineral, but with ripe fruit and a long, drying finish. Orange Sauvignon Blanc (one month with skins) is golden and hazy, not dominated by this distinctive variety's usual aromas, but rather bringing chamomile and hints of ginger and orange; it is tangy, with some phenolic grip, textural, savoury and long.

The Chardonnays vary significantly from vintage to vintage, as is to be expected from this winery's approach. Their 2021 is saline and savoury, with ripe pear, clear minerality and crisp acidity; it is satisfactory, long and complex. 2022 is so diverse: golden, very honeyed and toasty, ripe, intensely savoury and very long, with attenuated varietal character, but so flavoursome. A very interesting product is the blend of Chardonnay and Moscato Antigo (Moscato Branco): golden, a bit hazy, perfumed (white flowers, lychee, ripe apple, pineapple), soft, with good weight in the mouth.

Rosé from Pinot Noir (80 per cent) and Cabernet Franc is dark pink, brimming with ripe red fruit, complex with savouriness and a saline touch, so fresh and intense, asking to be drunk with good food. Pinot Noir exudes ripe red fruit with great purity amidst hints of earth; it has a clear, mouth-watering acidity and is savoury, with gentle tannins. Cabernet Franc is a true gem: high varietal typicity, with lots of pencil shavings, capsicum and ripe blackcurrant, tingling acidity and high savouriness. Vivente da Francisca, labelled Blanc de Noir (Pinot), is, in fact, a very pale onion-skin rosé; this ancestral method sparkler, although having a lower pressure than traditional method examples, is fizzy and bone dry, with the proverbial savouriness of Vivente's wines. It combines fresh and ripe red fruit with moderate autolysis and petrichor notes.

Also in Serra Gaúcha

- Vitivinícola Don Affonso, Caxias do Sul (www.donaffonso.com.br)
- Vinícola Arbugeri, Caxias do Sul (vinicolaarbugeri.com.br/)
- Área 15, Bento Gonçalves (vinicolaarea15.com.br/loja-virtual)
- Artse Vinhos, Caixias do Sul (www.artsevinhos.com.br)
- Audace Wine, Bento Gonçalves (www.audacewine.com)
- Berkano Premium Wines, Bento Gonçalves (www.berkano.com.br/)
- Orgalindo Bettú Vinhos Nobres (WhatsApp (+55) 54 99900 2003)
- Vinhos Bettú, Garibaldi (vinhosbettu.com.br/)
- Quinta Don Bonifácio, Garibaldi (contato@quintadonbonifacio.com.br)
- Vinícola Buffon, Bento Gonçalves (www.vinicolabuffon.com.br/)
- Vinícola La Cantina, Garibaldi (www.lacantina.com.br)
- Cão Perdigueiro, Caixias do Sul (@caoperdigueiro)
- Catafesta Indústria De Vinhos, São Marcos (administrativo@catafesta.com.br)
- Cheti, headquarters in Brasília, DF (www.cheti.com.br)
- Vinhos D'Motter (Irmãos Motter), Caxias do Sul (dmotter@vinhosdmotter.com.br)
- Casa Dorigon, Bento Gonçalves (www.casadorigon.com.br/)
- Cave dos Frades, Vila Flores (comercial@cavedosfrades.com.br)
- Lote Frighetto, Caixias do Sul (@lotefrighetto)
- Garbo Enologia Criativa, Bento Gonçalves (garboenologiacriativa.com.br/)
- Espumantes Georges Aubert, Garibaldi (loja.espumantesgeorgesaubert.com.br/)
- Vinícola Gheller, Guaporé (vinicolagheller.lojaintegrada.com.br/)
- Vinícola Dom Hermínio, Caxias do Sul (diego@domherminio.com.br)
- Hex Von Wein, Picada Café (www.hexvonwein.com.br)
- Inclusive Wine, headquarters in Porto Alegre (www.inclusivewine.com.br)

- Vinícola Jolimont, Canela (www.vinicolajolimont.com.br)
- Likewine, headquarters in Belo Horizonte, MG (www.likewinestore.com)
- Lovara Vinhas e Vinhos, Bento Gonçalves (vinicolalovara.com/)
- Vinícola Lovatel, Bento Gonçalves (www.vinicolalovatel.com.br)
- Vinícola Lugares, Carlos Barbosa (www.vinicolalugares.com.br/)
- Machado & Crivelari, Garibaldi (sac@twpbusiness.com.br)
- Vinícola Marson, Cotiporã (www.vinicolamarson.com.br/)
- Vinhos Don Miguel, Garibaldi (vinicola@donmiguel.com.br)
- Casa Muterle, Antonio Prado (contato@casamuterle.com.br)
- Casa Olivo 1033, Antonio Prado (www.casaolivo1033.com.br)
- Vinhos Penzo, São Valentim do Sul (@flavioluizpenzo)
- Petronius Beverages, Caixias do Sul (contato@petroniusbev.com.br)
- Casa Possamai, Bento Gonçalves (www.casapossamai.com.br/)
- Vinícola Casa Postal, Bento Gonçalves (casapostal@casapostal.com.br)
- Cave di Pozza, Caxias do Sul (www.cavedipozza.com.br)
- Primo Fior, Antonio Prado (@vinhosprimofior)
- Quinta do Lobo Vinhos Autorais, Bento Gonçalves (@quintadolobo)
- Vinícola Ravanello, Gramado (www.vinicolaravanello.com.br)
- Adega Refinaria, Bento Gonçalves (@adegarefinariaterroirsdobrasil)
- Vinhos Rotava/Vinícola Monte Rosário (vinicolarotava@gmail.com)
- Vinícola Salvati & Sirena, Bento Gonçalves (salvatisirena.com.br/)
- Vinhos Sanabria, headquarters in Brasília, DF (www.vinhossanabria.com.br/sobre)
- Vinícola Monte Sant'ana, São Marcos (www.montesantana.com.br)
- Vinícola Santini, Caxias do Sul (www.vinicolasantini.com/)
- Casa Seganfredo, Gramado (www.casaseganfredo.com.br)
- Vinícola Sinuelo, São Marcos (adegasinuelo@yahoo.com.br)
- Vinha Solo, Caxias do Sul (www.vinhasolo.com.br/)
- Vinícola Stopassola, Gramado (www.vinicolastopassola.com.br)
- Cantina Tonet, Caxias do Sul (www.cantinatonet.com.br)
- Vaccaro Vinhos e Espumantes, Garibaldi (vinhosvaccaro.com.br/)
- Verace Vinhos e Espumantes, Bento Gonçalves (sac@vinoverace.com.br)
- Vistamontes Vinícola, Bento Gonçalves (www.vistamontes.com.br)
- Yoo Wines, Caixias do Sul (yoo-wines.zerofila.com.br/)
- Vinícola Zanella, Antonio Prado (www.vinicolazanella.com.br)
- Vinhos Zanrosso, Caxias do Sul (vinhoszanrosso.com.br/)

9

OTHER AREAS OF RIO GRANDE DO SUL

CAMPANHA GAÚCHA

While Serra Gaúcha is a hilly region at altitude, with steep inclinations, a good deal of woodland and plenty of rain, Campanha Gaúcha is quite different – a flatter terrain, lower lying, and with less rain and scarce forests. Here we are in the *pampas* (one of the Brazilian biomes), which is very flat, or among *coxilhas* (rolling hills). Etymologically, the term *campanha* has the same origin and meaning as *Champagne* (the region), from the Latin *campania* for large, open expanses with very few trees. The word *pampa*, of Quechua origin, means the same. Historically used as grazing fields for cows and sheep (which continues successfully), this is, indeed, the land of large farms, the *estâncias*, traditional *gaúchos*, *crioulo* horses, open-air, rustic *churrasco*, bitter *chimarrão*, cultural traditions, glorious sunsets, hot summers and cold winters.

A brief history

Half of Campanha Gaúcha's borders are international – Argentina to the west and Uruguay to the south. Here, Portuguese-speaking Brazil meets its Spanish-speaking neighbours; the local dialect and accent reflect this proximity. Campanha is the largest part of the region known locally as *Fronteira*, or frontier, and is marked by a fearsome history of revolutions and fights. The oldest town in Rio Grande do Sul, São Borja, was founded by the Jesuits in 1682 as a part of the Missions (or *reduções*) and played an important role in primitive viticulture in Brazil (see History of wine in Brazil, page 13). Although legally not a part of the IP Campanha Gaúcha, it is very close and belongs to the *Fronteira*. Here, the most famous Brazilian politician ever, Getúlio Vargas, long-term president (and then dictator) of the country was born. He took his own life in 1954. São Borja was also the hometown of another president, João Goulart, who was was deposed by the military in 1964. Unlucky, both.

As we've already seen, wine was produced in Campanha Gaúcha by the Jesuits in the seventeeth century and then by the Portuguese in the eighteenth century. After some time, due to Uruguayan influence just across the border, from 1880 onwards, successful vineyards were established in some frontier towns, all trained/trellised using vertical systems. The first registered winery in Brazil was established at Candiota in 1892. Although the most extensive vineyards in Rio Grande do Sul were, briefly (1890–1910) those of Campanha Gaúcha, the *labrusca*-based wines from Serra Gaúcha overtook them and viticulture was almost totally abandoned in the region.

A much more recent wine history started in the 1970s. The renowned oenologist Harold P. Olmo (UC Davis) visited Rio Grande do Sul in 1972 and 1973 after an invitation from the Californian winery Almadén (founded in 1852 and then a part of National Distillers). This process was helped by Carlos Daudt, a Brazilian postgraduate student of Olmo's at Davis. Although retired from Santa Maria University, Daudt is alive and well, with a vineyard in Santa Maria and making his wines at nearby Velho Amâncio.

Almadén acquired land in Campanha Gaúcha (a total of 63 hectares) and imported 65,000 Californian vines, planting and trying many different cultivars and rootstocks. An evaluation was made by a team of Brazilian oenologists led by Antonio Santin, with the best-performing cultivars being selected, as well as the preferred rootstock, SO4. Almadén, then, bought much more land at Sant'Ana do Livramento (1,200 hectares), planting extensive vineyards. Olmo continued to come here yearly until 1988. The first wines were commercially launched in 1984.

Almadén was bought by Seagram in 1989, and the first varietals appeared in 1993. In 2001, Seagram sold the land, winery and brands in Brazil to Pernod Ricard. In 2009, Almadén became a part of the Miolo Wine Group – which has another important property at Candiota, also within Campanha Gaúcha. The great success of Almadén attracted other producers (such as Salton in 1995, as well as local landowners), with significant growth seen in the 2000s. The process continued in 2010 with the establishment of a producers' association, *Associação Vinhos da Campanha* (www.vinhosdacampanha.com.br/) – no acronyms here, despite the Brazilian fondness for them – culminating with the IP status being granted in 2020. This IP was born from the coordinated work of no less than 194 professionals of all levels, integrating several universities and, again, under the invaluable leadership of Embrapa.

Distances here are much greater than in Serra Gaúcha. If one drives from Candiota, in the extreme east of Campanha Gaúcha, to Uruguaiana, in the extreme west, the distance by road is 441 kilometres. But note: to drive from Porto Alegre, the state capital and main airport, to Candiota, adds another 402 kilometres. Take your time and break up your trip, knowing that you can first visit vineyards and wineries at Bagé/Candiota, and then, one or two days later, at Sant'Ana do Livramento, 162 kilometres to the west.

The most important Campanha Gaúcha cities are as follows:

- Bagé and Uruguaiana had the same population in 2022: around 117,000 inhabitants. Bagé is well known for promoting the International Churrasco Feast and horse-raising. The best stud farms in Brazil are here, especially for English thoroughbred horses. It is very close to Candiota and Miolo's Seival vineyards and winery. The Dom Diogo de Souza Museum, exhibiting many items that illustrate the history of Rio Grande do Sul and the *Fronteira*, can be found in a beautiful nineteenth-century building, a former hospital built by the Sociedade Beneficente Portuguesa (Portuguese Beneficent Society). Bagé has ample, well-planned avenues and streets and is a convenient location for visiting wineries at nearby Dom Pedrito.
- Uruguaiana has few vineyards, but it is an interesting place to visit on the Uruguay River. Cross it through the Getúlio Vargas (you will find his name at countless places in Brazil) International Bridge, and you'll be in Paso de los Libres, Argentina, despite the river's name. But, having a total area of 5,700 square kilometres, Uruguaiana also borders Uruguay. A large rice producer, the city is also important for livestock and various export businesses. This is a good place for shopping, especially at duty-free shops (where tax is lower) on either side of the border.
- Sant'Ana do Livramento (population 84,421) is another frontier town bordering Uruguay. Here, you do not even need to cross a river,

but rather a street, to be at Rivera, in Uruguay. Again, it is a good place for shopping. This is the seat of Almadén, the largest vineyard and winery in Campanha Gaúcha, and Cordilheira de Sant'Ana, another pioneer wine producer.

Campanha Gaúcha is the second-largest wine region in Rio Grande do Sul – in volume, not in surface area. In terms of the latter, it is the biggest, with 44,365 square kilometres and 14 townships.

Climate and soils

Campanha Gaúcha is Brazil's southernmost wine region, located between the parallels 29°S and 32°S. Latitude, here, compensates for lower altitudes (100–360 metres). Generally, soils are highly weathered, texturally sandy and slightly acidic, with good drainage, low organic matter content and low fertility. However, this is just a generalization, as the region is large enough to show an ample variety of soil types. The most frequent SiBCS soil classes are *neossolos, planossolos* and *chernossolos*. Erosion can be a problem despite the flat relief. Inter-row planting is invaluable. According to Köppen's classification, the climate is Cfa (subtropical). According to the MCC system, it is HI+2 (warm), DI-1 (sub-humid) and CI-1 (temperate nights). Some subregions, however, are drier, with DI up to +1. There is plenty of sunlight at the end of the

Campanha Gaúcha's open expanses and vines

growing season: up to 15 hours a day. This, plus the generally moderate (compared to Serra Gaúcha) rainfall (average 1,475 millimetres per year, but lower from November to January), ensures complete grape ripening. There are enough hours of cold to allow complete dormancy of most vines at Sant'Ana do Livramento and Bagé; at Uruguaiana, however, not all varieties achieve this. Spring frosts and hail are not infrequent. As usual, fungal diseases (downy mildew, cluster rots, anthracnose, excoriosis, powdery mildew) are the main threats. Generally speaking, climatic conditions in Campanha Gaúcha are better for vine growing than in Serra Gaúcha: the plants are healthier, fewer treatments are required, vines live longer and fruit quality is superior.

Planted areas and wine types

The total planted area at Campanha Gaúcha in 2015 was 1,560 hectares, all *vinifera* vines. SIVIBE statistics are still incomplete; hence, the numbers for 2015 are used here. The most planted varieties, in decreasing order, were Cabernet Sauvignon (309 hectares), Chardonnay (286), Tannat (164), Merlot (144), Pinot Noir (119), Sauvignon Blanc (82), Riesling Itálico (58), Cabernet Franc (49), Gewurztraminer (28), Pinotage (24), Viognier (24), Tempranillo (23), Trebbiano (22), Alicante Bouschet (20), Moscato Branco (20), Chenin Blanc (20) and Pinot Gris (18). With 36 different cultivars planted, many others exist, including Alvarinho, Ancellotta, Arinarnoa, Colombard, Flora, Gamay, Malbec, Marselan, Petit Verdot, Riesling, Semillon, Syrah and Touriga Nacional.

According to the producers' association, Campanha Gaúcha crafts 31 per cent of all *vinhos finos* made in Brazil. Whereas many believe that Serra Gaúcha excels in sparkling wines as a speciality, there is, as yet, no given wine type associated with Campanha Gaúcha. Here, wines of all colours, both still and sparkling, are made. A warmer, drier climate explains why the local wines have more colour, alcohol, body and intensity of aromas and flavours than their Serra counterparts. Despite the modest production volumes, Gewurztraminer wines are, as expected, very aromatic and true to the variety, but in a lighter, fresher way than the dense Alsatian style. Cabernet Sauvignon does very well here, as its wines offer typicity, fruit and structure. Tannats are among the best in Brazil, on a par with those from Uruguay, especially when made from old vines, dating from the first plantings by Almadén back in the 1970s. These reds marry superbly with the beloved, plentiful *churrasco* (grilled or roasted beef or sheep), which is typical of the region and a combination certainly worth trying. But there are many more – these are outlined in more detail over the following pages covering the producers and their wines.

Campanha Gaúcha wineries

Batalha Vinhas e Vinhos ♀

Candiota

vinhosbatalha.com.br/

Partners Giovâni Peres, Gilberto Pozzan and Felipe Pozzan established this winery at the site of the Battle of Seival which took place in 1836 during a revolutionary war – *Guerra dos Farrapos*, or War of the Rags. The vineyard was planted in 2010 and has 6.5 hectares at an altitude of 320 metres, on parallel 31, and on sandy soils. It includes, interestingly, Saperavi; the wine, however, had not been launched at the time of writing this book. The wines are crafted at their winery under the technical direction of legendary oenologist Adolfo Lona. Total annual production averages 30,000 bottles. Still wines predominate, mostly red; 30 per cent are sparkling (all traditional method).

Although still undergoing building works, the winery gladly receives visitors from Monday to Saturday; no booking is required and tasting is free. If you plan to have lunch or dinner (usually a juicy *churrasco)*, book in advance. The winery is well situated on the highway linking Bagé to Pelotas, between Miolo Seival and Bueno Wines. I could taste some of their wines *in loco*, manager Patrícia Kaufmann being my host. Some months thereafter, however, the business was sold to other entrepreneurs (see Cerro de Pedra, page 170), retaining only the brand Ideologia.

Ideologia, a rosé from Merlot, Cabernet Sauvignon and Cabernet Franc, is made by direct pressing; it is a bone dry, fresh and gastronomic wine. Tannat is deep in colour, with intense aromas and flavours of chocolate, tobacco and ripe black fruit. It has a sturdy structure, but the tannins are already being tamed; this is a good wine for cellaring. Super-premium Entrevero is their top red blend (Merlot, Cabernet Sauvignon, Tannat); ripe, fresh and elegant, with a strong alcoholic and tannic structure, it is reminiscent of a very good Right Bank Bordeaux. Traditional method Brut is a *blanc de blancs* from Chardonnay. The base wine spends some time in oak; after at least 18 months with lees, it marries ripe fruit with good autolytic character.

Cerro de Pedra

Pinheiro Machado

vinicolacerrodepedra.com.br/

This new wine business was started when two entrepreneurs purchased Batalha Vinhas e Vinhos (the name of which was derived from a battle). One of these has, coincidently, the Batalha surname, being a large producer of olive oil at Campanha Gaúcha. Their vineyards (except those acquired from Batalha) are located at Pinheiro Machado. Although technically not belonging to Campanha Gaúcha, the winery is so near that, in practice, they do. Their wines are currently made at Pizzato winery (see page 118), under the technical expertise of oenologist Flávio Pizzato. All wines will be made in the purchased winery very shortly and they will be ready to start receiving visitors some time in 2025.

Chardonnay Jovem is fruity and unoaked, with ripe apple, pear and pineapple and a lively acidity. Cabernet Sauvignon Reserva does not show any pyrazines, displaying ripe but fresh fruit and moderate tannic structure, with non-intrusive vanilla from nine months in American oak barrels. Tannat Reserva is more restrained in the nose but opens up in the mouth with ripe black fruit, earth, savouriness and firm tannins, plus spice and cedar from ten months in French oak.

Bueno Wines

Candiota

buenowines.com.br/

Galvão Bueno, a well-known Brazilian sports commentator and staunch wine lover, founded his wine business at Candiota (Bella Vista Estate, very close to Miolo's Seival) in 2009. The first wines (from bought grapes) were launched in 2010. The name Bella Vista (beautiful view) reflects the elevated situation of the vineyards and the pretty buildings, which allow for an incredible view of the *pampas*. There are 31 hectares of vines: Cabernet Sauvignon (12.5), Merlot (6.5), Petit Verdot, Pinot Noir and Sauvignon Blanc (4 each). Bueno is a great fan of Petit Verdot, explaining why this variety is so important here. Bravo: the impressive wines support his preference.

Most soils are red and yellow *argissolos* (SiBCS). A complete draining system has been installed to avoid waterlogging. Resident oenologist Taiana Madeira, with the technical assistance of the famous Italian oenologist Roberto Cipresso (who comes periodically to Bella Vista and is Bueno's partner at a Tuscan winery), and agronomist/philosopher Edvard Theil Kohn, provide the expertise to nurture the vineyard and craft the wines. The legendary flying winemaker Michel Rolland has also been instrumental in creating one of their top red blends, Paralelo 31 GR. The team, encouraged by the perfectionist Galvão Bueno, is constantly conducting research on 70 different technical indexes. The wines are made at Miolo under the close supervision of Bueno's technicians. Total annual production averages 200,000 bottles, of which 70 per cent are still and the balance sparkling. There are no oenotouristic facilities, but they plan to open to visitors in 2026. I was warmly received by Taiana and Edvard (nicknamed Edinho) for a thorough tasting of the wines, enjoying the far-reaching, beautiful view of a lake and the rolling hills. They were, indeed, very interesting and well-informed companions.

Desirée Sauvignon Blanc, made from clones 242 (for aroma and acidity) and 530 (for ripeness), has clear varietal characteristics with great ripeness and good balance; it is a dry but rich wine that opens up in the mouth. Pinot Noir Reserva is true to the variety (clone 777): light in colour, full of perfectly ripe red berries, clear acidity and velvety tannins, with fine vanilla and toast. Petit Verdot Reserva is a jewel: deep purple, brimming with very ripe blackberries, slight hints of pyrazines, so spicy, with great freshness and an excellent structure of warming but balanced alcohol. It is a great food wine – to enjoy now or to cellar for five to eight years.

Paralelo 31 Gran Reserva (luxury price level) is a Bordeaux blend of Cabernet Sauvignon, Merlot and Petit Verdot; inky, very aromatic and completely ripe, but again so fresh and spicy, fleshy but highly elegant and ageworthy. This is a great wine, and again testimony to Petit Verdot's attributes. Anima (again luxury price level) is their iconic red, mostly Merlot (it is legally varietal) with some Petit Verdot; deeply coloured from 55 days of maceration, it is highly complex in the nose and mouth (plums, chocolate, tobacco, spice, elegant oak), with a great structure but such very fine and caressing tannins. It spends over two years in French oak barriques, plus one year in the bottle.

Desirée sparkling rosé is a very good Charmat from a blend of Cabernet Sauvignon, Merlot and Pinot Noir. Roberto Cipresso devised its winemaking protocol, leading to a pale pink colour, ripe red berry flavour, good structure and an attractive style.

Vinícola Campos de Cima ♀

Itaqui (north of Uruguaiana)

www.camposdecima.com.br/

Fazenda Campos de Cima is a very old (150 years) cattle-raising farm located at Maçambará, a tiny town about 50 kilometres east of Itaqui. In 2002, owner José Silva Ayub, a doctor, and his wife, Hortência, decided to establish a vineyard as the first step of a well-planned wine business. They created 15 hectares with imported planting material between 2002 and 2004. Today, there are 17 hectares in production, mainly Chardonnay, Cabernet Sauvignon, Merlot, Pinot Noir and Tannat. Interestingly, they have unusual (in Brazil) varieties: Arinto, Assyrtiko and Ruby Cabernet. The official wine business started in 2008, and the couple's two daughters, Vanessa and Manuela, are also partners. The first wine, a Tannat, still made by third parties, was launched in 2008. Manuela, an architect, designed the winery, which was built at Itaqui, where the first wines were crafted in 2014. French oenologist Michel Fabre oversaw the winery's establishment and purchasing of equipment (mostly Italian). Today, winemaking is led by oenologists Breno Tavares and Celito Guerra.

Annual production averages 50,000 bottles, of which 65 per cent are still wines (mainly reds). In 2014, they began exporting wines to the UK. Many wines are imaginatively named after local expressions, with pretty labels reproducing exclusive paintings by Felipe Constant. An oenotouristic project began in 2017 and a small guesthouse was built in 2018. Visitors can enjoy guided tours, tastings, meals, wine courses and events. They can also stay at the property. The winery areas for visitors are refined and comfortable and demonstrate impeccable good taste. Reservations are a must. There are flights from São Paulo to Uruguaiana (98 kilometres to the south). Campos de Cima has participated actively in the regional producers' association (Associação dos Vinhos da Campanha): Hortência as vice-president, then Pedro Candelária (Manuela's husband) as vice-president, and, up to June 2024, as president. I was warmly received by Dr Ayub, Hortência and Pedro, who showed me their flawlessly made wines.

Cepas Viognier has an evident varietal character; it is aromatic (roses, peach), has more acidity than usual for this grape, and is well structured, elegant and balanced. 3 Bocas white, a surprising blend of Arinto, Alvarinho and Assyrtiko, is a lively, crisp, sharp, mineral wine

with complex aromas. Thanks to its strong structure of acidity and flavours, it has many years of bottle ageing ahead to attain the tertiary
complexity of toast and honey. For me, this is one of the most interesting white wines made in Brazil.

Lúdicos Guriazita rosé, made from Cabernet Sauvignon and Merlot
by direct pressing and (usually) co-fermented, is light pink and bone
dry and has great gastronomic versatility. The 3 Bocas rosé is made
predominately from Pinot Noir, plus some Cabernet Sauvignon and
Merlot; it offers excellent fresh red fruit, crisp acidity and great elegance.

Red 3 Bocas, one of their biggest commercial successes, is made from
Tannat, Cabernet Franc and Petit Verdot. Unoaked, it is deeply coloured and fresh, with well-integrated alcohol, very ripe black fruit, hints of
pencil shavings and evident spiciness; its strong structure makes it the
perfect accompaniment to the typical beef dishes of Campanha Gaúcha.
Assinatura Pinot Noir is an elegant, savoury and well-structured version
of this grape; spending six months in French oak, there is no excessive
oakiness. Dos Netos is, unusually, a non-vintage blend of Tannat and
Ruby Cabernet, spending 12 months in oak; at 14.5% abv, it is spirity,
but the clear vanilla and toast are well balanced by the ripe blackberry
fruit. It will age well but can already be enjoyed at its full strength.

Prometido Safra dos Deuses (luxury price level) is their iconic red;
made only in exceptional vintages, like the present 2022 edition, it
blends Tannat, Syrah and Malbec. It has a deep colour, very high intensity and concentration, a full body and powerful tannins, albeit fine
grained. It demands years of bottle ageing to come together and show
its potential – an exceptional wine.

Reserva Nature (Chardonnay/Pinot Noir, traditional method) is
fruity and elegant but exhibits high savouriness and autolytic character
from 24-month autolysis. The Rosé version (Pinot Noir, Chardonnay)
has more structure and red berries, being bone dry and again elegant,
with a very slight tannic grip.

Cerros de Gaya/Vinícola Previtali ♀

Dom Pedrito

cerrosdegaya.com.br/

Dom Pedrito is just 73 kilometres to the north-west of Bagé. Here,
Dr André Previtali (a plastic surgeon of Italian descent) planted the
first vines in 2012 and 2013, on sandy, well-drained soil. The place
is called Três Cerros, hence the Cerros de Gaya name (Gaia being the

Greek name for the earth or land). Eight varieties are planted, mainly Chardonnay, Cabernet Sauvignon, Merlot, Pinot Noir and Tannat. The first commercial wines were from the 2018 vintage. The grapes are vinified at Peruzzo under the guidance of oenologist Alcides Javier González. A winery is being built, however.

Visitors are welcome to enjoy guided tours, including of the vineyards and olive groves, and tastings with cheese and charcuterie at a belvedere overlooking the *pampas*. They also have a pretty shop at Bagé, where the wines (and olive oil) can be tasted. Reservations are needed to visit the vineyard, but you can go straight to the shop (open every weekday, Saturday 10 a.m. to 1 p.m., but closed Sunday). I was warmly received by Dr André and his wife, Eveline, to taste the wines.

The Chardonnay is a bargain: buttery, with a good body, keeping acidity and clear varietal character. Humanidade Pinot Noir has ripe red fruit and keeps acidity well, with fine, soft tannins, all seasoned by discreet vanilla and toast. Igualdade Cabernet Sauvignon showcases ripe cassis, moderate acidity and fine tannins; it is ready to drink. Tannat is deep in colour, with an unusual but agreeable minty character. Sparkling traditional method Nature is 100 per cent Chardonnay, with clearly ripe tropical fruit, Brazilian style, and slight autolytic aromas and flavours.

Cordilheira de Sant'Ana ♀

Sant'Ana do Livramento

cordilheiradesantana.com.br/

After careful planning, oenologists Gladistão Omizzolo – who sadly passed away in 2023 – and Rosana Wagner, his wife, started their wine business in 1999, when they bought land (46 hectares) near Almadén. The soils are predominately sandstone, with moderate fertility. Omizzolo, by the way, played a role in the purchase of Almadén by Seagram in 1989. He was, therefore, very knowledgeable about the region and its potential. Here, the vines can undergo a full winter dormancy, but there is plenty of sunlight, as the air is quite limpid (low humidity). They didn't lose any time: the first vineyards were planted in 2000, the winery was started, and the first wines were launched in 2003. Several prizes at national events attested to their quality. Today, there are 20 hectares of vines and eight different varieties.

The scenic vineyard lies at the foot of beautiful Cerro Palomas, a distinguishing feature of the region's landscape. The winery is spotless; 10,000 bottles are produced annually. They do not make sparklers;

Cerro Palomas and Cordilheira de Sant'Ana's vineyard

65 per cent are reds, 30 per cent are white and 5 per cent are sweet fortified wines. The surroundings have a sedate, pastoral beauty. Visitors
are welcome seven days a week, and no previous booking is required
except for groups of over ten people. However, booking is necessary if
you want to have charcuterie or a typical light lunch to accompany the
wines. I was warmly received by Rosana and her dedicated, efficient
work fellows, Márcia and Afrânio, who spared no effort in helping me
taste their wines.

Gewurztraminer is, as expected, golden, very aromatic, full of lychee fruit and spicy flavours; we are not, however, in Alsace, and this
Brazilian wine is not heavy, with less unctuousness and more acidity
– you'll always be asking for another glass. Chardonnay is oaked, as 40
per cent of the wine stays in American and French oak barriques; this
is clearly evident and marries well with the wine's butteriness and ripe
fruit characters, with some mineral hints and a long length.

Reserva dos Pampas Rosé is a 100 per cent Cabernet Sauvignon from
saignée, hence its deep colour and good structure; it is aimed at those
who love pink wines with some sweetness (20 grams per litre residual sugar). They began making Touriga Nacional in 2014; despite being a varietal wine according to the 85 per cent rule, it has 8 per cent
Tannat, which strengthens its structure. Notwithstanding this, it is an

elegant, refined, fresh red. Super-premium Tannat reinforces the fact that this grape is very at home in Campanha Gaúcha: deep in colour, sinewy in tannins, it spends 32 months in 300-litre casks of American and French oak, softening the strong structure. Their Merlot is from the 2017 vintage, with garnet rims; ripe plums, vanilla, toast, coffee and leather fit into a fresh, elegant structure with fine-grained tannins. Super-premium Cabernet Sauvignon 2005 (yes, 2005): despite the age, it keeps a youthful colour, being, however, predominately tertiary in aromas and flavours. Fruit (cassis) and pyrazines are present, and so are the tannins, fine grained but firm; allied to the fresh acidity, they allow for a few more years of cellaring.

The top red wine, Dom Gladistão, honours the memory of Rosana's husband. It is, unusually, a blend of three vintages (2005, 2020, 2022) and four varieties (Cabernet Sauvignon, Tannat, Merlot, Touriga Nacional). Deeply coloured, with a high intensity and concentration of aromas and flavours within a very strong structure of acidity and tannins, it is an exceptional wine.

Rubi dos Pampas is a sweet, fortified, late-harvest Tannat with nearly 100 grams per litre residual sugar, very well balanced by the fresh acidity and ripe dark fruit, tobacco and chocolate.

Dunamis Vinhos e Vinhedos

Dom Pedrito

www.dunamisvinhos.com.br/

Agronomist José Antonio Peterle, of Italian descent, moved from Serra Gaúcha to Dom Pedrito in 1981. Two years later, he started a career as a rural producer. Vine growing, however, began quite later, in 2002. This is a family business: besides José Antonio, his son Thiago, an oenologist, daughter Carolina, plus nephew Celso also work here. The Três Cerros vineyard is planted at an altitude of 340 metres on sandy-clayey, well-drained, poor soil. Eight different varieties are grown, but they also have an experimental vineyard with about 60 cultivars being tested. Their winery is being finished. Winemaking – the wines are currently made at the Batalha winery, in Candiota – is overseen by enthusiastic oenologist Vinícius Cercato. They have a shop in Gramado, the charming tourist town in Serra Gaúcha. Of note: Dunamis uniquely crafts a white Merlot (*blanc de noirs*) and a sparkling Pinot Grigio. I was kindly received by Thiago, Vinícius and Celso at Batalha to taste several wines.

White Merlot is made using hyper-oxidation to eliminate colouring matter; pale, soft, with a good body and a bit unctuous, it is a unique wine. Arinarnoa (Cabernet Sauvignon × Tannat crossing) is inky, with very ripe blackberry fruit, herbs and mint; fresh, spicy and full bodied, with sinewy tannins, albeit fine grained – a good example of this uncommon variety. Cabernet Franc is very easy drinking and has fresh acidity, ripe fruit and hints of graphite and pyrazines. Teroldego also has a strong colour, exhibiting ripe blackberries, with vanilla and cedar from 12 months in oak barriques; freshness and spice are due to 15 per cent whole cluster. Super-premium Tannat Gran Reserva spends 20 months in barrels (American and French) and reveals sweet, very ripe fruit, vanilla, toast and the familiar strong structure of this grape. TARR is their iconic red, a blend of Tannats from 2015 and 2018; inky and spicy, with fine oakiness, a powerful structure of warming alcohol, sinewy tannins, and full bodied – cellar for ten-plus years.

Nature Blanc de Blanc (100 per cent Chardonnay) saw no malolactic fermentation, and hence keeps a racy acidity; after an 18-month autolysis, the biscuity character is very clear and fine. The very interesting sparkling Pinot Grigio Extra-Brut, made by the traditional method, is tasty, with high varietal typicity; the autolytic character is discreet but harmonizes well with the exuberance of ripe pear from the variety.

Vinícola Guatambu ♀

Dom Pedrito

www.guatambuvinhos.com.br/

Estância Guatambu belongs to the Pötter family of German descent, who have been developing their agribusiness since 1958. Grapes, however, only appeared on their radar in the early 2000s. On *luvissolos*, their vineyard was started in 2003, using planting material imported from France and Italy. Under the direction of agronomist Gabriela Pötter, daughter of the owner Valter Pötter, a pioneering vineyard of half a hectare was started. The results were so good that commercial planting followed. Today, a total of 20.5 hectares has Chardonnay, Gewurztraminer, Sauvignon Blanc, Cabernet Sauvignon, Merlot, Pinot Noir, Tannat and Tempranillo.

The winery, conveniently located on a highway leading to Dom Pedrito and Bagé, was opened in 2013. It has over 3,000 square metres, with oenotouristic facilities that include an auditorium and events spaces. Gabriela and Amélia Leite conduct the oenological works under the assessorship of Alejandro Cardozo. A comprehensive series of oenot-ouristic activities are on offer; reservations are necessary. One of these is the 'Dia Épico', which involves various activities (folkloric dances and music, a hearty lunch with barbecued beef, and tasting the wines). All installations are spotless and show impeccable good taste; no effort has been spared in creating this world-class complex. It was a great pleasure to be received by Gabriela and her efficient oenological companions, Amélia and Jean Zambrano.

Luar do Pampa Gewurztraminer is an elegant rendition of this charac-terful grape; they manage to get a low pH (3.25), balancing very well with the aromatic richness and leading to a wine you want to keep drinking. Concretum Chardonnay is fermented in concrete amphorae, where the wine stays for two months, followed by stabilization in stainless-steel vats. It is complex, mineral, fresh and lengthy but with good varietal typicity.

Rastros do Pampa Cabernet Sauvignon shows very ripe fruit, bal-anced by fine-grained, soft tannins, amongst discreet oakiness of coco-nut, vanilla and toast. Concretum Tannat is also fermented and matured (six months) in concrete amphorae, with a very long maceration time. It is well extracted, dense and complex, with slightly rustic tannins, this being more a style than a defect. Lendas do Pampa Tempranillo is a very elegant wine with good varietal characteristics (ripe red berries, leather, fine and soft tannins), well married to vanilla and toast from French oak. Lendas do Pampa Tannat is deep purple and displays ripe black fruit, leather, tobacco, chocolate, brown sugar and animal hints. They have managed (by using selected yeast) to obtain a low pH (3.3) for this powerful red wine, hence making it fresh; it is long, concentrated and ageworthy – a truly memorable Tannat from Campanha Gaúcha. Épicos Edição 8, their iconic red, is a multi-vintage blend (2020, 2021, 2023); despite its great intensity, concentration and complexity, it maintains a wonderful elegance – it is a truly exceptional wine.

Traditional method Nature (Chardonnay) spends at least nine months on lees; 20 per cent of the base wine spends time in oak barri-ques, which impart volume and some butteriness. It is creamy, with ca-ressing foam; slight notes of vanilla mingle with ripe but elegant tropical fruit. The very unusual red sparkler from Merlot is Brut. The colour is pale red, which is very beautiful to see; after a 12-month autolysis, high acidity is maintained and the wine has an excellent structure. It is highly recommended that you pair this wine with *feijoada*, the famous hearty Brazilian pork dish.

Miolo Wine Group 🍷

Candiota (Seival) and Sant'Ana do Livramento (Almadén)

www.miolo.com.br/

Seival

Miolo started this sector of their several divisions in 2000 when equipment was installed at Estância (farm) Fortaleza do Seival. Today, there is an impressive total of 200 hectares of vines on clayey soils. Here, harvesting mechanically at night has been pioneered. Miolo has also innovated by planting Portuguese varieties at Seival, from which some of its best reds are crafted. As with Almadén, visiting reveals astounding views of a sea of vines planted on rolling hills. The winery is also large, although not as big as Almadén's.

The wines produced at both wineries go, in tankers, to Miolo's main installations at Serra Gaúcha to be finished and bottled. Total annual production is about 1.7 million bottles. Visits can be scheduled through Miolo's website, although there is no proper oenotouristic structure. An existing shop, however, is a convenient place to buy the group's many products. I was very well received by Bruna Schmidt, who was in charge of oenotouristic activities (and at the laboratory at harvest time) when I visited to taste their wines.

Sauvignon Blanc Reserva Colheita Noturna is bone dry, with good varietal character, especially in the mouth. Pinot Grigio Reserva is somewhat neutral and simple in the nose (like the Italian archetypes) but impresses well in the mouth. Both are good everyday whites. Single Vineyard Alvarinho brings citrus and peach, is very sharp and mineral, has a good structure, and is quite true to the variety.

Wild Gamay, from the 2024 harvest (tasted at the end of April 2024), was the first red from this vintage launched worldwide. Like a Beaujolais Nouveau, it is deep purple and brimming with bubblegum, cherry and banana aromas and flavours. It is refreshing and delicious – drink it (cold) as early as possible after sales start! Reserva Tempranillo is medium ruby, with ripe red fruit, vanilla and some coconut from six months in used oak barriques, soft, cheek-impressing tannins, moderate acidity, and a medium length. Single Vineyard Pinot Noir is ripe and fruity, with evident vanilla and toast (due to one year in barriques), good freshness and very soft tannins. Single Vineyard Touriga Nacional has been launched following significant demand from knowledgeable customers;

with a deep colour, it brings violets, mandarin and ripe blackberry within a fine, elegant structure, as becomes this noble variety. Quinta do Seival is a blend of Touriga Nacional and Tinta Roriz (that is, Tempranillo); intense and concentrated, with a strong structure framed by ripe black fruit and fine oak (12 months, new), it will improve from cellaring to acquire tertiary complexity. Sebrumo is Miolo's top Cabernet Sauvignon; very ripe cassis and blackberries, slight pyrazines, and a strong structure of alcohol (15% abv) and fine-grained tannins lead to a long length. Sesmarias is the most expensive wine made by this large group; made from six different cultivars, it offers all that is expected of a great wine: full intensity, concentration, body, structure, oak (18 months, new), alcohol (15.5% abv), length and a very long ageing potential.

Almadén

As already noted, this large concern (www.almaden.com.br/) was bought by Miolo in 2009. It has been thoroughly updated and refurbished. The vineyard is extensive, the largest continuous area in the country, with 450 hectares in production and some expansion taking place. Here, in 2011, Miolo pioneered mechanical harvesting in Brazil. The vineyard is divided into 138 mapped parcels, of which 111 deliver grapes to be processed at the large winery (which can store up to 8.5 million litres). Twenty-five varieties are planted here, including less well-known cultivars such as Aspiran Bouschet, Ekigaina, French Colombard and Petite Sirah.

There is an extensive line of entry-level, inexpensive varietals sold throughout Brazil. Some of these are off-dry or demi-sec to meet the needs of consumers with a sweet tooth. All wines made here are certified vegan. Visitors are welcome to a guided tour that includes the vineyard, the winery, a museum and a tasting of four wines. The museum is very interesting, serving as an excellent introduction to the visit. There is a beautiful view from a large deck overlooking the vineyards – perfect for selfies and to take pictures to post online! You can take advantage of their duty-free shop of wine, where taxes (and prices) are reduced. This is because Sant'ana do Livramento lies on the border with Uruguay, having several tax-free businesses. I was very well received by a team led by the chief oenologist, Daniel Alonso Martins, to taste wines very close to Cerro Palomas. This emblematic mountain inspires so many pictures.

The inexpensive line of varietals, all closed by screw caps, is aimed at younger groups of consumers who are looking for uncomplicated wines. Riesling is, in fact, a varietal from Riesling Itálico, but it has a small percentage of Riesling proper; it brings fresh citrus and apple with low alcohol. Gewurztraminer is true to this aromatic variety, albeit lighter and fresher than Alsatian models; it is indeed a bargain.

Cabernet Sauvignon is fruity, easy drinking and soft in tannins. Marselan 50 Years is dark, also ripe, with a good structure of somewhat grippy tannins. Tannat brings the typical tannic structure of this grape, again offering a great deal for the low price. Tempranillo 50 years is ripe and fruity, with good varietal typicity. Trebbiano Wild, as the name suggests, is spontaneously fermented; savoury, fresh and crisp, with slight salinity and some caramel hints, it is rare and a very gastronomic wine. Single Vineyard Gewurztraminer is very aromatic and floral, full of lychee fruit, and rich in the mouth. Single Vineyard Riesling Johannisberg is a rare varietal from this great grape, seldom grown in Brazil; it exhibits the usual steely acidity, low alcohol, and aromas and flavours of citrus, green apple and petrol hints.

Single Vineyard Cabernet Franc has high varietal typicity: pencil shavings, fresh blackberries and green bell pepper, with a high acidity and firm tannins. Super-premium Vinhas Velhas Tannat is made from 40-year-old vines planted when Almadén was established here; it has a very deep colour and offers tobacco, chocolate, ripe blackberries, toast and vanilla. It is a rich, powerful wine with high acidity and alcohol (albeit well balanced), with a formidable tannic structure and capable of ageing gracefully for many years.

For more on the Miolo Wine Group, see also pages 115 and 322.

Estancia Paraizo ♀

Bagé

www.estanciaparaizo.com/

This *estância* (cattle farm), belonging to the Mercio family of Portuguese descent, has existed since 1790. The present owner, Thomaz, belongs to the ninth generation of this Azorean family. He and his wife, Monica, continue to raise cattle and sheep. They started a vineyard in 2000 to expand their work. Today, wines are crafted from 5.5 hectares of Cabernet Sauvignon and Syrah, planted on *argissolos* and *luvissolos*, deep to very deep soils with good drainage and moderate fertility. The altitude (380 metres) is among the highest in Campanha Gaúcha. Ample diurnal variations during the growing season, plenty of wind and low winter temperatures (allowing complete dormancy of the vines) all contribute to grape quality.

Their Syrah planting material came originally from South Africa, and this is, in fact, the first Syrah vineyard officially registered in Brazil. Total annual production averages 15,000 bottles under the technical direction of oenologist Fernanda Dall'Astta (also a gifted chef). They plan to build a winery using one of their old stone buildings. Currently, the wines are crafted by third parties. Visitors can drive 41 kilometres from Bagé to enjoy the bucolic surroundings and historic buildings of the *estância*, where no less than 106 different bird species exist. Tastings with appetizers and meals are available, always through prior booking. Fernanda received me warmly on a beautiful late afternoon to taste some of their red wines.

Don Thomaz y Victoria Cabernet Sauvignon is fresh and elegant, with a medium body and fine-grained tannins, the varietal character enhanced by not seeing any oak. Camilo I Syrah, a bit unexpectedly for Campanha Gaúcha, is more reminiscent of a northern Rhône wine than the New World style: so fresh (pH 3.46, tartaric acid 7.03 grams per litre), minty, peppery, with ripe blackberry fruit and smoke. Cova de Toro is their blend of the two varieties; 70 per cent Syrah is enough to put forward this variety's characters more than Cabernet's; again, a very fresh, gastronomic wine with animal, smoky and spicy hints.

Peruzzo Vinhas & Vinhos ♀

Bagé

www.vinicolaperuzzo.com.br/

The Peruzzos, long-term landowners at Bagé, decided to start a wine business in 2000; they planted their vineyard in 2003 and the first wines were launched in 2006. Planting material was imported from France, Italy and Portugal to form a 14-hectare vineyard. Here, on sandy-clayey soil, five varieties are grown (Chardonnay, Cabernet Franc, Cabernet Sauvignon, Marselan and Merlot). Grapes are also bought from other parties. No time was lost: in 2008, their winery was ready. It delivers about 40,000 bottles annually. As they can process up to 50,000 litres, wines from other producers are also made here. Éder Peruzzo and Ariel Pereira are in charge of oenological activities. Eighty per cent of the wines are still (reds predominating), and the balance is made up of sparklers. Peruzzo has shops both in Bagé and Vale dos Vinhedos. They receive visitors for tastings; you can enjoy meals paired with their wines at their Bagé shop (booking required).

Chardonnay, moderately aromatic, reveals itself in the mouth with ripe apple, peach and pineapple hints, plus a touch of spice and vanilla (from oak staves during fermentation), surrounded by fresh acidity. Arinarnoa is inky and aromatic, with ripe blackberry and hints of herbaceousness, enlivening acidity and good tannic grip, but the tannins are fine; it is a very interesting wine from this unusual but promising variety. Cabernet Franc is a powerful wine, dark and intense in aromas and flavours (ripe blackberries, capsicum, pencil shavings); its strong structure of alcohol (14% abv), high acidity and grippy tannins mean it will improve in the bottle for several years.

Routhier & Darricarrère/Província de São Pedro

Rosário do Sul

www.redvin.com.br/

This wine business was founded in 2002 at Rosário do Sul (106 kilometres north of Sant'Ana do Livramento) by French brothers Pierre and Jean-Daniel Darricarrère, plus Canadian Michel Routhier. A 6-hectare vineyard was planted with Chardonnay and Cabernet Sauvignon on poor, sandy soil. This was later augmented with Alicante Bouschet and Petit Manseng. The first commercial vintage was in 2008. Since then, Julio Gostisa has entered the business; today, he leads the commercial activities with Patrick (viticulture) and Anthony (winemaking) Darricarrère. They produce about 30,000 bottles annually, of which 80 per cent are still wines (reds and rosés predominating). Traditional method sparklers comprise 20 per cent of the total production. Some of the wines are included in the wine lists of top Brazilian restaurants (such as the Michelin-starred DOM). There is no oenotouristic set-up.

Three different Cabernet Sauvignon wines are made. ReD has a good varietal character, with ripe cassis and blackberries, plus hints of green bell pepper, toast and spice; the acidity is refreshing and the tannins very soft. Salamanca do Jarau is made (from a single vineyard, with spontaneous fermentation) only in outstanding vintages; it displays a perfect balance between the clear varietal characteristics (ripe cassis, mint, capsicum) and the solid structure of acidity, concentration and tannins. So polished, it is a fine wine indeed. Routhier Code Name (luxury price level) has a medium-ruby colour with garnet rims. It brings very ripe blackcurrant and capsicum; medium bodied and savoury, it has a firm structure of fresh acidity and sleek, fine-grained tannins – a very elegant and classy wine.

Bodega Sossego 🍷

Uruguaiana

www.bodegasossego.com.br/

At Estância do Sossego, owned by the Ormazabal Moura family, not far from Uruguaiana, Bradford cattle and pastures share space with the vineyard, established in 2005 (over 5 hectares) on clayey-rocky soils. Their brand is crafted from these, but they also buy in grapes. According to René Ormazabal Moura, the owner, a special partnership exists with the Dom Giovanni winery (in Pinto Bandeira), where their wines are made. The total annual production is 20,000 bottles, under the technical expertise of oenologist Marcelo Alves. Visitors are welcome to stroll in the vineyard, taste the wines with accompanying light dishes, and potentially enjoy a beautiful sunset. Booking is strictly required, as visits are allowed only twice a month.

Bodega Sossego is their entry-level line, meant for everyday drinking. The white, blending Sauvignon Blanc and Chardonnay, is simple, fruity, aromatic and fresh. Rosé (Cabernet Sauvignon and Pinot Noir) is bone dry and fruity, with some savouriness, and is very food friendly. The red version, or Tinto, has an unusual blend: Cabernets Franc and Sauvignon, plus Sauvignon Blanc; light in colour, alcohol and structure, it is fresh and fruity.

The Camp4ña (no typos here) line brings more ambitious wines. Unoaked Chardonnay is a very ripe, full bodied, big, alcoholic wine with moderate acidity and a long length. Oaked Chardonnay has very ripe fruit; maturing in American oak barrels, where malolactic fermentation occurs, it is buttery and full of vanilla with coconut hints. Cabernet Sauvignon brings ripe fruit (we are in Campanha Gaúcha!), balanced by fresh acidity, with a high level of grippy tannins, needing time.

Camp4ña Blanc de Blancs Brut is a blend of Chardonnay grapes from Uruguaiana and Pinto Bandeira; made by the traditional method, with 12 months with lees, it offers a good mix of ripe fruit and autolytic characters.

Terra Fiel

Bento Gonçalves (head office)

www.terrafiel.com.br

Paula Schenato saw her grandfather make wine at home until he was 90. This inspired her to earn degrees in biology and oenology to make her own wines. After achieving an MSc degree, with a stint of six years at Embrapa and working at several wineries, she started her personal project, selling the first wines in 2020. Using grapes from Campanha Gaúcha (still wines) and Serra Gaúcha (sparkling), Paula crafts the products herself at a cooperative (Nova Aliança). She prefers modern, youthful wines with moderate extraction and oakiness, all sold at attractive prices.

Terroir Chardonnay has a deep lemon colour, with discreet aromas of ripe apple, pear, pineapple, hints of butter, vanilla and spice; fresh but ripe, it has a good texture. Pinot Noir is brimming with ripe red berries, hints of undergrowth and earth, which impart complexity; it is fresh and juicy. Brut Rosé (Chardonnay/Pinot Noir, traditional method, 20-month autolysis) has an onion-skin colour and displays fresh red berries, apple and pear, with evident dough and patisserie. It is savoury, well structured and food friendly.

Vinhetica

Sant'Ana do Livramento

www.vinhetica.com.br

After travelling through several Brazilian regions, Frenchman Gaspar Desurmont settled at Sant'Ana do Livramento where he decided to craft wines with minimal intervention. Together with his partners, Jean-Pierre and Cyril Bernard, their goal is to produce wines that faithfully express the immensely diversified Brazilian terroirs. Owning 82 hectares of land, they have planted 14 varieties, including Assyrtiko, Saperavi and Nebbiolo. Besides wines from Campanha Gaúcha, they also have products from Serra Gaúcha, Campos de Cima da Serra and Santa Catarina. Desurmont has chosen to use Brazilian woods to age many wines: *grápia* (or *garapeira*), *cabreúva, jequitibá, putumuju, cedrinho, amburana, bálsamo* and *castanha*. This is a work in progress, according to him (see page 63). Besides the Vinhetica line, they have also recently launched Terroir da Vigia, comprising wines made with minimal intervention: spontaneous fermentation, no additions and very low sulphites. They also use Brazilian woods in this line. The annual production of both lines is 60,000 bottles.

Cyril Bernard was my kind host at their office in São Paulo to taste some of the wines. These were all fresh and well balanced, with moderate alcohol, savoury and gastronomic, in line with the French philosophy of winemaking and wine purposes. They are also moderately priced (how welcome!). Vinhetica Sauvignon Blanc (Campos de Cima da Serra) is aged both in oak and Brazilian woods (*jequitibá*, *grápia*); the overt varietal character is subdued here, replaced by honeyed hints, perfume and good texture, with a slightly bitter bite on the finish. Vinhetica Terroir de Rosé (Campanha Gaúcha; Cabernet Franc and Merlot) is darker than Provençal examples; it is ripe (red fruits), dry and well structured (some tannic grip is felt) – it calls to be drunk with food.

Vinhetica Pinot Noir (Campos de Cima da Serra and Serra Gaúcha) is partly fermented (native yeast) and matured in *jequitibá* foudres for 12 months. It has a deep colour and a firm tannic structure for Pinot Noir; besides ripe fruit (here more black than red), it is floral, earthy and fresh. No wood aromas appear, as *jequitibá* is neutral in this sense. Terroir da Vigia Fortáo da Vigia, although a blend, including Baga, Cabernet Franc, Petit Verdot and Saperavi, is almost a varietal Tannat; it is matured in six different Brazilian woods. Dark, fresh, complex and strongly structured, it brings discreet, ripe black fruit, earth, violets and mint. Terroir da Vigia Georgiano da Vigia is 100 per cent Saperavi. This alone would suffice to attract plenty of interest. But the wine offers much more: an inky colour, complex aromas and flavours of ripe black fruit, violets, mint and earth, with a sinewy, powerful structure of acidity and tannins, demanding time in the bottle. Truly a big wine and one of a kind.

Vinhetica Terroir d'Effervescence Brut Rosé (Serra Gaúcha) is made from Pinot Noir, Chardonnay and Riesling Itálico; after a minimum 12-month autolysis, it is very biscuity and bready, and such flavours marry well with a crisp acidity and fresh red berries.

Also in Campanha Gaúcha

- Casa Barrios, Sant'Ana do Livramento (casabarrios.net)
- Vinícola Costanza, Bagé (santacostanza.com.br)
- Nova Aliança Cooperativa Vinícola, based in Flores da Cunha, Serra Gaúcha (novaalianca.coop.br/)
- Vinhos Dom Pedrito, Dom Pedrito (contato@vinhosdompedrito. com.br)
- Vinhos Yby, headquarters in Venâncio (www.vinhosyby.com)
- Vinhedo Zampieri Fernandes, Sant'Ana do Livramento (@vinhedo zampierifernandes/)

SERRA DO SUDESTE

Approximately midway between Serra Gaúcha and Campanha Gaúcha, the region known as Serra do Sudeste has become important in viticulture. Although mentioned frequently, this is not an officially delimited area, that is, with limits defined by the federal government or as an *Indicação de Procedência* (IP). Serra Gaúcha is a Viticultural Zone and Campanha Gaúcha is an IP. Until 2019, when it was closed, the Instituto Brasileiro do Vinho (IBRAVIN), or Brazilian Wine Institute, was linked to the sector's wineries, cooperatives and unions. It had delineated the region (and Campos de Cima da Serra) in 2010. Notwithstanding this lack of legal borders, the fact is that two townships in this new region, Encruzilhada do Sul and Pinheiro Machado, have a significant grape production and have become important in Rio Grande do Sul and nationally. Several publications by Embrapa take for granted that Serra do Sudeste and Campos de Cima da Serra are wine regions, and the general and specialized Brazilian press consider them as such, and so must we.

More or less as in Campanha Gaúcha, vineyards in Serra do Sudeste had already started appearing in the 1970s. Then, the search for areas with better climates and less expensive land than Serra Gaúcha began. Climatic studies by Silveira da Mota (Federal University of Pelotas) pointed to both regions. In 1976, the now defunct Companhia Vinícola Rio-Grandense planted, with the invaluable assistance of Onofre Pimentel, a vineyard at Pinheiro Machado, presently owned by Terrasul (from Flores da Cunha, Serra Gaúcha). They were followed by Heublein, then showing vinous interest in Serra Gaúcha. With time, other wineries from Serra Gaúcha (such as Lídio Carraro, Valduga, Angheben and Chandon) bought land and/or planted new vineyards in the region. Almost all grapes from here are sent to and vinified at Serra Gaúcha. Bento Gonçalves lies about 250 kilometres north of Encruzilhada do Sul. The still wines, however, are frequently labelled with a link to their true origin, Serra do Sudeste. This helps to sell them as superior products from a differentiated terroir.

Climate and soils

Climatically, the region has the same MCC classification as Serra Gaúcha: HI+1 (warm temperate), DI-2 (humid), CI-1 (temperate nights). However, there is less rain during the growth season and the diurnal temperature variation is significant. Main weather hazards include spring frosts and hailstorms. As usual, the most important diseases are downy mildew and cluster rots. The region lies on a granite bedrock formation, the *Escudo Cristalino Sul-Riograndense*. Altitudes range from 400 to 500 metres above sea level. Soil studies found that the most frequent SiBCS soil classes are *cambissolos*, *neossolos* and *argissolos*. As for texture, they are frequently sandy or gravelly, with good drainage. The mountainous relief and soil shallowness indicate erosion as a common problem.

Planted areas and wine types

According to SIVIBE, the region (comprising the townships of Encruzilhada do Sul, with 427.5 hectares, and Pinheiro Machado, with 100.6) had 528.1 hectares of planted vineyards in 2022. The overwhelming majority were *vinifera* varieties. The most planted cultivars, in descending order, were Pinot Noir (121 hectares), Chardonnay (116), Merlot (45), Cabernet Sauvignon (38), Riesling Itálico (30), Malbec (18), Marselan (17), Cabernet Franc (16), Tannat (10), Touriga Nacional (9), and Sauvignon Blanc (8). Other varieties, with smaller planted areas, included (from a long list) Alicante Bouschet, Ancellotta, Arinarnoa, Gewurztraminer, Sangiovese, Tempranillo and Viognier.

This reflects some facts. Firstly, the region provides Serra Gaúcha with grapes to make base wines for classical-style sparklers (Pinot Noir, Chardonnay and Riesling Itálico). Chandon (LVMH group), based at Serra Gaúcha, has 288 hectares of vineyards in Serra do Sudeste. Secondly, the mix of red grapes, except for the predominance of Pinot Noir, is very similar. Thirdly, the evident importance of aromatic white grapes seen in Serra Gaúcha is not repeated here.

According to Embrapa, and generally speaking, the still white wines made from Serra do Sudeste's grapes are lightly coloured, with subtle, delicate floral and fruity notes, fresh (due to moderate to high acidity), with medium to high alcohol and body and good length, and can be kept for up to five to six years. Still reds have a medium to deep colour, with medium aromatic intensity (fruit predominating: raspberry, cherry, blackberry, blackcurrant), a good structure (including medium to high alcohol), moderate acidity and long length, and the ability to age up to ten years in the bottle.

Serra do Sudeste wineries ♀

Brocardo Vinhedos & Vinho

Encruzilhada do Sul

@brocardovinhos

Euclides Brocardo has grown grapes at Serra do Sudeste since 2000. The family owns 21 hectares of vineyards on granitic, well-drained, sandy soil. Daughter Gabriela, formerly a tea sommelier, decided to switch to wine. After a first successful experimental vinification – a surprise homage to Euclides – she has produced wines commercially since 2020. The wines (8,000 bottles a year) are made at EBV, under her direction, by Alejandro Cardozo. Production is almost evenly divided between still and sparkling wines. The sparklers have achieved high marks in the *Descorchados* wine guide. Visitors (booking advised in advance) can stroll the vineyards and taste the wines, eventually pairing these with a lamb barbecue.

All the wines I tasted were ripe but moderate in alcohol, and showed good varietal typicity. Pedroso Chardonnay, unoaked, puts forward ripe pear and some pineapple; it is very fresh and textural, with slight unctuosity. Oaked Chardonnay (25 per cent of the wine spent four months in oak barrels) shows good integration of wood and fruit; it is ripe, savoury, buttery, textural and long. Rosé (70 per cent Muscat of Hamburg, 30 per cent Pinot Noir, direct pressing) is a true star: pale and intensely aromatic, brimming with white flowers, lychees and red berries; tingling acidity brings it alive. With a good body and long length, it is one of a kind.

Pinot Noir, unoaked, has fresh but ripe red berries with great purity of fruit, plus hints of earth and undergrowth; its vital acidity and vigorous tannic structure allow cellaring. Helena Nature (Pinot Noir, 12-month autolysis) has bread and dough framing fresh red berries; it is bone dry, well structured and savoury, saline at the end, and so food friendly. Marina Brut Rosé (Chardonnay, Pinot Noir), made by the traditional method with 15-month autolysis, is pale pink, displaying ripe red berries, patisserie and savoury notes. The Pinot Noir imparts an excellent structure; the wine is fresh, rich and food friendly.

Manus Vinhas e Vinhos

Encruzilhada do Sul

www.manusvinhasevinhos.com.br

This firm has produced grapes for third parties since 2000, owning 34 hectares with 20 grape varieties. These include, notably, Assyrtiko and Feteasca Neagra. Teroldego is also important; Professor Idalêncio Angheben (see page 141) brought the planting material from Trentino. They are planted on granitic soils, some of the oldest in Rio Grande do Sul, at 410 metres above sea level. Since 2020, however, they have had their own wines, made in Bento Gonçalves under the supervision of oenologist Monica Rossetti. They work with Embrapa, developing projects on precision viticulture and native yeast. Several scientific papers have been produced so far. As Gustavo Bertolini, one of the owners, and nephew of Idalêncio, explained, several native yeasts have been cultivated. Some of their wines are inoculated with these, exclusively from the *Saccharomyces* genus. Manus offers some very unusual bottlings of a very good quality. They plan to start making wines at their winery in 2026. It is possible to taste their wines in Bento Gonçalves (booking required).

Virgo unoaked Chardonnay, which doesn't undergo malolactic fermentation, has crisp acidity, clear mineral hints and some savouriness in a Chablis-like style, if riper. Liberum Alvarinho uses grapes from a Rías Baixas clone and is fermented with one of their selected yeasts; it is very aromatic, with ripe peach and citrus, perfumed and has a good structure; with a long length, it bears a closer resemblance to Albariño than Portuguese Alvarinho. Clássico Chardonnay is fermented and matured in French oak tonneaux, being riper and less acidic than Virgo. It is buttery, oak is evident but not overwhelming, and the wine is long and complex. Liberum Rosé is a unique blend of Barbera, Touriga Nacional and Feteasca Neagra, unlikely to be found anywhere else. It has a crisp acidity, perceptible phenolic grip and gastronomic merit.

Liberum Clairet is not commonplace: a claret-styled wine (hard to tell whether this is a dark rosé or a pale red) with very ripe red fruit; it is fresh and delicious. Clássico Pinot Noir is ripe, perfumed and elegant, with some earth, undergrowth, discreet vanilla and cedar – a classy wine. Clássico Touriga Nacional (luxury price level, as are the next two Clássicos) brings the expected characteristics of ripe blackberry, violets, mandarin peel and earth, having the proverbial elegance of this superb variety. With a strong structure of acidity and tannins, it will age well. Clássico Nebbiolo is again varietally true: moderate colour, ripe red fruit, hints of roses and dust, savoury, full bodied, and with high acidity and grippy tannins. It will reward cellaring. Clássico Teroldego has a deep colour, floral notes of ripe black fruit, high acidity and firm, sinewy tannins; long and complex, it also needs time to come together.

Nature Blanc de Blancs is a traditional method sparkler, 100 per cent Chardonnay, spending 12 months with its lees; hence, the good autolytic notes, combined with ripe fruit and high freshness with a delicate mousse. Another uncommon wine: Liberum Vermentino Extra-Brut; made by the traditional method, with 12 months of autolysis, it is very fresh, nutty, almost full bodied, textural and very interesting.

Vinícola Hermann

Pinto Machado

www.vinicolahermann.com.br

Adolar Leo Hermann, owner of one of Brazil's most important wine importers (Decanter), and using the expertise of Anselmo Mendes (of Portuguese Alvarinho fame), bought vineyards at Serra do Sudeste in 2009. These had been planted by Portuguese businessmen in 2002. Hermann kept some of the Portuguese varieties and planted Chardonnay and Pinot Noir to make base wines for sparklers. Using such grapes, wines are made at Serra Gaúcha by third parties under the technical direction of oenologist Mike Rosa. Hermann pioneered *sur lie* undisgorged sparkling wines in Brazil with Lírica Crua, still one of the most successful products of this kind. About 200,000 bottles are produced annually.

Alvarinho Jovem is crisp, fruity and youthful, with good varietal characteristics of peach and citrus. Bossa Tempranillo is ripe, evidently fruity, with discreet vanilla and spice from six months in used oak barrels. Lírica is their line of traditional method sparklers (all Chardonnay and Pinot Noir). Undisgorged Crua white started its successful career in 2013; sold after 12 months with lees, it is hazy, fresh, ripe in fruit, savoury, biscuity and complex, with a fine mousse. Crua Rosé has less fruit but more structure and savouriness. Brut white has a nice proportion of fruit and bready characters after a 12-month autolysis, enveloped by a crisp acidity. Brut rosé brings riper fruit (red berries) and more structure.

Also in Serra do Sudeste

- Bodega Czarnobay, Encruzilhada do Sul (www.bodegaczarnobay.com. br/)
- Vinhas do Tempo, winery in Monte Belo (www.vinhasdotempo.com.br)
- Vinhedo Pedras Altas, Pedras Altas (www.vinhedopedrasaltas.com.br)

CAMPOS DE CIMA DA SERRA

The limits of this region, like those of Serra do Sudeste, were defined by IBRAVIN in 2010. Also, similarly to Serra do Sudeste, grape production for *vinhos finos* is centred around two cities: Vacaria and Muitos Capões. One neighbouring township (Monte Alegre dos Campos), however, has some planted areas of *vinifera* grapes (despite producing largely Bordô and other *labrusca* grapes) and is included in the statistics here.

The late Raul Anselmo Randon (who died in 2018), an entrepreneur from Caxias do Sul, in Serra Gaúcha, was highly successful with a company specializing in truck trailers and truck chassis adaptation, diversifying afterwards to agribusiness. He was, for some time, the largest apple producer in Brazil. With very different interests, and after a trip to Italy, he began to produce an excellent, high-quality hard cheese, *Gran Formaggio*, much like a Grana Padano. Not content, after consulting with the Miolo family from Serra Gaúcha he started a vineyard at Muitos Capões in 2001. In a few years, the wine brand RAR (vinified by Miolo) was launched and again became a successful product. This can be considered the start of viticulture at Campos de Cima da Serra. Other producers (such as Sozo in 2001 and Aracuri in 2005) followed suit, forming what is today a firmly established region. With specialized support from Embrapa, it has already initiated the long process of trying to be certified as a geographical indication. They plan, ambitiously, to go straight to DO, skipping the IP stage.

The most important city in Campos de Cima is Vacaria (population 64,187 in 2022). The best tourist destinations, however, are the National Parks of Serra Geral and Aparados da Serra at Cambará do Sul. Astounding canyons can be visited, with spectacular views and a recently installed (2023) zipline (known in Brazil as a *tirolesa)* providing an adventurous ride over the very deep Fortaleza Canyon.

Climate and soils

This region's name reflects some of its characteristics: *Campos* (or fields, as it is relatively flat) *de Cima* (highland) *da Serra* (Gaúcha; geographically, albeit not for wine, it belongs to the Serra). It is, in fact, the highest wine region in Rio Grande do Sul (above 900 metres). Altitude explains why it is the coldest area in the state; snow is relatively frequent in some years. The climatic classification (MCC) is HI-1 (temperate), DI-2 (humid), CI+1 (cold nights). Early and late frosts and hail are the principal weather hazards. As usual in humid regions, fungal diseases are the main threats in the vineyards: downy mildew and cluster rots, plus excoriosis and anthracnose. From 2018 to 2022, it rained an average of 1,754 millimetres annually at Vacaria. Predominant soil types (SiBCS classes) are *latossolos* and *cambissolos*, both dystrophic (that is, infertile). They are usually deep, with good drainage.

Planted areas and wine types

According to SIVIBE (2022 data), the total planted area of *vinifera* and *vinifera*-like varieties (like BRS Lorena), including three towns (Vacaria, Muitos Capões and Monte Alegre dos Campos), was 147 hectares. The most planted cultivars, in descending order, were Merlot, Cabernet Sauvignon, Chardonnay, Pinot Noir, Sauvignon Blanc, Moscato Giallo, Malvasia de Cândia, BRS Lorena and Gewurztraminer. Other varieties exist, however, such as Alvarinho, Verdelho, Tinta Roriz and Touriga Nacional.

According to Embrapa, and quite generally, white wines tend to have a light to medium colour, with moderate to high aromatic intensity; flavours and alcohol are moderate and acidity is crisp and high, balancing the other components and allowing medium-term keeping and ageing. Reds have a medium to deep colour, medium aromatic and flavour potency (with enough complexity, albeit fruit predominates), showing enough structure (fresh acidity, high tannin content, medium alcohol) to permit several years of keeping and improving in the bottle. Long ripening periods favour sugar accumulation, so much so that it is possible to find red wines up to a whopping 16% abv. Notwithstanding this, elegance is the most relevant characteristic of most wines produced here, allied to freshness and fruit purity. Pinot Noir does exceptionally well here, being one of the staples of viticulture at Campos de Cima da Serra.

Campos de Cima da Serra wineries

Aracuri Vinhos Finos

Muitos Capões ♀

www.aracuri.com.br/

Henrique Aliprandini and João Meyer, who are apple producers, decided to diversify and planted a vineyard in 2005. They now own 12 hectares at 960 metres on low-fertility soil, benefitting from plenty of wind, which reduces humidity and disease. Aracuri is the Indigenous name for a local parrot, *charão* in Portuguese, meaning 'bird of the tall tree' – this being the typical southern Brazilian pine tree or *Araucaria*. The annual harvest reaches 50 tons. Chardonnay, Sauvignon Blanc, Cabernet Sauvignon, Merlot and Pinot Noir are planted. From these, they craft (at select third parties in Serra Gaúcha) several lines of wines under the technical expertise of oenologist Paula Schenato. Although they still don't have an oenotouristic set-up, visitors are welcome (weather permitting) to visit the pleasant garden amongst *jabuticaba* trees at their administrative facilities in Vacaria. There, I was warmly and competently received by Cláudia Nunes, an agricultural engineer (but who is, in truth, a factotum in the firm), and was able to taste their wines. Visitors are indeed welcome, as long as the visit is booked in advance.

Campos Altos Cabernet Sauvignon, unoaked, is an easy-drinking wine. It is fresh and devoid of herbaceousness but shows good varietal typicity. Aracuri Sauvignon Blanc demonstrates the region's style for this cultivar: more elegant than explosive in aromas and flavours, crisp and with high varietal typicity. Aracuri Chardonnay sees no oak and undergoes partial malolactic fermentation; it has an evident varietal character and is fresh, fruity and elegant. The Aracuri white blend mixes the former two grapes; although Chardonnay is 75 per cent, Sauvignon Blanc appears very clearly in aromas and flavours, whereas its companion adds body and structure.

Pinot Noir is a dark, savoury, structured, charmingly fruity example of this variety; albeit good to drink now, a few years of bottle ageing will serve it well. Aracuri Cabernet Sauvignon is a youthful wine with good varietal character, reflecting the cool origin: elegant, fresh and fluid, with ripe cassis, correct oak character (six months in used French barrels), and sleek, fine-grained tannins. Collector Cabernet Sauvignon is dark and intensely aromatic, with a firm structure of fine tannins

Aracuri vineyard

and invigorating acidity. The oak (12 months, French, second use) is seamlessly integrated. It can improve and keep in the bottle for five to six years. Reduto, their super-premium wine, is 100 per cent Merlot, multi-vintage, and made from dehydrated grapes. These are harvested very ripe and undergo 20–25 days of *appassimento*. This is a deeply coloured wine with intense aromas and flavours of raisined fruit, a sturdy structure of sinewy tannins, healthy acidity and high alcohol. It is a big, complex wine suitable for long cellaring.

Aracuri Brut (Chardonnay, long Charmat method) is fresh, fruity and elegant, with a touch of autolysis. The traditional method sparklers take advantage of the sound quality of Pinot Noir from Aracuri's vineyards. Nature, Blanc de Noir (Pinot Noir), somewhat austere in the nose, grows up in the mouth, being rich, well structured, with some savouriness and clear autolytic character. Rosé Nature is also Pinot Noir (24-month autolysis). It is a dark pink wine, rich in ripe red berries, so dry and exceedingly fresh. Sur Lie, undisgorged, again Pinot Noir, is savoury, with a saline touch, complex and concentrated and has great gastronomic versatility.

Vinícola Campestre (Zanotto) ♀

Vacaria

www.vinicolacampestre.com.br

The brand Pérgola, owned by the Zanotto family, has been the sales leader in Brazil for nine consecutive years in the category of *vinhos de mesa*. This is a long-standing business (about 50 years) at Campestre da Serra, 50 kilometres south of Vacaria and belonging to Serra Gaúcha. Their *vinhos finos* branch at Vacaria started in 2017, when they bought the large, deactivated installations of a former slaughterhouse. This has been remarkably transformed into a beautiful vineyard/winery, including a large oenotouristic complex. The year 2020 marked their entry into the *vinhos finos* market under the guidance of oenologist André Donatti. Now, they own 33 hectares of *vinifera* vineyards with 17 varieties. Besides the usual cultivars (Chardonnay, Moscato Giallo, Sauvignon Blanc, Cabernet Sauvignon, Malbec, Merlot, Pinot Noir, Syrah, Tannat), they also have less common varieties: Gewurztraminer, Ancellotta, Montepulciano, Rebo and Sangiovese. They do not buy grapes to make *vinhos finos*. The annual production of these is 150,000 bottles. More than half (60 per cent) comprises sparkling wines, of which almost all are Charmat or Asti-like. Oenotourism is well developed, including vineyards and winery tours, tastings, events and an Italian restaurant, Villa Campestre. It is a joy to visit Campestre and its world-class complex.

Zanotto Sauvignon Blanc is typical of Campos de Cima da Serra, where such varietals are not exuberant but fresh and elegant. The Reserva version displays very good oak integration. Gran Reserva Chardonnay is barrel fermented, with no malolactic fermentation, keeping a crisp acidity; the oak is clear.

Varietal Syrah is savoury and spicy, and a good example of a cool-climate wine from this cultivar. Zanotto Varietal Pinot Noir, unoaked, has pure, fresh fruit, and is easy, soft and lively. The Reserva version spends 12 months in second-use barriques, is very ripe and shows good structure and typicity. Reserva Corte 2020 (a blend of four red grapes) is a very ripe wine, with a high, warming 16% abv. I tasted a barrel sample of a Gran Reserva Tannat with the same alcohol level, which revealed how well grapes ripen in this terroir. Some wines are labelled as 'Roots – Vinificação Integral'. The Merlot version offers this variety's rich, typical black fruits; partially barrel fermented, it is full and concentrated and will age well. Roots Rebo is an exclusive delight: dense but fresh, fruity, well structured and with a seamless oak integration; it will improve after spending up to five to six years in the bottle. Charmat Brut (Chardonnay, 11.3 grams per litre residual sugar) is soft and fruity.

Família Lemos de Almeida Vinhas e Vinhos 🍷

Muitos Capões

www.familialemosdealmeida.com.br/

Lemos de Almeida is an exception in Rio Grande do Sul: a winery whose origin has nothing to do with Italy, as its founder and owner, Agamenon Lemos de Almeida, has Portuguese roots (from the Azores). He started the business in 2005, when their vineyard was planted, and leads it with his daughter Bibiana. The first wines were from the 2012 vintage. Today, they use only grapes from their vineyards: 12 hectares, from which 100,000 bottles are produced yearly, under the technical expertise of oenologist Delto Garibaldi. Portuguese varieties are, as expected, important here (25 per cent of the vineyard), although the most planted cultivars are Merlot and Pinot Noir. There is a very good oenot-ouristic set-up, including reproductions of Azorean style buildings – the *Villa Açoriana* – and an events centre. Portuguese decorated wall tiles, embroidery and artworks add to the interesting vineyard and winery tour. All visits must be booked. They also have a wine shop at Vacaria, where I could taste many of their wines.

Capella dos Campos is their entry-level line. Sauvignon Blanc has a distinct style, being very ripe, with a fuller body and less acidity than the usual Campos de Cima da Serra wines from this variety. Verdelho is pale and aromatic, with fresh pear and citrus, crisp acidity and good varietal typicity. Alvarinho is very ripe at almost 15% abv and typical: lots of ripe peaches, with hints of minerality and saltiness, full bodied and firmly structured.

Capella Pinot Noir is fruity and youthful, brimming with fresh red berries and well balanced by the agreeable acidity. It is a delicious un-oaked wine. Touriga Nacional is a darker wine with a more substantial structure and aromas and flavours of blackberries and violets. Casais Açorianos is an interesting rosé blend of Touriga Nacional and Tinta Roriz; pale pink, very dry, with crisp acidity, fresh red fruits and a perceptible tannic structure, it is a good alternative to Provence rosés. Família Lemos de Almeida are oaked wines. Chardonnay is a well-structured, savoury wine with evident oakiness. Pinot Noir (24 months in French oak barriques, second use) is a savoury red, displaying considerable structure of acidity and tannins that will allow it to age gracefully. Touriga Nacional/Tinta Roriz blend, again matured for two years in used oak, offers smoke, tobacco, violets, vanilla and toast; its fresh acidity and stout tannic structure also permit cellaring, albeit drinking very well today. Sparkling Villa Açoriana Nature, so finely bubbly, is bone dry, flinty, crisp and with moderate autolytic character.

Vinícola Rar ♀

Vacaria

www.rar.ind.br/marcas/rar-vinhos

As we have seen, the late Raul Anselmo Randon played a central role in starting viticulture at Campos de Cima da Serra (see page 192). They have vineyards at Muitos Capões and Vacaria. Miolo crafts RAR's wines at Serra Gaúcha. The firm partners with Masi, the famous Veneto producer, to sell some of their wines (from Argentina and Italy). There is a pretty store at Vacaria (Spaccio Randon), where the wines can be tasted and bought, along with many food delicacies (such as their excellent Gran Formaggio cheese). Technical visits can be scheduled; my host was the amiable and enthusiastic sommelier Carlos, nicknamed 'Chitão'.

Avvento Rosé from Pinot Noir is light pink (five to six-hour maceration), dry, refreshing and fruity. Collezione Gewurztraminer is quite distinguished, as it is made from grapes that are usually partly botrytized (about 20 per cent). It shows the variety's typically deep colour, intense aromatics (lychee, tropical fruit) and moderate acidity; off-dry and long, it is a perfect match for spicy, exotic dishes.

Collezione Pinot Noir is perfumed, clean and elegant, so typical of this cool-climate region; it spends six months in used French oak barrels. Riserva di Famiglia is a Bordeaux blend matured for one year in new French oak barriques. It is very well structured, with ripe fruit and clean acidity, and it is a serious wine that will improve in the bottle for seven to eight years. Don Raul (luxury price level) is 100 per cent Merlot from *appassimento*, a blend of three outstanding vintages (2012, 2018, 2020). The grapes dry indoors for six to seven weeks, and the wine stays for 30 months in second-use French oak barrels. An Amarone-like product, benefitting from the expertise of Masi, it is deeply coloured, intensely aromatic and concentrated, off-dry, warm (15% abv) and full bodied, with a long, rich, complex finish – an outstanding wine.

Avvento Brut (Chardonnay/Pinot Noir, Charmat) is intensely fruity but keeps stimulating acidity. Cuvée Raul Brut has equal proportions of Chardonnay and Pinot Noir, and undergoes a 12-month autolysis (traditional method); it is a good example of the Brazilian style of such wines: at once fruity and fresh but retaining elegance, with a moderate autolytic character. Nature has the same varietal proportion but is kept on lees for 18 months; with a deeper colour, it shows more biscuit and bready character, especially evident in the mouth.

Vinhos Sopra

Vacaria

@vinhosopra

The Varaschin family is a traditional Campos de Cima da Serra apple producer. In 2008, Ermano Varaschin honoured his Italian ancestors and planted 3.5 hectares of vineyards at 950 metres above sea level. They grow Sauvignon Blanc, Chardonnay, Pinot Noir and Merlot. The wines (about 4,000 bottles a year) are made under the supervision of oenologist Alejandro Cardozo at his EBV business, in Caxias do Sul.

Sauvignon Blanc escapes from the stereotype of overt aromatics, being more subdued in the nose; it has a good volume and texture (from long lees contact) in the mouth, is fresh but ripe, bringing white guava and mango – more elegant than exuberant. Chardonnay points to its cool climate (for Brazil) origin: pale, discreet in the nose, but showing ripe pear and apple, with hints of pineapple, and very fresh and slender. Riguardo is their premium Merlot; from biodynamic grapes, it shows a deep ruby colour, having a moderate aromatic intensity of ripe plums, violet, toast and some coconut and vanilla notes; it is very fresh in the mouth, with soft, fine tannins.

Sozo Vinhos Finos de Altitude ♀

Vacaria

www.sozovinhos.com.br

José Sozo grew up in a 'colonial' environment at Flores da Cunha, in Serra Gaúcha. A colony is a group of descendants of Italian immigrants living in rural zones. His father, Carmine, made wine domestically, and José developed a fondness for the drink when he was very young. After a successful career as a business administrator, he settled at Vacaria in 1988. Together with Raul Randon, he participated in pioneering initiatives to kickstart viticulture in Campos de Cima da Serra. He started to plant his vineyard – the second in the region – in 2001, at Monte Alegre dos Campos (near Vacaria), at 980 metres, on basaltic soil. The first wine was launched in 2004. The traditional French (or 'international') varieties were cultivated from the vineyard's inception. From 2017, they were followed by Italian cultivars, and, more recently, other grapes from

Georgia, Portugal, Greece and, again, Italy are being tried. José's son, Rodrigo, after living and working abroad for 25 years, returned to Rio Grande do Sul and currently plays an active part in the business. José Sozo is a seasoned, cultivated person and a gentlemanly host. Tastings and visits to the vineyards can be arranged directly with Mr Sozo.

Portal dos Carvalhos Fumé Blanc is an oaked Sauvignon Blanc that has spent nine months in barriques; it is an elegant, perfumed wine with deftly managed oakiness, which is not at all invasive. Orange (the wine's name) is an orange wine made from Sauvignon Blanc and Chardonnay, mixing two vintages and spending an average of ten months on skins; it is golden, brimming with umami, so savoury and with a saline touch.

The charming Clarete is a lightly coloured red, a blend of Sozo's Sangiovese and Chardonnay by the Don Affonso winery (Serra Gaúcha), very fruity, delicious, hard to resist, so fresh, and excellent to accompany pasta with tomato-based sauces. Terroir Barbera Piemonte is deeply coloured, bringing ripe fruit, mouth-watering acidity and soft tannins, which are typical of this variety. Terroir Pinot Noir shows how well the variety performs in this region: it's perfumed, fruity and fresh, but with a very good tannic structure (however silky), allowing it to improve in the bottle to gain tertiary complexity.

Sozo Blanc de Blancs Nature is a traditional method (24-month autolysis) Chardonnay sparkler, bone dry, crisp, steely and food friendly.

OTHER RIO GRANDE DO SUL REGIONS

Some other areas of Rio Grande do Sul make wines from *vinifera* and *labrusca* varieties. The planted areas for *vinhos finos* are not large, but many products show a growing level of quality and deserve close attention.

Alto Uruguai

Alto Uruguai, or Northwest Rio Grande do Sul, is a thriving new region with wineries located in several towns (Ametista do Sul, Crissiumal, Entre-Ijuís, Itatiba do Sul, Santo Ângelo, Sarandi and Três Palmeiras). One city, Chapecó, in the south-west of the neighbouring state, Santa Catarina, also has a winery and may be included here.

Viticulture started at Alto Uruguai at about the turn of the century. The legendary oenologist Adolfo Lona, who was then working for Bacardi-Martini, aided by Evalde Filippon, assisted local proprietors in Ametista do Sul in planting vineyards. The support of Silvio Poncio, then mayor of Ametista, was invaluable, according to Filippon. The results were so good that Lona launched a line of red wines named 'Terroir', including a Cabernet Sauvignon from the region. Since then, other entrepreneurs have followed this example. The name 'Alto Uruguai' is deceptive. The 'Uruguai', here, does not relate to the country Uruguay, but rather the homonymous river, whose source is in Brazil. This majestic, scenic river flows west and makes up a good part of the frontier between Rio Grande do Sul and Santa Catarina before it becomes the border between Brazil and Argentina. It ends at the Río de la Plata, the large estuary formed by the mighty Uruguai and Paraná rivers. The most planted *vinifera* grapes at Alto Uruguai are Chardonnay, Moscato, Cabernet Sauvignon, Merlot, Pinot Noir and Tannat. Both still and sparkling wines of all colours are produced, up until now in relatively small quantities compared to, for example, Serra Gaúcha.

Missões

Missões is a new region with a few producers in towns like Entre-Ijuís, Santo Ângelo, and São Borja. They claim a common historical heritage: the Jesuitic Missions, where viticulture and winemaking started in the state, and the importance of the original inhabitants, the Guaranis (several wine labels honour them).

The producers from the Northwest and Missões have joined together and created the expression 'Terroir NoMi' to identify the provenance of their wines. They are considering an IP certification, albeit their number (eight wineries) is still tiny.

Vale Central

Vale Central – yes, Rio Grande do Sul also has one, like Chile and California, but it is much smaller in vinous terms. The activity here is centred around the large city of Santa Maria (population 271,633 in 2022), in the heart of Rio Grande do Sul, including the small towns of Itaara and São João do Polêsine. Viticulture also began with the arrival of Italian immigrants; this was the fourth colony established in Rio Grande do Sul (and the first outside of Serra Gaúcha) in the nineteenth century. Planted areas, like the number of wineries, are small. They include the usual characters, like Cabernet Sauvignon, Merlot and Tannat, but also less common varieties like Traminer and Montepulciano.

Porto Alegre

Around Porto Alegre – despite the unfavourable climate (too warm, too humid) – areas surrounding the state capital already have a long history of viticulture and winemaking. The late Oscar Guglielmone (tragically killed in 1993 by a resentful employee), from Viamão (almost a suburb of Porto Alegre), became famous in the 1980s. One of his artisanal wines, a Nebbiolo, was deemed the best Brazilian red wine by the team of *Guia Quatro Rodas*, a nationwide tourist guidebook, then edited yearly and now unfortunately out of print. His Adega Medieval winery has also gone (so many sad losses), but a few brave winemakers still produce wine at Viamão, albeit in minuscule amounts. A growing number of urban wineries in the capital have joined them. These use grapes from several origins to craft their wines.

Other Rio Grande do Sul wineries

Adolfo Lona Vinhos e Espumantes ♀

Porto Alegre

www.adolfolona.com.br/

The Argentine (or, more appropriately, after decades of living and working here, Brazilian) oenologist Adolfo Lona is an important personality in the national vinous scene. He came here in 1973 to work at Martini & Rossi. At that time, this company (besides their primary vermouth business) owned the Chateau Duvalier brand, a national success custom-made for Martini by Companhia Vinícola Rio-Grandense. Lona was to oversee the process and assess the building of a new wine facility at Garibaldi. So he did; at this new plant, he launched the very successful De Gréville sparkler line and the Baron de Lantier brand of still wines, made from 1985 to 2002. Some of their Bordeaux blends became legendary in Brazil due to their quality and longevity. He also pioneered the concept of terroir, launching the *Série Regionais*, which included wines from Garibaldi, Pinheiro Machado and Ametista do Sul a long time ago. Lona was also instrumental in promoting wine lovers' associations, such as the Confraria De Lantier, which contributed to the dissemination of wine culture in the country.

Lona left the company, then Bacardi-Martini, in 2001 and established his own sparkling and still wines business in 2004. He purchases wines from Serra Gaúcha and Campanha Gaúcha, produces Charmat wines at third parties and finishes his traditional method *espumantes* at his urban winery in Porto Alegre. Here, 15,000 bottles of traditional method sparklers are made annually. Charmat products total 45,000 bottles and still wines 26,700. All this amounts to 86,700 bottles a year. Lona's wines are included in the wine charts of top Brazilian restaurants, such as Fasano, Claude Troisgros and Locanda Della Mimosa. New installations were added on the eve of the day I visited this dear old friend. Visitors can shop, taste wines and take wine courses. Booking is advised.

Brut Charmat is made from Chardonnay (with no malolactic fermentation in the base wine) and Pinot Noir, remaining four months with its lees in the tank, plus at least four more months in the bottle. It is very fruity, fresh and elegant. Regarding the Charmat method, Lona

Adolfo Lona

believes it allows the production of lower-cost sparklers that are creamy and easy to drink, excellent for teasing the appetite and cleansing the palate. He thinks sparkling wines should be drunk more frequently during meals, as they allow a better perception of food flavours.

Baron, a red blend made to honour the legendary Baron de Lantier, is made predominately from Cabernet Sauvignon (51 per cent), plus Merlot (34 per cent) and Tannat – all from Campanha Gaúcha. It is dark and ripe, showcasing red and black fruit, complex, layered, and with very fine grained, almost velvety tannins; so round, elegant and well made – a great red wine indeed, exuding class and quality.

Vinícola Ametista ♀

Ametista do Sul (Alto Uruguai)

vinicolaametista.com.br/

Silvio Cesar Poncio, owner of amethyst mines and former mayor of Ametista do Sul, founded this winery in 2009. A very agreeable person, Silvio says he has tried to diversify the town's economy, which is otherwise centred on mining and tourism. He dreams of crafting products of excellence renowned for their quality. The winery is appropriately named, as it is located in the town boasting the title 'World Capital of Amethyst'. There are many mines here, which are very interesting to visit. This winery uses a decommissioned mine to mature its wines 300 metres beneath the surface. Here, the temperature is a steady 16–18°C, with 50–70 per cent humidity. They own 10 hectares of *vinifera*: Chardonnay, Moscato Giallo, Sauvignon Blanc, Cabernet Sauvignon, Malbec, Merlot, Pinot Noir and Tannat. Soils are pebbly, mineral and well drained.

At Ametista do Sul, the climate leads to an earlier harvest than at Serra Gaúcha (from early January to mid-February). This does not prevent a complete ripening; it is common for reds to attain 14% abv or more. They use a very new, shiny winery to make an annual average of 40,000 bottles of *vinhos finos*, under the baton of oenologist AndersonSchmitz. Still wines comprise 88 per cent of their production, with reds predominating. Sparklers are made using the traditional method only. The oenotouristic facilities are excellent – it was such a pleasure to visit their facilities and I was warmly received by Cleci, their enthusiastic and welcoming sommelier.

Ágata Sauvignon Blanc tends more to elegance and freshness (despite malolactic fermentation) and shows good varietal character.

Wines ageing in a disused mine, Vinícola Ametista

Chardonnay (whole-cluster pressing), with a clear expression of the cultivar, has some vanilla from oak cubes. Pink Cabernet Sauvignon, direct press but not pale (eight hours of skin contact), is very fresh (no malo), fruity and well structured.

The Ágata de Fogo line comprises only reds, spending 12 months in used French oak barrels. Merlot has a deep colour and considerable tannic structure with moderate acidity. Malbec is deep purple, with intense typical ripe plum and chocolate aromas, yet keeping freshness and elegance. Ágata 10 anos is a premium line made only in outstanding vintages, spending 18 months in new oak. Tannat has a deep colour, evident oaky character and strong tannic structure; ageworthy, it needs time. Cabernet Sauvignon is true to the variety, with lots of colour, ripe fruit and seamless oak integration.

Ágata de Fogo Brut Champenoise (Chardonnay/Pinot Noir) is fresh and fruity, with a good deal of autolytic character from an 18-month autolysis.

Vinícola Cannion

São José dos Ausentes
cannion.com.br/

Alexandre de Carvalho and his wife, Fabiana Nelson, are a brave pair. After visiting São José dos Ausentes, in the cold highlands (1,200 metres above sea level) in the north-east corner of Rio Grande do Sul (a continuum with Serra Catarinense), they became fascinated by the region's beauty and bought a property. After consulting the oenologist Jefferson Sancineto Nunes (see Vinicola Pericó, page 230), they planted a pioneering vineyard about 800 metres away from the astounding canyon Amola Faca. This demanded two years of soil correction, as there was a lot of peat and high acidity. They planted some unusual PIWI varieties developed at Udine University in Italy (Sauvignon Rytos, Cabernet Eidos and Merlot Kanthus), as well as Soreli (another Udine cross), Alvarinho, Gewurztraminer, Cabernet Franc, Montepulciano, Nebbiolo, Sangiovese, Syrah and Teroldego. Until the vineyard is well established in this new region, they are buying grapes from other parts of Rio Grande do Sul to make their wines, labelled Experimentus, at third parties.

Riesling (Itálico) is a good example of how in Brazil this variety can generate fruity (ripe pear, apple), fresh white wines with a soft texture and medium body. Chardonnay, unoaked, is true to the variety: soft, ripe fruit, hints of pineapple, moderate alcohol and fresh acidity. Tannat shows how this cultivar does not need to be overtly tannic; it is ready to drink, with black fruit and earthiness, good acidity and a savoury end. Cabernet Sauvignon Reserva has some Alicante Bouschet, and it shows: deep colour, softer tannins and very ripe fruit, all well integrated with the evident but fine oak. Charmat Brut is fruity, fresh and easy drinking. Traditional method Brut is very Brazilian: clear ripe fruit, great freshness and creamy mousse, with some complexity from a 24-month autolysis.

Vinícola Cárdenas

Mariana Pimentel

www.vinicolacardenas.com.br

Renato Cárdenas planted the first vineyards in 2010 outside the main vinous roads of Rio Grande do Sul, about 75 kilometres to the south of Porto Alegre. Sixty different varieties were initially planted and tested on granitic soil. The first wines appeared in 2018. He defines the winery as 'boutique', although 16 hectares are now planted, and has earned several prizes for some of his bottlings. Cárdena's wines are made by third parties under close supervision. They have innovated, devising a beautiful, trademark amphora-like ceramic bottle which prevents light reaching the wine inside.

Meninas do Vinhedo Pinot Noir has ample intensity and concentration of ripe red berries, mouth-watering acidity, and a complexity imparted by earth, cedar and hints of vanilla. Meninas do Vinhedo Petit Verdot is spicy and fresh, with fine oak aromas balancing the ripe black fruit. Meninas do Vinhedo red blend is predominately Merlot, plus Syrah and Petit Verdot; it is deep-dark, the latter two varieties imparting an evident spiciness and structure to Merlot's rich fruit; oak treatment is deft and moderate, and the fresh acidity makes the wine so fluid. Meninas do Vinhedo Tannat translates this variety's character well: moderate intensity of ripe black fruit, earth, some spice and violets, its six months in oak contributing with cedar and vanilla, all within Tannat's strong structure of clear acidity and firm (albeit fine) tannins – a balanced, savoury drink, bone dry and asking to be enjoyed with food.

Amphora Rebo (luxury price level) is deeply coloured, with a high intensity and concentration of very ripe berries, mint, vanilla and cedar; rich in the mouth, it is fresh and soft in tannins, with a long length – it really stands out. Amphora Merlot is remarkable for its velvety tannins, and one of the smoothest, most caressing wines I have ever tasted. Now six years old, it still shows ripe plums and blackberries, dusty hints, vanilla, spice and tertiary components of leather and earth.

Domus Mea ♀

São João do Polêsine (Vale Central)

domusmea.com.br/

São João do Polêsine, a small town, has a district named Recanto Maestro, the site of luxury condominiums and other activities. This was all started about 30 years ago – when there was next to nothing there – by Antonio Meneghetti, an Italian ex-friar, artist and founder of the so-called Ontopsychology. A complete resort and aqua park, the Termas Romanas, take advantage of naturally warm and saline waters. All this is quite close (35 kilometres) to Santa Maria.

It is said that a pupil of Meneghetti's, Edi Kante, who produced wine at Friuli-Venezia-Giulia, was challenged by the master to make wine here. He accepted and started the Domus Mea winery at Recanto Maestro in 2007. Planting material, including Traminer and Montepulciano, was brought from Italy. In 2017, however, Kante sold the vineyard to Sergio Marin, Wesley Lacerda and Ademar da Silva Jr. Kante continues as the consultant oenologist, although Marcos Vian, helped by Elisandro Bortoluzzi, leads most of the work. The experienced agronomist Silvano

Michelon takes care of the vineyard. Soils have a thin layer of sand on a thick stratus of clay, which retains water. This has demanded a complex drainage system to avoid waterlogging. Many of their wines show some salinity, making one wonder whether the region's warm, saline thermal waters have some influence on this.

Within the exuberant greenness of the pretty hills of the area, great care was taken to construct the reception building, a beautiful garden with a lake, and the modern winery, where all the equipment is Italian. During Kante's first years, the decision was made to produce predominately white wines; hence, Chardonnay, Pinot Grigio, Sauvignon Blanc and Traminer have been chosen. Montepulciano, however, was also planted with success. The new owners introduced Merlot, Malbec and Tannat. Total annual production is 25,000 bottles. Visitors are welcome to taste the wines and enjoy the garden and the beautiful surroundings; reservations are advised (open seven days a week). I was very kindly received by Luis Eduardo Dias, who started work here six years ago.

Sauvignon Blanc is more elegant than exuberant and tropical; it is delicate, very crisp and slender, though the varietal character is evident. The same relatively low aromatic power happens with their Traminer/ Pinot Grigio, a co-fermented field blend; in the mouth, it is quite substantial, with a good structure and body.

Pink Pinot Noir is so very crisp that you think it is fizzy (it is not), with saline notes and a high gastronomic versatility. Montepulciano is dark and full of black fruit, with a strong structure of acidity and tannins, typical of this grape. Primus red blend (Merlot/Malbec/Tannat) has a deep colour, ripe blackberries, strong tannic structure, high acidity and a full body – it needs time and will certainly improve in the bottle.

Traditional method Nature (Chardonnay, Riesling Itálico), six-month autolysis, has a good autolytic character and some salinity and is very crisp and elegant. It was a privilege to taste their first commercial wine, a 2008 Chardonnay: it is very alive, still displaying clear ripe fruit and high acidity amidst hints of honey and beeswax.

Vinícola Fin ♀

Entre-Ijuís
www.vinicolafin.com.br

Belonging to the third generation of an Italian family that arrived in 1876, Jorge Fin, once a bank clerk, is at the helm here, crafting wines and grape juice. It is a real pleasure to talk to him – take your time and enjoy his conversation. He and his wife welcome visitors to their pretty vineyard and winery. They own 12 hectares of vines, crafting 60,000 bottles of wine yearly, of which 70 per cent are still (predominately red), 20 per cent sparklers and 10 per cent dessert wines. Those visiting São Miguel das Missões and the outstanding Jesuitic ruins (not to be missed – stay at the excellent Tenondé Park Hotel) will need to drive a mere 38 kilometres to enjoy the Fins' warm hospitality and fine wines. Do not miss Ancellotta, one of their specialities, and the sweet fortified wine. Oenotouristic facilities are available, including a deck over a lake, where sipping wine while the sun sets is a great way to end a day. You can taste up to three of their wines for free, seven days a week, without a prior reservation. More extensive tastings must be booked in advance, however.

Moscato Charrua (despite the name, it is 100 per cent Lorena), unfiltered, is very aromatic, floral, fruity and a bargain. Fin Malbec is a fresher, more elegant rendition of this grape, compared to Argentinian products, yet shows a clear varietal character of plums and chocolate. Tannat Reserva brings the powerful tannic structure of this cultivar, but the wine has enough fruit to balance the usual austerity. Tannat Gran Reserva, made from overripe grapes, is deeply coloured, full bodied, strongly structured and complex (notes of clove, tobacco, animal hints, fully ripe blackberries), with a long length. Marselan Gran Reserva, also made from overripe grapes, displays this variety's succulent, ripe berries and soft, velvety tannins. For those who want to know Marselan, or for its lovers, *ne plus ultra*. Ancellotta Gran Reserva do Produtor is again so typical of the variety, rich, soft, full bodied and spicy from six months in French oak.

Sparkling Moscatel, from Moscatos Giallo and Branco, is an excellent example of how well Brazil makes such wines: very agreeably fresh, less sweet than Asti, delicious and easy drinking. Porto das Missões, despite the label stating 'Vinho Licoroso Rosado Doce', is in truth red, the colour much like that of tawny Port; made from a blend of red grapes and fortified at 18% abv, it ages well in seven to eight years (part in old oak, part in stainless steel); an interesting, complex and intense dessert wine.

Vinhos Finos Malgarim ♀

São Borja

www.malgarimvinhos.com.br/

Sérgio Malgarim started a vineyard in 2001 with French planting material at Quinta do Sino, in São Borja. This town (the cradle of two Brazilian presidents) touches, in fact, the north-westernmost limit of Campanha Gaúcha (though it's not included in this IP). Malgarim highlights belonging to the Missões territory – where the Jesuits initiated viticulture in Rio Grande do Sul. He built his winery according to Missões' style, all made in beautiful, hand-carved red sandstone. The varieties grown are Cabernet Sauvignon, Merlot, Sangiovese and Tempranillo. Sérgio decided to plant Tempranillo to honour the history of the missions, established by Spanish priests, and Sangiovese due to his Italian roots. A few grapes, such as Riesling Itálico, are bought from third parties. Sérgio's son Daniel leads the winemaking, while his father is a gifted viticulturist. Their wines are all labelled after names linked to the rich but tragic history of the Indigenous people of this region, the Guaranis. Sérgio is always ready to talk about wines in general and his region in particular. Expect to spend a long time (which passes quickly, so agreeable is his conversation) with him discussing wine. Visitors are welcome for indoor and outdoor tastings in their pretty, bucolic surroundings, about 11 kilometres from São Borja. Reservation is necessary.

Sangiovese has a good varietal typicity: moderate colour, aromas and flavours of sour cherries and earth, vivid acidity, and medium body – but it shows its local origins through finer, softer tannins than its Italian counterparts. Arapysandú Tempranillo, fermented and matured in new American oak barrels, shows it clearly: high intensity of vanilla and coconut, here well married to ripe red berries, however with fresh acidity, soft tannins and a long length – echoes of Spain. Sepé Assemblage, a blend of four grapes, is a powerful, broad red; very ripe fruit marries well with evident oakiness from 12 months in American oak barrels. It is rich, warming (15.5% abv) and full bodied, has a muscular tannic structure and will age well.

Cantina Mincarone

Porto Alegre

@cantina_mincarone

Mincarone, an urban winery in Porto Alegre, was started in 2017 by Lizete and José Augusto Vicari. Currently, Caio Mincarone and his mother, Ana, lead the business. Small (albeit numerous) batches of minimal intervention wines are crafted from bought grapes. Most whites are made on skins in the 'orange' style. If you want your own label, they can also help you. Caio is the creator of the pretty labels.

Minca Ripasso Gewurztraminer is an orange wine from this characterful grape. Onion skin in colour, it is strongly aromatic: lychee, roses, papaya and ginger. It is bone dry and very concentrated, has some tannic grip and good freshness, and lingers in the mouth. True to the variety, Cabernet Franc has intense aromas of pencil shavings, violets, capsicum, cassis and hints of dust. It is very fresh, savoury, slender and savoury.

Vinícola Pianegonda ♀

Viamão

www.pianegonda.com.br/

This small winery purchases grapes from Vila Flores (Serra Gaúcha) to craft their products besides those grown locally. Several types of tastings, plus picnics, are offered to visitors to their beautiful surroundings – always through prior booking.

Vermentino is pale, bringing herbs, citrus and ripe peach. Fresh and textural, it opens in the glass and has a saline finish. Bruxaria Claret (from co-fermented Tannat, Nebbiolo and Alvarinho) is pale red and offers ripe red berries and floral hints. It is crisp and bone dry and with a lively tannic grip – it calls to be savoured with food.

Quinta Barroca da Tília ♀

Viamão

quintabarrocadatilia.com.br/

Agronomist Eduardo Giovannini, the author of a good book called *Manual de Viticultura*, worked at several important Brazilian wineries before deciding to buy land – at Viamão, close to Porto Alegre. This is a relatively small property, with 4 hectares of vineyards planted on sandy soil with multiple varieties. Total annual production is about 27,000 bottles. They make blended wines, almost field blends, which are not repeated year after year. Some varietals, however, are also produced. Although there are no oenotouristic facilities as such, visitors are welcome to taste the wines, providing they book first.

Luca is a rare blend: Caladoc, Malbec and Marselan. A part of the wine has not undergone malolactic fermentation, keeping it fresh. It is vinous and complex, exhibiting ripe and sweet black fruit, discreet cedar and toast, soft tannins, a full body, many layers, complexity and a long length.

Vinhos da Rua do Urtigão 🍷

Taquara

@vinhosdaruadourtigao

The Kunz family, led by Rubem Ernesto (plus his wife, Valéria, and children Tatiana and Rodrigo), started to make low-intervention wines in 2014. At first, they used third-party installations, but in 2019, their winery became functional. They buy grapes from selected producers (mostly organic or biodynamic) in Campos de Cima da Serra, Serra Gaúcha and Serra do Sudeste. Rubem embraced the philosophy of winemakers like Jolie, Chauvet, Lapierre and Overnoy, crafting small lots of minimal-intervention wines. Total annual production is about 4,000 bottles, of which only 10 per cent is sparkling. All wines have attractive labels, some with artwork from Valéria Kunz. They are not open to the general public, but small groups can visit for booked tastings.

All the wines I tasted were savoury, food friendly, spontaneously fermented and unfiltered. Inanna Alvarinho is golden, mineral and peachy; it is dense and textural but ripe, rich and fresh. Take your time and let it open up in the glass. Evah Gamay is a claret with a beautiful, light red colour; bone dry, with low alcohol, it is so fresh. Do not expect the traditional aromas of bubblegum or bananas from Gamay; here, fresh red berries appear. Animus Pinot Noir is moderate in colour, alcohol and tannins; it is redolent of fresh red berries, sour cherry and earth. Urtigão Poeira Cabernet Franc is very strong in varietal traits: capsicum, graphite, cassis, mouth-watering acidity and firm tannic structure. It is an electric, tense, rewarding wine. Outono Merlot, vinified with carbonic maceration, is floral, with considerable body and good tannic structure. Rüya Nebbiolo shows varietal fidelity: light colour, very perfumed, mixing fresh strawberries with flowers and earth; it has high acidity and a muscular tannic structure, demanding time to soften. One advantage: it is moderate in alcohol.

Soliman Vinícola Boutique 🍷

Itatiba do Sul (Alto Uruguai)

www.vinicolasoliman.com.br/

Rogério Soliman and his wife, Vanessa Bancer, founded this winery in 2005. They were pioneers in this area, which had previously been unknown for wine. The vineyards (5.5 hectares) are planted on stony, clayey soil at 800 metres, comprising eight varieties of French and Italian origin. The first wines were launched in 2012. Despite their brief existence, some of their products have achieved significant prizes and good evaluations by eminent chefs, such as Claude Troisgros.

The Römerwein wines are beautifully bottled and wrapped with personalized labels. All wines point to the owners' great care regarding labels (many inspired by chess), capsules and other details. Marcos Vian, the oenologist, leads the annual production of 20,000 bottles (mostly still reds). Serious wine lovers can participate in their 'Meu Vinho Experience', during which, over 18 months, all grape-growing and winemaking steps can be observed and each person receives their own final product. Visits, tastings and picnics in the wine garden are also available (book first).

Rainha Gran Chardonnay (of the Römerwein series) is golden, displaying very ripe fruit (apple, pineapple) amidst overt oakiness (vanilla, coconut, spice). Dense, warming (14% abv), concentrated and long, it will satisfy fans of ripe, New World, oaked Chardonnays. Torre Blends (four red varieties) brings red and black berries with hints of capsicum, coffee, vanilla and spice (12 months in French oak barrels); the tannins are ripe and fine. The wine is fresh, well balanced and food friendly. Torre Gran Reserva Sur Lie, from Cabernet Sauvignon and Tannat, is dark, with very ripe black fruit and strong aromas of vanilla, spice and cedar (15 months in new French oak barrels). It can be cellared for a long time due to fresh acidity and strong, grippy tannins. Rainha Montepulciano (Römerwein) offers ripe blackberries with hints of mint, fine herbs, spice, earth, violets, vanilla and toast. Its refreshing acidity and solid tannic structure make it complex, well balanced and ageworthy.

Casa Tertúlia ♀

Três de Maio (Alto Uruguai)

vinicolacasatertulia.com.br/

The Hilgert family, of German descent, migrated (for a second time) from the outskirts of Porto Alegre to the north-western part of Rio Grande do Sul, the Alto Uruguai, a place then called *Colônias Novas* (New Colonies). Here, they became landowners. This is not a traditional vine-growing region but rather a new one, so establishing a winery here involved experimentation, research and study. Viviane Hilgert became an oenologist at Bento Gonçalves, then returned to her homeland when Casa Tertúlia was born. *Tertúlia*, in Portuguese, is a conversation – certainly better with wine! Visitors are welcome through booked tastings and dinner (when dishes are paired with their wines).

Moscato de Alexandria is quite unusual in variety and style: golden, dry and a bit hazy from long lees contact. It is intensely aromatic (white flowers, lychee, grape, orange peel), moderately fresh, complex, concentrated and a bit phenolic in its finish. Textural and long, it is highly recommended – perhaps the best dry Muscat in Brazil.

Tertúlia Cabernet Sauvignon Safra Histórica is almost garnet in colour, with high varietal typicity (cassis, capsicum, fresh acidity, fine-grained tannins), elegant and lean, and so food friendly. Super-premium Marselan Safra Histórica, unoaked, is dark, very ripe and plummy, with a strong structure of tannins, allowing it to develop well in the bottle. The wine named IA (Inteligência Artificial), according to Gabriel Hilgert, was crafted using an algorithm he developed. It is a multi-vintage blend of Merlot, Marselan, Teroldego and Cabernet Sauvignon. Ruby with garnet rims, it brings tertiary flavours of leather, dried fruit and spice amidst some ripe black fruit, mint, herbs and basil. The tannins are firm but fine, and the wine is savoury, complex and layered.

Alliance Brut (Charmat method), unusually crafted from Chardonnay, Pinot Noir, Glera and Riesling Itálico, is fruity, fresh, easy going and delicious.

Vinícola Velho Amâncio 🍷

Santa Maria/Itaara (Vale Central)
velhoamancio.com.br/

One of a few Rio Grande do Sul's wineries without Italian roots, this winery has Portuguese origins: the immigrant Amâncio Pires de Arruda, who arrived at Santa Maria in 1885. He started his drinks business, however, fabricating *cachaça* after buying the property now owned by his heirs. The family kept the distillery for decades. Amâncio's grandson Rubens Fogaça, a mechanical engineer who worked for Volkswagen and throughout Brazil, returned to Itaara and started to make wine in 1987. Their vineyard is planted predominately on *neossolo* - a young, sandy soil with basalt deposits and low fertility. A total of 8.4 hectares of vines is cultivated, with five varieties (Chardonnay, Cabernet Sauvignon, Merlot, Pinot Noir and, interestingly, Syrah).

A small part of the vineyard lies at São Sepé, about 69 kilometres to the south. Here, the vines are decades old. They were part of the viticultural experiments by Almadén when it started exploring Rio Grande do Sul to establish itself here. At the time, oenologist Carlos Eugenio Daudt was instrumental in this research. After retiring from academic activities, he now lives, coincidentally, in front of Velho Amâncio and cultivates some vines. From these, a few wines, labelled Vinhos da Toka, are made at this winery. Unfortunately, this is not a commercial activity. Velho Amâncio also purchases some grapes from Campanha Gaúcha.

Today, the business is led by the agronomist Aline Fogaça, who holds a doctorate in Food Science and belongs to the fourth generation of this family. Rubens, her father, assesses her. They craft about 30,000 bottles annually, equally divided between still (predominately red) and sparkling (more traditional than Charmat) wines. Through modern and sustainable practices, Aline seeks to express the uniqueness of Vale Central, a region where two biomes meet: the Atlantic Forest and the Pampas. She sees sparkling wines as a true Brazilian vocation growing in importance. Visitors can visit the shop and taste their products. Aline often offers wine courses and guided tastings. They boast a beautiful building made of basalt stones, with a floor painted with pictures of vines. Larger tastings take place at gigantic tables made from enormous one-piece planks of the precious Brazilian wood *angelim pedra*. Rubens and Aline are extremely agreeable hosts, genuinely enjoying conversation about all things vinous. I had the fortune of tasting many of their wines on a Sunday night. Direct flights from São Paulo serve Santa Maria.

Caliandra Chardonnay, unoaked, has ripe fruit, clear varietal typicity, moderate acidity and a very good texture. Caliandra Syrah rosé, made through direct pressing and brief skin contact, is pale and bone dry, with elegant red fruit and crisp acidity.

Estação is a Bordeaux blend where Cabernet Sauvignon predominates, which shows well in the bottle: slight, elegant pyrazines, fine tannins, moderate colour and body. Terras Baixas Pinot Noir, from vines over 20 years old, has a moderate colour but is very ripe in fruit. Terras Baixas Merlot/Cabernet Sauvignon, from São Sepé grapes, is very alive in tannins and fruit, albeit the current wine being sold is from 2018 (in fact, it needs a few more years in the bottle to round up). Super-premium Garganta do Diabo (Devil's Throat), named after a remarkable road bridge that can be seen from the winery, is also a Bordeaux blend, its grapes being planted on higher terrain with more sunlight. This shows through perfect ripeness, great balance and ageing capacity.

The traditional method sparklers are named Vivelam (from Vinícola Velho Amâncio). La Vie Brut Rosé (12-month autolysis) is very pale – from Chardonnay and a dash of Syrah; it is fruity, fresh and well balanced. Its white Brut companion is similar: so Brazilian in its evident fruitiness, balanced by the moderate autolytic character, and very fresh. Unique Brut brings more complexity from a 36-month autolysis and is a tad drier than La Vie. Unique Extra Brut is much more autolytic in character, so complex, and reminiscent of a good Champagne. Vivelam 50 Nature (50-month autolysis), bone dry, vivid and sharp, is like a good vintage Champagne, needing more time in the bottle to better express itself.

Vinícola Weber ♀

Crissiumal (Alto Uruguai)

www.vinicolaweber.com.br/

This winery was founded by members of the Weber family (of German descent) in 1999, but vineyards existed here before this, with the first vintage being sold in 2000. The present owner, Delci Wermeier Weber, leads the business with his daughter Taciana Weber (the oenologist) and Henrique Gottens. There are 20 hectares planted on well-drained soil with balanced fertility, mostly Chardonnay, Cabernet Franc, Marselan, Merlot and Pinot Noir. About 10,000 bottles are crafted annually, of which 60 per cent are still (half reds, the balance equally divided between whites and rosés) and 40 per cent are sparkling (also equally divided into Moscatel, Charmat, traditional method and pétillant naturel). Visitors are welcome, but advance booking is needed. The visit includes a stroll amidst the beautiful vineyards adorned with flowers and palm trees, seeing the winery and a tasting. You may also enjoy a well-kept garden while tasting the wines and also a restaurant. They have a shop at the winery, too.

Henrique, a very dynamic and knowledgeable professional, and mainstay of this winery, received me to taste their wines. They craft microlots of certain wines, later sold as parts of their lines. I tasted Eu Floria (meaning 'I blossomed') white, a Sauvignon Blanc/Chardonnay blend: so fresh, fruity, light and delicious – as the French say, *gouleyant*! Eu Floria rosé, made by direct pressing (four hours of skin contact) from Pinot Noir and Marselan, is dry, fresh and fruity, and again hard to resist.

A new blend of Tannat, Marselan and Merlot is to become an entry-level red wine; it is a charming, well-made, everyday wine, and so fruity.

Instantes Cabernet Franc demonstrates how well this cultivar does here; with high varietal typicity (graphite, blackberries, green bell pepper, fresh acidity), spending six months in French oak barriques, it has a sturdy structure and will age well. A very interesting red wine is a blend of Tannat, Cabernet Franc and Malbec; with a very small production (225 litres), it spends six months in barrels made of the Brazilian wood *cabreúva*: blackberries, spice, refreshing acidity, strong tannins, tobacco, honey and floral hints, and sweet wood – truly original.

Symphonie Brut is made from Chardonnay and Riesling (the German grape, not Riesling Itálico) by the tank method; it is round, fruity and fresh. Sur Lie Rosé, 100 per cent Pinot Noir, undisgorged, is sold after 36 months on lees; it is fat, dense, very leesy and savoury, a complex example of its kind. Lotus Moscatel is another example of how well Brazil crafts these sparklers: from Moscato Bianco, Moscato Giallo and – yes – Poloskei Muskotaly (a hybrid of Hungarian origin), it is fresh, fine and elegant.

Tannat Licoroso is a fortified, moderately sweet red wine; a characterful brandy is used to arrest fermentation, and this shows up as cognac-like aromas and flavours.

Also in Rio Grande do Sul

- Altos Paraíso Vinhedos, Camaquã (altosparaiso.com.br/)
- Antonio Dias Vinhos de Terroir, Três Palmeiras, Alto Uruguai (www.vinhosantoniodias.com.br)
- Audaz Vinhos, Novo Hamburgo (@audazvinhos)
- Villa Bari, Porto Alegre (villabari.com.br/)
- Vinícola Bennato, Rolante (vinhosesucosbennato@yahoo.com.br)
- Vinícola Don Carlos/Novos Caminhos, Santo Ângelo (www.novoscaminhoswine.com.br)
- Cooperametista Vinhos e Sucos, Ametista do Sul, Alto Uruguai (www.cooperametista.com.br/)
- Vinhos Ferigollo, Frederico Westphalen, Alto Uruguai (clevertonferigollo@gmail.com)
- Vinícola Don Gentil, Sarandi, Alto Uruguai (www.dongentil.com.br/)
- Guahyba Estate Wines, Guaíba (www.facebook.com/guahybavinhos)
- Bodega Köetz (rogerkoetz@gmail.com)
- Vinícola Louscher, Três Palmeiras, Alto Uruguai (@vinicolalouscher)
- Vinhedo de Lucca Caçapava do Sul, Vale Central (@neusadelucca)
- Máscara de Ferro, Porto Alegre (atendimento@mascaradeferro.com)

- Montes Vinhos de Autor (zecabackes@gmail.com)
- Outro Vinho, headquarters in Monte Belo (outrovinho.com.br/)
- Cave Poseidon, Porto Alegre (WhatsApp (+55) 51 99112 7333)
- Ruiz Gastaldo Vinícola Urbana, Porto Alegre (contato@ruizgastaldo. com.br)
- Suspeito Vinho, Porto Alegre (falecom@suspeitovinho.com)
- Casa Tassinary, Colinas (casatassinary@gmail.com)
- Cantina Vinallegro, Lajeado (cantinavinallegro@cantinavinallegro. com.br)
- Vitis Insanis, Taquara (kunz@tca.com.br)
- Vivá Vinhos, São Francisco de Paula (@vivavinhosnaturais)

10

THE SOUTH: SANTA CATARINA AND PARANÁ

SANTA CATARINA

This beautiful Brazilian state is sandwiched between Rio Grande do Sul to the south and Paraná to the north. To the west, it borders Argentina; to the east, it has a long coastline washed by the Atlantic Ocean. Measuring 95,736 square kilometres, its population (in 2022) was 7.61 million. The human development index (HDI) was 0.792 in 2021 (0.754 for Brazil).

A brief history

The demonym is *catarinense*, but there is also the curious denomination *barriga verde* (green belly). This is derived from the colour of the corsets of soldiers who left the region in 1753 to conquer Rio Grande do Sul for the Portuguese crown, thus ensuring the unity of Brazil. This more or less coincided with the arrival of about 5,000 Portuguese immigrants from the Azores and Madeira. They settled in the area of the present capital, Florianópolis. It is not known whether they established successful viticulture.

Santa Catarina, unlike Rio Grande do Sul, had more German than Italian immigrants. Though Germans were instrumental in promoting industrialization, the same did not happen to wine. It was, in fact, the Italians who, arriving from Veneto and Lombardia (as well as Serra Gaúcha) in the Atlantic valleys of the state in the nineteenth century, began viticulture and winemaking. Subsequently, some of their descendants migrated westwards and took viticulture with them, albeit on a small scale.

Not much happened until the 1990s, except the introduction of some *vinifera* varieties. Then, thanks to governmental action through Empresa de Pesquisa Agropecuária e Extensão Rural de Santa Catarina (Epagri), Santa Catarina's agricultural agency, regions favourable to viticulture were searched for and found. In 1994, the first winery of this new era, Panceri, was established in Tangará. New vineyards and winemaking facilities appeared, especially at São Joaquim, in Serra Catarinense. The producers founded an association for altitude wines in 2005, including three regions that now integrate the IP Vinhos de Altitude. The IP status was granted in 2021. In the same year, the older region where Goethe grapes are cultivated also achieved this.

Santa Catarina has much to offer wine lovers, as oenotourism is well developed. There is no lack of non-vinous tourist attractions in the state, however. More than five million tourists visit annually, many foreigners (mainly Argentineans). There are a lot of beaches – at the capital, Florianópolis, but also at Balneário Camboriú, Bombinhas (the Brazilian diving capital), Itapema, Garopaba and Imbituba, among others. Surfing is widely practised.

The strong German heritage attracts visitors to larger cities like Joinville and Blumenau (where Oktoberfest is celebrated annually) and to smaller, rural and more isolated towns, such as Pomerode and Treze Tílias. There is much to see and do: aquatic parks, a Disneyland-like facility (Beto Carrero World), extreme sports, and rafting and canyoning at Timbó.

Climate and soils

Santa Catarina is famous for having some of the coldest places in Brazil, where it snows almost every year. One of the best-known winter towns is São Joaquim, the most important wine centre. To get there by car from Florianópolis, one drives along a spectacular road, climbing the Serra do Rio do Rastro, with over 280 breathtaking twists and turns and astounding ocean and mountain views. After the ascent, you arrive at a scenic highland full of Brazilian pine trees (*Araucaria angustifolia*, the Paraná pine) in the very heart of Serra Catarinense, the state's leading fine wine centre. Not that this is the only one – the very large geographical indication, or IP, Vinhos de Altitude, includes other areas. There are also other smaller regions besides this IP, such as Alto Uruguai, Vale do Tijucas and Vales da Uva Goethe.

Before IP status was finally granted in 2021, some names were used to designate the area – for example, Planalto Catarinense (still seen on some maps). Embrapa played an important role, although Epagri led the process, which also involved other institutions. This extensive IP encompasses no less than 29 townships and measures 19,676 square kilometres. The common denominator is altitude. This is even included in the regulations, as no one growing grapes under 840 metres can use the IP name on the label. Altitude ranges from 900 to 1,400 metres. The terrain is either mountain or highland. The climate (Köppen) is almost entirely Cfb (humid tropical, oceanic, without dry season, temperate summer). Using the MCC system, however, results in no less than seven different classifications within the IP. Yet it is possible to observe that the main São Joaquim subregion has a predominant class as follows: HI-2 (cold), DI-2 (humid), CI+1 (cool nights). The second most important subregion, around Videira (which means 'vine' in Portuguese), on the other hand, mostly has the class HI+1 (temperate warm), DI-2 (humid), CI-1 (temperate nights). Frosts – both at the end of winter and in spring – are always a threat. Hailstorms are also a risk. All MCC classes are DI-2 (that is, humid). The high rainfall means that fungal diseases (especially downy mildew) are the main viticultural threats, as in the rest of Brazil's South.

The main SiBCS soil classes are *neossolos* (young, shallow), *cambissolos* (young, shallow and erosion-prone), and *nitossolos* (old, clayey, fertile). High humidity and low temperatures impart a yellowish colour. Soil washing and the parental rock (basalt) lead to high acidity and aluminium content, demanding correction. Despite the shallowness of the topsoil, it allows the growth of vines, which do not have a deep radicular system. As the organic matter content is frequently high (giving the soil a clear colour transition between horizons) and humidity is not low, the vines tend to have a strong vegetative vigour. This demands expertise in canopy management.

Planted areas and wine types

According to Epagri, the most planted *vinifera* cultivars in 2019 were (in descending order): Cabernet Sauvignon, Merlot, Sauvignon Blanc, Chardonnay, Pinot Noir, Sangiovese, Malbec, Montepulciano and Cabernet Franc. Many other varieties are cultivated, though, albeit in small areas. According to Embrapa, the total amount of *vinifera* vines is around 300 hectares.

Still white wines from this IP tend to have medium colour intensity, medium to high aromatic power and flavour concentration, medium to high alcohol content, high acidity, good complexity, and medium to long length. They can age and improve in the medium term. The reds are moderate to deeply coloured, with moderate aromatic intensity and medium to high flavour concentration; the structure is strong, thanks to high acidity and medium to high alcohol, plus a high level of tannins; they have an intermediate to long length and can age and improve in the bottle over several years.

The westernmost portion of this IP, at the centre of Santa Catarina state, is also known as Vale do Rio do Peixe, named after a tributary of the Uruguai River. The town of Pinheiro Preto is important in wine production, making about 10 million litres of wines annually. Although most of this is *vinho de mesa*, many wineries also produce *vinifera* wines, predominately from Cabernet Sauvignon, Merlot, Tannat, Moscato Giallo and other Muscats (which generate sweet, Asti-like sparkling wines). In many cases, the grapes come from Rio Grande do Sul. The wines are mainly entry-level, very affordable products. *Vinhos finos* of very good quality are made at Água Doce, Tangará, Treze Tílias and Videira.

IP Vinhos de Altitude de Santa Catarina wineries

Abreu Garcia Vinhos de Altitude ♀

Campo Belo do Sul

www.abreugarcia.com.br

Campo Belo do Sul sits more or less midway between Serra Catarinense proper and the Vale do Rio do Peixe. Here, at Fazenda Campo Belo, the winery was founded in 2006 by Ernani Garcia. Much-valued over-sight was guaranteed by Professor Aparecido Silva (Federal University of Santa Catarina) and the experienced oenologist Jean-Pierre Rosier. Vineyards are planted at 950 metres, comprising seven varieties, including the unusual Vermentino. The oenologist is Leonardo Ferrari. They have a shop in Florianópolis. Visitors can enjoy tastings (paired with food or not) and special meals, as well as beautiful views from a wine bar on top of a hill. Reservation required.

Geo Vermentino exhibits the typical textural density of this variety, with ripe peach, apricot and moderate acidity. Unoaked Chardonnay has a superb texture and body from eight months with lees and *bâton-nage* in tanks; it is so ripe and true to the variety, yet keeps a refreshing acidity. Ami Sauvignon Blanc, made with grapes from two distinct terroirs, is very aromatic, with tropical fruit, albeit mixed with cool-climate grassy notes – it's racy and satisfying. Oaked Chardonnay is a complex, again textural and ripe, wine with evident but non-intrusive flavours from 20 months in new French oak barrels. It is very well structured and Burgundian in character.

Abreu Garcia Rosé, a blend of Pinot Noir, Malbec and some Vermentino, is very pale, almost white; ripe in fruit, bone dry, it has more body and texture than Provençal examples. Pinot Noir is complex, the ripe but fresh fruit blending well with leather, undergrowth and earth; a strong structure of acidity and fine-grained tannins mean it will age gracefully. Cabernet Sauvignon/Merlot is very Bordeaux-like, with a sturdy structure, ripe fruit, freshness and complexity from 18 months in new French oak.

Geo Brut sparkling Vermentino is, indeed, one of a kind; crisp, structured and creamy, but a bit grippy, with floral and exotic fruit characters. It does not show evident autolytic elements, despite its 40 months with lees, except for excellent savouriness. Highly recommended.

Altopiano Vinhas e Vinhos ♀

São Joaquim

@altopianovinhasevinhos

Altopiano, a recent wine business at Serra Catarinense, is a brand of wines belonging to Joelson Fronza, owner of Osteria La Campagnaga, a restaurant and events centre at Rio do Sul (200 kilometres to the north). He bought a property in São Joaquim and started to plant a vineyard in 2019. Today, 1.8 hectares are planted with seven varieties, mainly Italian, including rare (in Brazil) Pecorino and Sagrantino. There is a brand-new facility to receive visitors, with a beautiful stone and wood building. Built on the top of a hill, it has an amazing view. The wines are made at Villa Francioni, under the expertise of oenologist Edson Andrade. They produce 10,000 bottles annually. Visitors can taste the wines, which may have imaginative names (book in advance).

Pink Montepulciano is very pale, with fresh red fruit balanced by outstanding acidity; a lightweight, elegant wine. Mi'Mpassis ('You make me mad', in Italian dialect) is a varietal Vermentino; bone dry, with citrus, peach and herbs, it has rewarding acidity and some phenolic grip. L'Incontro is an oaked Sangiovese; pale red and Chianti-like, it is savoury and mouth-watering and has a good tannic structure – drink with pasta or pizza. Dame de Pù ('Give me more') Montepulciano has ripe, sweet black fruit, hints of tobacco and savouriness; it is easy going and delicious. Baùco ('Crazy') Cabernet Franc spends 12 months in new American and French oak barrels; moderately coloured, it is very aromatic (ripe blackberry and blackcurrant, pencil shavings, slight capsicum, vanilla, cedar). Its 14% abv is well balanced by the other components; it ends fresh and dry.

D'Alture Vinícola Boutique ♀

São Joaquim

www.dalture.com.br/

The family of Roberto Chávez has made wine in Tarija Valley, Bolivia, for over a century. He searched for high-altitude vineyards in Brazil and selected Serra Catarinense, buying vineyards there in 2008. These have been improved and they have a total of 14 hectares. Annually, they make 45,000 bottles of wine. There is a good set-up, including cottages, to receive visitors (book first).

Blanc de Blancs, a still wine, is made from Chardonnay, Viognier and Sauvignon Blanc; although not very aromatic in the nose, it improves much in the mouth, showing a firm structure of acidity and body. Santa Izabel Oak, 100 per cent Sauvignon Blanc, spends 14 months in used French oak barrels. It is very savoury and oaky indeed. Santas Stella e Martina Rosé, a varietal from Pinot Noir and minor proportions of other grapes, has 9 per cent of its volume matured in used oak; it has a good structure with a perceptible tannic grip.

El Poeta Gran Reserva Bordeaux blend spends 18 months in oak barrels, has high, warming alcohol and very, very ripe fruit with a strong structure ideal for ageing. Sine Metu do Alquimista is a complex red blend, including Bordeaux grapes, Montepulciano and Sangiovese; it is particularly rich in liquorice aromas, plus overripe black fruit, and high, warming alcohol; its muscular tannic structure allows cellaring.

Vinícola Hiragami

São Joaquim

www.hiragami.com.br/

Fumio Hiragami, born in Japan, arrived in Brazil in 1959. He grew up here and worked hard on farms. In 1974, he settled at São Joaquim to develop a project on apple growing. This later included other fruit (kiwi, pear) and a general agricultural store. Wine, however, entered his life in 2001 (first studies), leading to vineyard planting in 2006. One of the highest in Brazil (1,427 metres), the vineyard comprises Sauvignon Blanc, Cabernet Sauvignon and Merlot. Hiragami makes 35,000 bottles of wine annually at Villa Francioni under oenologist Arlindo Menoncin. This is remarkable: a Japanese person crafting wine in Brazil from French grapes. Such is the beauty of this drink! There are no oenotouristic activities, but they have a shop at São Joaquim (open 9am–7pm).

Sauvignon Blanc is a crisp, cool-climate example, moderately aromatic, with little tropical fruit. Sur Lie Sauvignon Blanc stays 77 days with its fine lees, with *bâtonnage*, imparting a textural character and even some grip; it has a good length. Oak Sauvignon Blanc undergoes the same time with lees, plus three months in oak barrels; it brings moderate notes of white guava, peach and grass and hints of vanilla and spice, being very round.

Cabernet Sauvignon offers ripe cassis, capsicum, fresh acidity, medium body and sleek tannins. Deep in colour, Merlot exhibits ripe blackberry, chocolate, coffee, vanilla and toast (15 months in oak) with a good structure.

Kanpai Nature is unusual: 100 per cent Sauvignon Blanc made using the traditional method. With a six-month autolysis, this attenuates the varietal characters but not the vivid, piercing acidity; bone dry, this wine is food friendly. Kanpai Brut Rosé is also unusual (only Cabernet Sauvignon); made by the Charmat method, it is fruity, refreshing and easy drinking.

Colheita Tardia, a dessert wine from late-harvested Sauvignon Blanc, is not overly sweet; the fresh acidity makes it very easy drinking. Another version is Licoroso; also from overripe grapes, it is fortified to 17% abv and spends 18 months in oak barrels; it is golden, with aromas and flavours of preserve, orange peel and some nuttiness.

Vinícola Kranz ♀

Treze Tílias

www.vinicolakranz.com.br

Walter Kranz was an executive at Mercedes-Benz for a long time, having supervised factory developments in Brazil, Mexico and China (where he lived and married). After leaving this peripatetic lifestyle, he returned to his hometown, Treze Tílias. This small town, perhaps better called *Dreizehnlinden* (Thirteen Linden), was founded by Austrian immigrants in a mountainous region in 1933 in west Santa Catarina. This is a charming and successful tourist destination where the Austrian (mostly

Tyrolean) heritage is very important, especially in architecture, gastronomy and drinks – there are several breweries.

Walter Kranz, however, decided to establish a winery here in 2007. He is very welcoming, someone who is happy to engage in agreeable and interesting conversation. Also a gifted woodworker and cook, he produces jams, charcuterie, cider and both *vinhos de mesa* and *vinhos finos*. The latter are mainly crafted from grapes bought at Santa Catarina and Campanha Gaúcha. He tends to make wines with long maturation periods (even his cider spends one year in the autoclave). He offers, for example, Kranz Diamond (luxury price level), a Chardonnay from 2011, now having spent more than nine years in French oak barrels and bottled on demand. Expect, therefore, to taste much more than just young, fruity wines. Lots are small and widely varied according to provenance, vintage and maturation period. Several wines are sold in 3-litre bag-in-boxes. Visitors are welcome and no booking is necessary unless for technical tastings. The beautiful shop and winery are located in the very centre of Treze Tílias.

Silver Sauvignon Blanc has been made in oxidative style; it is golden, savoury and fresh. I tasted two Malbecs, one of the house's specialities. The 2010 was, as expected, complex, with tertiary components of earth and leather. Despite the still powerful tannic structure, it retained elegance and finesse. The 2018 (which won first place in an important Brazilian wine contest) keeps youthful dark fruit (plums), violets, spice and vanilla, and its strong tannic structure does not hamper a generally more elegant than powerful style. Luxury Gran Reserva Platinum Cabernet Sauvignon has a high varietal typicity and stout structure, being complex but elegant. Charmat Brut rosé is 100 per cent Malbec, with a very prolonged (for tank method) contact with its lees – 20 months. This wine is unusual: instead of the easy-going fruit expected from a Charmat, it is savoury and quite phenolic.

Leone di Venezia ♀

São Joaquim

www.leonedivenezia.com.br/

Saul Bianco, grandson of the Italian immigrant Guerino Bianco, has wine in his blood. After working for 32 years as an agronomist, he decided to start his own wine business. He lived for one year in Italy, learning about oenology at Conegliano. Living at Florianópolis, choosing Serra Catarinense seemed logical, so he bought land at São Joaquim and started his vineyard in 2008, using Italian planting material. At 1,280 metres, the soil is predominately *cambissolo bruno*, acid and fertile. The total area is 5 hectares, comprising Italian varieties (Montepulciano, Sangiovese, Refosco, Gewurztraminer, Garganega and others). Some grapes are purchased elsewhere, but they are always Italian cultivars. In 2013, the winery was started; completed in 2016, its architecture was inspired by a palace in Treviso, Veneto. Oenologist Maikely Paim Amoros directs the winemaking activities. The annual production is 22,000 bottles, of which 90 per cent are still (reds predominating). Most of the wines are sold to visitors. Tours and tastings include *sabrage* and picnics where you can enjoy the splendid view (book in advance).

Maikely, a very friendly and well-informed professional, welcomed me to taste the wines. Rialto is a white blend of four Italian varieties, harvested at different maturation points: pale, with moderate citric aromas, elegant, a bit nutty, and with a piercing, mouth-watering acidity. It would be perfect with a platter of oysters. Garganega is golden, almondy, honeyed, with vanilla and toast from eight months in American oak, perfectly integrated and keeping refreshing acidity. Oro Vecchio, vinified as an orange wine, is a blend with 35 per cent Gewurztraminer; it is almost pink, very aromatic and floral, with lychees and mandarin peel. It has a solid structure of acidity, perceptible phenolics, and a long, long length.

Sangiovese has a very deep colour for this variety; spending eight months in American and French oak, it has a firm structure of cheek-puckering tannins and sharp acidity. Its style reminded me of a Brunello or Chianti Gran Selezione – a wine to age. They have two different Montepulciano wines. The varietal is very ripe, with high alcohol; deeply coloured, it offers blackberries, plums, balsamic notes, plus vanilla and toast from 14 months in oak. Super-premium Mastino, from their best Montepulciano parcels, undergoes a longer maceration and matures for 24 months in oak; it is inky and oaky, has a potent structure, and is a big wine that will age well. Sud + Sud blends two southern Italian grapes, Primitivo and Aglianico. It is another big, warming, dark wine with very ripe fruit, a full body and moderate acidity. It spends 12 months in oak, and this is easily apparent. Refosco – a variety relatively unknown outside Veneto and Friuli – is deep purple, with exotic aromas and flavours of spice, fine herbs and dark fruits; a high acidity finishes with sinewy tannins. The 15.5% abv provides a Herculean structure, demanding time.

From the vat, I tasted their version of a Ripasso; they mixed Montepulciano wine with the used skins, which imparted both colour and raisined fruit, besides increasing the wine's already high alcohol content. Also from the vat, their exclusive wine: a Garganega Recioto (much like Recioto di Soave): deep gold, it has a very rich nose of ripe peach, nectarine, honey and beeswax; the fresh acidity balances its 55 grams per litre of sugar well. Its 16.5% abv is achieved naturally, without fortification. Delicious!

Vinhedos do Monte Agudo ♀

São Joaquim

www.monteagudo.com.br/

Leônidas Ferraz, a paediatrician, and Alceu Muller, a rural producer, founded Monte Agudo in 2004. Their vineyards were started from French planting material in 2005. At 1,280 metres, they yield 5–7 tons per hectare. Today, Leônidas' daughter Patrícia leads the business with her brothers Léo and Carol. Wines are competently made under their direction at Santa Augusta. Several oenotouristic activities are offered: tastings, sunset tastings, picnics and full meals (booking required).

Vivaz Sauvignon Blanc has an overt varietal character (passion fruit, guava, herbs and citrus); its crisp acidity is balanced by good texture from long lees contact. Chardonnay (labelled Unoaked) is a faithful example of this variety's characteristics: very clean, ripe pear, apple and some pineapple, and with excellent texture. Expressões de Altitude Chardonnay, barrel fermented, stays 14 months in barrels, but there is no blinding of its ripe fruit by the oak. This is seamlessly integrated, and the butteriness and creaminess from malolactic fermentation add complexity to this very satisfying wine.

Sublime Rosé, Merlot with 10 per cent Malbec, is made by direct pressing (two hours of skin contact). It is fruity, juicy, balanced by excellent acidity, and food friendly. Cabernet Sauvignon/Merlot could be labelled as a varietal wine (Cabernet 85 per cent); it showcases, however, the enrichening effect of Merlot on the highly typical varietal character of its companion, hence balancing the cassis, green bell pepper hints and more slender body with ripe plum and chocolate. It is an elegant, Bordeaux-like wine.

Sinfonia Extra-Brut (Chardonnay) is crafted through a long Charmat process; with ripe fruit, it is a light, refreshing drink. The pink version

(Merlot with a dash of Malbec) brings a lot of ripe red berries, great freshness and a fine mousse.

Eko is a sweet, fortified (17.5% abv), oak-aged Chardonnay; it is golden, honeyed, toasty and fresh, with moderate sweetness and a long length. Alida Nature (Chardonnay) is a traditional method sparkler with a prolonged 40-month autolysis; bone dry and crisp, it seamlessly joins ripe pear, citrus and white flowers to rich bread and brioche, ending with a saline, complex finish. It has a unique, pretty, cast-metal cap – a great souvenir.

Vinícola Panceri 🍷

Tangará

www.panceri.com.br

Nilo Panceri and sons, Celso and Luiz, were grape growers until they founded their winery in 1990. Nilo died in 1994, and his heirs began to think about planting *vinifera* grapes. Celso Panceri is a restless entrepreneur – he made several trips abroad to learn how to plan the growth of the business. Theirs was the first winery in Santa Catarina to export wines, in 2006. He was awarded several prizes for his initiatives. Being at the helm, he launched the first commercial vintage of *vinhos finos* in 2003. Progress has been very significant since then. The vineyards are planted at Serra do Marari, at about 1,000 metres, in a very isolated spot with drying winds, so lowering the incidence of fungal disease. The surroundings are, indeed, beautiful. Some of the wines come with interactive tags with QR codes, providing links for online videos. Visitors are welcome, and the oenotouristic structure is new, pleasant and in very good taste.

Celso and his daughters, Estefânia and Emanoela, are excellent hosts. When going there – and it is well worth doing this – be careful to drive first to the small town of Ibiam, which is not far from Tangará. Configure your navigation app to avoid unpaved roads.

Barbera is a lovely wine, brimming with red berries, mouth-watering acidity, soft tannins and very good cultivar typicity. Reserva Cabernet Sauvignon is bone dry and fresh but keeps varietal character and fine and silky tannins. Panceri 30 Anos is a blend of Teroldego, Tannat and Ancellotta, with very ripe blackberries surrounded by spice and toast. It is tannic and full bodied, with a long bottle life ahead. Passito is 100 per cent Moscato Bianco, fortified to 15.5% abv after some skin maceration; copper-coloured, with intense dried orange peel aromas and flavours and very sweet, it shows that Brazil could produce more dessert wines.

Panceri is well known for producing some sparklers based solely on Sauvignon Blanc, something unusual anywhere in the country. Their traditional method Brut (12.1 grams per litre residual sugar), eight-month autolysis, is fresh and fruity, with the Sauvignon Blanc not overwhelming. Trinta Anos Brut (10.6 grams per litre) is much more complex and golden, and quite autolytic, but still crisp and crunchy after 84 months with lees.

Vinícola Pericó ♀

São Joaquim

www.vinicolaperico.com.br

Pericó, one of the oldest wineries at Serra Catarinense, was founded in 2002 by Wandér Weege, a successful textile entrepreneur. The winery was sold in 2018 to two businessmen from Santa Catarina (Carlinhos Bogo Jr and Diego Censi, the majority owner) and the Frenchman Gauthier Gheysen. It was the first to produce sparklers here and the first (and only) to make an icewine in 2009. The vineyards (15 hectares), within the 447-hectare property, are planted on basaltic soil at high altitude (1,300 metres). The soil is fertile and with a lot of clay, free-draining and with low amounts of phosphorus (requiring correction). The planting density is around 5,000 vines per hectare. During the long growing season, days are sunny (although rain is not infrequent) and nights are cool, allowing for slow flavour development while keeping the clear acidity of this region.

The wines (150,000 bottles per year) are made under the highly competent oenologist Jefferson Sancineto Nunes, a very experienced but open-minded professional who has worked for Pericó since the beginning. Visitors are welcome from Tuesday to Saturday (guided tastings take place Thursday to Saturday). A fine restaurant and light platters to accompany the wines are available. Everything must be booked in advance. Vale do Pericó lies between São Joaquim and Urubici; to reach there from São Joaquim calls for over an hour of driving, partly on unpaved roads (around 15 kilometres). The roads, however, were being paved and improved when I visited Pericó (September 2024); when finished (in 2025), they will make the trip much less of an adventure. A visit is worthwhile, anyway, as the region is exceedingly beautiful and the installations here first-rate – not to mention the high-quality dishes created by the talented chef and the excellent wines on offer.

Visiting Pericó and enjoying Sancineto's enthusiasm and deep knowledge of oenology and the region was a pleasure. The freshness of Vigneto Sauvignon Blanc is assured by a glass stopper; according to Sancineto, this is less permeable to oxygen even than screw caps with tin seals. For this wine, the harvest is timed by dosing citric acid into the juice, among other parameters, aiming for a finished wine that offers racy acidity, youth, elegance and high varietal typicity, but not the exuberance of tropical fruit. This seems to be the personality of Sauvignon Blancs in this region. Plume Chardonnay begins its fermentation in a stainless-steel tank, then finishes the process (when density is about 1,050) in Allier oak barrels (second and third use) for four months. The result is a perfect balance between the ripe but fresh fruit and the oak. The wine is elegant and very long. Taipa Rosé comes in the same beautiful bottle as the Vigneto; Cabernet Sauvignon (70 per cent) and Merlot

Jefferson Sancineto Nunes

are harvested at the right time for making rosé, the grapes being cooled to 5°C before processing, thus minimizing enzymatic activity and extraction. No malolactic fermentation is allowed; the wine is fruity, sharp and refreshing.

Basaltino Pinot Noir is an elegant rendition of this variety, which performs so well at Serra Catarinense: there's ripe red fruit balanced by deftly managed oak – a delicious wine. Basalto, a Bordeaux blend of 70 per cent Cabernet Sauvignon with Merlot, stages for one year in French oak. Jefferson explained, interestingly, that red wines at Pericó are removed from barriques when 50 per cent of the tannins have polymerized, as shown by laboratory tests. They do not launch the wines commercially unless this polymerization reaches 56 per cent of the total tannins. Basalto shows a good concentration and intensity of ripe blackcurrant, capsicum, chocolate, vanilla, spice and toast, and its structure allows it to improve in the bottle for three to five years. Minerato Merlot (luxury price level) blends lots of ripe black fruit, chocolate, vanilla and spice with a strong tannic structure; offering great drinking now, it will, however, improve in the bottle for at least five years. Benedictum Cabernet Sauvignon brings very ripe cassis, slight capsicum, a vigorous structure of fine-grained tannins and rewarding acidity; it matures for 15 months in second-use Allier barriques of medium toast. Vinte-Vinte is a Bordeaux blend from a memorable vintage (2020, hence its name); layer upon layer of perfectly ripe black fruit, chocolate, spice and vanilla are seasoned with clear mint notes. Its sturdy structure allows it to age gracefully. Altitude Colheita Tardia is a late-harvest Cabernet Sauvignon, fortified to 17.5% abv with brandy made by Pericó; it is dark pink, with strong aromas and flavours of overripe fruit, honeyed notes and sweet spice. It is very long indeed and not at all overly sweet.

Doradus Sur Lie is a sparkler of exception: traditional method, undisgorged, with no less than 84 months with lees; a bit hazy, it is at once very complex and elegant, with plenty of ripe pineapple, brioche and patisserie. Despite the maturation time, there were no signs of oxidation. Pericó uses only stainless-steel crown caps; as Jefferson explained, this closure is the tightest of all and stops oxygen entering the bottle; the wine, moreover, enjoys the freshness initiated by its lees. Doradus is absolutely delicious.

Piccola Fattoria 🍷

São Joaquim

@piccolafattoria

The oenologist Joelmir Grassi and his wife, Taís, started this small wine business in 2019. After working more than a decade for other wineries, with a stint at Zenato (Italy), and having taken part in winemaking activities since childhood, Joelmir bought land at 1,430 metres (one of the highest in this high region), very near São Joaquim. It has since snowed regularly here. After preparing the formerly abandoned terrain, they began planting vines in 2020 (today, they have a bit more than 1 hectare). They consider themselves *garagistes*, crafting 4,500 bottles yearly. They welcome visitors (book in advance) to their small but pretty tasting room and open-air deck (the view is astounding).

Joelmir, with whom I had a pleasant and informative chat, showed me his wines. Natural fermentation and a reduction of inputs are the rule. Tala Sauvignon Blanc is fermented in Perle Blanche Nadalié barriques, where it stays for ten months; unfined and unfiltered, it is golden, savoury, aromatic, toasty, spicy, saline and quite textural.

Joelmir buys grapes from Suzin to craft his Ziro Merlot; it is a light, fresh rendition, which reminded me of north-eastern Italian Merlots. It is good to drink with pasta or pizza and has a good structure of acidity and tannins. Ziro Syrah (grapes from Bassetti) is an elegant, cool-climate, European-style wine that is minty, peppery, fresh and medium bodied. Ziro Sangiovese is very typical: moderate colour, aromas and flavours of sour cherry, tomato and earth; it is savoury, well structured and food friendly. Tala Pinot Noir is very dark and firmly structured for this variety; ripe, savoury and complex, it will age well. Ziro Cabernet Sauvignon has a deep colour; acidity and tannins are high, but the latter are sleek and fine grained; its 14 months in oak lead to well-integrated notes of vanilla, toast and cedar.

Quinta da Neve 🍷

São Joaquim

www.quintadaneve.com.br/

Quinta da Neve ('neve' means snow) came to life in 1999 as the pioneering vineyard planted at Lomba Seca, São Joaquim. For many years, it was controlled by the Decanter wine importer (see Vinícola Hermann, page 191). In 2021, five partners, led by engineer Gérson de

Borba Dias, bought the business. The whole property has 87 hectares. The winery has been refurbished and its annual production can reach 60,000 bottles, under oenologist Betina de Bem. The owners plan to build an oenotouristic complex. There's already a tasting room and a space for events (booking required).

Rosa da Neve is a pink blend of Pinot Noir and Sangiovese made by directly pressing specially harvested destemmed grapes. It is pale, with ripe fruit and some savouriness, with a surprising structure, so dry and fresh. Leão Baio, a blend of Merlot, Malbec, Montepulciano and Sangiovese, is easy drinking, fruity, fresh and delicious. Sangiovese, a cuvée of three vintages, presents the variety's typical characters: bone dry, savoury, earthy and well structured. Montepulciano is a big wine, high in intensity, concentration, alcohol, ripeness and structure; complex and complete, it is again testament to Montepulciano's success in this region. Vinhas Velhas Cabernet Sauvignon (luxury price level) comes from the oldest vineyard at Serra Catarinense (planted in 1999). Varietally typical, it offers ripe cassis, hints of capsicum, rewarding acidity, and a strong alcoholic and tannic structure, albeit sleek and fine grained; it will age beautifully. Sur Lie (Chardonnay), an undisgorged sparkler, had undergone 18 months with lees when tasted: hazy, savoury and full of ripe fruit, biscuit and brioche.

Vinícola Santa Augusta ♀

Videira

santaaugusta.com.br/

Two entrepreneurs founded this winery in 2006, initially as a hobby to be led by their daughters. They had made their first wine in 2005 at Epagri, Santa Catarina's agronomical research organ. The business grew, demanding an extensive restructuring in 2020. Significant changes were made to labels, brands and processes, so improving quality. Three hectares of vineyards are planted at over 1,000 metres, comprising Sauvignon Blanc, Moscato Giallo and Malbec. They also buy grapes. Although the altitude favours acidity and flavours, high humidity is a problem, demanding protection of the vines with plastic covers. Luiz Filipe Farias is their oenologist. However, crafting wines for third parties is the most important part of their business. While they produce 60,000 litres of their own wines annually, they make 600,000 for others. Santa Augusta makes predominately (60 per cent) sparkling wines, mostly Charmat and Moscatel. Still wines are chiefly white.

The winery is located in the pretty, rural surroundings of Videira, and there's a wine garden and agreeable tasting room. Group visits are welcome (book in advance). I was very well received there by owner and sommelier Francieli De Nardi. Bottles and labels are beautiful and very well finished.

Tapera Sauvignon Blanc shows the terroir: instead of overt tropical fruit, this is more discreet and restrained, but crisp and delicate. Santa Augusta Pinot Noir Rosé, in a pretty, unconventional bottle, is made by direct pressing; the short skin contact (three to four hours) provides a pale pink colour; fresh red berries fill the palate and the wine is bone dry and fresh. Fenice Sauvignon Blanc spends six months in second-use French oak barrels; the oak character is moderate, well balanced by varietal aromas and flavours, with some savouriness, good structure and complexity. Fenice Merlot is a deep ruby colour, full of blackberries, with voluminous tannins integrating its good structure with acidity and flavours; the oakiness (24 months in barriques, mostly French) is not intrusive.

Santa Augusta Moscatel has a lower residual sugar (60 grams per litre) than Asti, with high aromatic intensity and a lovely balance of acidity, sweetness and flavours. It is a very good and elegant fizzy Moscatel. Traditional method Brut (Chardonnay/Pinot Noir, 12-month autolysis) is a good Brazilian sparkler, with clear fruitiness of citrus, pear and pineapple, amongst brioche and bread.

Vinícola Suzin ♀

São Joaquim

www.vinicolasuzin.com.br/

Suzin, one of the pioneers at Serra Catarinense, was founded in 2001 by Zelindo Suzin, now 86, and his sons Everson and Jeferson. The 10-hectare vineyard is planted at 1,200 metres, 20 kilometres from São Joaquim, and comprises nine varieties (French and Italian). Wines are currently made by Santa Augusta (Videira), but a winery is being built. Everson holds an MSc in oenology. About 50,000 bottles of wine are made annually. At a wine bar, visitors are welcome for tastings (booking required).

Jeferson and Sabrina, Everson's wife, welcomed me to their beautiful wine bar in São Joaquim during a cold, foggy night to taste their wines. One thing to note, and they confirmed this, is that Suzin's main style is that of big, strong, ripe and alcoholic reds.

Suzin Sauvignon Blanc, aromatically discreet, is intense in the mouth, where citrus, peach, white guava and herbs are balanced by crisp acidity; it is textural and ripe. Suzin Rosé, a red blend, is pale, fresh, light and fruity. Alecrim Tinto, a Bordeaux blend, spends 12–18 months in oak; harmonious and well structured, it is a bargain. Pinot Noir is a light, fresh and fruity rendition of this lovely grape with moderate oakiness.

The following varietal wines spend 24 months in oak, having 14–15% abv. Cabernet Sauvignon is dark, ripe, warm, minty and full bodied, with no hint of pyrazines. Merlot puts forward very ripe blackberry, chocolate and coffee, framing a full body and already amicable tannins with a long length. Malbec is again so ripe, full of plums, moderately tannic, powerful, chocolatey and dense. Rebo is riper still, with concentrated black fruit and a muscular structure, and is very long and satisfying. Cabernet Franc exhibits mint, pencil shavings and ripe cassis; its high, fluid acidity imparts elegance and associates with sturdy tannins, ensuring it will age well. Petit Verdot is dark and spicy, with a sinewy structure of tannins and acidity; it's complex and ageworthy. Intrigante Lote III, a blend of five varieties, is once again a ripe, powerful, warm red, very tannic, demanding more bottle time to round off its edges. Montepulciano, with a huge 15.8% abv, uses new oak only (French and American); it's super-ripe and full of blackberry fruit, chocolate, tobacco and balsamic notes. The high intensity, concentration and structure demonstrate how well Montepulciano performs at Serra Catarinense. Seu Zelindo (the patriarch's name) Lote III is made from the same varieties as Intrigante, plus Cabernet Franc; dark, intense and strongly structured, with oak more evident, this is a wine to cellar.

Charmat Brut Rosé, made from Merlot and Malbec, offers fresh and ripe red fruit; it is simple and perfect for informal occasions.

Vinícola Thera ♀

Bom Retiro, Serra Catarinense
www.vinicolathera.com.br/

João Paulo de Freitas inherited this vast (800-hectare) property from his father Dilor (who died in 2004), the creator of Villa Francioni. Indeed, Dilor's pioneering vineyards were here, at Bom Retiro (about 100 kilometres north of São Joaquim). João christened the wine business after his mother Theresa's nickname. He improved the vineyard, which now has 24 hectares, and created a complex for oenotourism, including a guesthouse (with a restaurant), wine bar and even a condominium.

Here, each owner can make their particular wines. A new, beautiful and well-finished winery opened in 2024.

Viticulture and winemaking are directed with great competence by the experienced oenologist Átila Zavarize. The winery can process up to 300,000 litres of wine annually, but present production is 100,000 bottles. They intend to plant another 10 hectares, focusing on Italian varieties. Visitors are welcome to tour the vineyards and winery or to experience the wines at three well-furbished tasting rooms (open Thursday to Sunday; booking required). The surroundings and buildings are all beautiful and functional.

Mr Freitas and Átila received me very well at Thera to taste some of their wines. Sauvignon Blanc is a good example of how the variety behaves in this cool region; instead of explosive tropical fruit, it brings a more discreet profile, with high freshness and a very good texture from eight to ten months with its fine lees. An older Sauvignon Blanc shows that these wines can gain complexity with mineral and petrol notes. Chardonnay is a very elegant rendition of the variety, its ripe fruit being well balanced by deft, moderate oakiness (20 per cent of the wine is fermented and matured in used French oak barrels). Again, a six-year-old wine demonstrates good ageing potential, being nutty, toasty and honeyed. A sample of their brand-new Semillon, not yet launched, had a

Átila Zavarize (left) and João Paulo de Freitas

rich, unctuous texture balanced by high, mouth-watering acidity. Átila explained that they intend to craft a white Bordeaux blend soon. Thera Rosé, made from the direct pressing of Merlot, Cabernet Franc and a dash of Syrah, is very pale, with ripe red fruit and the usual pronounced acidity of this cool-climate region.

Very promising was a vat sample of their Syrah (not yet launched): bone dry, sleek and peppery, with discreet vanilla and toast (50 per cent is matured in 500-litre French oak barrels, the balance in smaller containers). Anima is their Pinot Noir from young vines: fruit predominates, ripe and fresh, with discreet oakiness. Thera Pinot Noir (luxury price level) from older vines is darker, more structured, more complex, and really ageworthy and outstanding in great vintages (such as 2020). Pieno is a blend of Sangiovese and Montepulciano, with high acidity, stout tannic structure and gastronomic attributes. Madai (Merlot, Cabernet Franc, Malbec and Syrah) is rich in fruity aromas and flavours, balanced by high acidity and moderate oak. Thera Merlot is legally varietal but has a significant percentage of Cabernet Franc; it is a complex, dark and strongly structured wine with ripe black fruit, chocolate and coffee.

Traditional method Auguri Brut (Chardonnay/Pinot Noir), 18-month autolysis, is fresh, elegant, fruity and biscuity. Auguri Blanc de Blancs Extra-Brut is razor-sharp and very dry, with cutting acidity (a very low pH) and evident autolytic character. Luxury Thera Nature (36-month autolysis) is bone dry, with high acidity, a very fine and abundant mousse, class and elegance. It is an outstanding sparkler.

Villa Francioni ♀

São Joaquim

www.villafrancioni.com.br/

Dilor de Freitas was a highly successful businessman, owning factories producing floor and wall tiles at Criciúma, a prosperous industrial city and the centre of coal mining activities in Brazil. Passionate about wine, he decided, after many trips to Europe, to buy land and start a vineyard in the late 1990s. The first site was Serra Catarinense, until then devoid of vines, at a site between Bom Retiro and Urubici (see Vinícola Thera, page 236). In the early 2000s, however, Dilor bought more land and began Villa Francioni at São Joaquim. A complete winery was built in record time (finished in 2004); it is one of Brazil's prettiest and most ingenious, and worth visiting. Dilor, unfortunately, died in August of the same year, so couldn't enjoy the results of his great efforts. The business, however, continued, with the present Thera passing to his oldest son and Francioni to the others.

This is an impressive winery: gravity dictates all grape and must movements. Visitors can view all winemaking stages without entering the work space through a well-devised sequence of stairs that connects six floors (don't worry, there is an elevator). Today, from 40 hectares of vineyards, they craft 120,000 bottles of wine annually. The large winery (4,400 square metres) can produce up to 300,000 bottles, hence they vinify for third parties. Visitors are welcome for guided tours and four different tastings (book first).

The oenologist Edson Andrade was a great host when I visited Villa Francioni. He has been here for a long time. All wines have a focus on high quality – as did the majority I tasted in the region. Villa Francioni's Sauvignon Blanc is more intense and aromatic than is usual in Serra Catarinense, especially in the mouth, where it is textural and long. Villa Francioni Rosé, made from eight different grapes by *saignée*, with very short contact, is fermented with a special yeast called Elegance. Pale pink, brimming with red berries, it is bone dry and well structured, with some tannic grip. In a beautiful bottle, it has become Villa Francioni's biggest commercial success since it was launched about 20 years ago, corresponding to 40 per cent of all wine sales.

Villa Francioni Chardonnay spends 12 months in new French oak barriques; as Eduardo explained, these are Nadalié's Perle Blanche, specifically for white wines, with a light toast. The wine ferments in tanks until specific gravity is 1,005; it then goes to the barrels to finish the fermentation and mature with fine lees and *bâtonnage*. It is very elegant; the oak (toast, vanilla, spice) is perfectly integrated with the variety's typical aromas and flavours of ripe apple and pear, as well as the buttery notes from malolactic fermentation, which does not impair the freshness.

Joaquim red, a Cabernet Sauvignon/Merlot blend, spends ten months in third-use French oak barrels; Cabernet predominates, with cassis and capsicum, and the tannins are sleek and fine. Like many oenologists here, Eduardo thinks Cabernet Sauvignon needs a lot of care to ripen properly; it expresses excessive pyrazines when not tended correctly. Francesco is a blend of five varieties, Merlot predominating, with a dash of Syrah; after 14 months in oak and one-and-a-half to two years in the bottle, it is deeply coloured, with ripe fruit and tannins, showing excellent balance. Like Joaquim, it is a bargain (especially the 2020, a great vintage). Villa Francioni Tinto, a Bordeaux blend, remains 18 months in new French oak, plus two to three years in the bottle. The perfect ripeness of fruit marries well with the non-invasive oaky characters and fine acidity; the tannins are velvety and the wine truly elegant. Michelli (luxury price level) is quite different: 80 per cent Sangiovese is joined by Cabernet Sauvignon and Merlot. After 36 months in new French oak, plus the same time in the bottle, it has moderate colour, overt oaky characters, a robust structure and refreshing acidity, with high savouriness and Sangiovese's sour cherry, dust and tea leaves; an excellent wine. Agripina is 100 per cent Nebbiolo, comprising wines from four vintages (as this grape is very hard to cultivate here). It shows great varietal typicity: moderate colour, perfumed roses, cherries and hints of tar, and very muscular tannins.

Villa Francioni Colheita Tardia is their dessert wine from overripe Sauvignon Blanc grapes (harvested about 20 days after those for dry wines); the grapes show some botrytis. Despite its 16.8% abv, it is unfortified and no special yeast is used – but the fermentation is very long. It remains for four years in barrels, as revealed by the golden colour; there is some nuttiness and caramel, preserved fruit and honey. It is complex, layered and not at all cloying, thanks to the high acidity.

Villaggio Bassetti Vinhos de Altitude 🍷

São Joaquim

www.villaggiobassetti.com.br/

This winery was founded in 2005 by the chemical engineer and editor José Eduardo Pioli Bassetti after a long search to find a satisfactory region. The first vintage was in 2008. There are 11 hectares of vineyards at about 1,300 metres, planted to Sauvignon Blanc, Pinot Noir, Merlot and Cabernet Sauvignon, plus a pioneering Syrah over-grafted on rootstocks (when previously it was Pinot Noir). Since 2011 the winery has produced 26,000 bottles yearly under oenologist Diogo Ascari. Visitors can taste the wines, stroll through the vineyards and enjoy guided tours (booking required). The surroundings are beautiful and the large area with paved roads is easy to reach.

Leonardo Nunes, the commercial manager, and Diogo showed me great hospitality when I visited to taste their wines.

Sauvignon Blanc has a distinct style: very ripe, low pyrazines and more to pineapple and peach than passion fruit. Rosé, crafted through direct pressing predominately from Sangiovese, is pale, bone dry, savoury and fresh. Dona Enny is an oaked Sauvignon Blanc, 100 per cent fermented and matured (up to 12 months) in barrels. It is golden and displays a seamless integration between the clear oak and the typical flavours, being textural, complex and very long.

Claret is a seldom encountered character: a pale red wine from a blend of four varieties, harvested earlier than is usual for reds; it is low in alcohol, light and refreshing, cool to drink, and gastronomically versatile. Ana Cristina Pinot Noir undergoes spontaneous fermentation and one-year maturation in new and used French oak barrels. It is bone dry, mouth-watering, complex and well structured. Gio Syrah has potent aromas of ripe fruit and black pepper, with a sturdy structure of acidity and tannins; it is savoury and demonstrates how well this variety adapts to the region's cool climate. Montepioli is a Cabernet Sauvignon/Merlot blend that spends one year in oak (Cabernet predominates strongly); it's bone dry and fresh, showing clear capsicum, and well structured – it resembles a good Bordeaux. Super-premium Primeiro Cabernet Sauvignon ferments in oak barrels, where it stays for 22 months, plus the same time in the bottle; it is very ripe, almost devoid of pyrazine notes, full bodied, with sleek, fine-grained tannins and a long length – a special wine to cellar.

Villaggio Conti ♀

São Joaquim

www.villaggioconti.com.br/

Humberto Conti, a food engineer, studied in Italy. With a great passion for wine, he started his vineyard (advised by peninsular professionals) with Italian varieties between São Joaquim and Urubici in 2009, just beside Pericó. The planted area covers 8 hectares, nearly everything Italian, including a very unusual Pignolo. This grape was on the verge of extinction in Italy, where plantings are very small. In Brazil, Conti is unique in this regard. The business is led by Humberto and his sons, Enrico, Bruno and Luca. Oenologist Camila Martins oversees winemaking. They have a well-equipped winery, where Bruno does most of the work. They are happy to offer tastings and accommodate a visit to the vineyard (booking required).

Humberto and Bruno received me for a tasting of several of their wines. Humberto thinks that since most wine producers in Brazil have Italian roots, it is only natural that Italian cultivars are chosen.

However, this goes against the common practice, as international grapes of French origin predominate in the country. Villaggio Conti's wines are a colourful, welcoming and varied lot (see also Leone di Venezia, page 226). Bruno highlighted Montepulciano as a successful grape at Serra Catarinense, with areas planted to these vines increasing. It is well adapted to the region, where conditions allow a long and slow growing season. The variety is, indeed, late-maturing, being picked until early May. Montepulciano has good yields because it produces two clusters per cane. Its thick skins offer a prized resistance to fungal diseases, besides providing plenty of colour and structure. Grecchetto resists diseases differently: its big clusters are very open, allowing the air to circulate and dry the grapes. As for Pignolo, my hosts explained that this is a very, very difficult grape to grow, much more so than even Pinot Nero: issues include fragile wood, a high susceptibility to disease, and low production. The resulting wine compensates for this, however – not to mention its utter rarity. The Contis must be praised for the price of their wines, most of which are, in my opinion, a real bargain. Top Brazilian restaurants stock some of their products.

Grecchetto, like most of the winery's whites, is not pressed but produced (like some rosés) by *saignée*. It is pale and has low aromatic power but shows citrus, minerality and savouriness in the mouth, being very fresh. Ribolla Gialla ferments for two to six months in new oak (French and American) barriques, undergoing lees contact with *bâtonnage*; it is a rich wine with ripe stone fruit, savouriness and an excellent texture.

Arancione is one of their orange wines: a blend of Grecchetto, Vermentino, Ribolla and Malvasia di Candia. Vermentino and Ribolla are frequently co-fermented to make this wine, whereas Malvasia is never more than 30 per cent of the blend due to its intense aromas. Skin contact is about 90 days, unprotected, hence the wine's orange colour. It is not fined (most of their wines are not). It is spicy and aromatic, with hints of basil, fine herbs and dried fruit, and layered, complex and long.

Conti Tutto is a non-vintage red blend of Sangiovese, Montepulciano and Teroldego; very fruity, but with a good structure of acidity and tannins, exhibiting an Italian personality, as do all Conti's wines. Rosso d'Altezza is Sangiovese from four different clones; spending 14 months in used oak, it is true to the variety (sour cherry, tea leaves, earth, dust), rather like a good Chianti. Don Guino is 100 per cent Montepulciano; it matures for 14 months in used oak barrels. It is deeply coloured and has a firm structure of tannins and acidity, plus a high concentration of aromas and flavours. It is savoury, very satisfactory and food friendly. Super-premium Pignolo is inky, dark, high in aromatic intensity and flavour concentration (blackberry, liquorice), very savoury, with tannins still grippy and needing time (it will age very well); layered, complex, this is an outstanding, highly recommended wine.

Villaggio Grando ⚲

Água Doce

www.vinicolavg.com.br/

Maurício Grando started to plant vineyards in 2000, in a region formerly new to viticulture, at an altitude of about 1,300 metres. Before this, he had been visited by a French Armagnac producer, who noted favourable conditions for viticulture there. With the assistance of oenologist Jean-Pierre Rosier (formerly at Epagri and an important character in the history of wine in Santa Catarina), an experimental vineyard had already been planted in 1998. The varieties showing the best adaptation were selected to start the commercial plantings. The first commercial vintage was in 2004. The vineyard has been expanded to 31 hectares, generating 150,000 bottles of wine per year. Of these, 80 per cent are still wines. Lara Malon is the oenologist and the Portuguese Antonio Saramago is a consultant. The average annual temperature is 14.6°C, and there is plenty of sunlight. Harvest here can continue up until May, or even June for late-harvest wines. The winery, where Maurício's son Guilherme Grando, enthusiastic and cordial, is a pivotal staff member, welcomes visitors and has a very good set-up for oenotourism within breathtaking surroundings. There, you can have picnics, book parties and meals, walk through the vineyards, visit the winery, and taste the wines on their own or with tasty appetizers (booking advised).

Chardonnay shows high varietal typicity; spending one year in French oak barrels, there is seamless integration between primary and secondary aromas and flavours. Elegant, it is more Burgundian than tropical. MCG Chardonnay (luxury price level) is a special edition named after Maurício; it stayed 36 months in French oak. The wine displays a very high flavour intensity and concentration, being very buttery and oaky, with a long length – by no means a shy character.

Pinot Noir is fresh, elegant and predominately fruity but also displays leather, earth and vanilla/toast/cedar from three years in French oak barrels. Cabernet Sauvignon, a light rendition of this grape, shows good varietal expression, fresh acidity and sleek tannins; it matured for four months in French and another four in American oak. Innominabile Lote 9 is a blend of seven red grapes from different vintages, spending one year in oak; it brings a mix of red and black berries, spice and floral aromas; with excellent acidity and good tannic structure, it is complex and ageworthy.

Traditional method Brut (Chardonnay, Pinot Noir), 12-month autolysis, is fruity, mineral and slightly bready; it leaves the mouth fresh and dry and has good gastronomic versatility. Marilla Licoroso is a real rarity in Brazil: a sweet dessert wine from Petit Manseng and Gros Manseng. Made from overripe grapes, it is rounded by spending three years in oak barrels; copper-coloured, spirity (fortified to 17.5% abv with a brandy produced in this same winery), its lovely, complex aromas and flavours seem to be a mix of Setúbal and Jurançon: dried apricots, dried orange peel, honey, vanilla and much more.

Vinícola Vivalti 🍷

São Joaquim

www.vinicolavivalti.com.br

Vicente Donini, a successful entrepreneur from the textile industry, is very fond of wines. Despite, as he says, the unfavourable tax treatment of Brazilian wines by the government, he still founded this winery, buying a property of 52 hectares at São Joaquim in 2014. It already had 3.5 hectares of vines. Vicente expanded the vineyards, using Italian planting material, to over 12 hectares (with four more on the way). The vines grow at up to 1,360 metres on clay-rich basaltic soil. A winery was built in 2021 under the solid expertise of oenologist Átila Zavarize. There is a beautiful oenotouristic space, and visitors are welcome for tastings and gazebo use (booking required). Their plans include a much larger facility comprised of an events space, hotel and residential area.

Átila was the host for my wine-tasting experience. Alvarinho is a complete wine; 20 per cent of it spends eight to ten months in oak barrels. The variety's high acidity is well balanced by the typical peach, citrus and mineral notes, with a good texture (up to eight hours of skin contact). Bone-dry, it is more like a Portuguese Alvarinho than a Rías Baixas Albariño. Átila has learned much from Anselmo Mendes, the famous Portuguese oenologist and a supreme master in the Minho region. Super-premium Maceratto is their orange Alvarinho: spontaneously fermented, it remains on its skins for 45 days when malolactic fermentation occurs. It is, indeed, orange and aromatic, with a firm structure of acidity and phenolics, and very long in the mouth, with a drying finish. The blend of their premium Vivalti Rosé is not usually revealed. Still, Zavarize told me (and you, the readers) that it is an unusual mix of Sangiovese and Touriga Nacional. It is a very pale pink drink with intense aromas of fresh raspberry; a good texture comes from 10–12 months on its lees. It is bone dry, with some phenolic grip – an excellent rosé.

Pinot Noir is intense, mouth-watering and highly typical. One-third comes from using whole clusters, contributing to good structure and minty notes. Super-premium Sangiovese is elegant, fresh and varietally typical, showing sour cherry, dust and tea leaves. Also in the super-premium range is a Touriga Nacional made with grapes from three or four different harvest dates in the same vintage. Átila aims to combine higher acidity (earlier) with more ripeness (late) and the remaining structure and characters from the rest of the harvest; part of the lot is spontaneously fermented, and the wine has moderate extraction through *pigeage*. The result is a beauty: elegant and refined, with fruit simultaneously ripe and fresh, showcasing Touriga's violet, mandarin, blackberry and mint. Marselan is inky, with very ripe black and red fruit, a touch of animal character, and mintiness. It has a good structure of acidity and tannins and is exotic and diverse, if a little charmingly rustic. Montepulciano is dark and ripe, exuding blackberries and floral aromas, with good muscle and well-integrated vanilla and cedar from 12 months in French oak (mainly used). The recently launched Supertoscano is a non-vintage Cabernet Sauvignon-dominant blend; Sangiovese and Merlot make up the rest. This wine is made only when wines from outstanding vintages are available. It undergoes maturation in 225-, 300- and 500-litre French oak barrels. It is exquisite, complex, powerful and well structured, and will age well.

Also in the Vinhos de Altitude zone

- Vinícola Adega Patrício, Pinheiro Preto ♀ (@vinho_adega_patricio_oficial)
- Vinícola Alleanza, Pinheiro Preto (www.vinicolaalleanza.com.br)

- Vinícola Berto Aguiar, Curitibanos (@vinicolabertoaguiar)
- Casal Piccoli, Pinheiro Preto (www.casalpiccoli.com.br/home)
- Cata Terroirs, Urupema (cataterroirs.com.br/)
- Vinícola Fama, São Joaquim (@vinicolafama)
- Vinícola Farina, Pinheiro Preto (www.vinicolafarina.com.br)
- Fattoria São Joaquim, São Joaquim (@fattoriasaojoaquim)
- Fellini Wines, Camboriú (@felliniwines)
- Vinícola Gaudio, Urupema @vinicolagaudio)
- Vinícola Longa Vida, Pinheiro Preto ♀ (www.vinicolalongavida. com.br)
- Vinícola Monte Vecchio, Tangará ♀ (www.vinicolamontevecchio. com.br)
- Vinícola Quinta Das Araucárias, São Joaquim (vinicolaquinta dasaraucarias@hotmail.com)
- Vinhos Randon, Pinheiro Preto (bebidasrandon.com.br/home.php)
- Vinícola Da Serra, Pinheiro Preto ♀ (www.vinicoladaserra.com.br/)
- Vinícola Serra Do Sol, Urubici ♀ (serradosolvinhosfinos.com.br/)
- Vinícola Taipa Mayer, Urupema (@taipamayer)
- Vila Romana, Pinheiro Preto (www.vilaromana.ind.br)
- Vinícola Zago, Videira ♀ (www.vinicolazago.com.br)
- Vinícola Zanella Back, São Joaquim ♀ (@zanella_back_vinhos)

IP VALES DA UVA GOETHE

As the name implies, this small region within Santa Catarina state relies on a single grape variety, which regulations stipulate as mandatory: Goethe. This American hybrid is a cross between Muscat of Hamburg and Carter.

The Italian immigrant Benedetto Marengo arrived in Brazil in 1885. He established himself in São Paulo, where he bought land and planted several grape varieties. One of these was Goethe, brought from the US. Another Italian, the lawyer Giuseppe Caruso MacDonald, worked for the Italian consulate at Florianópolis. He was in charge of overseeing Italian colonies in the south of the state. He seemingly liked the area, because he settled in Urussanga, giving rise to a family that persists to this day. He founded a winery here in 1913, the first in Santa Catarina to produce wine industrially. Its activities stopped in 1994. The buildings still exist, but need care and maintenance.

Between the 1930s and 1950s, the local Goethe grape wine was very successful in Brazil, so much so that President Getúlio Vargas served it during receptions at the presidential Catete Palace in Rio de Janeiro. Urussanga was, then, the wine capital of Santa Catarina. Vargas promoted the region and founded an oenological institute. A period of decadence followed when coal mines were established, thus attracting manpower. The Second World War, when Italy was numbered amongst Brazil's enemies, dealt another blow to the region's viticulture. Wine production became little more than a trickle until a renaissance took place, starting in the 1970s. Two important people at this time were Genésio Mazon and Hedi Damian, who founded new wineries.

In the 1990s, the old oenological institute became an experimental station, now a part of Epagri. New wineries appeared, and an association (ProGoethe) was founded in 2005. Epagri took care of the historical and cultural aspects (under agronomist Sérgio Maestrelli) and the technical approach was overseen by oenologist Stevan Arcari. IP status was granted in 2012, including eight townships, and 55 hectares are now planted with this rare variety.

The most important town is Urussanga, 190 kilometres south of Florianópolis. It is close to the spectacular Rio do Rastro road leading to São Joaquim, though at a lower altitude. Lying just 50 kilometres from the sea, cool marine breezes dry and refresh the area, compensating for the high humidity. For those travelling from the state capital to Serra Catarinense and the IP Vinhos de Altitude, stopping at Vales da Uva Goethe is definitely worthwhile.

The Goethe grape is more resistant to disease than *vinifera* varieties and has adapted very well to the environment. Its two clones, Goethe Clássica (pink skin) and Goethe Primo (white), both with the same genetics, give rise to white wines devoid of foxiness, very fresh and aromatic (tropical fruit), and with an enticing mineral character. They are a true Brazilian vinous speciality, worth trying and quite affordable.

IP Vales da Uva Goethe wineries

Vinícola Casa Del Nonno ♀

Urussanga

www.casadelnonno.com.br

This winery was founded in 1975 by Hedi Damian and Flávio Mariot; today, their descendants, Renato and Matheus Mariot Damian (the oenologist), continue to lead the family business. Besides local Goethe grapes, they also buy fruit from partners at Serra Catarinense. Visitors are welcome; there is no need to book if you only wish to taste the wines (closed on Sundays).

Nobile Goethe is aromatic: floral, citrus, pear and peach, with mineral notes and a clear saline finish. Light, with low alcohol, and crisp, it is an excellent wine for a summer afternoon. Peccato Bianco is the lightly oaked, off-dry version, where some vanilla and spice marry well with the fruit, keeping the salinity. Traditional method Goethe Nature offers ripe peach and melon; it is bone dry and has good autolytic notes (36-month autolysis). The finish is saline and mineral. The Brut version has fewer autolytic notes (12-month autolysis), bringing ripe peach, pear and melon; it is crisp, creamy and mouth coating, ending with a mineral note.

Also in Vales da Uva Goethe

- Vinícola Bianco, Orleans ♀ (@vinicolabianco)
- Vinícola De Noni, Urussanga ♀ (@denonivinhos)
- Vigna Mazon Pousada e Vinícola, Urussanga ♀ (www.mazon.com. br)
- Vinhos Quarezemin, Içara ♀ (vinhosquarezemin.com/)
- Vinhos Trevisol, Urussanga (vinhostrevisol.com.br/)

VALE DO RIO TIJUCAS

A small wine region exists in the Tijucas River valley around Nova Trento. The production is primarily *vinho de mesa* from American hybrids, but there are some incipient vineyards of *vinifera* grapes developed by Epagri. Some *vinho fino* is also produced with grapes brought from Serra Gaúcha. Nova Trento, 90 kilometres north-west of Florianópolis, is best known as a religious (Catholic) centre, attracting pilgrims from many places who visit the sanctuary of Santa Paulina.

Vale do Rio Tijucas wineries

- Vinícola Castel, Nova Trento ♀ (@vinicolacasteloficial)
- Vinícola Girola, Nova Trento ♀ (www.vinhosgirola.com.br/)

ALTO URUGUAI

Some vineyards around the city of Chapecó are integrated into the Alto Uruguai wine region – please refer to Other Rio Grande do Sul regions, page 200. In Chapecó itself, you will find the winery Família Viel, Chapecó (familiaviel.com.br/).

Also in Santa Catarina

- Quinta Da Figueira Vinhos Disruptivos, Florianópolis (@quinta dafigueira)

PARANÁ

The northernmost state of Brazil's South region borders Santa Catarina and Argentina to the south, São Paulo to the north, Paraguay and Mato Grosso do Sul state to the west, and the Atlantic Ocean to the east. The total area is 199,308 square kilometres and the population is 11.4 million (2022). The human development index (HDI) was 0.769 in 2021 (0.754 for Brazil). The state's demonym is *paranaense*.

Tourist attractions abound here. The state capital, Curitiba (population 1.77 million), is a cosmopolitan and civilized city with many exceedingly beautiful parks and cultural points (such as the Botanical Garden, the Oscar Niemeyer Museum and the Ópera de Arame). A scenic hop-on, hop-off panoramic bus visits the main city attractions. You can take a train from Curitiba to Morretes, traversing the Serra do Mar mountain range amidst luxuriant forests with spectacular views. You will cross several breathtaking bridges over deep abysses, down to Morretes near the Atlantic, where the hearty traditional dish *barreado* can be enjoyed. Go back to Curitiba by bus or car via the old, stone-paved Graciosa road, with its rich history and twists and turns. By all means, visit the Iguaçu Falls, one of the 'New 7 Wonders of Nature' and the largest collection of waterfalls on Earth. Go to the Vila Velha Geological Park, which has dozens of sandstone cliffs not far from Curitiba.

A brief history

Except for wood extraction, nothing important happened in Paraná during the first half of the sixteenth century. In the second half of that century, however, when the state partially belonged to the Spanish Crown,

Jesuit missionaries arrived in its western parts. They founded towns and established 'reductions' – that is, settlements for the Indigenous people – where the grapevine was cultivated and wine made, especially for use at Mass. Brazilian and Portuguese from São Paulo invaded the area in the seventeenth century to claim it for Portugal and destroyed the reductions.

Paraná became the land of *tropeiros*, who moved cattle from Rio Grande do Sul to São Paulo. It was a part of the state of São Paulo until 1853, when Emperor Dom Pedro II made it a province of the Brazilian Empire. Like the other southern states, Paraná received a strong influx of immigrants, especially from Europe (Portuguese, Polish, German, Dutch, Ukrainian and Italian) and, later, also from Japan. With the arrival of railways, the wood industry became very important. The state had enormous amounts of the Brazilian pine tree, *Araucaria angustifolia*, which grows with a straight trunk, providing regular timber. It is estimated that more than 100 million trees of this kind have been felled, so much so that the threat of extinction has become real. This forced a ban on *Araucaria* logging, thus preserving the symbolic tree of Paraná. Not that the tree is only found in Paraná – whoever travels from

Vineyard and Araucaria trees at Vinícola Legado

the southern parts of Minas Gerais down to Rio Grande do Sul will see these beautiful trees in cooler regions. It is, however, everywhere in Paraná. The tree produces a kind of nut called *pinhão* (pine nut), which is delicious to eat onced cooked and part of the regional cuisine. A great pairing: try the nuts with sweet fortified reds, like Port, or any of its Brazilian renditions. From the end of the nineteenth century, coffee became a very important agricultural product, especially in the northern parts of Paraná.

After the Jesuits were expelled, winemaking didn't appear in Paraná again for about two centuries. It reappeared in 1870 when immigrants from Alsace and Vevey (Switzerland) formed the colony of Superaguy on the state's coastline near the border with São Paulo. A total of six wineries existed, supplying wine to both states. At about the same time, Italian immigrants settled around Curitiba, mainly in Colombo, planting vines and making wine. Not unlike so many other places, here too *labrusca* varieties were preferred due to their disease resistance and productivity. Following this, new regions, like the Southwest (Italian and German immigrants) and the North (Japanese), were developed for viticulture, both for table and wine grapes. Vineyards prospered around Curitiba until the 1960s, when disease, real-estate factors and competition from Serra Gaúcha forced a drastic reduction in the planted area. It was only in the 1990s that viticulture for *vinhos finos* started to flourish once more.

It must be kept in mind, however, that viticulture is highly scattered in the state and that *vinifera* plantings are still in the minority. No trustworthy statistics are available, but the total planted area of such varieties will likely not reach 50 hectares. Notwithstanding this, brave producers have improved the quality of their wines, and these deserve some recognition.

Climate and soils

Based on Köppen's classification, Paraná has just two climate classes: Cfa (humid tropical, oceanic, without dry season, hot summer) and Cfb (humid tropical, oceanic, without dry season, temperate summer). It is certain, then, that there is plenty of rain and that high humidity can be a problem. However, a more detailed evaluation (Ricce and collaborators, 2011), using the MCC System, pointed to seven different classes. Again, all had a Dryness Index of -2 (that is, humid). However, some were comparable with those of other regions successfully making wine (such as Rio Grande do Sul, Santa Catarina, Slovenia, and areas in Germany and Switzerland). In the north of the state, table grape production uses double pruning to obtain two growth cycles and two harvests yearly. Such a scheme has started to be applied to wine grapes grown to produce *vinhos finos.* As for soils, the predominant orders (SiBCS) are *latossolos, neossolos* and *cambissolos.* As usual, most are acidic and demand correction.

The state has an IP for wines, Bituruna. However, most wines here are made from hybrid grapes, especially Casca Grossa (thick skin). Some wineries at this IP also make *vinhos finos.* The state has an association of wine producers, Vinopar. Their website (vinopar.com.br/) provides helpful information about Paraná wines.

Paraná wineries

Vinícola Legado ♀

Campo Largo (metropolitan region of Curitiba)

vinicolalegado.com.br/

Just 30 kilometres from Curitiba, the very knowledgeable and cultivated Heloise Merolli (DipWSET) planted a vineyard in a beautiful location boasting virgin woods. Oenology is led by José Luiz Marcon Filho, PhD, a scholar who earned a sandwich doctorate at the University of Auckland. Both are keen to study all aspects of viticulture at their particular terroir – and to translate it into good sustainable practices. I could perceive this when I visited them and saw how well their vines are doing despite the humid climate. Cover crops are used instead of herbicides, and their practices can be adequately described as *lutte raisonnée.* They have been particularly successful with Viognier, Merlot and – yes! – Fiano. Fiano in Brazil and in Paraná. Who would think that? Heloise told me that she was very fond of this Campanian cultivar, so she brought planting material from Italy and, fortunately, succeeded in making the vines prosper here. Despite the moderate yields (averaging 2.4 kilograms per vine), the resulting wines have been rewarding. Legado is within easy reach via well-paved roads, and there is an excellent set-up for oenotourism, including picnics. Lighter wines are labelled Sapienza ('Wisdom', in Italian), and those with more structure and oak treatment are named Sfizio ('Whim'). Sparklers have an evocative name: Flair.

Sapienza Viognier is fresher and lighter than French examples, but it offers classical floral, peachy and honeyed flavours, expressing its particular terroir well. Rosé Merlot, from *saignée,* is dark pink, bone dry

and very fresh, with some savouriness. Merlot is unoaked and fermented protectively at a low (for a red) 22–23°C, hence bringing fruit to
the front – its style is akin to a good Valpolicella. Sfizio Fiano is crafted
protectively in stainless steel; it has floral, nutty and honeyed aromas
and is well structured and intense in the mouth. I was fortunate to taste
2013: dense, complex, waxy, almost oily, and outstanding. Fiano all'An-
tica is a very different interpretation: an orange wine with four-month
skin contact, made under oxidative conditions; it is golden, complex,
savoury and very fresh, and balances the flavours and acidity well – it is
really food friendly.

Sfizio Viognier ferments in stainless steel but with oak staves. This
contact continues for four months thereafter, on lees, in a reductive
environment. It is a savoury, spicy wine in which the varietal characters appear less evident than in Sapienza, but there is more structure
and complexity. Sfizio Merlot has a longer fermentation time than
its entry-level brother and undergoes more extraction (pumping over)
and some oak treatment. It reminds me of Italian reds and is simultaneously fresh and ripe, bone dry, with complex aromas and flavours
of blackberries, mocha and spice. Their top, luxury Sfizio Lote 13 is a
multi-vintage *appassimento* wine, 100 per cent Merlot; whole clusters
dry indoors in plastic boxes for 20 to 30 days, attaining up to 25 Brix.
A specific yeast is used to ferment it. Malolactic fermentation takes

Heloise and José Luiz at their Viognier vineyard

up to a year to complete, and the wine undergoes barrel maturation for an average of four years. No wonder it is a very complex, dense, concentrated wine, with plenty of dried fruit, tobacco, chocolate and slight volatile acidity (typical of its kind), but not heavy, thanks to excellent acidity.

Flair sparkling wines are all made using the traditional method. The varieties used to craft the base wines are unusual. Brut white, 100 per cent Viognier, is very aromatic, especially in the autolytic characters (over three years with lees), keeping freshness with considerable structure. Brut rosé is 100 per cent Merlot; it is light pink, again intense in aromas and flavours, biscuity, savoury, complex and mature.

Vinícola Araucária

São José dos Pinhais ♀
vinicolaaraucaria.com.br/

This winery was founded in 2007 by a quartet of friends. The vineyards are located within a scenic, rural environment not far from Curitiba, at altitude (980 metres), on soils with clay and limestone. The star amongst red grapes here is Cabernet Franc. At their state-of-the-art winery, the oenologist Marcos Vian guides the making of their wines from local and bought grapes. There is an excellent set-up for receiving visitors, including a top restaurant (Gralha Azul) and a brand-new hotel.

Gralha Azul Cabernet Franc is a fresh example of this variety, displaying unmistakable aromas and flavours of pencil shavings, blackberries, hints of capsicum, plus spice and vanilla from six months in used oak barriques. Angustifólia Chardonnay, lightly oaked, is very fruity, with touches of white flowers and spice, being an elegant and typical example of the variety. Merlot is a deeply coloured wine with ripe black fruit and an evident oak character (12 months in barrels). Cabernet Sauvignon has less colour, exhibiting aromatic cassis amidst invigorating acidity and a firm structure of fine-grained tannins. Poty Lazarotto Nature is Chardonnay, Pinot Noir and a touch of Viognier; after 40-month autolysis, it is pale, with fine bubbles, bone dry, and so fresh.

Vinícola RH

Mariópolis ♀
www.vinicolarh.com.br/

This particular winery is located in a small town, Mariópolis, near the border between Paraná and Santa Catarina, 434 kilometres west of

Curitiba. Enthusiastic couple Vaner Herget (a dentist) and Odilete Rotava (agronomist) planted 2.5 hectares in 2008 with Chardonnay and Pinot Noir. The predominant soil type is *latossolo vermelho* – that is, red, clayey and fertile. They had already started planning their business, however, in 2000, and began selling wines in 2005. Vinícola RH crafts only traditional method sparkling wines, some of which have earned prizes at national contests. Producing only sparklers, according to the couple, was both an opportunity to specialize and also dictated by the climate. At Mariópolis, it is challenging to achieve grape maturity to produce good still wines. But, as in Champagne, the conditions favour the creation of base wines for sparklers. Oenologist Marcos Vian provides the technical advice, but Vaner oversees most winemaking tasks. They can process up to 25,000 litres of wine annually; the present production is 15,000 bottles. An important differential advantage of RH is their stock of reserve wines from several vintages at various autolysis lengths. Visitors are welcome to tour the vineyards, learn about the production process and taste the wines (booking required).

Brut (Chardonnay, 28-month autolysis) has a remarkable, crisp, sharp acidity, so well balanced by ripe, but by no means overripe, fruit and clear autolytic character – a very elegant, satisfying sparkler. Extra-Brut (Chardonnay/Pinot Noir, 40-month autolysis) is steely, sharp and dry, bringing citrus, green apple and savoury flavours of bread and toast, with some salinity on the finish. Nature Black (Chardonnay/Pinot Noir, 65-month autolysis) has overt dried fruit, bread, brioche and patisserie, besides savoury and saline notes; it is complex, layered and so long. Extra-Brut Medalha (Chardonnay/Pinot Noir), after no less than 84 months with lees, is richly autolytic, with intense and concentrated flavours of bread, dough and brioche; bone dry and crisp, it is indeed complex and savoury.

Also in Paraná

- Vinícola Bertoletti, Bituruna (vinicolabertoletti.com.br/)
- Vinícola Betiatto, Francisco Beltrão 🍷 (vinicolabetiatto.com/)
- Vinícola Bordignon, Palotina (near the Argentinean border) 🍷 (vinicolabordignon.com.br/)
- Vinícola Casa Carnasciali, Apucarana 🍷 (@ vinicolacasacarnasciali)
- Cave Colinas de Pedra, Piraquara (near Curitiba) 🍷 (cavecolinas depedra.com.br/)

- Vinícola Crevelim, Maringá (@vinhos_crevelim)
- Vinícola Dezem, Toledo ♀ (vinicoladezem.commercesuite.com.br/)
- Vinícola Família Fardo, Quatro Barras (metropolitan area of Curitiba) ♀ (familiafardo.com.br/)
- Vinícola Franco Italiano, Colombo (near Curitiba) ♀ (www.franco italiano.com.br/)
- Vinícola La Dorni, Bandeirantes ♀ (ladorni.com.br/)
- Tenuta Lopedote, Bituruna ♀ (@tenutalopedote)
- Vinícola Sanber, Bituruna ♀ (www.vinicolasanber.com.br/)
- Vinícola Di Sandi, Bituruna (loja.disandi.com.br/)
- Unus Mundus Vinhos Autorais, São Luiz do Puruná (@unus mundusvinhosautorais)

11

THE SOUTHEAST

This region, comprising the states of São Paulo, Minas Gerais, Rio de Janeiro and Espírito Santo, is the locomotive of the country's economy. It also has the largest population: 84.8 million, or 41.8 per cent of Brazil's total. The two biggest cities are here: São Paulo and Rio de Janeiro.

To the benefit of viticulture, a vast part of the Southeast is at altitude. This moderates the climate, bringing more sunlight and wind. In terms of the types of relief found in the region, we see *serras* (mountain ranges), *planaltos* (highlands), *chapadas* (flat highlands), *patamares* (areas intermediate between higher and lower terrains), *depressões* (not beneath sea level but rather just below neighbouring areas), *tabuleiros* (low-lying areas near the coast, at about 20–40 metres' altitude) and *planícies* (plains). In the Southeast, vineyards are located in *planaltos*, *chapadas*, *serras* and *patamares*.

DPWH IN THE SOUTHEAST

Despite a long history of winemaking, beginning in the sixteenth century, wine production only began to improve and grow in the region after double pruning and winter harvesting (DPWH) was introduced. As a result, this very particular viticultural practice is considered first. It is not exclusive to the Southeast, but in terms of area and volume, it is almost as if it were.

DPWH management is a Brazilian speciality viticultural practice described in the chapter on Viticulture (see page 42). It is restricted neither to a single state nor to a single Brazilian region, being practised wherever climatic conditions allow.

I am fortunate to live and work in the town where this revolutionary technique began: Três Corações, in the south of Minas Gerais state. Here, where Pelé (the greatest soccer player of all time) was born, the first experimental vineyard to try this approach to vine management was planted in 2001 at a coffee farm (Fazenda da Fé) belonging to wine enthusiast Dr Marcos Arruda Vieira. This happened because he was associated with the 'father' – or should I say the 'Pelé'? – of DPWH in Brazil, oenologist Murillo Albuquerque Regina, plus two French partners. They founded the first wine firm, Vinícola Estrada Real. Murillo has a doctorate from Bordeaux University and a post-doctorate from ENTAV, France. He was a researcher at Epamig (the Embrapa equivalent inMinas Gerais state). Without his pioneering work with this 'cycle inversion' (as it is sometimes called here) technique, it is likely that a very significant expansion of Brazilian wine regions would not have taken place.

The experiments pointed to Sauvignon Blanc and Syrah as the most suitable varieties for DPWH, leading to a commercial vineyard. The first wine from this origin was launched in 2010: Primeira Estrada Syrah. Even before this launch, other brave new growers had appeared, attracted by the sound quality of the pioneering pre-commercial wine editions. Such was the case for Vinícola Guaspari, which planted their first vineyards in 2006 in Espírito Santo do Pinhal, just across the border between southern Minas Gerais and São Paulo state. Vinhos Maria Maria planted their first vineyards in 2009, 96 kilometres from Três Corações and again at a coffee farm. The resounding success of such wineries in these two states in Brazil's Southeast attracted the attention of other entrepreneurs. Many other vineyards were planted, almost always under Murillo Regina's close assessment and attention. This happened mainly at Minas Gerais and São Paulo, but also elsewhere, including Goiás, Mato Grosso, Mato Grosso do Sul, Rio de Janeiro, Espírito Santo and Bahia states, and even around the country's capital, Brasília, in the Federal District. DPWH, therefore, has reached many places in Brazil and is still growing. The following section summarizes briefly how this approach to viticulture is managed.

One of the most significant issues with traditional grape growing in the Southern Hemisphere north of the classical latitude interval (between 30 and 50 degrees) is the climate: too warm, too humid. Remember that under traditional management, grapes are harvested from January to March, when DPWH regions are very warm or hot, with plenty of rainfall. It is hard to grow good grapes for wine in such conditions. If, as will be seen, the climate is at least very dry (as in São Francisco Valley),

Murillo Albuquerque Regina

tropical viticulture is feasible. But what about other, more humid regions – a vast expanse of Brazil's Central Highlands? In this case, Murillo and his followers used a double pruning system. Besides the usual pruning in August (Southern Hemisphere), known as 'formation pruning', there is also a summer pruning (January or February), the 'production pruning' – hence, 'double pruning' (which some call, albeit incorrectly, 'inverted pruning'). The first pruning is severe and short, with only single-bud spurs remaining. A new growth cycle ensues. A green harvest eliminates clusters in October or November. The production pruning is followed by applying 6% hydrogen cyanamide (Dormex®) to break bud dormancy and avoid apical dominance. This allows the grapes to mature fully in the winter – hence, 'winter harvesting' (June to August) and my proposed initialism DPWH. There are, therefore, two growth cycles and one harvest per year (there is no significant production in the 'normal' cycle).

Identifying sites suitable for DPWH

When I earned my Wine & Spirit Education Trust (WSET) Level 5 (Honours Diploma) degree (I was the last graduate of this discontinued qualification), my research project was entitled *Critical Analysis and Possible Expansion of Double Pruning and Winter Harvest (DPWH) in Brazil and other countries*. For Brazil, I did an extensive search, including over 1,400 climatic stations, to find places with a climate that could potentially allow DPWH. This signified that MCC climate classes should be similar to southern Minas Gerais, albeit not mandatorily identical. Places with less rainfall were also included, but those with over 100 millimetres of rain in total in the last two months of the cycle (RL2M, a shorthand I created for this important parameter) were excluded. The limits for minimal average temperature in the month of harvest (Cool night Index: CI) were determined as 10–14°C. Less than this, and it would be too cool for good grape maturation; more than this, and it is too warm. I also investigated the cycle's thermal amplitude in the last two months (TALM), which is relevant to grape quality. Climatic data from six months (potential vegetative cycle: pruning to harvesting) were analysed for each region, beginning in December, January, February or March, searching for a climatic cycle that could fulfil the selection criteria suitable for DPWH. The best cycle could be selected without dogmatically establishing a January to June cycle. The regions selected as suitable for DPWH were described in terms of altitude, latitude, longitude, rainfall, RL2M, average maximum and minimum temperature, TALM, evapotranspiration (ETP), Heliothermal Index (HI), Dryness Index (DI), CI and MCC climate classification.

I found 184 places in 11 states with climates suitable for DPWH (see map opposite). The latitudes (South) ranged from 7.83 to 23.77; the longitudes (West) ranged from 38.12 to 59.45. Of all 184 sites, only one was under 400 metres (average 759 metres). A sub-humid DI predominated (71 per cent), followed by moderately dry (21 per cent); however, even at the humid sites there was – as a selection criterion – less than 100 millimetres of RL2M. The predominant HI was warm (58 per cent), followed by temperate warm (38 per cent). By default, only two classes of CI were found at the selected sites: CI+1 (64 per cent) and CI+2 (36 per cent). The TALM ranged from 9.2°C to 18°C (average 13.5°C). The states of Minas Gerais, São Paulo and Goiás were home to 159 (86 per cent) of all sites. This provided the common factors essential for DPWH: altitude and mild and dry winters. In many areas investigated for the work, the climate in the six-month cycle of DPWH is similar to that of some traditional wine-producing regions in Europe and other parts of the world.

Winter, where DPWH is feasible (a vast region), is dry and sunny and has warm days with cool to cold nights (high diurnal variation). Precious acidity is thus maintained, and a good level of polyphenols and aroma precursors is created. The macro-region is very large, more or less coinciding with the Brazilian Highlands, where the vineyards lie most-ly at altitude (600–1,200 metres). The predominant climate is temper-ate (subtropical), with Köppen types Cwa and Cwb. However, using the MCC system by Tonietto and Carbonneau results in several classes. Considering the winter viticultural cycle, the pioneering region (south of Minas Gerais) mainly has an MCC class of temperate warm, sub-humid, with cool to very cool nights (a mild winter in tropical condi-tions). Many Brazilian states have areas that allow this type of viticulture.

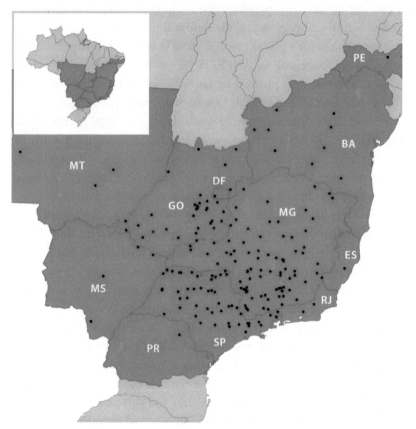

Map 9: Location of 184 places in 11 Brazilian states with a climate suitable for DPWH. BA: Bahia; DF: Distrito Federal; ES: Espírito Santo; GO: Goiás; MG: Minas Gerais; MS: Mato Grosso do Sul; MT: Mato Grosso; PR: Paraná; SP: São Paulo; RJ: Rio de Janeiro

As already noted, new players in the DPWH arena have multiplied. A producers' association – Associação Nacional de Produtores de Vinhos de Inverno (ANPROVIN) – was founded in 2016 and, as of now (2025), includes 50 wineries. Data from their site (www.anprovin. com.br) indicates that 450 hectares have been planted, producing 1.1 million bottles per year. The yield is low, which is partly explained by the fact that many of the vineyards are still very young (some are quite recent and have not started production yet) and partly by an inherently low productivity. DPWH vines have a lower production than those managed by less interventionist practices. According to Murillo Regina, although this depends on the variety, region, climate, irrigation or dry farming, among other factors, the average yields range between 6 and 8 tons per hectare. It is possible (albeit unproved) that such a fact may lead to better-quality grapes. Only time will tell.

However, the total planted area of DPWH vineyards is larger because not all wineries belong to ANPROVIN. As for varieties, they are all *vinifera*, and the most planted, by far, is Syrah, followed by Sauvignon Blanc – the best adapted to this type of management.

ANPROVIN has successfully applied for the first Indicação de Procedência (IP) of winter wines, calling it Sul de Minas (South of Minas Gerais), after the pioneering region (see page 76). Along the trajectory of their 15 years of commercial production, such wines have been proven to offer enough typicity and personality to point to a characteristic terroir. Syrah wines are more like those of northern Rhône than Australian examples in aromas and flavours: a complex mix of ripe black fruit, black pepper, smoky and animal notes. They are usually well structured, with clear acidity, broad tannins (usually fine grained and amicable), and medium to high alcohol. They marry well with oak. Despite the relatively short time in which to evaluate their ageing capability, many wines from the earlier vintages continue to drink very well and are improving. Sauvignon Blanc has a personality of its own, too: aromas and flavours sit midway between the exuberance of Marlborough products and the relative restraint of the Upper Loire, but always ripe and textured. Many show clear and agreeable notes of green coffee beans amongst the other typical aromas and flavours of this aromatic variety. It is tempting to think that this may be due to the proximity of many vineyards to coffee plantations – but this would require scientific investigation. On the other hand, it may perhaps serve as a link to origin during blind tastings.

Other cultivars, however, are also doing well, although with a little more difficulty and less productivity. Very good wines are on the market, made from Chenin Blanc, Viognier, Cabernet Franc, Cabernet Sauvignon, Malbec, Merlot and Pinot Noir. This is all a new process in development and needs time to evolve.

MINAS GERAIS

This state is the fourth largest in Brazil (586,514 square kilometres, bigger than France) and the second in population (20.5 million). Its name – meaning 'General Mines' – comes from its importance for mineral extraction, which started in the seventeenth century when gold was discovered and provoked a large rush. Many cities were then founded, the arts flourished, and baroque churches were built. Fortunately, many are well preserved, as are some parts of the most important towns. The historic cities of Minas Gerais are a great tourist attraction, and not to be missed: Ouro Preto, Tiradentes, São João del-Rei, Congonhas, Mariana and Diamantina, among others. The demonym is *mineiro*, or 'miner'. People from here – my state – are reputedly reserved, discreet, shrewd and independent – but always very hospitable. As we say, *mineiros* work silently. But they really do, and the state has been very relevant politically in Brazil. The most important movement in attaining the country's independence arose here in the eighteenth century: the *Inconfidência Mineira*. The Portuguese suffocated this uprising, hanging its most representative leader, nicknamed *Tiradentes* (or 'pull teeth', as he was both soldier and dentist). Many records from this time are preserved in the state's historic cities, especially at the Museu da Inconfidência, in Ouro Preto.

Minas Gerais has a very varied regional cuisine, mostly pork- or chicken-based, with hearty dishes. Try *tutu à mineira* (bean purée with pork loin, crackling, braised kale, pork sausage and eggs), *torresmo* (crackling), *frango ao molho pardo* (chicken in blood sauce) and *frango com quiabo* (chicken with okra). All meals end with typical desserts: *ambrosia* (a milk, eggs, sugar and cinnamon treat), *baba de moça* (custard cream with eggs and coconut) or the ubiquitous 'Romeo and Juliet' (that is, *goiabada* or 'guava sweet' with fresh cheese) and, of course, a good coffee. Minas Gerais is Brazil's largest coffee producer and produces the best gourmet coffees. The state is also a source of top-quality cheese, some with geographical indications; many have won important international prizes.

There is no lack of tourist attractions. The state capital, Belo Horizonte (planned and built from scratch at the end of the nineteenth century), is a beautiful, cosmopolitan city (population 2.3 million) with many attractions. Go to Praça da Liberdade, Parque Municipal, Parque da Serra do Curral, Mercado Municipal and Museu de Artes e Ofícios; see a soccer match at Mineirão stadium; or go to concerts at Palácio das Artes or at the world-class Sala Minas Gerais, seat of the Minas Gerais Philharmonic Orchestra. Belo Horizonte – or just BH, or Belô – is not far from the historic cities. You can visit impressive caverns (Lapinha and Maquiné), the beautiful Serra do Cipó National Park (a well-preserved nature reserve, full of waterfalls) or the park of the Colégio Caraça. In the south of the state, many spa towns attract tourists, including the cities of Poços de Caldas, São Lourenço and Caxambu. Or visit Capitólio, at the Furnas Lake, for sports and to enjoy crystalline waters and beautiful cliffs.

A brief history

Given the great importance of religion and tradition in Minas Gerais from the beginning of its history, it is only natural to think that wine has been made here for a long time, at least for use in the Catholic Mass. Bringing wine from abroad, after all, was a mighty feat. Even taking merchandise from Rio de Janeiro to Minas Gerais demanded very slow, risky transportation on the backs of mules, following impossible tracks across the many mountains. The most important and pioneering track, as allowed by the Portuguese rulers, connected the seaside town of Paraty, south of Rio, to Villa Rica (today, Ouro Preto), the very centre of mining. This became known as *Caminho Velho* (Old Way); it was legally permitted by the Crown – people also knew it as *Estrada Real* (Royal Road).

One of the first references to locally made wine comes from John Mawe, a British mineralogist and traveller. He was here between 1809 and 1810, visiting Villa Rica and the diamond deposits then being explored. This was unusual, as the Portuguese rulers did not allow foreigners to enter such regions. Mawe published a book in 1812, which is very interesting to read: *Travels in the Interior of Brazil, particularly in the Gold and Diamond Districts of that Country*, in which he claimed to be the first Englishman to go to such places. He visited a nearby pottery in Villa Rica and Mariana; when describing this, he wrote: 'I was here invited to taste some wine, made from grapes grown on the spot, which was excellent.' As this happened before the arrival of American hybrids, the wine must have been made from *vinifera* varieties brought by the Portuguese.

A little later (in around 1817), two German naturalists, Johann Baptist Von Spix and Carl Friedrich Von Martius, visited Minas Gerais and went up to its northern limits, near Bahia state. This is the *sertão* (outback) – not the mountainous, well watered and more fertile areas around Villa Rica, but rather like the present tropical viticulture area (that is, flat, vast and dry). They came to Brazil with the entourage of Archduchess Maria Leopoldina of Austria, who was to marry the future (from 1822) Pedro I, Emperor of Brazil. They explored the country's hinterland despite the innumerable difficulties. They observed that, in the *sertão*, irrigating vines allowed growers to produce a second crop in winter. More or less at the same time, another European scientist, Auguste de Saint-Hilaire, also travelled the country. He, too, found vines yielding two crops a year at Tejuco (now Diamantina) if irrigated. These were the first records of a phenomenon that would become fundamental to tropical viticulture and DPWH. Such facts are reported in a paper by João F. P. Meira, doctor in political sSciences and winemaker at Diamantina.

Wine likely continued to be made in those days, at least for liturgical purposes. However, the first commercial viticulture and winemaking registers date from the late nineteenth century.

With the focus on DPWH, it is sometimes forgotten that traditional viticulture has been practised for much longer in Minas Gerais, albeit offering more modest results. As in Rio Grande do Sul, the greater yield and stronger resistance of American and hybrid varieties led to their dominance. Only a few decades ago, *vinifera* grapes were significantly planted after many Brazilian wine consumers started to switch from *vinhos de mesa* to *vinhos finos*. Traditional viticulture persists, although it is being progressively dislodged by DPWH wines, which now dominate the scene.

One of Minas Gerais' oldest centres of viticulture and winemaking is the historic city of Diamantina (still making wine today). It was the seat of a bishopric in 1864 and, according to João Meira, the Church became, from 1871, a producer of wine, both for liturgical and economic reasons. A winery existed within the grounds surrounding the bishop's palace. It produced a wine appropriately named *Vinho do Palácio*, or 'Palace Wine', to be used at the Catholic Mass and for selling to the general public. In 1920, Diamantina had 12 wine-linked businesses, and the total official production was 33,000 litres. Part of such wine came from small producers from other professions (such as doctors and teachers). A larger enterprise, Mil Oitavas, appeared in 1944; it was owned by Portuguese immigrants and made wine until 1960. As in many other places, most grapes were American hybrids, such as Isabel, Herbemont and Niágara. From the late 1960s to the early 2000s, however, there was a decline in viticulture and wine production. This began to change with DPWH practices, allowing a rebirth of wines from Diamantina.

However, the most important centre of traditional viticulture in Minas Gerais is far away from Diamantina (about 750 kilometres by car), in the towns of Caldas and Andradas, in the state's south, near the border with São Paulo. According to the prolific scholar and writer Júlio Seabra Inglez de Sousa, commercial viticulture started at Caldas in 1860, when hybrid varieties were introduced. As usual, Isabel was at the forefront, later accompanied by Concord, Catawba, Martha and, importantly (from 1904 onwards), York Madeira. Curiously, the latter was brought from Portugal, not from the US, under the name *Folha de Figo* (Fig Leaf). It also made strides at Rio Grande do Sul, where it was soon renamed 'Bordô'.

An important regional character was the 'colonel' José Francisco de Oliveira. He was not in the military. In Brazil, until the first half of the twentieth century, all rich and important landowners were nick-named 'colonels'. At Caracol (later Andradas), he planted many different varieties, most of them American hybrids, and made wines, one of which earned a prize at Ouro Preto, then the capital of Minas Gerais. Unfortunately, the first documented recording of phylloxera in Brazil was made at the colonel's vineyards in 1893 by a technician from the Instituto Agronômico de Campinas (Campinas Agronomical Institute). Then, Italian immigrants made another entrance. They arrived in Andradas at the start of the twentieth century, bringing their wine traditions with them, with between 400 and 500 families buying small rural properties, as in Rio Grande do Sul. They made wine first for domestic consumption. Production soon increased and sales began. The production volume, always from American hybrids (Jacquez at the forefront, not Isabel), reached an apex in the 1950s and then began declining steadily.

According to Thalassa Kalil, only seven *cantinas* (wineries) existed in 2012. Of these, two were the most important, but they used 80 per cent of grapes from Rio Grande do Sul to make their wines. Since then, a shift from hybrids to *vinifera* has taken place, not least due to market demands. This has been favoured by the appearance of DPWH, the theoretical foundations (and some practical applications) of which were developed by Murillo Regina precisely at Epamig, in Caldas (near Andradas). With such developments, a renaissance has been experienced in both towns.

Geology, climate and soils

The relief is predominately mountainous, especially in the south, and dominated by Serra da Mantiqueira. One of the highest peaks in Brazil, however, is located not in Minas Gerais' southern regions but rather on its border with Espírito Santo state: the Pico da Bandeira, at 2,891 metres. Minas Gerais constitutes a large portion of the Brazilian Highlands.

When I researched new regions with climatic potential for DPWH, which included Minas Gerais, the sites showing favourable results had an altitude (median) of 860 metres. The median MCC values were HI 2,305 (temperate warm), DI 64.5 (sub-humid) and CI 12.3 (cool nights). According to Köppen-Geiger's classification, almost all the regions already making wine belong to classes Cwa (humid subtropical, dry winter and hot summer) and Cwb (humid subtropical, dry winter and temperate summer). Minas Gerais, however, is a very large state, with many regions at altitude and a series of climate types. The north is flatter, warmer and drier than the centre or the south, where DPWH is concentrated.

Again, the vastness brings significant variability to soils. However, it is possible to generalize that, in DPWH regions, the predominant class is *latossolos*. Soils usually have low fertility and high aluminium content, demanding correction (lime, fertilizers). Especially at Minas Gerais, they tend to have a red, yellow or yellow-red colour derived from iron oxides. They are usually quite acidic, with low base saturation. As they display good porosity and permeability, waterlogging is not a common problem.

Varieties planted today

Data from the state-maintained Emater-MG, which assists rural producers, account for the total planted area of wine grapes being 403.9

hectares in the same year. This has more than doubled since 2015 and keeps increasing. However, such data include both DPWH (the majority) and traditional viticulture. They also encompass *vinhos finos* (again the largest part) and *vinhos de mesa*. The most planted varieties are Syrah and (at a distant second) Sauvignon Blanc. A small traditional viticulture hub exists at Andradas and Caldas. At Caldas, where the winter is a bit too cold for DPWH, Chardonnay and sparkling wines are doing well.

Minas Gerais wineries

Alma Mineira ♀

Senador José Bento

almamineiravinicola.com.br/

Welles Pascoal, an agronomist, grows coffee at his farm in Senador José Bento, a little town in southern Minas Gerais. He fell in love with wines, viticulture and DPWH, so much so that a vineyard was planted and a winery recently established. They have 15 hectares at 900 metres, comprising seven different varieties. Currently, however, only Syrah and Sauvignon Blanc wines are made. Their winery can process up to 100,000 litres annually. Total production (2024) was 15,000 bottles under the direction of Cléber Gurgel. Visitors are welcome for tastings, plus there's a restaurant and the Hotel Refúgio Alma Mineira (booking necessary).

Brumado Sauvignon Blanc is very ripe, unctuous and warm at 14.5% abv; stone fruit and floral aromas mix with some passion fruit and white guava. Felício Syrah is dark, very ripe, with black fruit, black pepper and smoke; warm (15% abv), it has a strong structure and good varietal typicity. The oaked version (14 months in new French oak barrels) is Felício Pascoal: inky, with clear vanilla and spice, the oak mixing very well with ripe berries and pepper. It is dense, full bodied, long and ageworthy.

Vinícola Alma Rios ♀

Patos de Minas

@vinicolaalmarios

Mauricio Rios, a doctor and wine lover with a Level 3 WSET qualification, planted a vineyard at 1,000 metres' altitude, close to Patos de Minas (400 kilometres west of Belo Horizonte). DPWH is used to manage Sauvignon Blanc, Cabernet Franc, Cabernet Sauvignon,

Marselan and Syrah. The year 2023 was their first vintage/vinification. Vinifiq makes the wines in Espírito Santo do Pinhal, São Paulo. Tours and tastings can be booked (Saturdays); visitors can also see ostriches, llamas, birds and armadillos.

Sauvignon Blanc is crisp, light, citric and grassy: an agreeable every-day wine. Cabernet Sauvignon Rosé is dark pink, bringing ripe red berries. It is bone dry, fresh, well structured, textured and food friendly, so distinct from the Provençal style. Cabernet Franc is dark and extracted and shows ripe blackberries and cherries, with hints of capsicum, earth and smoke. The tannins are firm, and the finish has a slightly bitter bite.

Vinícola Alto do Gavião/Campo de Estrelas

Vieiras

www.altodogaviao.com.br/

Vieiras is a small town in the Zona da Mata region, near Muriaé, about 340 kilometres to the south-east of Belo Horizonte. Here, at Fazenda Mundo Novo, owned by four partners, a 2-hectare DPWH vineyard was initially planted in 2017 at 800 metres' altitude. Fourteen varieties are grown. The first commercial vintage was 2023. The wines (4,000 bottles a year) are made at Vinícola Inconfidência, Rio de Janeiro (see page 307).

Super Syrah (from 2023) has this variety and Touriga Nacional in equal proportions. Almost black in colour, it has aromas and flavours of raisins, dried figs and preserves. It is full bodied with firm tannins, low acidity and high, spirity alcohol – for lovers of powerful, super-ripe reds. From the vat (2024): Syrah has ripe fruit, is full bodied and well structured, with a warming alcohol. Bordeaux Blend (the two Cabernets and Merlot) brings very ripe black fruit, fruit cake, slight pyrazine hints, fine tannins and warm (but well-integrated) alcohol.

Vinícola Artesã

São Gonçalo do Sapucaí

vinicolaartesa.com.br/home

The town of São Gonçalo do Sapucaí, 260 kilometres north of São Paulo, is becoming a kind of vineyard capital for southern Minas Gerais. Eight growers operate there. Roberta Cavalcanti and Luis Toledo, certified oenologists who are knowledgeable and focused, bought land here specifically for planting vineyards at over 900 metres. Half of the property is for the vines (6 hectares). The other is for keeping or restoring an ecologically sound environment. They divided the vineyard into two different areas. The Mosaico vineyard, with a great variety of soils, has been subdivided into five parcels according to altitude and soil. Here, five varieties are in production: Sauvignon Blanc, Cabernet Sauvignon, Cabernet Franc, Petit Verdot and Syrah, all planted in 2016 at a density of 4,000 vines per hectare. The Alto Mar vineyard lies on a steep granitic slope (up to 1,000 metres) and is exclusively planted with Syrah at 6,000 vines per hectare. All planting material was certified by ENTAV-INRA; rootstocks have been carefully selected to marry soil, water needs, varieties and desired styles. Yields are low, less than 4 tons per hectare. Luis states that most DPWH wines have a high potassium content; consequently, the pH is usually high. This does not mean, however, that acidity is low. Their white or red wines have a high acid content. Under their close supervision, the wines are made at Vitacea Enológica (Caldas) or Barbara Eliodora. Annual production is about 15,000 bottles. There is no set-up for receiving visitors.

Mar de Morros Sauvignon Blanc is very aromatic and fruity, with great varietal typicity and a crisp, almost tart acidity. Mar de Morros Syrah brings varietal characteristics of blackberries, black pepper and savouriness, being so very fresh. Rococó is a blend of almost equal parts Cabernet Sauvignon and Cabernet Franc, with clear but fine pyrazine aromas and flavours, bringing high typicity. It spends 13 months in new French oak barriques (Tronçais and Allier, medium toast), the wood characters of vanilla, toast and spice being clear but very well integrated; this, plus the high acidity and supple tannins, provides a very good structure for ageing. Íngreme Syrah spends 14 months in Allier barrels (medium-long toast); it displays great elegance and a harmonious balance between the oak and evident varietal character. It has a very good concentration, body, and acidity and tannin structure, and calls for several years of cellaring to acquire tertiary complexity.

Vinícola Barbara Eliodora ♀

São Gonçalo do Sapucaí

vinicolabarbaraeliodora.com.br/

Guilherme Bernardes Filho, owner of a farm where milk production was previously the most important activity, is one of the wine lovers taken by the 'winter wine fever'. After tasting the pioneering Primeira Estrada Syrah, he was so impressed by its quality that he decided to make his own wines. Assessed by Murillo Regina, he began planting a vineyard in 2015, between 916 and 941 metres, at São Gonçalo do Sapucaí, the first in a town which is now thriving with viticulture. Today, 18 hectares are planted with seven varieties. Currently, Sauvignon Blanc and Syrah are used to make their wines. A winery, restaurant and wine bar complex was quickly built. Former dairy installations were refurbished and improved to accommodate the winery. Here, oenologist Isabela Peregrino directs the making of the wines, many of which have earned international prizes. Thirty-thousand bottles are produced annually, but the winery has a much larger capacity (up to 80,000), so wines from other producers are also made here. Visitors are welcome to visit the impressive and beautiful installations, enjoy a guided tour and taste the wines, accompanied by regional cheeses (Thursday to Sunday). Booking is required, although the shop is open seven days a week. The winery is well placed beside the important Fernão Dias BR-381 highway connecting São Paulo (263 kilometres to the south) to Belo Horizonte (326 kilometres to the north).

Sauvignon Blanc reflects very well the characteristics taken on by this variety in southern Minas Gerais, brimming with flavours of green coffee beans, ripe tropical fruit, discreet grass and capsicum; it has a long finish. Syrah Rosé Flor, made by direct pressing from free-run juice only, is dark pink and fresh, with lots of fruit; bone dry, with some slight tannic grip, it is a very gastronomic wine. Unoaked 'Clássico' Syrah again reflects its origin and variety so well: deep purple, with ripe fruit amidst earthy, leathery, smoky aromas. Gran Reserva Syrah is made from older parcels than the former red wine, being more concentrated and structured; spending 14 months in French oak barrels, there is a harmonious integration of all characters, resulting in a strong, age-worthy wine.

Vinícola Campo de Estrelas

Vieiras

@vinicolacampodeestrelas

This new enterprise belongs to nine partners. They planted 7 hectares with 11 varieties. The first vintage produced 6,000 bottles, made by Inconfidência, Rio de Janeiro, under the direction of oenologist Mario Lucas Ieggli.

I tasted (from the barrel) a field blend (co-vinified) of Syrah, Touriga Nacional and Tannat. It is inky, showing ripe black fruits, pepper and hints of violets. There is a good acidity and a potent tannic structure, demanding time to polymerize and soften; it will age very well.

Casa Geraldo ♀

Andradas

www.casageraldo.com/

Geraldo Marcon, of Italian descent, founded a winery at Andradas in 1969 when he bought land to grow vines. For many years, this remained a small business, selling its products to third parties. Geraldo died in 1978 and his son Luiz Carlos took the helm. Some years later, Luiz brought his three sons (Carlos Geraldo, Luiz Henrique and Michel) into the growing business. A very successful brand of *vinhos de mesa*, Campino, was introduced in 1993. The grapes were brought from Rio Grande do Sul, as local production could not meet the increasing demand. As this included *vinhos finos*, it led to a new brand, Casa Geraldo, which was introduced in 2000 – always with grapes from Rio Grande do Sul. Luiz Carlos retired in 2010; his sons saw the potential of DPWH management and began to plant *vinifera* varieties at Andradas and surrounding areas. This venture grew steadily, too; today, they have 52 hectares of vineyards in production, plus 8 hectares at the pre-production stage and 20 more planned.

The most important cultivars are Syrah, Cabernet Sauvignon, Cabernet Franc, Merlot, Viognier and Moscato Giallo. Most vineyards are at 900–950 metres, on rocky red *latossolos*. Casa Geraldo is no small concern, crafting about 350,000 bottles per year. At their winery, wines at all price points are produced. A pioneering oenotouristic complex was started in 2003; this was much improved in 2015. Visitors are welcome to visit the superb facilities to taste the wines or have a complete experience, including guided tours of the vineyards (using a vintage bus, the *jardineira*) and the winery, as well as lunch with pairing wines. You can enjoy an astounding view of the vineyards, some of which are terraced, from a belvedere (see cover photo). There is a large restaurant (open Friday to Sunday) and a wine shop. Reservations are advised for the more extended tours, which take place on Saturdays.

I was very well received by Fábio Silva, the manager, to see the premises and taste many wines from their extensive line. Alma Sauvignon Blanc is great value; it is clean and crisp, with high varietal typicity. Arte Chardonnay is crafted from grapes of two origins, Divinolândia (São Paulo) and Andradas, spending six months in 600-litre used oak casks;

it is buttery and well structured, with the oak showing clearly. With a brief four-month stage in French oak barrels, the exuberance of the grape variety used for their Sauvignon Blanc Reserva is made more elegant by the non-invasive, agreeable spice and vanilla. Terroir Viognier, a blend of three vintages matured for 15 months in French oak, has a good acidity for this variety; it's peachy and honeyed, offering a different, fresher style of Viognier.

3 Tons Rosé, a blend of red grapes from the region and Serra Gaúcha, is fresh, fruity and a bargain. It is the same for the red version, which is off-dry, openly fruity and very soft. Relicário Reserva, a blend of Marselan and Touriga Nacional, is inky and ripe, mixing earth and herbs with violets and mandarin; it is rich and full bodied, with fine tannins. The Reserva Signature line offers varietal wines. Syrah Rosé from *saignée* has the expected dark pink colour and stronger structure from this process; however, it retains excellent fruitiness balanced by complete dryness. Syrah Jatobá, made through semi-carbonic maceration, is juicy and full of ripe fruit with a slight savouriness. Signature Merlot Reserva, fermented in concrete eggs, with 20 per cent undergoing oak maturation, is predominately fruity and plummy, with fine, soft tannins. Signature Cabernet Franc Reserva offers good varietal typicity and fresh acidity. Signature Cabernet Sauvignon Reserva has a sleek, agile structure of acidity and fine tannins. Signature Syrah Reserva expresses well the suitability of this cultivar to DPWH: it's ripe, peppery, smoky and savoury, with excellent structure. Pinot Noir Reserva brings predominately ripe red fruit with round tannins; it is juicy and succulent, demonstrating that this demanding grape can do well under DPWH management. The Terroir Gran Reserva line brings the same three varietals, spending about one year in French and American oak barrels. To me, the Cabernet Franc seemed the best, so vivid and vibrant, with well-integrated oak and a strong structure of tannins and acidity, to age and develop its high concentration and intensity of flavours. Merlot is very ripe, dense, strong and well balanced. Cabernet Sauvignon is like a deeper, stronger version of the Signature Reserva example. Syrah Gran Reserva, from older vines (20 years), spends a year in French and American oak; it is full bodied, warm, dense and strongly structured, with a long bottle life ahead. Liberdade (luxury price level), their top red, is a very elegant and fresh Bordeaux blend with a fine balance and a strong structure.

Lily Brut Rosé, made by the Charmat process from Pinot Noir, is full of ripe red cherry and raspberry; it is crisp, round and delicious.

Casa Geraldo traditional method sparklers, either Brut Tradicional (24-month autolysis) or Nature (30 months), made from Chardonnay and Pinot Noir grown at nearby Divinolândia (1,300 metres' altitude), are very Brazilian: fresh, fruity, easy going and well made, with bready complexity provided by the long autolysis. A very interesting sparkler is their Sauvignon Blanc, which is produced by modifying the Asti process, whereby the must is fermented in autoclaves to Brut dryness. The result is that this grape's crisp acidity is multiplied, preserving its strong personality – a gift for those who enjoy exploring the diversity of sparkling wines. It is a very agreeable summer wine. Moscato Late Harvest (from Moscato Giallo) is great value: it is very aromatic and fresh, with a high intensity of floral and fruity aromas and flavours, not at all cloying.

The recent Cais line offers fortified reds made in a similar way to Port except the wines are crafted from *passerillée* grapes of French varieties and have a lower 17% abv. After a five-year maturation in used oak barriques, Ruby is indeed 'Porty', warm, round and dark. Tawny spends 14 years in oak; hence, it is lighter in colour, almondy and complex.

Cave das Vertentes

Santo Antonio do Amparo
@cavedasvertentes

Recently established at Santo Antonio do Amparo, about 180 kilometres south of Belo Horizonte, this business owns 4 hectares of vineyards (Syrah and Sauvignon Blanc), planted in 2018. The terroir has benefitted from low rainfall from mid-March onwards, but this may also be a problem, so irrigation might be important, according to owner Bruno. Soils are red *latossolos*, with a clayey texture. Besides downy and powdery mildew, birds are also a problem and netting is necessary to protect the ripening grapes. The grapes are sent to Vitacea (at Caldas) to be vinified. Total production is about 6,000 bottles.

Ver. Te Sauvignon Blanc, very ripe at 14.5% abv, is very fresh, with green aromatics. Ver. Te Syrah rosé (made by *saignée)* is a dark pink, dense, well-structured (tannins are perceptible), full-bodied wine, which is more like a Tavel than Provence. Ver. Te Syrah reveals the typicity of DPWH Syrah from Mina Gerais: dark, dense, full bodied, with clear savouriness and smokiness, its sinewy tannins and fresh acidity provide good ageing potential. Ver. Te oaked Syrah spends 12 months in first-use French oak barriques, with excellent oak integration.

Estrada Real 🍷

Caldas

www.vinicolaestradareal.com.br

It was here that the DPWH revolution started. The pioneering vineyards using this technique, first an experimental area and then the first commercial section, were planted by Murillo Regina at Três Corações, at a coffee farm belonging to Dr Marcos Arruda. This all began in 2001. When the first Syrah wines made their debut, their quality and typicity were so resounding that other producers soon followed suit. These vines continue to perform very well. For a while, this was the only vineyard of the Estrada Real winery. Today, there are vineyards at Caldas (Chardonnay, in partnership with Maria Maria) and São Gonçalo do Sapucaí (in partnership with Davo). Estrada Real now belongs to Murillo and partners, who also own Vitacea. This business has two divisions: a nursery (licensed by ENTAV and other international developers), selling vines to the whole country, and a winery. Both are located at Caldas, where their wines are made (80,000 bottles annually). They also produce wines for many other DPWH growers. At Sítio Carvalho Branco, in Caldas, a brand-new wine bar and restaurant has recently opened. On top of a hill, visitors can enjoy dazzling views of this mountainous part of southern Minas Gerais, while drinking wine and eating fine food. Visitors are welcome (booking advised).

Sauvignon Blanc is the best white variety in DPWH. Estrada Real's Sauvignon Blanc (grapes from São Gonçalo) has an unmistakable varietal character but points to its origins – neither overtly aromatic as a New Zealand rendition nor green and mineral like Sancerre or Pouilly-Fumé, but rather well structured, ripe and keeping fresh acidity. Syrah Rosé is made by *saignée* (thus benefitting the red wine) and is, as expected, dark pink, very fruity and well structured.

Syrah has three versions. The first (just called Syrah) is made from grapes from Três Corações (75 per cent) and São Gonçalo; it is unoaked and exhibits the traits that make DPWH Syrahs so distinctive: deep colour, full ripeness of dark fruit, and high but well-integrated alcohol, all balanced by fresh acidity and lovely hints of smoke, black pepper and savouriness. Gran Reserva, from vines planted in 2004 at Três Corações, spends one year in used French oak barriques; it brings the same characteristics as the unoaked version, plus softer, velvety tannins and seamlessly integrated cedar, toast and vanilla. The top Syrah wine is luxury-level Prógono. Murillo found that, at Três Corações, older vines using 110 Richter as the rootstock produced grapes of such excellent quality that, in an exceptional vintage, justified a microlot vinification to craft a great wine. He called it Prógono – that is, the precursor or leader. It is a big, premium wine, intense in every way: deep colour, strong aromatics and flavours, a full body, 15.5% abv, clear fine French oak, fresh acidity and a long length. It can be cellared for many years.

Maria Maria ♀

Boa Esperança

vinhosmariamaria.com.br

Eduardo Junqueira Nogueira Jr, owner of Fazenda Capetinga, a coffee farm at 840 metres, had a heart attack in 2006. His doctor prescribed healthier foods, including one glass of red wine each day. Eduardo, a strong-minded man, decided straightaway to make wines himself. Meeting Murillo Regina, DPWH was adopted and a vineyard plant-ed in 2009. The first wines appeared in 2013. Eduardo is a friend of the famous Brazilian composer and singer Milton Nascimento. One of Milton's best-known songs is 'Maria Maria' – hence the winery's name. Syrah and Sauvignon Blanc (23 hectares) are doing well. Cabernet Sauvignon and Chardonnay, on the other hand, had yields so low that they were overgrafted with Syrah. Their wines (80,000 bottles a year,

Vineyard and coffee grove side by side at Maria Maria

crafted at Vitacea Enológica, where Eduardo is a partner) are named after women in their family or friends. Visitors are welcome, but booking in advance is vital. Try to book a wine tasting, a hearty, very tasty lunch of traditional food (pay close attention to the chicken with palm heart), and a coffee tasting – an experience that lasts many hours and satisfies all the senses.

Sauvignon Blanc is ripe, aromatic (green coffee beans, ripe guava) and well structured, with a good body. This is one of Brazil's best renditions of the characterful variety. Syrah Rosé (*saignée*, two-and-a-half hours of skin contact) is not at all pale, offering plenty of ripe red berries framed by considerable structure. It is a very gastronomic wine. Syrah (unoaked) is purple, very aromatic, savoury and complex. It's fresh, well structured and full of ripe blackberries, smoke, pepper and animal hints. This is a textbook example of DPWH Syrah. Gran Reserva Syrah spends 12 months in French and American oak barrels (new and second use). It is inky, very ripe, dense and full bodied, with warming but well-integrated alcohol and the typical Syrah descriptors of black fruit, smoke and black pepper, besides vanilla, tobacco and toast. Full, rich, concentrated and well structured, this is a big wine that will benefit from cellaring. Sous les Escaliers Nature, made by the traditional method from Chardonnay (Caldas), with 36-month autolysis, is fruity, bone dry, fresh and savoury.

Vinícola Munira ♀

Três Corações

@vinhedoquintadocedro

It is a great pleasure for me to see that, in my town, where the pioneering DPWH vineyard was planted, another wine business has been founded. The owner, Dr Hugo Couto, was first guided by his father Gilson, an agronomist, and by the same agronomical technician working at Fazenda da Fé, where the aforementioned first vineyard is located. He planted 2 hectares of Syrah and 0.5 hectares of Sauvignon Blanc. The first vintage was 2020. Only Syrah is in commercial production, and the wine is made in Epamig under the supervision of oenologist Lucas Amaral. An average of 3,500 bottles are produced each year. The property has a beautiful events space where tasting and vineyard tours can be booked.

Munira Syrah is a good example of DPWH wines from its champion variety. It has ripe dark berries, smoke, black pepper, a good tannic structure and high alcohol (well balanced by the fruit).

Vinícola dos Montes ♀

Santana dos Montes

@vinhodosmontes

Santana dos Montes is a small town 140 kilometres south of Belo Horizonte. Here, you will find a tourist complex that includes Fazenda Guarará, a rural hotel, a brewery (Cerveja da Loba), *cachaça*-making facilities and vineyards. The latter comprise 3.8 hectares, planted in 2007, at 720 metres, where Syrah is the main star. The vines are managed by DPWH. Mildew is the main viticultural problem here. The first wines appeared in 2011 and are made by Epamig, at Caldas (about 1,300 bottles a year). Visitors can enjoy the very comfortable hotel, with many leisure options, and taste the wine.

Syrah is deeply coloured, with very good varietal typicity: ripe blackberries, black pepper, savouriness and smoke.

Vinícola Pioli ♀

Jacutinga

vinicolapioli.com.br/

Jacutinga, a town in southern Minas Gerais, is better known for its knitwear industry. Pioli planted the vineyard and built their winery (where they have crafted wines since 2021). Today, 12 hectares are planted to Syrah and Sauvignon Blanc, the usual varieties in DPWH, but also

Vinícola Munira's vineyard, Três Corações

to Chardonnay, Viognier, Cabernet Franc, Cabernet Sauvignon, Petit Verdot and Pinot Noir. They produce about 35,000 bottles annually under the technical guidance of oenologist Cristian Sepulveda. Visitors are welcome for tours and tastings (booking advised).

Syrah Rosé is not a *saignée* wine, as is usual in this region; made from specially harvested grapes by direct pressing, it is pale, fresh, fruity and easy drinking. Pinot Noir is bone dry, savoury, not overly fruity and quite oaky. Pioli Syrah is their unoaked version; as a typical DPWH Syrah, it is very ripe, smoky, savoury and full bodied, with 14.6% abv. Barracão Pretenzioso, a blend of Syrah, Cabernet Sauvignon and Pinot Noir, is complex, fresh, well structured and layered, showing well-balanced new French oak. Solar Pretenzioso Syrah, made with grapes from a specific, high terroir, is a big wine: super-ripe, keeping however good acidity, with 15% abv, complex, oaky and with a firm structure, allowing it to age well. Barracão Incitante is a Syrah from another parcel: also a big wine, with 15% abv, but now so savoury and peppery, with animal notes and very ripe black fruit.

Sacramentos Vinifer

Sacramento

sacramentosvinifer.com/

Jorge Donadelli, landowner at Serra da Canastra, together with son Jorgito and daughter Sabina, founded this wine business influenced by family traditions. Under the guidance of Murillo Regina, a vineyard was planted in 2019 (at 1,100 metres) with Syrah and Sauvignon Blanc (1 hectare each); these were later complemented by Viognier and Garnacha. The first two varieties are used for their current wines. Ample diurnal variations during winter ensure favourable conditions for achieving good grape quality under DPWH management. The grapes are transported (in refrigerated trucks) to Caxias do Sul, where the oenologist and winemaker Alejandro Cardozo crafts the wines at EBV. He and the Donadellis defined their desired style of Syrah as one of tension, freshness and elegance. Cardozo uses a sizeable 70 per cent portion of whole clusters to make the wine. Much to their surprise, the first edition of the wine has been elected the best Syrah in Brazil, as well as earning prizes abroad. However, the Sacramentos brand is not limited to DPWH wines, as they have also launched wines made from grapes grown at other selected Brazilian terroirs. The property is somewhat remote, 450 kilometres west of Belo Horizonte by car or

515 kilometres north-west of São Paulo. They plan to build a winery as soon as possible.

Jorgito is sympathetic, open, conversational and resolute in acquiring wine knowledge. He was my student at a WSET Level 3 course. He gladly showed me his wines. Sabina Sauvignon Blanc is fermented in 2,000-litre oak foudres, after which it is stabilized in vats. It is a typical DPWH Sauvignon Blanc, showing perfect ripeness. There is no overt tropical fruit, just the necessary amount to balance the green coffee beans, grass and capsicum flavours.

Il Dolce Far Niente is a pink Pinot Noir from Serra Gaúcha; delicate, fresh and uncomplicated, it is an everyday wine. Sabina Syrah undergoes a complex winemaking process; three parcels are fermented separately, with different yeasts; as noted above, 70 per cent whole clusters are used; the blend matures in large oak foudres over four months. The result is a fresh wine with a sturdy structure of acidity and tannins, layered and elegant, with ripe blackberry and pepper, plus hints of smoke, mint, vanilla and cedar. It is, indeed, different from most DPWH Syrahs.

Antonella Charmat Brut is made unusually from Glera, Chardonnay, Trebbiano and Riesling Itálico; it is fruity, crisp and easy going. Il Dolce Far Niente Chenin Blanc Nature is a pét nat, bringing the variety's typical bruised-apple aromas and remarkable acidity; it is savoury and complex.

Stella Valentino ♀

Andradas

stellavalentino.com.br/

The Stella family began in Brazil with the Venetian immigrant Valentino at the end of the nineteenth century. They settled at Andradas (then named Caracol), and wine, as usual, became a part of their daily life. The fourth-generation descendant José Procópio Stella, an agronomist, started to make *vinhos finos* in 2002. In 2017, the first vintage of DPWH wines appeared. Now, 7 hectares of vineyards are planted at 930–1,000 metres on volcanic soil. Procópio is very good at explaining the terroir and the wines. Some *vinhos de mesa* are also made from Moscato Embrapa and Lorena, and devoid of 'foxy' aromas. Lorena is managed conventionally and harvested in the summer. Procópio holds Lorena in high esteem due to its resistance, yields and quality. Isabela Peregrino is the oenologist (Stella Valentino has its own winery). The oenotouristic facilities include a cosy wine bar in the basement of a very old farmhouse surrounded by woods. Tastings with paired dishes are offered at weekends and must be booked in advance.

Lonoris Sauvignon Blanc is crisp, not overtly aromatic, bone dry and lightweight. Malus is a pink Tempranillo made by direct pressing. It is very pale, dry and fruity, and quite versatile gastronomically. Modestus Syrah shows the usual characteristics of DPWH Syrahs of southern Minas Gerais: spicy, smoky and well structured. The oaked version is Gran Modestus, a strongly structured wine with full varietal character and a warming 15.4% alcohol, well balanced by the ripe fruit and high concentration. Tempranillo Gran Reserva has a good typicity of this somewhat unusual (for Minas Gerais) variety. It displays seamless integration with the evident oak (American, 12 months), as in traditional Riojas, being more elegant than muscular. Zia Bella dry Lorena is intensely aromatic, floral and fresh – a real bargain. Zia Nata is also Lorena, but in a sweet version, fortified to 15.5% abv, with 60 grams per litre residual sugar and not cloying at all.

Vinícola Luiz Porto 🍷

Tiradentes

luizportovinhosfinos.com.br/

Luiz Porto, owner of a farm at Cordislândia (a small town in southern Minas Gerais), specialized in coffee and Mangalarga horses – but was a long-time wine lover. When DPWH appeared, he lost no time, planting 45,000 vines in 2004 using French material. The winery, however, was only ready in 2012. Luiz, unfortunately, passed away at Christmas of the same year. His youngest son, Luiz Porto Jr, took over the business. The wines became very well known, especially their Cabernet Franc. However, various trials and tribulations forced them to move the winery to Tiradentes, a delightful historic city some 240 kilometres from Cordislândia. Today, the wines are made in Tiradentes, under Marcos Vian's technical expertise. Annual production is 80,000 bottles, vinifying grapes from Cordislândia and elsewhere. There is a good oenotouristic set-up where you can taste the wines after touring the winery.

I was very well received by Ana Elisa (public relations) to learn about the Tiradentes winery (I already knew of it when it was in Cordislândia) and taste some of the wines. Dom de Minas is their line of unoaked, less complex wines. Sauvignon Blanc is pale and aromatic, displaying tropical fruit (guava), a fresh acidity, and more body and structure than usual for this variety. Cabernet Franc has a good varietal typicity: raspberry, capsicum, fresh acidity and a light structure; it is a good everyday wine. Syrah is very perfumed and floral, with ripe blackberries and hints of black pepper, earth and smoke; its tannins are ripe and agreeable. Luiz Porto is their line of more structured, oaked wines. Chardonnay spends six months in American oak barrels, offering vanilla, coconut, ripe pear and apple, some butteriness and a good texture. Oak is by no means overwhelming, being well integrated into the wine.

Cabernet Franc Gran Reserva is dark, fresh and highly typical of the variety. It has a well-built structure of acidity, alcohol and tannins – it asks to be drunk with food. Cabernet Sauvignon Gran Reserva is so aromatic: there's tobacco, ripe cassis, hints of capsicum, clear vanilla and spice, again well integrated; its tannins are fine grained. Syrah Gran Reserva is inky, very peppery and complex (ripe blackberries, smoke, animal hints, vanilla and toast); it has an excellent tannic structure, being very round and amicable.

Tenuta Giarolla

Lavras

@tenutagiarolla

Lucas Giarolla, a doctor living and working in Lavras, and his wife (who works in real estate) planted a vineyard in 2021 in the small nearby town of Ijaci. Vitacea has assessed them. The first experimental vintage, 2023, yielded grapes vinified at Vinifiq/InnVernia (Espírito Santo do Pinhal, São Paulo).

Alba is a typical DPWH Sauvignon Blanc. It is aromatic and displays green coffee beans and lime, hints of tropical fruit and slight saline notes. It is ripe but fresh and textured, and has a good structure and even some unctuousness. Tramonto (Syrah/Cabernet Sauvignon) is a dark rosé, almost a claret (although made by direct pressing, it stayed 17 hours on skins and was not filtered), bringing ripe red berries, good structure and density, and moderate acidity. Not a lightweight rosé, it is a gastronomic experience and also versatile.

Also in Minas Gerais

- Vinícola Arpuro, Uberaba ♀ (www.arpuro.wine/)
- Vinícola Bambini, Cruzeiro da Fortaleza (@vinicolabambini)
- Vinícola Casa Bruxel, Patos de Minas (vinicolacasabruxel.com.br/home)

- Quinta do Campo Alegre, Diamantina ♀ (@quintadocampoalegre)
- Vinhas Cruzília, Cruzília (@vinhascruzilia)
- Quinta D'Alva, Diamantina ♀ (@quinta_d_alva)
- Epamig, Caldas (www.epamig.br)
- Vinícola Ferreira, Piranguçu ♀ (vinicolaferreira.com.br/)
- Vinícola Quinta da Lapa, Serro (@vinicola_quinta_da_lapa)
- Vinícola Lorenzo, Maria da Fé (vinicolalorenzo.com.br/)
- Quinta da Matriculada, Diamantina ♀ (@quintadamatriculada)
- Vinícola Mil Vidas, Ritápolis (www.vinicolamilvidas.com.br/)
- Vinícola Obstinado, Jacutinga ♀ (vinicolaobstinado.com.br/)
- Vinícola Paiva Aguiar, Araxá (@vinicolapaivaaguiar)
- Vinhos Casa Rodrigo, São João da Mata (@vinho.casarodrigo)
- Vale do Gongo Uvas e Vinhos, Grão Mogol (@valedogongo)
- Ventania Vinhedo e Vinhos, Caldas (@ventaniavinhedos)
- Vinícola Vesperata, Diamantina (@vinhovesperata)
- Vinhas Gerais, Campos Gerais (@vinhasgerais)

SÃO PAULO

The state of São Paulo, where the first wine in Brazil was made, is the country's most important producer of table grapes, with a planted area exceeding 7,000 hectares. It also has a rich, important and well-documented historical role, albeit pertaining mainly to *vinhos de mesa*. Since DPWH appeared, it has been practised successfully (and increasingly) here, marking a renaissance of the state's importance in Brazilian wines.

More than 20 per cent of all Brazilians (44.4 million people) live in São Paulo. The state, covering 248,219 square kilometres, is larger than the United Kingdom. It is the richest state in Brazil, generating about one-third of the country's economic wealth. This economic powerhouse is centred around diverse industries, including all kinds of vehicles, military and civilian aeroplanes, and much more. The demonym is *paulista*, whereas those born in São Paulo, the homonymous city, are *paulistanos*. People here are reputedly workaholics – their motto is *São Paulo não pode parar* (São Paulo cannot stop). This applies especially to São Paulo, the city – the largest in Brazil, by far, with 11.45 million inhabitants, or above 21 million if the whole urban region, encompassing several neighbouring cities, is also included. The official motto of the metropolis is, perhaps appropriately, *Non ducor, duco* (I'm not led, I lead).

A cosmopolitan city

In nowhere else in the country, if not in the world, is the term 'melting pot' more appropriate when describing the people who make up the population of both state and capital. A very large number of immigrants flocked here, from the Portuguese in the sixteenth century, to enslaved Africans, then to Spanish, German, French, Jewish, Japanese, many Italian and Lebanese, and, more recently, Koreans. In addition to those also coming from Central and South America, as well as again from Africa, the number is almost countless.

São Paulo is also populated by those coming from other Brazilian states, predominately the Northeast. This is reflected in the capital's cosmopolitanism, as becomes any city of equivalent size and importance. There is plenty to do in São Paulo. Having the busiest airport in Brazil (Guarulhos), it is very likely that your starting point will be here if you decide to visit the country. Consider, therefore, staying for a while: buy whatever you wish, either at glamorous shopping centres or *très chic* specialized street shops – or among the crowds at popular centres. You can choose from basic to luxury hotels.

Like other Brazilian states, São Paulo has many tourist attractions. Go to the splendid beaches at São Paulo state's northern coast. Get to know the large, sophisticated cities such as Campinas, Sorocaba, Ribeirão Preto, São José dos Campos, Santos (the biggest port in Brazil) and many others. Climb to Campos do Jordão, the highest town in Brazil at 1,628 metres and so very charming. Relax in the thermal waters of Olímpia or a good *hotel fazenda* (farm hotel). Visit the astoundingly beautiful Sala São Paulo to see OSESP (the best symphony orchestra in the Southern Hemisphere) or international soloists. View the whole city from Mirante do Vale, the highest building, on breathtaking belvederes with a glass floor. Stroll along Avenida Paulista (be careful of pickpockets, however) or visit Ibirapuera Park (suitable for jogging), Parque Augusta or Trianon Park. Enjoy the Museu do Ipiranga, the MASP (São Paulo Museum of Art), the Sacred Arts Museum, the Pinacoteca do Estado, the Museum of Portuguese Language, and so much more.

In São Paulo, you will find Brazil's most prominent wine importers and shops – and many wine bars. Food? You can find anything from any cuisine, starting with street food, hearty sandwiches at decades-old traditional bars, and ending with Michelin-starred expensive restaurants. Don't forget to look for Brazilian food establishments, of which there are plenty, where you'll be delighted by our richly varied gastronomy – pairing the dishes with Brazilian wines, for sure.

Viticulture and winemaking

Bear in mind, as a wine lover, that São Paulo is the cradle of viticulture and winemaking in Brazil. As we saw in Chapter 1 (see page 12), everything started here in 1551, when Brás Cubas successfully planted vines and made wine at Piratininga – part of the terrain where São Paulo, the city, lies today. Viticulture continued for over a century, but not as a prime economic activity; it was predominately for domestic consumption or complemented other crops. The wine's quality was probably poor, as some reports (like that of Fernão Cardim) advised that it should be boiled to avoid becoming sour, as it was 'too green'. No wonder – the local climate did not allow perfect grape ripening, so the resulting wine was too acidic and unstable. Boiling made it microbiologically cleaner and longer lasting. This local wine industry, restricted to the outer areas of the city of São Paulo, thrived for a while. Some landowners made up to 8,000 litres of wine a year. The wines were made from *vinifera* varieties of Portuguese origin: the Ferraes, Moscatel, Dedo de Dama, Bastardo and Galego.

This state of affairs lasted until the late seventeenth century when the gold rush to Minas Gerais drained manpower to the point that vinous activity virtually disappeared, according to Inglez de Sousa. This view, however, conflicts with other, more modern analyses, like that of Lia Romero in her MSc dissertation of 2004, from which I gleaned much helpful information. She states that viticulture continued in more or less the same way, not least in order to provide wine to the mining areas. Again, wine was not an important commodity, like coffee and sugar cane, and it was only in the nineteenth century that things started to change.

São Paulo may have been the cradle of another viticultural first: the introduction of American hybrids, first and foremost Isabel, to Brazil. According to one account of this momentous event, the Englishman John Rudge bought land and installed a farm called Morumbi (today an upper-class neighbourhood in São Paulo), planting the aforementioned variety with great success in 1860. This variety, together with other *labrusca* and *aestivalis*, would remain the mainstay of São Paulo's viticulture until at least the 1930s. Isabel is very productive; it can yield five times more grapes than *vinifera* cultivars, besides being much more resistant to disease. Its wines were – and are – consequently much less expensive than those made from European varieties. This explains why it has been so important in São Paulo and other regions.

The upper classes drank imported wines, but the lower classes could only buy cheaper products. Isabel's supremacy, however, was challenged by other hybrids of possibly better quality, such as Norton, Cynthiana, Jacquez and, later, Seibel 2. However, all wine made from such varieties was heavily criticized for being too acidic, herbaceous and, important-ly, *avulpinado* (that is, 'foxy'). Amador Cunha Bueno, writing in 1898, considered it 'an abominable beverage'. Part of such character could also be due to adulterations and frauds: the addition or mixing of a se-ries of substances, from water to *aguardente* (a distilled alcoholic spirit), through to tartaric acid, ethanol, glycerol, dyes (such as fuchsin) and other substances.

Although statistics are scarce and unreliable, Lia Romero states that São Paulo produced 12,600 hectolitres of wine in 1886 and 17,500 in 1889 – reducing to 7,820 in 1896. This decline can be attributed to the arrival of fungal diseases and phylloxera. Other factors includ-ed competition from foreign wines, poor viticultural and winemaking techniques, and a lack of state policies supporting this sector, unlike the coffee business. Even then, production rose again at the start of the twentieth century, to 31,789 hectolitres in 1926.

At about the end of the nineteenth century and the start of the twen-tieth, although viticulture was still relatively important within the city of São Paulo, other towns also became relevant. This was the case for Cunha and Sorocaba – but this is only of historical interest, as viticul-ture in such places completely disappeared afterwards (albeit returning to Cunha with DPWH). The same happened to the capital, where ur-ban expansion progressively extinguished viticulture. Grape growing in São Paulo state became important elsewhere.

Until 1888, when slavery was abolished in Brazil, this infamous man-power sustained agriculture in the country. The most important prod-ucts in São Paulo were sugar cane and coffee. The latter became an important export product; in fact, it was Brazil's most important ex-port for several decades. After 1888, a growing number of immigrants replaced the slaves working at the large coffee farms. Who, again, was important? The Italians – and their wine culture that permeates the his-tory of wine in Brazil from the nineteenth century onwards. Between 1886 and 1906, more than 800,000 Italian immigrants came to São

Paulo. Although most worked on coffee farms or dedicated themselves to urban occupations, many formed colonies, planted vines and made wine. This activity had almost disappeared, however, by the end of the nineteenth century, again due to diseases and other factors.

Another group of producers was formed by wealthy landowners who, loving wine, developed vineyards at their properties. Unlike the poor immigrants, who had only practical knowledge, they studied the subject in depth. They worried about alternatives to coffee production, being subjected to international crises, and many immigrants returning to their countries as they hadn't found the employment and earnings they'd hoped for here. Viticulture, therefore, was seen by them as both a means of diversifying and of consolidating the presence of the immigrants in the area. Some of their establishments became the predecessors of rural schools, considerably improving the formerly primitive viticultural practices.

An important point of advancement was the creation by the federal government (still a monarchy, in 1887) of the Imperial Agronomical School of Campinas, near São Paulo. The institution's name was changed in 1893 to Instituto Agronômico de Campinas – IAC (see p. 57). From the beginning, an oenological section has existed here, indicating the importance of this commodity in São Paulo. Already in 1892, more than 300 different grape varieties were being studied. IAC's work was instrumental in disseminating the indispensable practice of grafting on phylloxera-resistant rootstocks, such as Rupestris du Lot. At the start of the twentieth century, however, IAC focused its limited resources on more reliable and important agricultural products, like coffee.

Notwithstanding some effort, and the publication in 1900 of a pioneering book (*Manual do Vinicultor*, by Luiz Pereira Barreto), viticulture and winemaking in São Paulo continued until 1930, releasing wines of low quality – as we've seen. Many analyses from IAC's registers point to generalized imperfections and defects: low colour, disagreeable aromas and flavours (predominately 'foxy'), excessive acidity, turbidity, high volatile acidity, bitter aftertaste and other problems.

This situation started to change in the late 1930s. Difficulties with the coffee market led to the diversification of agriculture, and other products gained governmental attention. Table and wine grapes were among them, and a regional hub developed around the towns of São Roque and Jundiaí, not far from the capital. Romero states that, in 1947, about 1.9 million litres of wine were produced at São Roque, while Jundiaí made 6 million in 1955. These two centres produced almost the total amount of wine crafted in the state at that time. A shift from Isabel to Seibel 2 made the latter very important. Both centres were then characterized by small rural properties, either originating from the fractioning of former coffee farms or bought by individuals – many of them Italian immigrants or their descendants, especially at Jundiaí. Large estates, like the one belonging to Cinzano (the great vermouth maker) at São Roque, were exceptions, although others appeared with time. Such was the case of the De Vecchi wine industry, which boasted a vineyard of 360,000 vines in 1925 – mostly Seibel 2.

Less important townships complemented the two main centres: Vinhedo (vineyard in Portuguese), Itatiba and Amparo. Interestingly, no town from this group was further than 150 kilometres from São Paulo, the capital. Although there is scarce information about using *vinifera* cultivars to make wine, a group of more scholarly people was formed at Amparo in around 1935. They studied and introduced European varieties to the region, such as Italia (Pirovano 65) and Muscat of Hamburg. Very important was the creation, by IAC, of experimental stations at São Roque (1928) and Jundiaí (1936) to support and promote vinous activities in the region, not least by offering annual oenology courses. The São Roque station built an impressive variety collection: in 1954, it had more than 700 cultivars. The already mentioned Júlio Seabra Inglez de Sousa headed the station and wrote, in 1940, that they procured varieties to replace Seibel 2 – yet he noted other Seibel hybrids as alternatives, such as 5213, 5455, 5437, and 6905, all of which (except 6905) bring 'foxy' characteristics to the wine. The stations, especially São Roque's, were important in providing growers with much-needed improvement of all viticultural and winemaking techniques.

Climate and DPWH

When I researched new regions with climatic potential for DPWH, the state of São Paulo was included. The median altitude was 571 metres. The MCC indexes were: HI 2.594 (warm), DI 121.0 (sub-humid) and CI 12.1 (cool nights). Although the sheer size of the state prevents too much generalization, the results indicate lower altitude and more rain than the median for Minas Gerais. They are, however, adequate for DPWH. According to Köppen-Geiger's classification, the regions already making wine belong to classes Cfa (humid tropical, oceanic, without dry season, hot summer); Cfb (humid tropical, oceanic, without dry season, temperate summer); Cwa (humid subtropical, dry winter and hot summer); and Cwb (humid subtropical, dry winter and temperate summer).

Planted areas and wine types

São Paulo state presents a series of natural difficulties for traditional viticulture – that is, harvesting during summer: too much heat, too much rain, and high levels of disease pressure (especially of fungal origin). For such reasons, historically the most resistant cultivars, namely American and other hybrids, have dominated the scene. Not even this, however, has been enough to furnish the wineries with all the grapes they need. As a result, bringing grapes from other places – namely, Rio Grande do Sul – to be vinified primarily at São Roque has been and continues to be common practice. This situation has, however, begun to change with DPWH. From the early 2000s, wine growers started to plant new areas exclusively with *vinifera* grapes, now maturing to the desired levels thanks to winter harvesting. This has dramatically altered the quality of wines made in São Paulo, allowing for the appearance of new regions and a change in former practices at more traditional places. A series of towns, which had never made wine before, entered the stage: Espírito Santo do Pinhal, Itobi, Itaí, São Bento do Sapucaí, Ribeirão Branco and Ribeirão Preto. Others, which formerly had at least some participation in the vinous scene, have been revitalized: Jundiaí, São Roque, Amparo and Louveira. As with Minas Gerais, this is all in a state of flux and moving quickly – to the consumer's benefit.

There is no source of complete, reliable statistical data on the planted area of *vinifera* grapes in São Paulo. SIVIBE, a system still in development, provides few statistics. Besides being incomplete, those available at state agencies do not separate *vinifera* from other types. A private source, Luiz Otávio Peçanha from Enopira, Piracicaba (enopira.com.br/sao-paulo/), has done some good research and reached a total planted area of around 150 hectares. This, however, is not updated; the area presently planted may be larger. The town with the largest *vinifera* vineyard by far is Espírito Santo do Pinhal. Except for a small amount of *vinifera* wine produced at São Roque using the traditional growing season (summer harvest), almost every production, as already explained, is DPWH. The most planted varieties are Syrah, Sauvignon Blanc and Cabernet Franc. ANPROVIN listed 15 associated wineries from the state in 2025. São Paulo's government published a magazine on oenotouristic destinations in the state in 2024 (*Rotas do Vinho de São Paulo*).

According to this source, São Paulo has 49 wineries making *vinifera* products and open to the public.

São Paulo wineries

Vinícola Amana ♀

Espírito Santo do Pinhal

www.vinicolaamana.com.br/

A group of more than 40 partners/investors bought land and founded this winery in 2017. Today, they own about 100 hectares, of which 11 are planted with six varieties of *vinifera* grapes and coffee trees. They grow Chenin Blanc, something noteworthy for this region. DPWH is the adopted management system. They have a brand-new winery where the 2024 vintage has been processed. Until 2023, oenologist Cristian Sepulveda vinified the grapes at his Terra Nossa facilities (see page 302). He continues to oversee winemaking. They can produce up to 200,000 bottles annually. One can see and feel architectural mastery and fine craftsmanship everywhere. Local stone, wood and steel co-exist harmoniously. Visitors can enjoy the beautiful surroundings, tour the vineyard and winery, taste the wines at the wine bar or in a pretty garden and, soon, have meals at an indoor/outdoor restaurant. The wine shop is open Tuesday to Sunday, but booking is advised for guided tours (weekends).

I was warmly received by owner/manager Alexandre Develey, an agronomist, and hostess Aline to taste some of their wines. Chenin Blanc is, indeed, a star: very intense in aromas of ripe pear, apple and banana, with hints of honey, mouth-watering acidity, plus moderate vanilla and spice from five months (60 per cent of the wine) in 600-litre French oak tuns, it is also very textural and long. Amana Una is their oaked Sauvignon Blanc: despite the very clear varietal character, bringing aromas and flavours of green coffee beans, passion fruit, white guava and grass, it is well balanced by the moderate spice and vanilla from French oak, improving its complexity.

Amana unoaked Syrah, deep purple, offers the typical ripe black fruit of DPWH wines, along with the also typical flavours of smoke, pepper and hints of meat, all framed by a healthy structure of acidity and tannins. Amana Una oaked Syrah is inky, very aromatic, strongly minty and potent, and has clear oakiness – a wine to be cellared.

Bella Quinta Vinhos Finos 🍷

São Roque

@bellaquintavinhosfinos

This winery has been making wine since the 1920s; *vinhos finos,* however, started in 2005. Owner Gustavo Borges and oenologist Flávia Cavalcantti use Jundiaí and Serra Gaúcha grapes to produce between 10,000 and 15,000 bottles yearly, always in small lots. Some wines are vinified in amphorae. They make white wines from IAC Ribas, a variety bred by Instituto Agronômico de Campinas, a true rarity. Bella Quinta aims to craft minimal intervention wines. They also make *vinhos de mesa* and coolers. Visitors can taste the products at their wine shop, close to Góes. Gustavo is enthusiastic and evidently appreciates showcasing his wines and talking about them.

IAC Ribas (São Roque grapes, summer harvest) Macerado/Barricado ferments with wild yeast in stainless-steel vats and has some oak contact. It is unfiltered; hence, a bit hazy. Flavours are ripe pineapple, dried fruits and hints of nuts, dried leaves, dust and vanilla. It is bone dry, tangy and a bit phenolic. Ânfora Ribas is also vinified spontaneously with its skins, but now in earthenware amphorae in an oxidative style. It is savoury, bringing notes of herbs, minerals and a saline touch. It is bone dry, taut and food friendly. Ânfora Cabernet Franc/Merlot (also from São Roque and summer harvest, spontaneously fermented in amphorae) is a lightweight, elegant, fresh red wine. It is bone dry, fresh and lightly structured, offering black and red berries, earth, dried leaves and savoury elements.

Vinícola Castanho 🍷

Jundiaí

vinicolacastanho.com.br/

Aristides Leme da Silva purchased an existing vineyard at Jundiaí, 60 kilometres from São Paulo, thus founding this winery in 1968. Aristides' sons took over the business in 2007 when it crafted grappa, *cachaça,* liqueurs and fortified wines. In 2014, they started making *vinhos finos* and expanding the vineyard. Syrah was planted the following year. Today, they have 15,000 vines (including hybrids). Gustavo Leme da Silva is now at the helm of all operations, including oenology. Their annual production of *vinifera* wines is 15,000 bottles, made from local and purchased grapes (mostly from Serra Gaúcha). Visitors are welcome seven days a week for tours and tastings.

Chardonnay (grapes from Serra Gaúcha) is unoaked and does not undergo malolactic fermentation. It is lively, ripe and fruity (pear, apple) and has a good texture and excellent varietal typicity. Cave Chardonnay stays for six months in new French oak barrels, and this shows well through vanilla and spice, well married to ripe and sweet pear, apple, hints of pineapple and some butteriness. It is textured and well structured.

Luar Merlot/Tannat (Serra) is their entry-level red, showing ripe red and black fruit, some vanilla and toast (oak staves for four months); it is light and friendly. Cave Tre Corte uses grapes from Jundiaí (Syrah, Cabernet Franc) and the São Francisco Valley (Tempranillo). Ripe blackberry, tobacco, capsicum notes, olives and smoke link to cedar, vanilla and toast. Such characteristics are sustained by a firm structure, making it ageworthy. Poesia de Inverno Syrah (Jundiaí) has ripe blackberries, liquorice, figs and hints of black pepper allied to vanilla and cedar. The tannins are broad and soft. Dolce Lacrima is 100 per cent Lorena, fortified to 18% abv to retain 80 grams per litre residual sugar. It is intensely aromatic (lychee, roses, honey, papaya), fresh and long.

Hotel e Vinícola Davo 🍷

Ribeirão Branco

www.hotelevinicoladavo.com.br/

José Afonso Davo, owner of an important logistics firm, has built remarkable oenotouristic facilities at Ribeirão Branco, a small town in the south of São Paulo state. It is, indeed, a luxury complex (including a hotel, lakes and woods) amidst beautiful surroundings, comprising not only vineyards (at over 800 metres) and a winery but also several orchards of apples, peaches, plums and nectarines, plus a large olive grove (very good olive oil is produced). The winery is state of the art, processing locally planted grapes (Chardonnay, Sauvignon Blanc, Pinot Noir) and Syrah from southern Minas Gerais. Davo has partnered with Murillo Regina, planting a new vineyard at São Gonçalo do Sapucaí, at 900 metres' altitude, on red *latossolos* and managed by DPWH. With such company, the planted area of Grupo Vitacea grew to 60 hectares and the annual production capacity in 2022 was 200,000 bottles. Davo and partners are building a new oenotouristic complex and winery in São Gonçalo, where more than US$ 1.5 million is being invested. They plan to reach an annual production capacity of a million bottles. At Ribeirão Branco, visitors can enjoy a fine stay, visit the vineyard and winery, taste wines or eat at the restaurant. Booking required.

Unoaked and whole-cluster pressed, Davo's Chardonnay is true to the variety: moderate in aromas but full of ripe apple, pear and peach. After undergoing malolactic fermentation, it retains freshness but is textural with some creaminess and butter hints. Syrah Rosé, from São Gonçalo grapes, made by *saignée*, is (as expected) dark pink, strong in ripe red fruits and well structured, with evident acidity (no malolactic). Gran Reserva Syrah, also from São Gonçalo, is a big wine: inky and dense, with a seamless blend of fine French oak (12 months) and very ripe, concentrated black fruit, black pepper, smoke, tobacco and chocolate. Its muscular tannic structure, high alcohol and good acidity allow a long cellaring; it is a high-quality wine that opens up a peacock's tail of flavours in the glass. Nature, 100 per cent Chardonnay from Ribeirão Branco, whole-cluster pressed and undergoing 24-month autolysis, is a very elegant and balanced mix of ripe apple with some pineapple hints, brioche and biscuit, and crisp acidity; hard to stop drinking.

Vinícola Essenza ♀

Santo Antonio do Pinhal

espacoessenza.com.br/vinicolaboutique/

Santo Antonio do Pinhal is a lovely little town near Campos do Jordão and a very popular winter tourism destination. Essenza winery, part of a complex with a charcuterie, restaurant, and olive oil, fruit and trout production, has protected vines (0.5 hectares) at 1,200 metres in the town, plus 13 hectares in Maria da Fé (seven varieties). The wines (15,000 bottles annually) are made at Vitacea, Caldas, under oenologist Isabela Peregrino. Visitors can enjoy various experiences besides wine (Friday to Sunday; book in advance).

Sauvignon Blanc is crisp, light and elegant, more Loire-like than New Worldy. Alvarinho has citrus, peach and mineral notes; fresh and textural, it is true to the variety. Cabernet Franc shows ripe blackberry and cassis, with hints of liquorice; it is a youthful, fruity wine with a good tannic structure and gastronomic merits.

Vinícola Floresta São Pedro ♀

Espírito Santo do Pinhal

vinicolafloresta.com.br/

On a farm traditionally dedicated to coffee growing at Espírito Santo do Pinhal, Mário and Rita Barbosa, the owners, decided to plant a DPWH vineyard in 2010. There are 2 hectares of Syrah and 0.5 of Sauvignon

Blanc. The first wine, made in 2014, was promising, and they now vinify at Terra Nossa under the expert management of Cristian Sepulveda (annual production is 10,000 bottles). A wine bar is open at weekends and special meals are offered on certain dates (book in advance).

Sauvignon Blanc is so aromatic, brimming with tropical fruit (white guava, passion fruit), citrus and hints of aniseed; it is very ripe and concentrated and has more body and length than is usual for this variety. Rainha das Serras, unoaked, is deep purple with high varietal typicity. It is a prototypical DPWH Syrah, displaying very ripe blackberry and plum, smoke, black pepper, a full body and warming alcohol.

Vinícola Góes ♀

Canguera, São Roque

www.vinicolagoes.com.br/

This winery has a long history, starting in the early twentieth century. Góes has Portuguese, not Italian, roots. From 1910 to 1938, they produced wine artisanally after settling at Canguera, São Roque. In 1938, they started to sell wines in barrels, dispatching them via railway to their markets, mostly in São Paulo. A new winery, under Gumercindo Góes, was built in 1962, and the name Góes began to appear on the labels the following year. With sales growing, not enough local grapes were available, and they had to be purchased from Rio Grande do Sul. Góes and the Venturini family bought a winery at Flores da Cunha, Serra Gaúcha, in 1989. Until then, only *vinhos de mesa* were produced – and they are still an essential part of their sales. In the late 1990s, however, *vinhos finos* appeared. Today, the firm is led by four Góes brothers and their sons. Fábio Góes oversees oenological activities. They own 32 hectares of *vinifera* vines, but they continue to buy grapes from selected partners. Most vineyards are planted on red and yellow, clayey *latossolos*. Góes makes 40,000 bottles of *vinhos finos* annually. A large range of labels is available, some wines are offered in cans, and they also craft coolers and grape juice. Oenotouristic installations include restaurants and an events space, receiving 6,000 visitors (average) each weekend for several different activities.

Tempos de Góes Sauvignon Blanc (DPWH grapes from São Roque) has crisp acidity and good varietal character, especially in the mouth. One of the very few Verdelhos in Brazil (see also Lemos de Almeida, Rio Grande do Sul, page 197), Lotes de Coleção is soft and mouth coating, with clear oakiness from staves – a good alternative to Chardonnay or

Encruzado. Maestria Chardonnay (grapes from Divinolândia, summer harvest) spends 12 months in new French oak barrels, which give it vanilla and spice. These marry well with ripe pineapple flavours, cream and butter; the wine is well structured and long.

Góes Concreto is a Cabernet Franc/Syrah blend staging for five months in concrete eggs. It has leather, smoke and some animal notes, besides ripe black fruit. Structurally, it has a vital acidity and meaty tannins. Lotes de Coleção Petit Verdot is made from DPWH São Roque grapes; it is so spicy and fresh, displaying ripe blackberries, cedar and toast, framed by a considerable structure of acidity, firm tannins and good concentration. Góes Tempos Philosophia Cabernet Franc (DPWH, São Roque) brings ripe raspberry and cassis, spice, pencil shavings, vanilla and toast (it spends 12 months in new French oak barriques). It has a lively acidity and solid but fine-grained tannins, and will age well.

Saint-Tropez Brut white (Chardonnay from Divinolândia), made by the Charmat method, is ripe, fruity (apple, pear) and fresh. Its easily perceived degree of residual sugar at the upper levels of the Brut category makes it easy to drink. The Rosé version (Cabernet Franc and Chardonnay) has ripe red berries, hints of caramel and a good structure to accompany food. Saint-Tropez Moscatel Rosé gets its pretty pink colour from Muscat of Hamburg; it is fruity, floral and not overly sweet; it would go well with a fruit pie.

Gumercindo de Góes Licoroso is a rarity: a sweet, fortified wine made from Lorena grapes and aged for eight years in oak barrels. It is amber in colour and splendidly aromatic, its aromas reminiscent of an aged white Port: dried fruit, nuts, caramel. It is complex and layered, and has an unbelievable length. This is a serious candidate to figure among the best Brazilian dessert wines.

Vinícola Guaspari 🍷

Espírito Santo do Pinhal

vinicolaguaspari.com.br/

Paulo Brito, the controller of Aura Minerals, acquired a large (850 hectares) coffee farm in the early 2000s inside the urban zone of Espírito Santo do Pinhal. Near the Minas Gerais border, this small town lies just 25 kilometres from Andradas or 78 from Caldas (and 190 from São Paulo). Brito and his wife, from the Guaspari family, intended to use the property for leisure purposes only. Still, they decided to start a high-end wine business after discovering Murillo Regina and DPWH. In 2006, a vineyard was planted on granitic soils at 900 metres. In 2008, an experimental vinification galvanized their efforts, as the wine was considered very good. In the same year, their winery was built. Everything grew considerably after this; today, they have 50 hectares of vineyards (one of the largest among DPWH producers), all drip-irrigated. The grapes are vinified under several labels, many of which have won important prizes in Brazil and abroad. Many parcels were named after an expression beginning with 'Vista' (view). The wines from such parcels, or single vineyards, are correspondingly named. The differences can be noted when tasting wines from the same variety (as Syrah) but from distinct parcels. These are due to different altitudes, soils, inclinations and other features.

Today, 100,000 bottles of wine are made annually. This, however, does not exploit the full potential of their vineyards. Viticultural activities are supervised by the Portuguese Paulo Macedo and Raquel Scaramussa at the property. Gustavo González, from Napa Valley, is the oenological director, while Ana Paula Sossai works locally. Guaspari has an exemplary oenotouristic set-up and a large, attractive wine bar was recently opened. Everything here shows exquisite good taste and is very beautiful and comfortable. Visitors can tour the vineyards and winery and taste the wines (reservation strictly required).

Vale da Pedra Syrah is made from grapes grown in several places on the whole property. It is a prototypical DPWH Syrah: deeply coloured, with very ripe black fruit, pepper, smoke, 15% abv, a full body and a firm tannic structure. Vista da Serra Syrah can be considered a single-vineyard wine; perfectly ripe, with clear but well-balanced oak aromas of vanilla and spice (24 months in French oak barrels, 50 per cent new), it is more elegant and better structured in tannins and acidity than the Vale da Pedra – ideal for long cellaring. Vista da Mata is a blend of Cabernets (Sauvignon and Franc); the varietal descriptors of cassis, capsicum and pencil shavings are easily noted, the wine having a fresh acidity, high but well-balanced alcohol and a solid structure of fine-grained, sleek tannins. It is an elegant, complex wine.

Vinícola InnVernia ♀

Espírito Santo do Pinhal
www.innvernia.com/

Eduardo Cruz and Marcelo Luchesi founded their wine business in 2020 at Espírito Santo do Pinhal. Several wines are made with grapes from other regions: Campanha Gaúcha, Serra Catarinense and São Francisco Valley. Their local vineyard, however, is starting to produce commercially. They plan to launch an exclusive Nerello Mascalese in 2025. According to Eduardo Cruz, other unusual grapes are being tested: Rkatsiteli, Corvinone, Rondinella and Nero d'Avola. Sangiovese and Rebo are planted at their vineyard in Santa Catarina (Bom Retiro). Due to their natural approach to viticulture, they lost many vines in the first years. The sturdy survivors – the fittest – are now thriving. They avoid chemical inputs, favouring green crops, chicken manure, careful fertigation and rock powder. The same approach is adopted in winemaking: native yeast, low additions, no filtration. Eduardo Camerati (Chile) and Alphonse de Rose (Napa Valley) are the oenologists directing the annual production of 16,000 bottles. InnVernia also acts as a custom crush (under the name Vinifiq) for other growers. Visitors can taste the wines (besides other activities) and booking is required.

Sauvignon Blanc is a lightweight version of this characterful variety: pale, crisp, bone dry, moderate in alcohol and lemony, with guava flavours and hints of grass. Chardonnay Premium (Campanha grapes spontaneously fermented) mixes the clearly ripe fruit (pear, pineapple) with vanilla and spice from deftly managed, not overwhelming oak. It has buttery hints and is dense and textural. CarbonPure Pinot Noir uses semi-carbonic maceration and native yeast; it is pale, very fruity (ripe raspberry), with a touch of kirsch and sweet spice. Fresh and very soft, drink it cold – delicious! Syrah Reserva (Vale do São Francisco) is made partially (30 per cent) from raisined grapes; the *appassimento* happens inside a ventilated greenhouse. The wine is inky and very ripe; its preserved black fruit mixes with Syrah's smoky and peppery hints. Very warm at 16% abv, it has a solid tannic structure, being so long and complex; it opens up slowly in the glass. This is a mighty, ageworthy wine.

Vinícola Lattarini ♀

Santo Antonio do Jardim
vinicolalattarini.com.br/

Márcio Lattarini, a landowner and coffee grower from the third generation of this family of Italian descent, established his vineyard (starting in 2019) at Santo Antonio do Jardim. This small town lies between Andradas (Minas Gerais) and Espírito Santo do Pinhal (São Paulo). There is also a vineyard in Campestre, Minas Gerais. Márcio is a firm, determined and clear-minded person. He has a test field planted with

43 different varieties. As he explained to me, he thinks some of them are inappropriate for DPWH and, in truth, call for more experimentation and the trialling of different management schemes. Considering the relatively short history of DPWH, he may well have a point. They already have a winery; hence, the whole cycle of wine is within their domain. Lattarini has recently opened (October 2024) an excellent, comfortable oenotouristic space, where visitors can taste the wines and enjoy meals.

Granito Chenin Blanc has a clear varietal identity: ripe apple, pear and honey, with mineral hints, crisp acidity and a good texture. Granito Rosé, 100 per cent Pinot Nero (the name is adopted because this is an Italian clone), is not at all pale. It offers fresh red berries and is bone dry and low in alcohol. Enjoy it cold on a summer's afternoon.

Artemísia is their entry-level Syrah; with ripe blackberries and peppery notes, it has a fresh acidity and soft tannins, and is ready to drink. Cabriolet 9 Castas, indeed crafted from nine different red varieties (French, Italian and Portuguese), is a kind of field blend, as all the grapes are co-fermented. It sees no oak, and the extraction is light, bringing ripe but fresh red and black fruit with a soft tannic structure – a very interesting wine. Lattarini Syrah remains for six months in stainless-steel vats with oak staves; it's deeply coloured and minty, with very ripe black fruit, pepper and smoke. It has a strong structure of alcohol, acidity and firm tannins. Reserva Syrah passes 12 months in new French oak barrels of medium toast; it is inky, very ripe in fruit, full bodied, concentrated (blackberry, pepper, smoke, hints of bacon) and long. It will age well.

Vinícola L'Origine 🍷

Santo Antonio do Jardim

@vinicolalorigine

Márcio Tadashi and his wife, Stella, native to the area, fulfilled an old dream by returning after decades of living and working elsewhere. They now live on land belonging to Tadashi's family, where a vineyard has existed for many years. Here, the present team, of five owners of Terra Nossa, led by the oenologist Cristian Sepulveda, started their business. As Stella explains so well, they had no land, no vineyards and no winery. So, they leased land from Tadashi's grandmother, planted the vines and started selling wines *en primeur* to those who trusted them (Tadashi included, despite Stella's fears). The revenue was used to buy equipment, and the first wines were born. Since then, the team has purchased land of their own (see Terra Nossa, page 302). Their lease ended and

Tadashi took over the Syrah vineyard, also planting Viognier. Today, the couple have a brand of wines (made at Terra Nossa) appropriately named L'Origine. Visitors (booking essential) can enjoy the beautiful view and quiet rural surroundings while tasting the wines. Both Márcio and Stella are wonderful hosts with whom conversation flows easily and pleasantly.

Viognier is what you expect from this attractive variety: ripe, aromatic, perfumed and full of white roses and peach, with moderate acidity, almost full bodied, and a good texture. They have two Syrahs. One is not matured in barrels but has oak staves while in the tank. It is very peppery, clearly varietal, ripe but fresh, with sleek tannins. The other stays in new French oak barrels for 12 months. This brings a clear oak character of vanilla and cedar, seamlessly integrated into the ripe black fruit; a solid structure of tannins and acidity will allow this wine to age well. It is more elegant than powerful.

Vinícola Mirante do Vale

São Sebastião da Grama

www.vinicolamirantedovale.com.br

Fazenda (Farm) do Recreio lies at São Sebastião da Grama, a little town that, although very close to Poços de Caldas (in Minas Gerais), is actually within the borders of São Paulo state. Here, Homero Teixeira de Macedo purchased a farm in 2006. His sons, Claudio, Diogo and Maria, started viticulture in 2016. At altitude (1,360 metres), on the volcanic soil of Vale da Grama, they planted Chardonnay (1.3 hectares) and Pinot Noir (0.5 hectares). Until now they have produced only traditional method Nature sparklers, which have won several prizes at national contests. Oenologist Lucas Amaral directs the winemaking, and the wines are crafted at Epamig in Caldas, Minas Gerais.

Nature Blanc de Blancs (Chardonnay) is crisp and steely but brings ripe apple and pear. It has a very fine and creamy mousse, plus complexity from an 18-month autolysis.

Casa Almeida Barreto

Espírito Santo do Pinhal

casaalmeidabarreto.com.br/vinhos

This new wine business was born inside a coffee farm, as frequently happens with DPWH wines. Gabriel Barreto, a former lawyer and now an oenologist, and his father planted a vineyard at altitude (1,300 metres).

Now totalling 5 hectares, it has Chardonnay, Viognier, Cabernet Franc, Cabernet Sauvignon and, unusually, Cinsault and Mourvèdre. The soils are *latossolos* of granitic origin, with sand and clay and high acidity. The wines are made at EBV, in Caxias do Sul, by Alejandro Fernández. Gabriel is keen to show his wines, describing how important music has been in his personal development, which influences the wines.

Chardonnay is crisp and mouth-watering; despite an initially high pH in the must, using selected yeast allowed correction, so much so that malolactic fermentation was not necessary; lees contact imparted a good texture. Viognier is a fresher version of this variety, albeit showing the usual white flowers and peach. Rosé is made by direct pressing from Syrah, Mourvèdre and Cinsault, all harvested especially for this wine. It is very tasty and fully flavoured and has a noteworthy structure. Cabernet Franc has a high varietal typicity, excellent structure and ripe blackcurrant, capsicum and graphite. Starting from 2021, their Syrahs show a stylistic change; the first year was a typical DPWH wine: savoury, smoky, complex and ripe. In 2023, the wine had more acidity and tension due to different yeast.

Villa Santa Maria ♀

São Bento do Sapucaí

villasantamaria.com.br/

São Bento do Sapucaí is a pretty little town in São Paulo state, a short distance from the busy tourist city of Campos do Jordão (180 kilometres from São Paulo). The surroundings in Serra da Mantiqueira are astonishingly beautiful, including the scenic Pedra do Baú peak. This dominates the landscape of the valley of the same name. In the early 2000s, the Carbonari family acquired land for a country house and soon decided to plant a vineyard and make wine. Having heard about DPWH, they obtained the assessorship of Murillo Regina, and the first vines were planted in 2005 at about 1,000 metres. Following a successful vintage in 2009, the vineyard was later expanded, totalling 60,000 vines. Today, they grow seven varieties. All the varieties, except Chardonnay, are managed through DPWH. The wines are made by Vitacea (Caldas, Minas Gerais) under oenologist Isabela Peregrino. In homage to their grandmother, Brandina, the wines were named after her. Besides tours and tastings, the tourist set-up includes a restaurant specializing in the delicious Italian dish *bruschetta*, (several delicacies on generous slices of bread). Booking is advised (closed Monday and Thursday).

Chardonnay is pale, with discreet aromas of citrus and green apple; it is lean, fresh and steely, with some mineral hints reminiscent of Chablis. Sauvignon Blanc has the usual aromatic power of this variety: pure and ripe guava, passion fruit, peach and grass notes. It is crisp but ripe and textural, a true DPWH Sauvignon Blanc. Rosé is a blend of Syrah and the two Cabernets, with a salmon colour. Ripe, concentrated red berries go well with a bone dry character.

Assemblage blends Syrah and Cabernet Sauvignon, bringing ripe blackberry and cassis. After some time in the glass, Syrah flavours open up and predominate: black pepper, smoke, leather, bacon and lots of liquorice. The wine is full, ripe, fresh and well structured. Assemblage Gran Reserva (Syrah/Merlot) is inky and ripe, showing black fruits (blackberry, plums, cassis), black pepper, vanilla, toast and chocolate. It has a strong structure of acidity, concentration and tannins. It is complex and ageworthy.

Casa Soncini

Itaí

www.casasoncini.com.br/

This winery is beautifully located, overlooking the large lake of the Avaré dam, about 300 kilometres west of São Paulo. The vineyard was started by Alfredo Soncini in 2017, at 600 metres, on clayey *latossolos*. Today, they grow the staples of DPWH, Syrah and Sauvignon Blanc, plus Viognier, Tannat and Tempranillo. The total planted area is 10 hectares. Their main viticultural problems are mildew and excess rain before winter. After a first test with vinification by Epamig in 2019, they installed their winery in 2021, starting sales in 2023. Present production is about 40,000 bottles per year. They aim to reduce alcohol levels through viticultural (de-leafing, harvest regulation) and winemaking (using special yeast, such as *Saccharomyces bayanus)* measures.

Sauvignon Blanc is pure, fresh and typical of the variety. Syrah Rosé, made by *saignée*, is dry and fruity. Syrah has two versions. The first, labelled just Syrah, spends six months in French oak barriques; it is spicy, smoky, with ripe blackberries, well balanced and elegant. Gran Syrah undergoes 18 months of new French oak maturation, imparting fine toast, spice and vanilla notes, adding complexity to the smoky, savoury and ripe fruit notes. Tempranillo, made in small quantities, is delicate and elegant, with fine tannins and moderate wood notes from six months in a blend of American and French oak barriques.

Vinícola Terra Nossa 🍷

Espírito Santo do Pinhal

vinicolaterranossa.com.br/

Terra Nossa was founded by a group of five partners led by the Chilean oenologist Cristian Sepulveda (not to be confused with Christian Sepúlveda from Bouchon, Chile). After stints in Italy and Napa Valley, Cristian and the other associates worked at Guaspari for some years. However, they left Guaspari to start a business of their own. After some time, they succeeded in buying land, planting vineyards, building a winery and opening an oenotouristic space within a beautiful rural setting surrounded by mountains. Besides offering viticultural services, they also have a custom crush winery, processing grapes from several growers. Some wines, however, are made under their own brand. Visitors can taste wines in a beautiful wine bar and enjoy guided tours of the vineyards and winery (booking required).

White Profano is an unusual blend of Chardonnay, Marsanne and Viognier. As expected, it is very textured, dense and almost unctuous, bringing flavours of sweet, ripe fruit (apple, pear and peach) amidst flowers and vanilla. Part of the wine stays nine months with the fine lees in French oak barrels. This is a distinct, elegant and well-balanced wine. Profano Rosé from Syrah, made by direct pressing, is pale, dry and crisp, with fresh raspberry flavours.

Profano is also the label of their 'youthful' Syrah, fermented in stainless-steel vats with oak staves; deep purple in colour, it brings ripe blackberries and has a full body, warming alcohol and strong structure. Cateto is a blend of Syrah (75 per cent, fermented in concrete) and Cabernet Sauvignon (in barrels). Cristian limits the temperature of the inoculated fermentation to 26°C, obtaining a clear fruitiness that mixes the characteristics of both grapes well. The wine exhibits DPWH Syrah flavours (smoke, bacon, strong alcohol, full body) combined with Cabernet's cassis and hints of capsicum. Its fresh acidity, strong but sleek tannins, and high alcohol provide enough structure for long cellaring. Terranossa Clássico Malbec, recently launched, demonstrates that this variety can also thrive under DPWH management. Cristian thinks, in fact, that Malbec can be more productive than Syrah. The wine is dark, ripe, plummy and chocolatey, but not heavy; its fresh acidity, moderate alcohol and agile tannins make it more elegant than powerful. This is a welcome novelty in DPWH.

Terras Altas ♀

Ribeirão Preto

vinicolaterrasaltas.com.br/

Ribeirão Preto is a large city (700,000 inhabitants), 310 kilometres north-west of São Paulo. Engineers and real-estate investors José Renato Magdalena and Fernando Horta, plus the agronomist Ricardo Baldo, all wine lovers, established a pioneering wine business here despite the warm climate. In 2016, they planted a DPWH vineyard on basaltic soils at 750 metres' altitude. Until now, only Syrah wines have been made at their brand-new winery. Visitors can tour the vineyards and winemaking facilities, tasting the wines. A good restaurant completes the oenotouristic set-up (booking advised).

Entre Rios Syrah is a deep purple colour. Very ripe, almost preserved blackberries mix with hints of pepper and smoke. The wine is full bodied and moderate in acidity and has a warming alcohol; its tannins are soft and framed by a high concentration of flavour.

Casa Verrone ♀

Itobi

www.casaverrone.com.br/

Itobi, a small town 235 kilometres north of São Paulo, is not far (70 kilometres) from Espírito Santo do Pinhal and the border with Minas Gerais. Here, Marcio Verrone started planting a DPWH vineyard in 2009 under the guidance of Epamig. The results were so encouraging that the vineyard was expanded; today, there are 15 hectares and 10 varieties. The terrain is hilly, stony and beautiful. Grapes from nearby Divinolândia are also used. The wines are made at their winery. Marcio established a partnership with Góes (see page 294) at the end of October 2024, the very day I visited Verrone. Visitors can tour the vineyards and winery, tasting wines at an agreeable wine bar, plus several types of bread, cheeses and charcuterie (booking required).

Marcio is enthusiastic and gentlemanly, and it was a great pleasure to talk to him. Viognier, matured in oak barrels (first used for reds, believe me), is a pale wine, offering the customary aromas of white flowers and peach, with vanilla and candy hints. It is fresher than, for example, a Viognier from Languedoc. Syrah Rosé is made by directly pressing specially harvested grapes; Marcio explained that the pressure at the press is so low that the process would better be called crushing. Notwithstanding this, the wine is not pale, with very ripe red berries; bone dry, fresh and delicious, it is indeed, as the French say, *gouleyant.*

Syrah Colheita's present style is unoaked. The wine is ripe, with a good intensity and concentration of blackberry, cassis, pepper and smoke. Speciale Syrah comes from older vines, spending 12 months in new and used French oak barrels. It is a ripe, intense, full, concentrated and powerful wine. It is very well balanced, very long and ageworthy. Tre Uve ('Three Grapes' in Italian) is a jewel. Made from equal proportions of Syrah, Grenache and Marselan, it is like a local version of GSM (Grenache–Syrah–Mourvèdre). A big wine, it resembles a good Châteauneuf-du-Pape: ripe, warm, full bodied and with soft tannins. Both oak and alcohol are perfectly integrated into this rich wine.

Casa Verrone Brut (Chardonnay/Pinot Noir), made by the traditional method, undergoes 18-month autolysis. It is elegant and fresh, but with the usual Brazilian fruit ripeness well integrated into the autolytic flavours. Nature Sauvignon Blanc Sur Lie, undisgorged, is a great surprise: the variety, the method and the style are, indeed, a welcome variation. It is very aromatic, almost exploding with white guava and opening up in the glass, with complexity brought by clear autolytic flavours (it is hazy). It is so refreshing and distinctive that it is difficult to stop drinking it.

I was also allowed to taste the Purple Cow. Marcio keeps a single barrel of wine, from which he takes samples for visitors to sip. The barrel, started in 2014, contains an undetermined mix of white, pink and (predominately) red wines, as it is always added to. in order to keep it full. The contents are not sold but rather reserved for visitors. When I went there, the wine was deeply coloured, its aromas resembling those of an aged Roussillon fortified wine. In the mouth, however, there was no sweetness at all; it was full of tertiary flavours. If you taste this, it will necessarily differ from what I tasted; it is a kind of *perpetuum,* a real oddity. That's another good reason to go to Casa Verrone.

Also in São Paulo

- 1300 Estate, Cunha (@1300estate)
- Alma Galiza/Fazenda Bagadá, São Roque ♀ (www.almagaliza.com/)
- Vinícola Arcano, Franca (@arcanovinicola)
- Vinícola Areia Branca, Amparo (@vinicolaareiabranca)
- Adega Beraldo di Cale, Jundiaí ♀ (beraldodicale.com.br/)
- Blend of Two Minds, Jarinu (bo2m.com.br/)

- Bramasole Vinho de Boutique, Indaiatuba ♀ (bramasole-vinho-de-boutique.negocio.site/)
- Vinícola Carmela, Amparo ♀ (www.vinicolacarmela.com.br/)
- Vinícola Casa da Árvore, São Roque (vinicolacasadaarvore.com.br/)
- Vinícola Ferracini, Penápolis ♀ (www.vinicolaferracini.com.br/)
- Vinícola Lucano, São Paulo ♀ (lucano.com.br/)
- Mantovanello Vinhos, Indaiatuba (@mantovanellovinhos)
- Vinícola Marchese di Ivrea, Ituverava ♀ (www.vinicolamarchesediivrea.com/)
- Vinícola Maria Herminda, Porto Feliz ♀ (www.vinicolamariaherminda.com.br/)
- Vinhos Micheletto, Louveira ♀ (vinhosmicheletto.com.br/)
- Vinícola Raízes do Baú, São Bento do Sapucaí ♀ (vinicolaraizesdobau.com.br/)
- Vinícola Refúgio, Bofete ♀ (vinicolarefugio.com.br/)
- Vinhos Sorocamirim, São Roque ♀ (@vinhos_sorocamirim)
- Adega Terra do Vinho, São Roque (www.adegaterradovinho.com.br/)
- Vinícola Terrassos, Amparo ♀ (www.terrassos.com.br)
- Casa Tés, São Sebastião da Grama (casates.com.br/)
- Vinícola Urbana, São Paulo ♀ (www.vinicolaurbana.com.br/)
- Vinícola Walachai, Campinas (@clauswalachai)
- Vinícola XV de Novembro, São Roque (vinicolaxvdenovembro.com.br/)

ESPÍRITO SANTO

Espírito Santo state is squeezed between the much larger Minas Gerais and the Atlantic Ocean, bordering Bahia to the north and Rio de Janeiro to the south. At 46,096 square kilometres (and 3.8 million inhabitants), it is the fourth-smallest state in Brazil. The area corresponds to half of Portugal. The demonym is *capixaba* or *espírito-santense*. There are many beautiful beaches, usually full of nearby *mineiros* (natives of Minas Gerais). The capital, Vitória (323,000 inhabitants), on the seaboard, is the tourist hub and worth visiting. The terrain goes up to the hinterland, where several pretty mountain towns can be found. It is the altitude that allows viticulture here. The main Köppen-Geiger climatic classes with regard to vinous activity are Cwa (humid subtropical, dry winter and hot summer) and Cwb (humid subtropical, dry winter and temperate summer).

Who founded the most important winemaking town here, Santa Teresa? Yes, Italian immigrants. They began arriving in about 1870, accompanied by those from Poland, Germany and other countries. Santa Teresa, a pretty little town near the state capital and airport hub, lies about 550–600 metres above sea level. Visit the Mello Leitão Museum within the National Institute of the Atlantic Forest. It was formerly the residence of Augusto Ruschi, a famous and brave environmentalist and author of very attractive books on Brazilian birds and orchids. Together with the beautiful Pedra Azul mountain region (also worth visiting and staying in), now at about 1,000 metres' altitude and with two wineries (at the towns of Venda Nova do Imigrante and Domingos Martins), Santa Teresa epitomizes the importance of elevation and DPWH for viticulture and winemaking.

Espírito Santo wineries

Cantina Mattiello

Santa Teresa

www.cantinamattiello.com.br

This winery was established in 1996 by Viviane Mattiello, the fourth generation of a family descended from Italian immigrant Attilio Mattiello. They also produce *vinhos de mesa*, liqueurs, juice, jams and ground coffee. Visitors are welcome for a guided tour with tasting. This happens only at weekends and holidays, and booking is essential. Grapes for their *vinhos finos* come from Senhor do Bomfim, Bahia. The wines are made under the assessorship of the ubiquitous oenologist Marcos Vian.

Piacere Reserva, a red blend (Cabernet Sauvignon/Malbec), has overt ripe fruit (cassis, plums), hints of tobacco, discreet oak and ripe, soft tannins. It is round and easy drinking. Piacere Brut is made from Chenin Blanc; it is fruity and tangy, with notes of honey and slight toast.

Also in Espírito Santo

- Casa dos Espumantes, Santa Teresa 🍷 (@casadosespumantes)
- Vinícola Tabocas, Santa Teresa (@tabocasvindegarage)

RIO DE JANEIRO

As with São Paulo, the state and its capital, in this case perhaps the best-known Brazilian city, are homonymous. In our country, people generally refer to the city as just 'Rio' and to the state as 'Estado do Rio'. The demonyms: *carioca* for the capital and *fluminense* for the state. Rio

(6.2 million inhabitants), the second-largest city after São Paulo, is an overwhelmingly important tourist destination in Brazil. It has, indeed, a countless number of attractions: the astounding natural beauty (which explains its nickname, *Cidade Maravilhosa*, or 'Wonderful City'), world-famous beaches (such as at Copacabana, Ipanema and Leblon), so many historic buildings (it was the country's capital until 1961), very fine hotels, restaurants, museums and so much more. And, of course, the legendary *carioca* easy-going way of life, including mandatorily sitting at one of the hundreds of seaboard bars, arriving from the beach at the end of the day (and deep into the night) to sip or guzzle ice-cold beer (ask for a *chope*) accompanied by some uncomplicated and tasty dishes (try *bolinho de bacalhau*, or codfish dumplings). Irresistible.

But back to wine: Rio de Janeiro (43,750 square kilometres) lies, along with Espírito Santo and São Paulo, within a coastal range of mountains, generally called Serra do Mar, which runs from Rio to the South. At Estado do Rio, the range provides a much milder climate than the capital's and offers very beautiful views of high peaks amongst a luxuriant forest, the Mata Atlântica. Several towns at altitude constitute rewarding tourist attractions not far from Rio: Petrópolis (the summer resort of former Emperor Dom Pedro II, hence its Imperial Museum), Itaipava, Teresópolis, Nova Friburgo and Areal.

The climate here is much like that of Espírito Santo: Cwa (humid subtropical, dry winter and hot summer) and Cwb (humid subtropical, dry winter and temperate summer). DPWH has enabled the emergence of new viticultural enterprises, again where they never existed before. Vineyards/wineries can be found at Areal, Pedro do Rio, São José do Vale do Rio Preto, Nova Friburgo and Teresópolis – the altitude ranges from just over 500 to above 1,000 metres. Currently, three wineries are equipped for processing their grapes, as well as those of other regional growers. Wine tourism is developing well, taking advantage of the proximity to Rio – although with a much milder climate.

Rio de Janeiro wineries

Vinícola Inconfidência 🍷

Paraíba do Sul

vinicolainconfidencia.com.br/

Angela and José Claudio Rego Aranha planted their vineyard in 2010, a pioneering feat in the state. At the start, they were assessed by Murillo Regina and his team. Since then, this role has passed to Floeno

Consultoria. Needless to say, DPWH is the adopted management system. Currently, more than 20,000 vines are in production under the technical supervision of agronomist André Luiz Gonçalves dos Santos. In 2019, they opened their winery, which is today led by oenologist Mario Lucas Ieggli. Depending on the vintage, their annual production can surpass 21,000 bottles. Their winery produces wines for other growers too, from Rio de Janeiro and Minas Gerais. Besides José Claudio, his sons Daniel, André and Maurício also take a lead in the business. Guided tours, including tastings, are available on Saturdays (book in advance).

Daniel Aranha and André Santos received me warmly to taste their wines as well as some they make for other growers. As a house philosophy, no wines labelled Inconfidência are oaked. João Carlos is an interesting and unusual blend of Syrah with 20 per cent Sauvignon Blanc. DPWH Syrah's character predominates, but pyrazine notes are also clear. The wine is fruity, fresh and delicious. Raphael Syrah has an intense and highly typical varietal profile: ripe black fruit, smoke, bacon and pepper, all framed by an excellent structure of acidity and tannins. Rubro is a blend of Syrah, Cabernet Franc, Cabernet Sauvignon and a dash of Merlot. It has a deep colour and combines Syrah's smokiness and Cabernet's capsicum and cassis very well. A solid structure of acidity and tannins allows cellaring. Bordalês is a Bordeaux blend: the two Cabernets and Merlot. Hints of green bell pepper and pencil shavings underline ripe blackberry and blackcurrant. Its tannins are quite alive but fine grained; this is a complex, ageworthy wine. Matheus Cabernet Franc balances (how well!) ripe fruit, capsicum, graphite and mineral hints. Its charmingly clear varietal character and robust structure express how good this cultivar can be in the region. Daniel and André think Cabernet Franc adapts itself to DPWH much better than Cabernet Sauvignon. Antonio's Cabernet Sauvignon is inky, dense and ripe and clearly manifests its varietal typicity: cassis, blackberry, capsicum, refreshing acidity and tannins so fine, albeit firm. Maria's Merlot has plenty of colour, ripe black fruit, fruit cake and tobacco. Sinewy tannins need more time to soften; this is a big, ageworthy Merlot.

Vinícola Família Eloy 🍷

Areal

@familia.eloy

This business was founded in 2019 by brothers Bernardo and José Carlos Eloy, backed up by father José Carlos. It is not just another vineyard or winery; they also built a condominium around a replica of a small Tuscan village, where visitors can enjoy the beautiful landscape and taste wine with German-style charcuterie. Besides the Areal vineyard, another is being developed at nearby Itaipava. All are managed through DPWH. Their wines are currently made at Inconfidência. Visitors are welcome at weekends (booking required).

Cabernet Franc has a medium ruby colour and is lightly structured; its clear varietal character and ripe fruit make it easy to drink. Syrah (from the vat) has a good typicity and moderate structure; the tannins demand more time to round up. Oaked Syrah (second-use French oak) has soft tannins, a medium body and strong vanilla and cedar.

Casa Rozental

Secretário (Petrópolis)

@casarozental

Célia and Marcelo Rozental, after careful planning, planted their terraced vineyard with Sauvignon Blanc, Cabernet Sauvignon and Syrah, which are managed through DPWH. The wines are made by Inconfidência, under the technical expertise of Mário Ieggli.

Syrah has a deep purple colour, ripe blackberry, hints of smoke and pepper, and soft, ripe tannins.

Also in Rio de Janeiro

- Vinícola Maturano, Teresópolis (vinicolamaturano.com/)
- Vinícola Tassinari, São José do Vale do Rio Preto (@vinicola.tassinari)
- Vinícola Terras Frias, Nova Friburgo ♀ (@vinicolaterrasfrias)
- Fattoria Vinhas Altas, Teresópolis ♀ (www.fattoriavinhasaltas.com/)

12

THE CENTRE-WEST

Three states form this vast (1.6 million square kilometres) region: Goiás, Mato Grosso and Mato Grosso do Sul, plus the Federal District around Brasília, the country's capital. It has a low demographic density, with 16.3 million inhabitants (10.1 inhabitants per square kilometres). Although predominately too warm or humid for viticulture, it has a sizeable area integrating the Brazilian Highlands. Here, altitude and dry winters permit DPWH, the reason behind the recent appearance of wineries.

GOIÁS

This central Brazilian state has a surface area of around 340,000 square kilometres (larger than Italy or Poland) and just over 7 million inhabitants. Its recorded story began in the seventeenth century when *bandeirantes* (slavers, explorers and fortune hunters who played a central role in increasing the lands dominated by white people in colonial Brazil) arrived searching for gold and diamonds. They founded a settlement in 1727, today the old town of Goiás (formerly Goiás Velho), which has a well-kept historical centre and is a UNESCO World Heritage Site. More or less at the same time, another town was founded: Pirenópolis, which also has many historic buildings. Goiás was the state capital until the 1930s when an entirely new city was built: Goiânia, now with 1.4 million inhabitants. An even more important new city was later built within the state: the country's capital, Brasília (see Federal District, page 313).

There is much to see and do in the state, after arriving either from nearby Brasília or Goiânia airports. Besides the many natural attractions, including thousands of waterfalls and caves, both within and outside state parks, plus many mountains, the state has perhaps the largest thermal complex in the world, at Caldas Novas. Also try to visit the large Araguaia River at Aruanã. Pirenópolis offers many traditional feasts, such as the 20-day *Festa do Divino* (which includes the colourful *Cavalhadas* and much traditional music), the Catholic Holy Week and Corpus Christi processions. A very traditional, impressive event of this kind takes place at Goiás: the *Procissão do Fogaréu* (Fire Procession), which starts just after midnight of the day before Good Friday, when masked people wearing long, white gowns and tall, pointed masks (as in Seville, Spain), purportedly disguised (strangely as it may appear) as Roman soldiers chasing and arresting Christ, carry large torches to the deep sound of drums. Impressive indeed!

Winemaking (as it pertains to *vinhos finos* at least) is, however, a much more recent development in Goiás state. Again, it was necessary to wait until DPWH made its appearance. Generally speaking, the climate does not favour traditional viticulture. It is only at regions combining altitude and Köppen-Geiger Cwa and Cwb climatic classes that DPWH can succeed. As at 2024, the townships with vineyards/wineries were Águas Lindas de Goiás (bordering the Federal District, c. 1,150 metres altitude), Cocalzinho de Goiás (close to both Brasília and Pirenópolis, at about 1,100 metres), Cristalina (c. 1,170 metres), Jaraguá (c. 640 metres), Itaberaí (c. 700 metres), Nazário (near Goiânia, c. 650 metres), Paraúna (c. 670 metres) and Rianápolis (c. 620 metres).

Goiás wineries

Vinícola Monte Castelo

Jaraguá

www.vinicolamontecastelo.com/

This business was founded in 2016 by two couples: Milton and Carolina Santana and Marco and Luciana Cano. Their 6.5-hectare, DPWH-managed vineyard is planted on sandy/stony soil. The cultivated varieties are Chenin Blanc, Sauvignon Blanc, Cabernet Franc, Cabernet Sauvignon, Marselan, Merlot, Petit Verdot, Syrah and Tempranillo. Since 2022, the wines have been made at São Patrício winery, less than 10 kilometres away, under the oenologist Bárbara Marques. Despite

Monte Castelo vineyard, Goiás

their short life, several wines have earned medals in national and international events.

Monte Castelo Syrah Reserva mixes varietal traits with oak (12
months in new and used French oak barrels): ripe blackberry, pepper,
vanilla and toast. Its grippy tannins, high concentration of flavours, and
warming alcohol compound a strong structure that allows it to age well.
Albhus Gran Reserva Syrah is deeply coloured, displaying overt characteristics of DPWH wines from this variety: ripe black fruit, smoke, pepper, leather and savouriness. These intermingle with vanilla and cedar
from 12 months in new French oak barrels, making the wine complex
and layered. Thick, fairly astringent tannins require more time to soften
this strongly structured, very good wine. Albhus Gran Reserva Cabernet
Sauvignon is inky, intense and varietally typical: ripe cassis, blackberries, mint and slight capsicum. Vanilla, spice and toast come from 12
months in new French oak barriques. It is fresh, concentrated and balanced; the 14.6% abv alcohol integrates well into the flavour concentration. Its sleek, fine tannins are still a bit grippy and demanding time;
this high-quality wine will age splendidly.

Vinícola São Patrício ♀

Rianápolis

vinicolasaopatricio.com.br/home-vinicola/

This new winery was founded in 2019, 235 kilometres west of Brasília. They have 6.5 hectares, comprising Chenin Blanc, Cabernet Franc, Cabernet Sauvignon, Marselan and Syrah, managed by DPWH. A new winery was established in 2024, where the wines are made under oenologist Bárbara Marques. Cristian Sepulveda (from Terra Nossa, São Paulo, where the first wines were made) is their assessor. Their wines are christened with the names of birds from the Araguaia River region. Visitors can enjoy guided tours of the vineyards and winery, with tastings, from Wednesday to Saturday (book first).

Cauré Syrah is a lighter version of the variety, with a medium ruby colour, ripe and fresh blackberry and raspberry, a medium body and alcohol. It is a wine for everyday consumption, fruity and easy to drink. Talha-Mar Syrah Reserva is overtly oaky (so much vanilla, spice and sawdust), but this integrates quite well into ripe fruit, fresh acidity and firm tannins. Udu Grande Reserva (Cabernet Sauvignon and Syrah) is dark, intense and complex, showing ripe cassis, blackberries, figs, capsicum, pepper and hints of smoke. It has a high flavour concentration, sinewy (but fine-grained) tannins, and a long length with a rewarding, satisfactory finish.

Also in Goiás

- Vinícola Assunção, Pirenópolis ♀ (@vinicolaassuncao)
- Fazenda Ercoara, Cristalina (@ercoara)
- Vinhedo Girassol, Cocalzinho de Goiás (@vinhedo.girassol)
- Casa Moura, Nazário (@vinicolacasamoura)
- Pireneus Vinhos e Vinhedos, Cocalzinho de Goiás (@pireneus vinhosvinhedos)
- Quartetto Vinhos e Vinhedos, Águas Lindas de Goiás (@quartetto vinhosevinhedos)

- Vinícola Serra das Galés, Paraúna (vinicolaserradasgales.com.br/)

FEDERAL DISTRICT

Being an enclave inside Goiás, it is no wonder that these areas share similar characteristics. Despite being the smallest administrative unit in Brazil, at 5,760 square kilometres, there is enough rural land around the country's capital, Brasília, to allow viticulture. Brasília is a planned city; its prominent architects, Oscar Niemeyer (for the buildings) and Lúcio Costa (for the city plan), were made famous through its design. The city was inaugurated in 1961, grew rapidly and now has 2.8 million inhabitants. It is a touristic attraction in itself, with handsome, modernistic works by Niemeyer (visit the Planalto and Alvorada palaces, the National Congress, other buildings encircling the Praça dos Três Poderes, and the astounding Metropolitan Cathedral), very large avenues, the Paranoá Lake and much more.

This is a cosmopolitan capital, where you can drink wines from everywhere in world at many restaurants (and pay dearly – this is a town for politicians, not dissimilar to Washington). Here, we are at an average altitude above 1,000 metres, at the heart of the Brazilian Highlands. This altitude, and the dry winters, make the area very good for DPWH. Ten wineries are established here (and in nearby Goiás state), some of which are already receiving visitors. As usual with the viticultural management, Syrah is the most planted variety, followed by Sauvignon Blanc.

Federal District wineries

Vinícola Brasília ♀

Brasília

@vinicolabrasilia

The ten producers of the Federal District joined together to build a brand-new winery, Vinícola Brasília, where US$ 3 million has been invested. The wines are made under the supervision of oenologist Marcos Vian. He, plus two other specialists (Anderson Schmitz and Valter Ferrari), is part of the team of Enovitis, a firm based at Monte Belo do Sul, in Rio Grande do Sul, which provides consulting services to many wineries in Brazil. Tastings can be booked, as well as visits to some associated producers.

Marchese Sauvignon Blanc is intensely aromatic, displaying ripe white guava, passion fruit, peach and citrus, with hints of cut grass and capsicum. It is rich and textural, with a New World style. Duetto Syrah is made from the grapes of two associates, Marchese Vinhos e Vinhedos and Fazenda Vista da Mata. It is ripe, bringing blackberry and notes of black pepper amidst strong, almost overwhelming, vanilla and cedar.

Also in the Federal District

Horus Vinhos do Planalto, Paranoá, Brasília (@horus.vv)

Oma Sena Vinhos e Vinhedos, Brasília (www.omasena.com.br/)

Villa Triacca Hotel Vinícola & Spa, Paranoá, Brasília 🍷 (www.villatriacca.com.br/)

Vinícola Casa Vitor, Brasília 🍷 (casavitor.com.br/)

MATO GROSSO DO SUL

This large (357,146 square kilometres) Centre-West state is not where you would expect to find a winery. The region is very important in agriculture (soya beans, corn, sugar cane) and cattle raising. Yet, there is one winery, and not in a reserved way, at Aquidauana, not far from the famous Pantanal. The latter is a well-known conservation area and definitely worth visiting. The town of Bonito is a place of astounding beauty within the National Park of Serra da Bodoquena. Here, you can find amazing landscapes, swim in rivers with crystalline water and full of fish, gaze in awe at caves with incredibly blue lakes, and see or enter many dolines (sinkholes) containing equally numerous waterfalls. This is a paradise for lovers of ecotourism. The winery, Vinícola Terroir Pantanal is located in Aquidauana (loja-terroirpantanal.paytour. com.br).

MATO GROSSO

Despite having a sizeable part of its large (902,207 square kilometres) territory included within the Amazônia Legal (a vast expanse of 5 million square kilometres encompassing several Brazilian states important in this context), an also considerable section of Mato Grosso state belongs to the Brazilian Highlands. At the very heart of South America (the geodesic centre of this continent is inside the Chapada dos Guimarães National Park), Mato Grosso has 3.7 million inhabitants and is very important in agriculture and cattle raising. The state capital and tourist hub is Cuiabá, with about 650,000 inhabitants.

The term *chapada* in Brazil is applied to a large area of highlands, with a relatively flat relief cut by many scarps. This leads to lots of waterfalls, caves and other attractive features. One of the most famous and visited is Chapada dos Guimarães, in Mato Grosso, which is protected by the homonymous national park measuring 33,000 square kilometres. At altitude (around 650 metres), winters are dry and mild, allowing DPWH. Presently, there is only one pioneering winery, Locanda Do Vale (www.locandadovale.com.br ♀) in the town of Chapada dos Guimarães. This is very near the state capital, Cuiabá. Visiting the Chapada is a very good ecotourism activity, allowing spectacular views of red sandstone cliffs, with caves, waterfalls, natural pools and numerous fauna. Why not, then, learn more about the local wine?

13

THE NORTHEAST

For a long time, the north-eastern states were among the least developed in Brazil. This applied especially to the *sertão* – deep into the country, away from the coastline. For centuries, a subsistence economy prevailed, based mainly on cattle raising. A lack of institutional organization, an almost complete absence of formal education, bad politics, land ownership concentration, paternalism, corruption and violence have all been compounded by an arid climate inland at the so-called *semi-árido*. Repeated droughts, recorded since the sixteenth century, brought famine and forced migration. For decades, desperate and impoverished people travelled south like goods loaded onto trucks – nicknamed *paus de arara* (macaw perches) – to try and secure a better future. Most succeeded, if achieving a better life compared to what they'd left behind can be considered successful. They took with them a very rich popular culture: music, food, poetry and mysticism, thus (somewhat paradoxically) enriching the places in which they chose to settle. This has changed, albeit slowly, thanks to institutional evolution, better development, industrialization, improvements in education and, fundamentally, water provision through irrigation. This allowed migrant people to escape the droughts and establish reliable agriculture – including fruit growing and grapes.

An important growth in tourism has also taken place. Tourism employs many people and improves their skills and income. The coastline is an almost endless series of beautiful beaches full of dunes, palm trees, warm water and many activities. Good to outstanding hotels, restaurants, resorts and beach bars provide satisfactory services and attract visitors all year round, both from Brazil and abroad. Foreigners receive a warm welcome and fare well due to favourable exchange rates. Wine tourism has also been implemented successfully.

The climate is, indeed, tropical, though with far less rain than, for example, the Amazon. You would not expect this to be a wine-producing region, but it is. Tropical viticulture is successful here (see IP Vale do São Francisco, page 75), which is perhaps unique in the world. DPWH, another Brazilian peculiarity, also has a role in northern Bahia. The country is, indeed, fortunate to have three distinct viticultural practices.

Unlike the South and the DPWH regions, tropical viticulture is concentrated in a smaller territory, comprising the nearby areas of Bahia and Pernambuco. Therefore, this chapter is not divided into states. It is also important to note how close the area is to the equator.

When discussing 'irrigation' in the Northeast, mention must be made of the São Francisco River, the primary water source for a large part of the *sertão*. Also known as 'the river of national integration', it begins at Serra da Canastra, in Minas Gerais. It runs north to Bahia, turns east, marks the border with Pernambuco, then divides the states of Alagoas and Sergipe until it flows into the Atlantic, so completing its long, 2,863-kilometre course. The São Francisco wine region is located where the river forms a frontier between Bahia and Pernambuco and where an impressive dam, Sobradinho, allows for vital electricity production and the formation of a very large reservoir, known as Sobradinho Lake. This, the largest artificial lake in Brazil, is 320 kilometres long, with an area of 4,214 square kilometres. Besides being an interesting tourist attraction, it also supplies a lot of irrigation projects.

Wine production, however, started in the region before the dam was built, as early as 1956, when Cinzano planted a vineyard to make base wine for vermouth at Floresta, some 300 kilometres down the São Francisco. The Cinzano facility was later sold and transferred to Santa Maria da Boa Vista, and the production was switched to vinegar. In 1958, Spaniard José Molina planted 10 hectares of *vinifera* and hybrid varieties.

However, the dam and lake allowed the establishment of a fruit-growing hub around the twin towns of Juazeiro (Bahia) and Petrolina (Pernambuco), the regional centre. This began just after the formation of the lake, in the 1970s. When you arrive at Petrolina by air (there are regular flights between São Paulo and this city), and the plane is coming in to land, you'll be under the impression that there are extensive vineyards in the region. As the aircraft descends further, however, you will see that much of what looks like vineyards is, in fact, a succession of mango and coconut groves beside the vines proper. Table grapes have been an essential product in the area from the beginning. Wine grapes have followed; the first wine made here was launched in 1985. Others followed suit in 2001, 2002, 2003 and 2004.

Governmental incentives have been important for the genesis of the wine industry in the region. The role of CODEVASF (a public company linked to a ministry) and Embrapa cannot be overemphasized here. They allowed the installation of the first winery, Vinícola do São Francisco, in the 1970s. The first wines were sold in bulk to Maison Forestier (owned by Seagram) in Serra Gaúcha, who bottled it under their own brand. Later, Vinícola launched its products under the label Botticelli, which persists to this day. The Italian names are not here by chance: the company was founded by Italian Franco Persico, owner of a large factory making steel tubes at Guarulhos (close to São Paulo).

Other wineries were established either by local investors or politicians, oenologists from Rio Grande do Sul or, importantly, by larger groups. These included, in 2002, the Terranova project of Miolo Wine Group, and Vinibrasil, now Vitivinícola Santa Maria (owned by the Portuguese Dão Sul, now Global Wines), in 2004. These two have been the biggest producers since then.

From 2013 to 2018, a large team led by Embrapa, including several universities, began a research and development project to improve the quality of the wines and build foundations for obtaining a geographical indication status. This was finally granted as an IP in 2022 (see Geographical indications, page 75).

IP VALE DO SÃO FRANCISCO

Tropical viticulture in Brazil is centred on this IP. This encompasses five townships and has a total area of 25,138 square kilometres, abutting the states of Pernambuco and Bahia. The area's relief is predominately flat, making viticulture easier. The altitude is more or less uniform, at about 350–420 metres. The predominant soil classes (SiBCS) are *argissolos* and *latossolos*, which require some correction.

The region benefits from its particular climate, which allows an average of up to 2.5 harvests per year (calculated as the average over ten years), from the abundance of irrigation water (indispensable here), lower land prices than in other wine regions, and the strong institutional support provided by federal and state governments. Importantly, manpower is also less expensive.

According to Alvares and collaborators, who developed a detailed map of Köppen climates for Brazil, the region is classified as Bsh – that is, semi-arid, with low latitude and low altitude. Using the MCC system, on the other hand, results in intra-annual variability, meaning that the climate class varies through the year. The variable index, however, is only DI, which can be -1 (sub-humid), +1 (moderately dry) or +2 (very dry). The other indexes are constant: HI+3 (very warm or hot) and CI-2 (warm nights).

Weather hazards are practically unknown: no frost, no hailstorms; as all viticulture is irrigated, drought is also not an issue. Powdery mildew can be a problem during the drier months, whereas rain may bring downy mildew and cluster rots. Grape moth has become a problem, however.

Tropical viticulture reigns here (see the *Viticulture* chapter, page 42, for more on this). It is, however, essential to remember that this allows more than one harvest per year, that the growth cycles can be adjusted to the climate type at each time of year, and that an almost uninterrupted supply of grapes can be thus obtained. The viticulturist may, for example, plan for a harvest during a cooler or drier month, thus

Large vineyards on flat terrain at Miolo's Terranova

influencing the wine's style. This is unique. Many vineyards are trained in a pergola system to protect the clusters from the abundant sunlight. Vertical shoot positioning (VSP) systems, here called *espaldeiras*, are also common. They demand specialized care. For example, the side that is more exposed to sunlight is seldom de-leafed, thus protecting the fruit.

According to Embrapa, about 500 hectares of grapes were planted in 2017 to craft *vinhos finos*. Table grapes and those for *vinhos de mesa* are not included in this amount, and their planted area is far greater. Chenin Blanc and the Muscat group are the most predominant white grapes; they are important for making sparkling wines. Arinto, Sauvignon Blanc, Verdejo, Viognier and other varieties are also planted. Sweet, low-alcohol, Asti-like sparkling wines make up a large percentage, and their base wines often include the Itália variety (see page 60). Sparklers constitute the majority of production here (over 60 per cent). Still white wines are made in minute amounts (1–2 per cent) and the balance is red. The reds are crafted largely from varieties better adapted to the particular conditions of the region: Syrah, Tempranillo, Touriga Nacional, Alicante Bouschet and Cabernet Sauvignon. Many other red varieties, however, are planted; some are already used commercially, while others are under trial, such as Barbera, Grenache, Malbec, Mourvèdre and Petite Sirah.

Pergola system and drip-irrigation lines at Rio Sol

The wines are predominately youthful, aromatic, floral and fruity, to be consumed within one to three years. Youthfulness and a fresh character are assured, as the supply of grapes is in constant flux. Well-structured red wines, however, are also made and can mature in the bottle for longer. These can be dark, rich, full bodied, with high alcohol but soft tannins, and, quite frequently, surprisingly fresh acidity.

Interestingly, a scientific paper by Lucena and co-workers, published in 2010, showed that red wines from this region have an unusually high phenolic content. The researchers found a total phenolic content in the region's red wines up to double that found in general reports. They reported that some wines could contain up to 5 grams Gallic acid equivalents. Figueiredo and co-workers (2017) corroborated this, demonstrating experimentally that the compounds could help combat hypertension. The latter authors hypothesize that the elevated levels of sunlight in the São Francisco Valley could lead to such high levels, which can have health benefits.

Northeast wineries

Miolo Wine Group: Vinícola Terranova ♀

Casa Nova, Bahia

www.miolo.com.br/linhas/terranova/

The *nissei* (son of Japanese fathers born in Brazil) Mamoru Yamamoto founded this property in 1980 as Fazenda Ouro Verde, intending to make wine. He had visited Israel, where similar environmental conditions are found. Professor Idalêncio Angheben, from Bento Gonçalves' Institute, and his pupil Ivair Toniolo assisted in planting the vineyard, and wine production was successful. Not quite, however, from a commercial stand-point. Due to heavy debts, Banco do Brasil had to take over the property. They sold it at auction in 2001 and it was acquired by Miolo. Yamamoto lived at the property until he died, in 2016, after becoming a producer of tea from the leaves of *Morus nigra* (black mulberry).

Miolo produces wines and grape juice at Terranova (the current name). The vineyards total a significant 200 hectares, primarily trained vertically. Harvest is almost wholly mechanical, as are other viticultural practices. The annual production is about 3 million bottles, with a primary focus on youthful sparklers, and the wines are sold nationwide. Sweet Moscatel is an important product, crafted chiefly from Itália (or Moscato Itália). Unlike most of their other planted varieties, Itália is trained as a pergola because the large, beautiful clusters suffer when exposed directly to the region's intense sunlight. Visitors can take an exciting boat trip on the river and lake, besides tasting and touring the vineyard and winery. Booking is essential.

I was very well received at Terranova by oenologists Miguel Ângelo Vicente Almeida and Eloiza Teixeira, both enthusiastic and fully dedicated to tropical viticulture. Miguel, from Portugal, has a lot of experience in Brazil and Miolo, as he worked at Seival for a long time. Afterwards, the firm invited him to take the lead at Terranova. They are always experimenting with new varieties. One of these is Mourvèdre, which has performed well. Although a component of blends until now, a varietal wine has been trialled and the results are encouraging. Another is Colombard, whose wines have a much-appreciated cutting acidity – and clear floral characters here. According to Miguel and Eloiza, Grenache is better for making base wines for rosé sparklers, as the wines are more pink than red in colour.

Syrah is the red star at Terranova; three different wines are made. Reserva, unoaked, showcases this variety's signature deep colour, blackberry, spice and good tannic structure. Single Vineyard has more structure, both of acidity and tannins, maturing in French oak barrels (second and third use). Super-premium Testardi is the top version: inky, dense, with high levels of tannins (which are amiable) and alcohol, and demanding bottle ageing. All three reds show a fresh acidity.

Terranova Brut white is a Blanc de Blancs from Chenin and Verdejo, while Brut Rosé is 100 per cent Grenache. Both are crafted by the Charmat method, having a residual sugar level of 10.5 grams per litre; very fruity, aromatic, fresh and inexpensive, they are youthful wines for everyday use. The pink version tastes drier (although the sugar level is the same as the white), perhaps due to a slight but perceptible tannic grip.

For more on the Miolo Wine Group, see also pages 115 and 179.

Rio Sol (Vitivinícola Santa Maria) ♀

Lagoa Grande, Pernambuco

www.vinhosriosol.com.br/principal/

This winery was founded in 2003 as Vinibrasil, a partnership between Dão Sul from Portugal (of the prestigious Cabriz brand) and the Expand group (then the largest wine importer in Brazil), plus the original vineyard owner (Grupo Raymundo da Fonte). The pioneering vineyards, as described by Adriano Miolo in the book *Vinhos do Brasil – do passado para o futuro*, were all planted with Syrah, over a large area – to make vinegar! Yes, vinegar, not wine. Today, the business belongs entirely to Global Wines, the current name of Dão Sul. They have 120 hectares of vines bordering the left bank of the mighty São Francisco River (here, 1 kilometre wide). There is a strong emphasis on organic farming. The dry climate helps lower chemical inputs, of course, but at Rio Sol, they are increasingly using more natural methods. They cultivate their own strains of beneficial bacteria, such as *Bacillus subtilis*, *B. thuringiensis* and *B. amyloliquefasciens*, not only to combat pests (botrytis, oidium, mildew, moths), but also to ameliorate the generation of nitrogen and increase the richness of the rhizosphere's microbiome. About 2 million bottles of wine are made annually. Rio Sol exports to the US, UK and Portugal. The Northeast is their primary market in Brazil, but their products can be found nationwide. Visitors can enjoy three different experiences (always book in advance).

Ricardo Henriques, an experienced Portuguese oenologist, is in charge of operations at Rio Sol. He received me very well when I visited the winery and tasted the wines. He has a deep understanding of the environment and the vineyards here, speaking authoritatively about his vines and wines. Despite the standard view that Syrah is the best red grape in the São Francisco Valley, Ricardo disagrees. He thinks, for example, that Touriga Nacional (an important grape at Rio Sol) behaves better and may result in superior wines. As for whites, he sees Arinto as perhaps the most promising variety, as it retains its flavours and crisp acidity here. Regarding acidity, by the way, some words are pertinent. As I mentioned earlier, the acidity of the wines is surprising in this tropical region. One would expect them to be somewhat flat, demanding strong correction. Miguel from Terranova and Ricardo both informed me that their consumption of tartaric acid to correct acidity is actually very low. Ricardo thinks this could be due to the high potassium content of the soil, which at once leads to a high pH and high levels of titratable acids. Whatever the reason, the fact is that one can expect fresh wines from the São Francisco Valley, something I noted myself.

Viognier/Chenin Blanc is a fruity, fresh white with the proverbial Viognier texture allied to Chenin's higher acidity; it is a good everyday wine. Tempranillo is unoaked, purplish, well extracted and devoid of raisiny flavours, and shows a firm tannic structure. Both wines are inexpensive and a genuine bargain. Reserva red blend (Cabernet Sauvignon, Syrah, Alicante Bouschet) undergoes about six months of maturation in oak barrels (predominately French) of second and third use. It has, as expected, a sturdy structure of tannins (fine grained) and acidity; the flavours range from ripe blackberries to spice and toast. The Gran Reserva line has more time in barrels (nine to twelve months), of which 70 per cent are new, mostly French, of different toasts, grains and origins. GR Alicante Bouschet has a deep colour, very ripe black fruit and a full body, keeping good acidity. GR Touriga Nacional is a jewel: elegant, with a high varietal typicity of violets, blackberries and mandarin hints; again, a true bargain. GR 8 (formerly Paralelo 8) is a complex blend of Touriga Nacional, Cabernet Sauvignon, Syrah, Tempranillo and Alicante Bouschet, and intended to have a European style, according to Ricardo; this translates through lively, but fine, tannins, a lovely acidity and some tertiary hints imparting complexity; a fine wine indeed.

Their inexpensive sparklers are made using the tank method. Brut white (Syrah and Arinto) is aromatic, fruity, fresh and dry (8.2 grams per litre residual sugar). Brut Rosé (Syrah, Tempranillo) ferments the base wines at a lower temperature than those of the white versions; although the residual sugar is the same, it feels drier, which is perhaps due to a slight tannic perception. Moscatel (Moscato Canelli) is a fine version of this highly successful category of Brazilian wines: so aromatic and fresh, not cloying, perfect to drink very cold on a summer's day. All the wines I tasted offer, in my opinion, a great deal for the price.

Grupo Verano Brasil

Petrolina

@grupoveranobrasil

Terroir do São Francisco/Garziera acquired part of the pioneering Fazenda Milano in 2021, and a group (T & T, recently changed to Verano Brasil) was formed, comprising Vinícola Terroir do São Francisco and Tropical Vitivinícola. Rodrigo Fabian, an oenologist, became one of the partners, along with the Garziera family. Jorge Garziera, from Garibaldi (Rio Grande do Sul), established himself for good at Lagoa Grande in 1978. An oenologist and businessman, he worked for Fazenda Milano/Botticelli. He subsequently started his own Garibaldina farm. This gave rise to Vinícola Terroir do São Francisco and its present winery, now owned by Garziera's daughters, Ana Catharina and Julianna.

The winery produces wines for Terroir and Tropical. This is not a small enterprise, boasting 50 hectares of irrigated vineyards, including both table and wine grapes. Their installed capacity allows them to make 3 million litres of wine annually. Flávio Durante is the chief oenologist. The wines are labelled VVSF Reservado and Tropical. Their focus is on simple, fruity, easy-drinking products. Most are sold within the Northeast; according to Flávio, this is what the market demands. Visitors are welcome (booking advised).

Tropical Vitivinícola (Fazenda Milano)

Santa Maria da Boa Vista, Pernambuco

tropicalvitivinicola.com.br/

Their brands are Garziera, Rio Valley and Vale das Colheitas. Rodrigo Fabian and Flávio Durante lead the oenological works. Despite an emphasis on entry-level products, they are starting to make oak-aged Reserva wines and a Charmat sparkler with a long autolysis time. Flávio explained that they take advantage of thermovinification to craft parcels of their wines, thus attaining more fruit and softness. I could taste some of the wines at their pretty facilities after touring the extensive vineyards of Fazenda Milano.

Garziera Chardonnay/Chenin Blanc is somewhat surprising, as growing Chardonnay in such a hot region seems unlikely. The wine, however, has a good typicity of both grapes, being fresh, light and fruity. Garziera Malbec is also easy going, fruity, soft and suitable for drinking lightly chilled. Rio Valley Brut (made by the tank method) is 60 per cent Chenin, the balance being Chardonnay and Sauvignon Blanc; like the other wines, it is fresh, fruity, youthful and light, suiting the local climate when drunk very cold. Rio Valley Moscatel Frisante, made from Itália and other grapes from the Muscat family, has a lower pressure (1.5 atmospheres), being made with the same Charmat process; it is sweet, low in alcohol (7% abv), floral and perfumed (also sold in cans). All these are entry-level, inexpensive, well-made drinks.

The newly launched Reserva line has more ambitious products. Chardonnay spends six months in French oak; it is very ripe and fruity, with moderate acidity, slight vanilla and toast, and a good length. Malbec also matures for half a year in oak; very fruity, medium in acidity, alcohol, body and oak characters, it is ready to drink now. Centenário Cabernet Sauvignon (premium) is a bigger wine: very ripe cassis and blackberry, a full body, warming 15% abv, a firm tannic structure and moderate acidity. Garziera Extra-Brut is 100 per cent Chardonnay made by the tank method; it offers very ripe fruit balanced by refreshing acidity.

DPWH IN BAHIA

Another famous and much-visited *chapada* in Brazil is Chapada Diamantina, located in the centre of Bahia state. There is a national and a state park here, plus other protected areas. The *chapada* is large, over 41,000 square kilometres, and encompasses 24 townships. The touristic hub is Lençóis, a little more than 400 kilometres (by car) from Salvador, the state capital. Salvador, by the way, is a big city, and there are many reasons to visit. The first Brazilian capital and one of its oldest cities, it has many historic attractions, beautiful beaches, excellent traditional food and much more to see and enjoy. Lençóis has an airport with regular commercial flights. From here, the two important towns linked to viticulture are Mucugê (about 150 kilometres to the south, by car) and Morro do Chapéu (around 160 kilometres to the north, also by car). They may seem improbable sites for viticulture, but altitude and DPWH have recently allowed the installation of some wineries. Their produce, albeit young, is quite promising. Mucugê lies about 1,100 metres above sea level, whereas Morro do Chapéu is slightly lower. It rains little from May to August, when average temperatures are under 20°C, falling to 15°C during the cool nights – precisely what DPWH needs. Syrah leads the plantings, accompanied by Sauvignon Blanc, Chardonnay, Malbec, Cabernet Franc and Cabernet Sauvignon.

Bahia wineries
Vinícola Uvva 🍷
Mucugê

www.vinicolauvva.com.br

The Borré family, of Norwegian descent and formerly from Rio Grande do Sul, settled at Chapada Diamantina during the 1980s. They own Fazenda Progresso, a vast property of 26,000 hectares at Mucugê, where coffee and potato farming have been the main activities. In 2010, however, French visitors prompted them to take up the challenge of starting a new wine region. DPWH allowed this, and, according to owner Fabiano Borré, they started planting their vineyard in 2012 at 1,150 metres on clayey-sandy soil with good drainage properties. Currently, 52 hectares are producing grapes, with nine different French varieties. The wines are crafted in their brand-new winery under the oenologist Marcelo Petroli. Their annual capacity is up to 260,000 bottles. However, at the moment, they are making less than half this. Different oenotouristic activities are offered: visiting, tasting or a whole experience, including harvesting (closed Mondays; booking advised). There is also a restaurant, Arenito, with a view of the surrounding mountains.

Sauvignon Blanc is a good example of this variety's DPWH wines: ripe, well structured, textural, fresh and aromatic. Unoaked Chardonnay has excellent varietal characteristics: ripe apple, hints of pineapple, cream and butter from malolactic fermentation, and a good structure. Microlote Chardonnay has a solid structure, is more complex, and oak treatment is elegant and not intrusive (85 per cent of the wine stays six months in French oak barrels with *bâtonnage*). Cordel is a red blend with Syrah predominating; very ripe, perfumed and peppery, it has lively acidity and oak flavours (spending eight months in barrels) well balanced by its black fruit characters. Super-premium Diamá is a Bordeaux blend with a predominance of Cabernet Sauvignon, passing 12 months in barrels; it is dark, very ripe, intense, concentrated, with a sinewy tannic structure, complex and lengthy. Nature is a traditional method sparkler from Chardonnay and Pinot Noir, spending 18 months in autolysis; this imparts clear brioche and bread characters, well integrated into ripe fruit and agreeable acidity.

PERNAMBUCO: OUTSIDE IP VALE DO SÃO FRANCISCO

As usual in Brazil, altitude allows vines to grow in unexpected places. One is Garanhuns (where President Lula was born), in Pernambuco. This town is found in the Borborema Highland (or plateau, which integrates the Brazilian Highlands) and is about 230 kilometres from the seaside capital, Recife. A single winery (Vale das Colinas) can be found here.

Also in the Northeast

- Adega Bianchetti Tedesco, Lagoa Grande, Pernambuco (@adega bianchettitedesco)
- Vinhos Botticelli, Santa Maria da Boa Vista, Pernambuco (vinhos botticelli.com.br/)
- Mandacaru Vinha e Vinhos, Lagoa Grande (@vinicolamandacaru)
- Vinícola Reconvexo, Morro do Chapéu (www.vinicolareconvexo. com.br/home)

- Vinícola Santa Maria, Morro do Chapéu (@vinicolasantamaria)
- Vale Das Colinas Vinhos e Vinhedos, Garanhuns (www.vinicolavale dascolinas.com.br/)
- Vinícola Terroir do São Francisco, Lagoa Grande (terroirdosaofrancisco. com.br/terroir-do-sao-francisco/)
- Vinícola Vaz (Vinhas do Morro), Morro do Chapéu (vinicolavaz.com/)

APPENDIX I: VINTAGES

Serra Gaúcha

Please note: There are almost no problems with the quality of base wines for sparklers and light white wines in any year.

2024 – A very difficult year due to excessive rainfall at flowering, lowering yield (41 per cent less than 2023) and quality. Youthful whites and base wines for sparklers were less affected. Not a good year for reds.

2023 – The biggest production ever (almost 100,000 tons). Being a La Niña year, there was a bit more rain than in 2022. Very good general quality.

2022 – High yield, less rain; very good quality for reds. Excessive heat around the harvest of grapes for base wines advanced the picking.

2021 – High yields and more rainfall than desired, leading to average quality.

2020 – Outstanding vintage, with little rainfall at the right time. The reds will age very well and are some of the best ever.

2019 – More rainfall led to increased yield and average quality.

2018 – Very good vintage. The weather conditions led to moderate yield and very good grape and wine quality. The reds are drinking well.

Older vintages of note: 1991, 1999, 2005, 2006, 2008, 2015

Campanha Gaúcha

2024 – A challenging year, dominated by El Niño, with abundant rain during ripening. Only the white grapes were spared, albeit not in the whole region.

2023 and 2022 – La Niña years, hence hot and warm. Excellent grape quality, leading to ripe and concentrated wines that will stand the test of time.

2021 – More rainfall, high yields; better for sparklers, whites, rosés and youthful reds.

2020 – As almost everywhere, a near-perfect vintage: warm, dry weather leading to excellent grape quality. The reds are drinking well but can be cellared for a long time.

2019 – Similar to 2021, with more rainfall and general quality not as good as 2018 and 2020.

2018 – Similar to 2020, there is an excellent balance of quantity and quality due to warm, dry weather and rainfall at the right time. The reds are delivering a lot now, but can be cellared.

Serra Catarinense

2024 – Challenging, as excessive rainfall lowered both yield and quality.

2023 – Advanced maturation and harvest, good general quality.

2022 – Little rain, very good quality, above average.

2021 – A normal year with average quantity and quality.

2020 – Historical: warm, dry, excellent maturation, outstanding wines.

2019 – As 2021, an average year.

2018 – Excellent vintage, among the top five in the last 20 years.

Northeast (tropical viticulture)

Due to its particular characteristics, there is very little vintage effect here.

DPWH regions

These are vast regions, so scattered that it is impossible to generalize. In any case, vintage effects are less important than they are in areas with traditional viticulture (the South). However, colder and drier years (such as 2021) can be better. The year 2020 was also a very good vintage in most places.

APPENDIX II: BRAZILIAN WINE IMPORTERS

EUROPE

Brazilian Wine House – Netherlands (brazilianwinehouse.com) – Casa Pedrucci, Don Guerino, Lídio Carraro, Miolo, Pizzato, Salton
Farsons Direct – Malta (farsonsdirect.com) – Miolo Wine Group
Systembolaget – Sweden (www.systembolaget.se) – Valduga, Terranova/ Miolo

UK

Atlantico (wholesaler) – Rio Sol
GoBrazil Wines (www.gobrazilwines.com) – Campos de Cima, Cooperativa Garibaldi, Don Guerino, Família Geisse, Guaspari, Miolo, Pizzato
Novel Wines (www.novelwines.co.uk/) – Pizzato
Vinvm (www.vinvm.co.uk) – Miolo, Valduga

USA

Aidil Wines & Liquors (aidilwines.com) – Rio Sol
Westchester Wine Warehouse (www.westchesterwine.com/) – Valduga
Wine for the World (www.wine4theworld.com) – Família Geisse
Wine.com (www.wine.com) – Salton

GLOSSARY

WINE TERMS AND BRAZILIAN EXPRESSIONS

Babo degree: the same as KMW (*Klosterneuburger Mostwaage*); the commonest grape must density scale used in Brazil. It is more precise than Brix.

Brix degree: (or just Brix) expresses a solution's density (specific gravity), e.g. grape must. As sugar is the predominant solid in the must, Brix (or another similar scale) is used to evaluate grape ripening and harvest times.

Caatinga: flat terrain with a semi-arid tropical climate.

Cachaça: cane sugar spirit.

Cantina: winery.

Cerrado: a kind of savanna.

Chapada: a flat highland.

Charmat: French term (also used in Brazil) for the method of making sparkling wines in which the second fermentation happens in pressurized tanks.

Churrasco: barbecue.

Cultivar: the same as 'variety' when applied to grapes.

Double pruning and winter harvesting (DPWH): *see* Winter viticulture.

Espaldeira: name used in Brazil to refer to all vertical training or vine-trellising systems, or VSP.

Espumante: a sparkling wine with a minimum pressure of 4.0 atmospheres.

Frisante: a sparkling wine with a pressure of 1.1–2.0 atmospheres.

Gaúcho: demonym for Rio Grande do Sul state.

Índio: Brazilian Portuguese name for the Indigenous people; not considered derogatory and is used by the people themselves.

Indústria Brasileira: made in Brazil.

Interspecific hybrid: *see Vitis* interspecific crossing.

Latada: name used in Brazil to refer to horizontal, pergola-like training and vine-trellising systems.

Lote: a piece of land.

Lutte raisonnée: or 'reasoned struggle', is a viticultural approach in which agrochemicals are used sparingly and only when absolutely necessary. There are no rules (as there are in organic or biodynamic approaches); the conscious grower's judgement governs decisions.

Mangue: mangrove.

Método tradicional: the traditional method of making sparkling wines, in which the second fermentation happens in the bottle.

Mineiro: demonym for Minas Gerais state.

Mistelle: unfermented grape juice to which alcohol is added.

Parreira: vine.

Paulista: demonym for São Paulo state.

Petrichor: an agreeable smell of rain falling on very dry soil.

Phytoregulators: or plant growth regulators, are substances similar to plant hormones used to modify or accelerate the vine's growth or maturation. Examples include abscisic acid, gibberellic acid, ethephon and hydrogen cyanamide.

Pico: peak.

Planalto: highland.

Reduções: or 'reductions', organized communities established by the Jesuits in southern Brazil in the early 1600s, where Indigenous people were converted and educated.

Rio: river.

Saúde!: this is what Brazilians say when making a toast.

Serra: mountain range.

Sertão: outback.

Sindicato: labour union.

Solo: soil.

Traditional method: *see Método tradicional*.

Traditional viticulture: in this book, this is the usual vine-cultivation cycle with a single summer or autumn harvest.

Tropical viticulture: practised in tropical regions, having more than one harvest yearly.

Tropeiro: drover.

Uva: grape.

Vinhedo: vineyard.

Vinho: wine.

Vinhos de mesa: in Brazil, wines mostly made from American hybrids such as Isabel.

Vinhos finos: in Brazil, wines which are crafted from *vinifera* varieties.

Vitis **interspecific crossing**: a hybrid resulting from crossing two different *Vitis* species (e.g. *Vitis vinifera* × *Vitis labrusca*; *V. vinifera* × a hybrid).

Vitis labrusca: American vine species, important as a phylloxera-resistant rootstock and as a genetic component of hybrids (e.g. Isabel, Concord, Niágara), used as table grapes, for making grape juice and to craft *vinhos de mesa*, which have a strong 'foxy' character.

Vitis vinifera: vine species with thousands of varieties used as table grapes, to make raisins, or as the raw material for most wines.

Winter viticulture, or double pruning and winter harvest (DPWH): a second pruning leads to a new growth cycle, and the harvest occurs during winter.

ORGANIZATION ABBREVIATIONS AND ACRONYMS

Brazilians love abbreviations, perhaps due to their Portuguese inheritance. The following are the most common wine-related examples and also include some acronyms.

ABE: Associação Brasileira de Enologia (Brazilian Association of Oenology)

abv: alcohol by volume

ANPROVIN: Associação Nacional dos Produtores de Vinhos de Inverno (National Association of Winter Wine Producers)

CI: Cool night Index

CNPUV: Centro Nacional de Pesquisa de Uva e Vinho (National Centre for Research on Grape and Wine)

CVE: Colégio de Viticultura e Enologia (Oenology and Viticulture School)

DI: Dryness Index

DO: Denominação de Origem (Denomination of Origin)

DPWH: Double Pruning and Winter Harvest

EEVE: Estação Experimental de Viticultura e Enologia (Experimental Station of Viticulture and Oenology)

Emater-MG: Empresa de Assistência Técnica e Extensão Rural de Minas Gerais (Minas Gerais Company of Technical Assistance and Rural Extension)

Emater-RS: Empresa de Assistência Técnica e Extensão Rural de Rio Grande do Sul (Rio Grande do Sul Company of Technical Assistance and Rural Extension)

Embrapa: Empresa Brasileira de Pesquisa Agropecuária (Brazilian Agricultural Research Corporation)

ENTAV-INRA: (from Établissement National Technique pour l'Amelioration de la Viticulture - Institut National de la Recherche Agronomique) – registered French trademark for viticultural material

Epagri: Empresa de Pesquisa Agropecuária e Extensão Rural de Santa Catarina (Santa Catarina Company of Agricultural and Livestock Research and Rural Extension)

Epamig: Empresa de Pesquisa Agropecuária de Minas Gerais (Minas Gerais Company of Agricultural and Livestock Research)

EPT: evapotranspiration

GDP: gross domestic product

HDI: human development index

HI: Heliothermal (or Huglin) Index

IAC: Instituto Agronômico de Campinas (Campinas Agronomic Institute)

IBGE: *I*nstituto Brasileiro de Geografia e Estatística (Brazilian Institute of Geography and Statistics)

IBPT: Instituto Brasileiro de Planejamento e Tributação (Brazilian Institute of Planning and Taxation)

IBRAVIN: Instituto Brasileiro do Vinho (Brazilian Wine Institute), now extinct

IG: Indicação Geográfica (geographical indication)

INPI: Instituto Nacional da Propriedade Industrial (National Institute of Industrial Property)

IP: Indicação de Procedência (provenance indication)

IVBAM: Instituto do Vinho, do Bordado e Do Artesanato da Madeira (Madeira Institute of Wine, Embroidery and Craftsmanship)

IVDP: Instituto dos Vinhos do Douro E Porto (Port and Douro Wines Institute)

IVV: Instituto da Vinha e do Vinho (Vine and Wine Institute)

LVMH: Louis Vuitton-Moët-Hennessy

MAPA: Ministério da Agricultura e Pecuária (Ministry of Agriculture and Livestock)

MCC: Multicriteria Climatic Classification System

OIV: International Organization of Vine and Wine

PIWI: Pilzwiderstandsfähig, or fungus-resistant hybrid

RL2M: Rain in the Last Two Months of the DPWH growing cycle

SiBCS: Sistema Brasileiro de Classificação de Solos (Brazilian System of Soil Classification)

SIVIBE: Sistema de Informações da Área de Vinhos e Bebidas (Information System on the Wine and Drinks Area)

TALM: Thermal Amplitude of the Last Month of the DPWH growing cycle

UVIBRA: União Brasileira de Vitivinicultura (Brazilian Viniviticulture Union)

VIVC: Vitis International Variety Catalogue

VSP: Vertical Shoot Positioning

WRBSR: World Reference Base for Soil Resources

WSET: Wine & Spirit Education Trust

Abbreviations of wine-producing states:

BA: Bahia; DF: Distrito Federal (Federal District); ES: Espírito Santo; GO: Goiás; MG: Minas Gerais; MS: Mato Grosso do Sul; MT: Mato Grosso; PE: Pernambuco; PR: Paraná; RJ: Rio de Janeiro; RS: Rio Grande do Sul; SC: Santa Catarina; SP: São Paulo

REFERENCES

Chapter 1: History of wine in Brazil

Cabral de Mello, C. E. *Presença do vinho no Brasil – um pouco de história* (in Portuguese). Editora de Cultura, São Paulo, 2007.

Chamberlain, H. Vistas e costumes da cidade e arredores do Rio de Janeiro em 1819–1820 (in Portuguese, translated by Rubens Borba de Moraes). Livraria Kosmos, Rio de Janeiro, 1943. Available for download at: http://www2.senado.leg.br/bdsf/handle/id/227375

Dal Pizzol, R. Inglez de Sousa, S. Memórias do Vinho Gaúcho. AGE, Porto Alegre, 2014. (3 vols.)

Sousa, G. S. Tratado Descriptivo do Brasil em 1587. Typographia de João Ignacio da Silva, Rio de Janeiro, 1879. Downloadable (in original ancient Portuguese) at: https://www2.senado.leg.br/bdsf/item/id/242787

Teixeira, D.M. A 'America' de Jodocus Hondius (1563–1612): um estudo das fontes iconográficas. Revista do IEB, 46:81-122, 2008. Downloadable (in Portuguese) at: https://www.revistas.usp.br/rieb/article/view/34601

Chapter 2: Layout of the country

White, R.G. *Soils for Fine Wines*. Oxford University Press, Oxford, 2003.

Chapter 3: Climate

Alvares, C. A. et al. Köppen's climate classification map for Brazil. *Meteorologische Zeitschrift.* 22:711-728, 2014. Available at: http://

www.dca.iag.usp.br/material/mftandra2/ACA0225/Alvares_etal_
Koppen_climate_classBrazil_MeteoZei_2014.pdf

Tonietto, J., Carbonneau, A. 'A multicriteria climatic classification system for grape-growing regions worldwide'. *Agricultural and Forest Meteorology*, 2004, 124 (1–2), pp.81-97.Available at: https://www.alice.cnptia.embrapa.br/bitstream/doc/1008614/1/1s2.0S01681923 04000115main.pdf

Chapter 4: Viticulture and winemaking

Anderson, K., Nelgen, S. Which winegrape varieties are grown where? University of Adelaide, 2020. Available at: https://www.adelaide.edu.au/press/titles/winegrapes.

Bois, B., Zito, S., Calonnec, A. Climate vs. grapevine pests and diseases worldwide: the first results of a global survey. OenoOne 2017, 51(3):133-139.

Cisilotto, B. et al. The Brazilian grapevine variety called 'Peverella' corresponds to the 'Boschera' variety. *Vitis* 2023, 62(4), 178–182. Available at: https://ojs.openagrar.de/index.php/VITIS/article/view/17137

Leão, P. C. S.; Riaz, S; Graziani, R.; Dangl, G.; Motoike, S. Y.; Walker, A. 2009, 'Characterization of a Brazilian grape germplasm collection using microsatellite markers'. *American Journal of Enology and Viticulture 2009*, 60(4): 517–24. Available at: http://www.cpatsa.embrapa.br:8080/public_eletronica/downloads/OPB2617.pdf

Martins, A. M. et al. Comparative agronomical, phenological and molecular analyses between the grape variety 'Moscato Branco' and accessions of Brazilian and French grape germplasm banks. IV Simpósio Brasileiro de Genética Molecular de Plantas, Bento Gonçalves, 2013. Available at: https://www.embrapa.br/en/busca-de-publicacoes/-/publicacao/979071/comparative-agronomical-phenological-and-molecular-analyses-between-the-grape-variety-moscato-branco-and-accessions-of-brazilian-and-french-grape-germplasm-banks.

Mello, L.M.R., Machado, C.A.E. Vitivinicultura brasileira: panorama 2021. *Embrapa Uva e Vinho*, 2022. Available at: https://www.infoteca.cnptia.embrapa.br/infoteca/bitstream/doc/1149674/1/Com-Tec-226.pdf.

Pereira, G. E., Tonietto, J. et al. Vinhos no Brasil: contrastes na geografia e no manejo das videiras nas três viticulturas do país. *Embrapa Uva e Vinho*, 2020. Available at: https://www.embrapa.br/en/busca-de-publicacoes/-/publicacao/1128174/vinhos-no-brasil-contrastes-na-geografia-e-no-manejo-das-videiras-nas-tres-viticulturas-do-pais#:~:text=Resumo%3A%20O%20Brasil%20%C3%A9%20o,e%20o%20manejo%20das%20videiras

Raimondi, S. et al. DNA-based genealogy reconstruction of Nebbiolo, Barbera and other ancient grapevine cultivars from northwestern Italy. Scientific Reports, 2020, 10(1):15782. doi: 10.1038/s41598-020-72799-6. Available at: https://www.ncbi.nlm.nih.gov/pmc/articles/PMC7519648/

Schuck, M. R. et al. Identificação molecular da uva 'Goethe' de Urussanga-SC por marcadores microssatélites. *Revista Brasileira de Fruticultura*, 2010, 32(3):825–831. Available at: https://www.scielo.br/j/rbf/a/zDRT6HsJ7nYqc859x8Xp4dr/?format=pdf&lang=pt.

Chapter 6: Brazilian wine law

Consolidação das Normas de Bebidas, Fermentado Acético, Vinho e Derivados da Uva e do Vinho. Anexo À Norma Interna Dipov Nº 01/2019. Cartilhão de Bebidas. 2ª Edição. Available at: https://www.gov.br/agricultura/pt-br/assuntos/inspecao/produtos-vegetal/legislacao-de-produtos-origem-vegetal/biblioteca-de-normas-vinhos-e-bebidas/AnexoNormaInternaDIPOV2Edicao.pdf

Chapter 7: Wine business

Bruch, K. L., Fensterseifer, J.E. Análise da tributação incidente na cadeia produtiva do vinho brasileiro. XLIII Congresso da SOBER, Ribeirão Preto, 2005. Available at: http://direitodovinho.org/arquivos/6.pdf

Chapter 8: Rio Grande do Sul: Serra Gaúcha

Miranda, E. E. de; (Coord.). Brasil em Relevo. Campinas: Embrapa Monitoramento por Satélite, 2005. Available at: <http://www.relev-obr.cnpm.embrapa.br>. Access: 20 May 2024.

Chapter 11: The Southeast

Cardim, F. *Tratados da Terra e Gente do Brasil.* J.Leite & Cia., Rio de Janeiro, 1925.

Inglez de Sousa, J. S. Vitivinicultura em Caldas, Minas Gerais: notas para sua história, 1950 and 1959. Compiled and edited by Celso Lago Paiva. Available for download (in Portuguese) at: https://www.researchgate.net/publication/313891852_A_historia_da_viticultura_em_Caldas_Minas_Gerais_Brasil

Inglez de Sousa, J. S. Uvas para o Brasil. Melhoramentos, São Paulo, 1969.

Kalil, T. O vinho em Andradas (MG): sabor, paisagem, lugar, memória e perspectivas na percepção dos produtores. Geograficidade, 2016. 6(2):50-70. Available for download (in Portuguese) at: https://periodicos.uff.br/geograficidade/article/view/12961

Mawe, J. Travels in the Interior of Brazil, particularly in the Gold and Diamond Districts of that Country. Longman, Hurst, Rees, Orme, and Brown, London, 1812. Original available for download at: https://www2.senado.leg.br/bdsf/handle/id/28/browse?type=author&value=Mawe%2C+John+1764-1829

Meira, J. F. P. Notes for a geographical history of wine in Diamantina (1817-2000). Revista Espinhaço, 2019. 8(2):58–70. Available for download (in Portuguese) at: https://www.academia.edu/43731949/Apontamentos_para_uma_geo_hist%C3%B3ria_do_vinho_em_Diamantina_1817_2000_

Romero, L. A. B. A vitivinicultura no estado de São Paulo (1880-1950). Dissertação de mestrado, Instituto de Economia da UNICAMP, 2004. Available for download (in Portuguese) at: https://www.abphe.org.br/uploads/Banco%20de%20Teses/a-vitivinicultura-no-estado-de-sao-paulo-1880-1950.pdf

Chapter 13: The Northeast

Ferreira, V. C. & Ferreira, M. M. *Vinhos do Brasil – do passado para o futuro.* Rio de Janciro, FGV Editora, 2016.

Figueiredo, E. A., et al. Antioxidant and antihypertensive effects of a chemically defined fractions of Syrah red wine on spontaneously hypertensive rats. *Nutrients*, 2017, 9:574.

Lucena, A. P. S., Nascimento, R. J. B., Maciel, J. A. C. et al. Antioxidant activity and phenolics content of selected Brazilian wines. *Journal of Food Composition and Analysis*, 2010, 23:30–36.

FURTHER READING

Although specialized books written in Portuguese are more common (albeit more are needed), those in English are scarce and short, as the following list shows.

In English

Barnes, Amanda. 'The Brazil Wine Guide'. *The South America Wine Guide*, 2022.

Deschamps, Lucien C. *Brazilian Wine Regions: A Connoisseur's Guide to History, Grape Varieties, Flavors and Wine Regions of Brazil.* Independent e-book edition, 2024.

Musumeci, Bernardo. *Wines in Brazil* series. Independent e-book edition, 2024. Regions already published: *Campanha Gaúcha, Garibaldi, Flores da Cunha.*

In Portuguese

Bueno, Silvana C. S. (editor) et al. *Vinhedo Paulista: História, Viticultura, Vinificação.* Campinas: CATI, 2010.

Burgos, Cristian. *Adega Brasil Guia de Vinhos.* São Paulo: Inner, 2024.

Cabral de Mello, Carlos E. *Presença do vinho no Brasil – um pouco de história.* São Paulo: Editora de Cultura, 2007.

Cordeiro, Michele Z. & Costa, Deisi. *Expedição Cultural Vou de Vinho.* Porto Alegre: Pró-Cultura, 2022.

Dal Pizzol, Rinaldo & Inglez de Souza, Sérgio. *Memórias do Vinho Gaúcho.* Porto Alegre: AGE, 2014. (3 volumes)

Dardeau, Rogerio. *Vinho Fino Brasileiro*. Rio de Janeiro: Mauad X, 2015.

Dardeau, Rogerio. *Gente, Lugares e Vinhos do Brasil* (2nd edn). Rio de Janeiro: Mauad X, 2023.

Ferreira, Valdinei. *Vinho e Mercado: Fazendo Negócios no Brasil*. Rio de Janeiro: FGV, 2019.

Ferreira, Valdinei C. & Ferreira, Marieta M. *Vinhos do Brasil, do Passado para o Futuro*. Rio de Janeiro: FGV Editora, 2016.

Figueiredo, José. *Velho Chico: vinhos regados de história*. Curaçá:Oxente, 2024.

Giovannini, Eduardo. *Manual de Viticultura*. Porto Alegre: Bookman, 2014.

Inglez de Sousa, Júlio S. *Uvas para o Brasil* (2nd edn). São Paulo: FEALQ, 1996.

Saldanha, R. M. *Vinho Brasileiro, Muito Prazer*. Rio de Janeiro: SENAC, 2019.

Salvo, M. *O Consumidor de Vinho no Brasil*. Urubici: Cinco Continentes, 2021.

Tapia, Patricio. *Guia Descorchados 2024*. São Paulo: Inner, 2024. Section on the wines of Brazil, Bolivia, Peru and Uruguay.

Venancio, Renato P. *Vinho e Colonização*. São Paulo: Alameda, 2023.

Waller, Michael. *101 Vinhos Brasileiros*. Porto Alegre: Ideograf, 2023.

INDEX

Notes: page references in bold refer to text boxes and those in italic refer to photographs, diagrams and tables.

More from The Classic Wine Library

The Classic Wine Library is a premium source of information for students of wine, sommeliers and others who work in the wine industry, but can easily be enjoyed by anybody with an enthusiasm for wine. All authors are expert in their subject, with years of experience in the wine industry, and many are Masters of Wine. The series is curated by an editorial board made up of Sarah Jane Evans MW, Richard Mayson and James Tidwell MS. Continue expanding your knowledge with the titles below.

The wines of Portugal

The wines of Portugal provides detailed descriptions of the demarcated wine regions, the growers and the wines they produce. From crisp Vinhos Verdes in the Atlantic north-west through the Douro, Dão and Lisbon to the big, bold reds of the Alentejo and newcomers from the Algarve, this book is an up-to-date appraisal of Portugal's vineyards and wine producers.

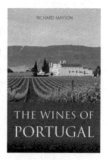

The wines of California

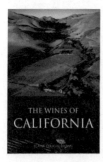

A concise, complete, smartly delivered and cohesive book that considers wine through the lens of social history. The book takes readers on a journey through the Golden State's wines, introducing the people who make them, and paying due attention to famous wine destinations such as Sonoma and Napa as well as exploring exciting lesser-known regions.

The wines of Australia

In *The wines of Australia*, sommelier Mark Davidson tastes his way round the new Australian wine world. He delves into the country's history, culture, growing environment and grape varieties before exploring the wine regions, with key producers introduced and their wines assessed. *The wines of Australia* captures the character of one of the most exciting wine-producing countries on the planet.

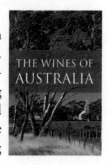

Browse the full list and buy online at
academieduvinlibrary.com